PENGUIN REFERENCE

MYTHS AND LEGENDS OF THE CELTS

Dr James MacKillop is an eminent scholar of Celtic history and culture, having been Visiting Fellow in Celtic Languages at Harvard University, Professor of English at the State University of New York, Visiting Professor at the Université de Rennes and President of the American Conference for Irish Studies. His many publications include the *Dictionary of Celtic Mythology* (1998), *Fionn mac Cumhaill* (1986) and *Irish Literature: A Reader* (1987, 2005). He is based in Syracuse, New York.

D1316273

JAMES MACKILLOP

Myths and Legends of the Celts

PENGUIN BOOKS

For Molly E. and Colin K.

PENGUIN BOOKS

Published by the Penguin Group
Penguin Books Ltd, 80 Strand, London WC2R ORL, England
Penguin Group (USA) Inc., 375 Hudson Street, New York, New York 10014, USA
Penguin Group (Canada), 90 Eglinton Avenue East, Suite 700, Toronto, Ontario, Canada M4P 2Y3
(a division of Pearson Penguin Canada Inc.)
Penguin Ireland, 25 St Stephen's Green, Dublin 2, Ireland
(a division of Penguin Books Ltd)
Penguin Group (Australia), 250 Camberwell Road, Camberwell, Victoria 3124, Australia
(a division of Pearson Australia Group Pty Ltd)
Penguin Books India Pvt Ltd, 11 Community Centre, Panchsheel Park, New Delhi – 110 017, India
Penguin Group (NZ), cnr Airborne and Rosedale Roads, Albany, Auckland 1310, New Zealand
(a division of Pearson New Zealand Ltd)
Penguin Books (South Africa) (Pty) Ltd, 24 Sturdee Avenue, Rosebank, Johannesburg 2196, South Africa

Penguin Books Ltd, Registered Offices: 80 Strand, London WC2R ORL, England

www.penguin.com

First published 2005
Published in paperback 2006
007

Copyright © James MacKillop, 2005
All rights reserved

The moral right of the author has been asserted

Set in 10.5/14 pt PostScript Linotype Sabon
Typeset by Rowland Phototypesetting Ltd, Bury St Edmunds, Suffolk
Printed in England by Clays Ltd, St Ives plc

Except in the United States of America, this book is sold subject
to the condition that it shall not, by way of trade or otherwise, be lent,
re-sold, hired out, or otherwise circulated without the publisher's
prior consent in any form of binding or cover other than that in
which it is published and without a similar condition including this
condition being imposed on the subsequent purchaser

ISBN-13: 978-0-141-01794-5

www.greenpenguin.co.uk

MIX
Paper from
responsible sources
FSC™ C018179

Penguin Books is committed to a sustainable
future for our business, our readers and our planet.
This book is made from Forest Stewardship
Council™ certified paper.

ALWAYS LEARNING   **PEARSON**

Contents

Acknowledgements   vii

Introduction   ix

PART ONE
Contexts

1 Names in the Dust: Searching for Celtic Deities   3

2 Remnants of Celtic Religion   25

3 Sacred Kingship in Early Ireland   48

4 Goddesses, Warrior Queens and Saints   66

5 Calendar Feasts   93

6 Otherworlds   107

PART TWO
Irish Myths

7 Irish Beginnings: the *Lebor Gabála Érenn*   127

8 The Irish Mythological Cycle   150

9 The Ulster Cycle, Part I   168

10 The Ulster Cycle, Part II: Cúchulainn and the Táin   191

11 The Fenian Cycle   219

12 The Cycles of the Kings   243

CONTENTS

PART THREE

Welsh and Oral Myths

13 British Roots and Welsh Traditions   261
14 Survivals in the Oral Traditions of Celtic Lands   284

Select Bibliography   305
Leading Names and Terms in Celtic Mythology   315
Index   350

Acknowledgements

Two valued friends read the typescript as it was being prepared and made countless useful suggestions. They are James E. Doan of Nova Southeastern University and Richard Marsh of Legendary Tours in Dublin. Lucy McDiarmid of Villanova University provided vital information at the inception of the project. Linda McNamara of Inter-Library Loan services at Onondaga Community College found obscure volumes even when they were not stocked by the Widener Library or the Library of Congress. David Lloyd of LeMoyne College gave critical advice on Welsh pronunciation.

The author and publisher would like to thank the following for permission to reproduce illustrations: Maiden Castle, Tara, The Uffington Horse (plates 1, 2, 13), copyright reserved Cambridge University Collection of Air Photographs; The Coligny Calendar (plate 3), Cliché Ch. Thioc, Musée gallo-romain de Lyon, France; Hallstatt Excavations, The Battersea Shield, The Gundestrup Cauldron, Miniature wagon from Mérida, Heads at Entremont (plates 4, 6, 7, 8, 9, 10, 14, 16), copyright © akg-images/Erich Lessing; The Book of Durrow (plate 5), copyright © The Board of Trinity College Dublin; The god Sucellus (plate 11), copyright © The Art Archive/Centre Archéologique de Glanum Saint-Rémy-de-Provence/Dagli Orti; The goddess Epona (plate 12), copyright © The Art Archive/Musée Alésia Alise Sainte Reine France/Dagli Orti; and Sheela-na-gigs in Kilpeck (plate 15), copyright © English Heritage.

Introduction

FINDING THE 'CELTS'

A word of uncommon resonance and ambiguity, 'Celt' may be the most poetic form ever given to us by scholars. Its root is easily traced to the Greek *Keltoí* that implies 'hidden', or the people hidden from the view of the more civilized. Not until about AD 1700 did learned people begin to apply the term 'Celtic' to the family of languages then spoken on the northwestern fringes of Europe: Irish, Scottish Gaelic, Manx, Welsh, Cornish and Breton. This origin in scholarly rather than spoken discourse explains why there is always some question about how it should be pronounced, with the cognoscenti always favouring the hard *c* 'kelt' for etymological reasons instead of the soft *c* 'selt' as one might expect from the usual pattern in English.

To complicate matters, the people we call Celts did not use the term at all until modern times and had no other expression to denote a linguistic community among themselves. The Greeks initially used *Keltoí* to indicate an ancient Gaulish people, distant ancestors of the French, north of what is today Marseille. Gradually, classical commentators began to apply the term to peoples speaking apparently kindred languages, from the Galatians of Asia Minor to the Gallaeci of the Iberian Peninsula in the west. In Julius Caesar's commentaries (first century BC), the Greek-derived Latin term *Celtae* was confined to the people of middle Gaul or central France, but other Romans used it to denote many of the continental populations we now describe as Celtic-speaking. Surprisingly, neither the Greek *Keltoí* nor the Latin *Celtae* referred to the populations of the British Isles, and no word in Old Irish or Old Welsh implies that speakers of those languages perceived a relationship between the two. When referring to themselves the several Celts often used terms incorporating the phoneme *gal-*, as in Gallia (Gaul), Galatia, Galicia (regions of both Spain and Poland) and Portu*gal*.

As a word merely denoting ancient, extinct languages, 'Celtic' was fairly widely known to informed English writers at an early date; Milton uses it in *Paradise Lost* (1667). But the notion that it could also describe the living languages of impoverished and despised peoples on the periphery of Europe was slow in coming. George Buchanan was ignored when he asserted (1582) that Scottish Gaelic was derived from ancient Celtic. In France, however, where the national history begins with the story of Gaulish resistance to Roman rule, several commentators discerned a survival or archaic language among the Bretons on their isolated peninsula in the northwest. Paul-Yves Pezron was much more persuasive in arguing for the continuity between ancient and modern in *Antiquité de la nation et la langue des Celtes* in 1703. Working concurrently with Pezron, the Welsh-born Edward Lhuyd or Lloyd (*c.*1660–1709), Keeper of the Ashmolean Museum, Oxford, had been studying the minority languages of the British Isles in the field. His *Archaeologia Britannia* (1707) introduced the word 'Celtic' in its modern definition into widespread use.

In little more than a half century almost any reader could be expected to have seen the word 'Celtic', following the hoopla accompanying James Macpherson's specious 'translations', *The Poems of Ossian* (1760–64). A young Highland Scottish schoolmaster, Macpherson purported to derive the *Poems* (produced in prose translation) from ancient Celtic documents, which later investigation proved to have been adapted from recent Scottish Gaelic ballads. Although so prolix that they cannot be read today without sustained ardour, *The Poems of Ossian* became an international rage, attracting admiration from such diverse figures as Thomas Jefferson and Johann von Goethe, who translated them into German. This created a fashion for the 'Ossianic', of haunted, rugged landscapes peopled by fatalistic, fair-haired warriors in chariots, which affected all the arts. At least thirty operas were composed on themes from *The Poems of Ossian*, and Ossian's image was idealized on hundreds of canvases. The name of Ossian's father, Fingal, was known across Europe by 1829 when Felix Mendelssohn's

Hebrides Overture was nicknamed the 'Fingal's Cave Overture'. The name of Ossian's son Oscar became so popular in Germany and Scandinavia that it was eventually borne by a succession of Danish kings. Concurrent with and related to Macpherson came the so-called Celtic Revival in English literature, 1760–1800, led by such Anglo-Welsh writers as Thomas Gray, whose poem 'The Bard' (1757) helped make that word, known in both Welsh and Irish, idiomatic in English.

Bards, crags, mists, harps, golden-tressed maidens, forgotten but recoverable magical feats: such was the Celtic world for the Romantic era. Antiquarianism, led often by enthusiasts rather than by what we would call archaeologists, began to turn attention to the Celtic fringe of northwestern Europe. Wide-eyed speculation attributed to the druids, priests of ancient Celtic religion described by Roman commentators, virtually all pre-Roman monuments, including the pre-Celtic (we now know) Stonehenge. It was also a time when a plaintive longing for a past more beautiful than the present prompted more sober-sided scholars to search out and translate the neglected texts of earlier Celtic tradition. Charlotte Brooke's *Reliques of Irish Poetry* (1789) established that Old Irish texts actually existed, even while the infatuation with Macpherson's chicanery and his even more bogus imitators drew attention to other traditions. Mid-way between sobriety and moonshine was Iolo Morganwg (*né* Edward Williams), a laudanum-addicted stonemason, who invented a society of poets and musicians, Gorsedd Beirdd Ynys Prydain (literally, the Throne/Assembly of Bards of the Isle of Britain); it was purportedly based on ancient models, to foster the culture and literature of Wales against the encroachments of the utilitarian Saxons. From this movement came the revival of the eisteddfod (1819), a nationalist popular celebration of traditional culture that would be imitated under other names – such as the Irish *feis* and Scottish Gaelic *mòd* – in other Celtic countries. A well-born Breton admirer of Macpherson and Morganwg, Théodore Hersart de La Villemarqué, gathered native materials for *Barzaz Breiz* (Breton Bards) in 1839. Although yet another pseudo-medievalist, his conscientiousness and superior grasp of the language furnished texts to launch the modern, written literary tradition in Breton.

All this led the word 'Celtic' to agglutinate connotations not yet supported by any evidence recovered from the ancient world, before there had been a single archaeological dig at any Celtic site. Because the reservoirs of Celtic culture were removed from the centres of modern civilization, not Dublin but Connemara, not Edinburgh but the Hebrides, not Paris but Finistère, and the Celtic languages had survived against odds for untold aeons, many observers found it easy to attribute to the Celts whatever was the opposite of advanced technological, commercial society. If Western culture at large was growing more materialistic, then the Celts must be more spiritual. Through this idealized inversion, the economic and sociological liabilities of poverty and isolation – hand-made utensils, amateur entertainments, unfashionable dress, slack work habits – came to be perceived as edifying assets.

Despite the modern deflation of romantic puffery, the origins of the Celtic languages are indeed still lost in the mists of early history. Imaginative speculation purports to find roots as far away as central Asia and northern China, but Celtic is certainly a branch of the Indo-European family of languages, which includes the Slavic, Germanic and Romance languages. It is necessarily more arduous to trace the language of a pre-literate society than it is to uncover physical evidence. Searching is made more difficult by the Celts' lack of a single, self-conscious ethnic identity or any unifying physical characteristics; Virgil (first century BC), memorably, saw them as tall and blond, but elsewhere they were reported shorter and darker. The Celts appear to have had something in common in terms of religion and social structure as well as material culture, but with wide variability.

The earliest Greek references to the *Keltoí*, then living along the Mediterranean coast, appear in documents from 560 to 500 BC. From such evidence modern scholars have determined that the first known Celts lived north of the Alps and in the Danube Valley, from the river's origins in Germany through what is today Austria, the Czech Republic, Slovakia and Hungary. The Celtic goddess Danu (linked with Ana, Anu) may give her name to the river. Celtic culture is first noted during the Iron Age, that last epoch of pre-history between the Bronze Age and the beginning of written records. At one time commentators speculated that the Celtic languages were spoken by people of the Urnfield culture, *c.* 1500–800 BC, a late Bronze Age development distinguished by techniques for burial of the dead. This theory can no longer be supported, but motifs of Urnfield origin are found in the oldest identifiably Celtic cultural era, that named for Hallstatt in what is today Austria.

Lying east of Salzburg in the magnificent mountains of the Salzkammergut, Lake Hallstatt and the adjacent salt-mining complex are today remote from main routes of transportation. But in the Late Bronze and Early Iron Ages, their huge reserves of salt made them a destination for travellers seeking the only food preservative known at that time. This same salt preserved skeletons of 980 bodies and many artifacts buried with them, giving nineteenth-century scholars the first great trove of Celtic material culture, including clothing, leather sacks and wooden implements. This evidence gives us the name Hallstatt for a period of culture, not a tribe or an ethnic group. Settlement of the mines and the lake shore began as early as 1200 BC and continued to as late as 600 BC, while the influence of Hallstatt designs flourished in Celtic Europe from c.800 to 450 BC. After decades of study of such items as weapons, buckets, and human and animal figures, scholars have determined four phases of Hallstatt art, lettered A, B, C and D. Modern viewers tend to admire the technical skill of execution of Hallstatt artefacts rather than their aesthetic distinction. They are generally severely geometrical with only rare examples of plant patterns, although bird motifs appear, perhaps an influence from Italy. There is little influence from the Greeks. At the same time, Hallstatt art can be extravagant, almost baroque.

Superseding the chevrons, zigzags and right angles of the Hallstatt era were the spirals, S-shapes and swirling rounded patterns of the La Tène epoch, named for an archaeological site (la tène: the shallows) on the eastern end of Lake Neuchâtel, in western Switzerland. Though underwater, the La Tène site yielded even more than Hallstatt had: 400 brooches, 270 spears, 27 wooden shields, 170 swords, not to mention such votive offerings as pigs, dogs, chariots and human beings. The precise function of the La Tène site, whether sanctuary, battlefield or marketplace, has never been determined. Intense human activity began at the Lake Neuchâtel shallows about 500 BC and extended until the beginning of Roman domination, 200 BC and after. Motifs from the more sophisticated La Tène style, recorded in three phases, I, II, and III, permeated continental Celtic settlements more widely than had the Hallstatt, extending also to the British Isles, where its influence persisted through Christianization to the time of the Norman conquest of Ireland in AD 1169.

During the first millennium BC, concurrent with the succession of Hallstatt and La Tène styles in art, came a decisive split into the two branches of the Celtic languages, usually described as the P-Celtic and Q-Celtic languages. The hard sound inherited from Indo-European that we represent with the letters *qu-*, for reasons unknown, came to be replaced by the sound of *p-*. We can illustrate this with contrasting examples from modern Q- and P- languages, Irish and Welsh, which still retain the same roots. The Irish word for head, *ceann*, is *pen* in Welsh. Likewise, *mac*, meaning son in Irish, is *map* in Welsh. At one time the split was thought to reflect migrations of different peoples across Europe, a position not supported by recent findings. Simple explanations are hard to come by. The substitution took place among peoples living in close proximity to one another as they migrated across Europe. As they settled in different areas either the P-Celt languages or the Q-Celts would become dominant while retaining trace patterns of the other family. Gaulish was largely P-Celtic with traces of Q-Celtic. The languages of ancient Britain were predominantly P-Celtic, as are the modern languages derived from them, sometimes designated Brythonic or Brittonic: Welsh, Cornish and Breton. Both Q-Celts and P-Celts settled in Ireland, with the Q-Celts becoming dominant. Q-Celtic invaders occupied much of Dyfed, in southern Wales, where their language was incorporated into the dominant language. Other Q-Celtic invaders, the Scotti, left northern Ireland for the islands and Highlands of Scotland where they established Scottish Gaelic, driving P-Celtic speakers into the Lowlands, where they became incorporated into populations speaking Scots or Lallans, related to English and thus part of the Germanic family of languages. Q-Celtic Irish settlers on the Isle of Man, sometimes dominated by Norse and Scottish rulers, spoke a language now known as Manx. Closely related, Irish, Scottish Gaelic and Manx are also known as the Goidelic languages after *Goídel*, the Old Irish word for the Irish people.

Conquered by the Romans, or by their allies, it was once assumed that the ancient continental Celtic languages had died out by the end of the Roman empire, although we now know that many pockets of

Celtic speakers survived to a much later date, thus the existence of two widely separated regions named Galicia, in northwestern Spain and in southern Poland. A taste for bagpipes, nurtured by romantic nationalists, still flourishes in northern Spain. But the greatest reservoir of Celtic culture is Ireland, protected from invaders by large expanses of seawater and barely visible from Britain. The oldest written Irish records are in the ogam (modern ogham) alphabet, a native system of notched parallel lines that are the equivalents of Roman letters. Writing using the Roman alphabet, in both Latin and the native Irish language, was brought to the island in the early fifth century by Christian missionaries, usually associated with St Patrick. As Roman legions abandoned the province of Britain in the middle of the fifth century, the rule of law receded from much of Europe, and travellers had no protection on Roman roads. This meant that Mediterranean learning was introduced and was then isolated during what used to be titled the 'Dark Ages', AD 600–1000. The Irish monks of this period followed their own rules rather than those of St Benedict of Nursia (c.480–c.543), founder of European monasticism. Often living independently, they scattered themselves widely over the map of Europe, providing tutors to illiterate continental kings. If the story of St Brendan is to be believed, they came to the New World as well.

There was no post-medieval Celtic nation until the creation of the Irish Free State in 1922, by which time the majority of that population had become English-speaking. Today only about 100,000 residents of the island of Ireland are fluent in the native language, despite intermittent support from the state to revive it. The situation in Wales and Brittany is much stronger, despite or perhaps because of a lack of long-term governmental support. More recent policies in both Britain and France have favoured preserving the languages. Scottish Gaelic continues in the mainland Highlands and is the dominant language on some of the islands in the Hebrides, as well as in areas of Nova Scotia in Canada. Cornish became extinct in the mid-eighteenth century, and the last Manx speaker died in 1974. Enthusiastic revivalists continue to learn, to speak and to sing, and to teach all the Celtic languages.

SOURCES OF OUR KNOWLEDGE

The ancient Celts left us scant written materials but many more artifacts than was once supposed. Unsympathetic, often patronizing
Greeks and Romans wrote about the Celts in great detail. After the fall
of the Roman empire and the coming of Christianity and monasticism,
surviving Celtic peoples established their own written traditions, at
first in Ireland and later in Wales. After Henry VIII's suppression of
the monasteries in the sixteenth century, enlightened nobles and other
patrons occasionally sponsored the recording of popular narratives
and poetry. Later in the nineteenth century and continuing into the
twentieth, learned travellers collected narratives in the field, often from
unlettered storytellers. Among students of Celtic myth and culture,
these several streams are known by different names. Materials uncovered by archaeologists are called 'the physical evidence'. Each year
there are more and more finds, many of them causing us to redefine
earlier suppositions. Declining in influence are the writings of Greek
and Roman observers, usually called the 'classical commentators',
now thought to be biased and short-sighted; their pronouncements are
increasingly seen to be at variance with the physical evidence. All texts
in Celtic languages since the introduction of Christianity are sometimes
described as the 'vernacular evidence', as if these were inferior to what
is known from the ancient world. The older written records, especially
as found in the great medieval codices, such as *The Book of the Dun
Cow* or *The Red Book of Hergest*, may be dubbed 'literary tradition'.
Materials from unlettered sources are called 'oral tradition', sparing
us the nuisance of deciding whether the item at hand is a folktale, a
legend or an instructive fable. Both narratives and characters, notably
the Irish Fionn mac Cumhaill, appear in contrasting portraits in literary
and oral traditions.

Knowledge of early Europe was stumbled upon before it was ever
methodically sought out. Early discoveries such as Hallstatt, Austria
(1846), are rightly named 'finds'. Little more than a decade later
(1858), enlightened amateurs plumbed the underwater site at La Tène
in Switzerland. Prominent ruins such as Tintagel in Cornwall and
ringforts such as Maiden Castle in Dorset became tourist attractions.

More telling was the large bronze calendar (first century BC) found at Coligny in eastern France, giving detailed information on a 64-month period in the most extensive of all surviving early examples of written Gaulish. The text suggests continuity with later Celtic languages; the autumn new year, known as *sam(h)ain* in Irish, is here *samonios*. Émile Espérandieu (1857–1939) led the search for further inscriptions, resulting in sixteen volumes of data published over fifty-nine years (1907–66). By the end of the twentieth century, researchers had examined more than a hundred sites in France, the Low Countries, Germany and the Danube valley, the burial mound at Hochdorf and the Gaulish 'city' of Alésia yielding abundantly. We even know a great deal about Celtic diet and personal grooming, thanks to the discovery of Lindow Man (1984), the body of a young, apparently sacrificial victim, preserved intact in a Cheshire peat bog, his last meal undigested.

The ever-mounting physical evidence of the ancient Celts portrays a society governed by laws, with complex social structures and a relatively strict morality. We now have detailed information about domestic accommodations, dress, diet, artisanship, agriculture and, especially, funerary rites. Abundant physical representation of what appear to be anthropomorphic deities often survives in sharp relief. The face of a god or goddess cannot, however, always be matched with a name. And even when we have names, some coordinated with those of classical commentators, we lack the narrative setting to make the Celtic deity a figure of action, as we do with Greek and Roman traditions.

Most discussed of the physical evidence is the celebrated Gundestrup Cauldron, named for the village of the Jutland Peninsula, Denmark, where it was found in a peat bog in 1880. Standing 14 inches high, 25.5 inches in diameter, capable of holding 28.5 gallons, the cauldron is made of 96 per cent pure silver, was originally gilded and weighs nearly 20 pounds. Ornate, detailed figures, some demonstrably of Celtic origin, such as its ram-headed snakes and the boar-headed war trumpet, decorate the seven outer and five inner plates, all of which are separable. Animals appear along with ordinary mortals and gods, conventionally seen as larger than human. A female deity flanked by wheels, as if riding in a cart, evokes Queen Medb of Connacht, as she is seen in medieval Irish narrative. A tall divine figure holding a man over a vat evokes the ferocious Teutates of Gaulish religion, accepting a human sacrifice. And, most impressively, a horned god, seated in what almost looks like a yogi's full lotus position, can now be identified with Cernunnos, a lord of nature, animals, fruit, grain and prosperity. Known elsewhere in more than thirty representations, Cernunnos may have been a principal god of the Continental Celts.

The succession of images on the cauldron, armed infantry and cavalry, a sacred tree, a spotted leopard, a small acolyte in a bull-horned helmet offering a chariot or cart wheel to the bust of a bearded god, all tease out the possibility of a narrative. Most scholars discern no continuity in the imagery, but one, Garrett Olmstead, has argued provocatively that the figures on the Gundestrup Cauldron can be seen as an anticipation of the episodes in the *Táin Bó Cuailnge* [The Cattle Raid of Cooley], the great epic of early Irish literature, of which Queen Medb is a leading figure.

Each new discovery of even the smallest artifact, together with each new evaluation of the physical record, enlarges our grasp of ancient Celtic life. This new knowledge tends to circumscribe and diminish what we have received from the ancient written record in Greek and Latin, the several dozen writers known as the classical commentators. Learned men in Athens and Rome seemed so familiar with the presence of the Celts that they felt no need to explain or contextualize any observations about them. Ephorus (fourth century BC) classified the Celts as one of the four principal barbarian peoples, along with the Scythians of eastern Europe, the Persians of Asia and the Libyans of Africa. The Greek 'Father of History', Herodotus (c.485–428 BC), recorded much of the Celts, as did the Roman historians Livy (58 BC–AD 17) and Tacitus (AD 55–117), whose purview included Roman Britain during the rule of his father-in-law Julius Agricola (AD 78–84). The philosopher Aristotle (384–322 BC) cited the Celts when discussing bravery. More valuable are the asides and digressions of Polybius (204–122 BC), who gives details of Celtic dress and living conditions as well as depicting the selfless heroism of raiders preying upon the Italian peninsula. Abundant particulars, despite his heavy-handed condescension, may be found in the *Geography* of the Greek Strabo (58 BC–AD 24) who lived in Rome. He found the Celts 'war-mad', though not fundamentally of evil character. Despite their strength and courage, Strabo wrote, the Celts were easily outwitted by their more cool-headed enemies.

Most informative of all the classical commentators is the Syrian-born Stoic philosopher Posidonius (c. 135–51 BC), who had lived in southern Gaul for a period, freeing him from reliance on self-serving travellers' reports. His surviving ethnographical observations comprise only an 86-page booklet in modern editions (1960, 1985), a goad to remind us of what he might have told us in still further commentary now lost. We know that Chapter 23 of his lost *History*, prepared before the first Transalpine War (131–125 BC), contained extensive, profound information, as a summary of it appears in such later writers as Strabo, Diodorus Siculus (first century BC) and Athenaeus (*fl.* AD 230). Some of Posidonius' commentaries strike parallels in early Irish and Welsh literature, especially his anticipation of bardic institutions and his description of the 'champion's portion', a ceremony at banquets which awarded the choicest portion of pork to the most exalted hero present.

Posidonius' views also inform the war commentary of Julius Caesar (100–44 BC), although they are not credited. Best remembered today as the introductory texts for beginning Latin students, Caesar's seven-volumed *De Bello Gallico* [Gallic War] nonetheless gives some of the closest observations we have of religious practices, notably of the druids, as well as Celtic social divisions. He perceived a Gaulish pantheon, with gods ranked according to function, but he called them by what he felt to be their Roman equivalents. Thus Gaulish Mercury stands ahead of Gaulish Apollo or Gaulish Jupiter. This became the imperial convention we now designate *interpretatio Romana* [Roman interpretation], leading to centuries of speculation over the true identity of Gaulish Mercury, Gaulish Apollo, etc. (see Chapter 2). Despite being one of the most partisan of writers (he was among the Celts to conquer them, 58–51 BC), Caesar revealed surprising sympathy for the common people, whom he found living like slaves, crushed with debts and taxes and abjectly subservient to powerful *equites* (knights or barons).

Ireland was known in the ancient world only in the geography of Ptolemy (second century AD), yet it affords a bridge between the earliest traditions and later survivals. By-passed by the Romans and the invading plunderers who followed them, the Irish retained their early family structures, social organization, and systems of inheritance and property for more than another millennium. We read about how this world was ordered in the Brehon Laws, named for the judges or brehons (Old Irish *breithem*) of early Ireland. Brehon Law has little in common with Roman Law, which lies at the foundation of law in most modern European states, but it does find parallels in the laws of the Welsh king Hywel Dda (d. 950).

Christianity had come to Ireland by the early 400s, before the collapse of Roman rule, and with it literacy, both in classical languages and also in Irish using Roman script. Thus during the bleak centuries between the Romans and the rise of medieval culture, Irish monasteries were the only places in Europe, north of Constantinople, where one might study Latin and Greek. During these heroic centuries of early Irish Christianity, Irish clergymen recorded many of the narratives discussed in this volume. Appearing first in documents now lost, they were later copied in the great medieval codices. Writing in Irish developed from the sixth to twelfth centuries, when native or Celtic monasticism flourished, but diminished after 1170, when monastic rule came under the domination of such continental orders as the Cistercians and the Dominicans. Surviving Welsh manuscripts, also produced by monks, date from later centuries, many of the oldest materials having been destroyed.

The great codices are leather-bound volumes made first of vellum, a parchment made of the skins of lambs, calves or young goats, and later of heavy paper. Each codex contains an assortment of narratives and other texts, in both the native language and Latin, assembled by the monks of a single community, such as Clonmacnoise on the Shannon River. Some codices are the work of a single hand. Internal evidence implies that many twelfth-century and later texts were copied from lost originals dating from centuries earlier. Most are designed to be attractive to the eye, though not so lavishly decorated as the earlier *Book of Durrow* (seventh century) or *Book of Kells* (eighth–ninth centuries), which are illuminated Gospels. Although the codices are cited here by their English titles, many learned commentators prefer their original Irish or Welsh titles, such as *The Book of the Dun Cow = Lebor na hUidre*; some scholars elect the disconcerting familiarity of citing the collection's Irish initials such as *LU* for *Lebor na hUidre*.

Materials appear within codices almost haphazardly, so that portions of great narratives such as the *Táin Bó Cuailnge* [Cattle Raid of Cooley], *Lebor Gabála* [Book of Invasions] or *Mabinogi*, might be spread over different collections. Sometimes, as in the case of the *Táin*, the narrative survives with significant variations from one codex to another.

Literary riches are unequally distributed. Pride of place among the Irish codices goes to *The Book of the Dun Cow* (begun before AD 1106), so named because it is thought to have been partly written on the hide of a cow that followed St Ciarán to his monastery at Clonmacnoise. The oldest codex entirely in Irish, *The Book of the Dun Cow* yields versions of the *Táin*, *Fled Bricrenn* [Briccriu's Feast], *Imram Brain* [The Voyage of Bran], *Tochmarc Étaíne* [The Wooing of Étaín], and Fenian materials. *The Book of Leinster* (1150 and after), possibly the work of a single scribe at the monastery of Terryglass, Co. Tipperary, provides a second version of the *Táin*, a large portion of the *Lebor Gabála* and tales of Tara, an ancient ceremonial site. Putting aside the Latin *Book of Armagh* (AD 807–8), containing the complete New Testament and a life of St Patrick, most of the others were compiled almost consecutively in a 100-year span: *The Book of Ballymote* (c.1390), *The Yellow Book of Lecan* (c.1393), *The Book of Lecan* (1397–1418), *The Book of Uí Maine* (late fourteenth–early fifteenth century) and *The Book of Fermoy* (fourteenth, fifteenth and sixteenth centuries).

A written Irish tradition, often treating of themes and characters from pre-Christian times, persisted for several centuries after the age of the great early collections despite increasing English interference with native life and attempts to suppress the language. Such stories as *Oidheadh Chlainne Tuireann* [The Tragic Story of the Children of Tuireann], while cited as early as the tenth century, were still circulating in paper manuscripts at the end of the seventeenth. Repression of Catholic learning in Ireland meant that some work was continued abroad, such as the huge *Duanaire Finn* [Poem Book of Fionn], compiled 1626–7 at Louvain in the Spanish Netherlands, in what is today Belgium.

No Welsh writing survives from the first millennium, although it certainly once existed, and the earliest Welsh codices date from a century after the Irish. The oldest is *The Black Book of Carmarthen* (*c.*1250), so named because of its cover and for a castle in southwestern Wales, followed by the *Book of Aneirin* (1265), named for the legendary sixth-century poet. Materials that we shall examine come mostly from the *White Book of Rhydderch* (*c.*1325) and the *Red Book of Hergest* (1382–1410)

No pre-Renaissance materials are known to have existed in Manx, Cornish or Breton, and the earliest known from Scottish Gaelic is *The Book of the Dean of Lismore* (early sixteenth century). Its compiler, James MacGregor (*c.*1480–1551), unfortunately assumed that no one would ever read Scottish Gaelic and so transcribed the poetry in a phonological script as the words might sound to someone living in the Scottish Lowlands. The Scots language, a dialect of English spoken in the Lowlands, is unrelated to Scottish Gaelic.

While all these documents are revered today as treasures, they were not always so kindly treated. Cromwell's soldiers in the seventeenth century cut up early Irish manuscripts to make tailors' patterns. The Welsh *White Book of Hergest* was destroyed by fire in the nineteenth century. And *The Book of the Dun Cow*, lost for centuries, might not be known today at all if it had not turned up in a bookshop in 1837.

Meanwhile, the contents of the early collections receded from consciousness, since only a tiny handful of people could read Irish or Welsh, and most texts were unavailable in English or French translation. Given the poverty and social disesteem of Celtic-speaking peoples, there was little motive to make the texts available until the implications of James Macpherson's *Ossian* phenomenon had settled in. Lady Charlotte Guest's English translation of the Welsh *Mabinogion* (1838–49) attracted a wide readership, including the Poet Laureate, Alfred Lord Tennyson. Translations from Old Irish could not begin until linguists, many of them German, recovered its grammar and vocabulary. The publications of the Ossianic Society (beginning 1853) and the establishment of learned journals such as *Revue Celtique* (1870–1934) put translations on library shelves but not necessarily into the hands of a wide readership. Standish James O'Grady, the first of many popularizers, injected colourful invention into what had been heavy-going scholarship with such works as *History of Ireland: The Heroic Period* (1878) and *Cuculain and His Contemporaries* (1880).

In another generation, William Butler Yeats, though he knew scant Irish, and Lady Gregory put figures from the earliest traditions on to the world stage.

The oldest written traditions, produced when only a tiny elite of the population was literate, must not be confused with what we now call 'folklore'. A term almost as difficult to define as 'mythology', the word 'folklore' first appeared in 1856 after two generations of collectors, beginning in Germany, had gathered materials from the oral traditions of the unlettered peasantry. Oral traditions may or may not relate to older written traditions and are sometimes sharply at variance with one another, as with the character of Fionn mac Cumhaill, subject of an immense number of stories, both written and recited, for many centuries. Stories from oral tradition, further, may fall into world-wide patterns of motif and episode and make astounding parallels with stories from distant parts of the world (see Stith Thompson, *The Folktale*, New York, 1936; Los Angeles, 1977).

In the Celtic countries collectors of oral traditions almost invariably sought to disseminate their findings in English or French. Welsh collections appeared first, with William Earl's *Welsh Legends* (1802) and William Howells' *Cambrian Superstitions* (1831). Among the first Irish compilations was *Researches in the South of Ireland* (1824) by Thomas Crofton Croker, the son of a British officer. Dozens of volumes would follow through the end of the twentieth century, and the Irish Folklore Commission (founded 1935) has more than half a million pages of oral transcription, and 10,000 hours of audio recordings. Work in other cultures emerged almost concurrently: Robert Hunt, *Popular Romances of the West of England* (1865) from Cornwall; François Marie Luzel, *Chants populaire da la Basse-Bretagne*, 2 vols (1868–74) from Brittany; and William Harrison, *A Mona Miscellany* (1869) from the Isle of Man. Two of the richest gatherings of oral narrative were found in Gaelic Scotland: John Francis Campbell, *Popular Tales of the West Highlands*, 4 vols (1861) and Archibald Campbell, *Waifs and Strays in Celtic Tradition*, 4 vols (1889–91).

INTERPRETATIONS AND REINTERPRETATIONS

As soon as texts became available, readers noted parallels between Celtic and classical heroes, so that Cúchulainn was quickly dubbed the 'Irish Heracles'. Matthew Arnold (1865) thought that the storytellers of the *Mabinogion* had plundered ancient myth just as medieval peasants had filched cut stones from Roman ruins to build their cottages. Yet it took many years before the several Celtic traditions, ancient and vernacular, written and oral, could be discussed at the same time or be constituted a 'mythology'. The ancient Celtic gods, not creatures of extensive narratives, relate only occasionally and obliquely to the characters in stories recorded in post-Christian times. Because of their bulk and antiquity, as well as the prestige given them in the generation of William Butler Yeats (1865–1939), early Irish narratives attracted the most scrutiny and generated the most interpretation. Nonetheless, as late as the mid-twentieth century, editors often preferred terms like 'early Irish literature' or 'Old Irish sagas and legends' rather than 'Celtic mythology'. The word 'literature' makes no assumption about the origin or function of narrative; 'legend' and 'saga' presume some rooting in fact or history. To call Celtic materials 'mythology' implies that they can stand comparison with stories of the Olympians, or of Achilles, Oedipus and Orpheus; increasingly, informed commentators have shown that they can.

As 'mythology' is a word of Greek origin (from *mythos*: 'word, speech or story'), it could be argued that only Greek stories are genuinely myths, just as *real* champagne comes only from France. So many stories are now deemed 'myth', from the Icelandic *Prose Edda* to those of the gods of the African Yoruba or Oceanic Maori, not to mention idiomatic uses like the 'myth' of *King Kong*, that the word has become almost impossible to define, or impossible to define simply and without many qualifications. We know a myth when we see it, and we know it is different from history. A myth is an anonymous, traditional story, usually originating in a pre-literate society, concerned with deities, heroes or ancestors who embody dimly perceived truths whose roots are in our innermost being. Some myths may explain the origin of the cosmos or of ourselves, or how living relates to dying, or why the weather changes. This explanatory function, aetiology, is not unique to myth and may also be found in religious dogma. Sometimes 'myth' can be defined as 'other people's religion'. That is because when we call a story a 'myth' we imply that someone, at some time, paid it great heed, which cannot always be said of the 'folktale'.

While the struggle to define 'mythology' more fully could easily fill this entire volume, of greater concern is what people have thought was contained in the material presented in the next several chapters. The earliest perception was that it was all history or related to history. The great Irish historian Geoffrey Keating (*c*.1580–*c*.1645/50) thought Cúchulainn and Fionn mac Cumhaill were flesh and blood human beings, an assumption still uttered popularly at the beginning of the twenty-first century. Certain historical figures, such as St Patrick or the Welsh Macsen Wledig (d. AD 388), may appear in early narratives many observers would describe as 'mythological'. But we can scarcely hope to find an historical antecedent to explain the resonance of personages such as the Irish Deirdre and Balor of the Evil Eye or the Welsh Rhiannon and Pwyll. The notion that gods and heroes of myth were somehow inflated out of living people is called euhemerism, after Euhemerus the Sicilian rhetorician (fourth century BC); the relation between myth and history is, as we shall see, infinitely more complex.

If the source for Irish and Welsh heroes was not actual human beings, the next place to look was to forgotten or repressed ancient gods. Sir John Rhŷs's lectures known under the short title *Celtic Heathendom* (1886) first sought to recover pagan knowledge ignored or perhaps distorted by Christian scribes. There was much to support his central thesis. The god the Romans designated Gaulish Mercury could be identified from place names as Lugos or Lugus, as the Gauls themselves would have known him. Lugos, in turn, can be linked to the Irish Lug Lámfhota and the Welsh Lleu Llaw Gyffes. As illuminating as Rhŷs's efforts were, he worked before some key texts became available, and he tended to push his thesis harder than subsequent research would support. Though *Celtic Heathendom* is little cited today, he influenced two generations of scholars, among them W. J. Gruffydd in *Math Vab Mathonwy* (1928) and *Rhiannon* (1953), and the prolific Irish commentators Myles Dillon and Gerard Murphy. The inclination to find lost divinities behind any number of warriors or kings also infuses T. F. O'Rahilly's monumental *Early Irish History and Mythology* (1946). Although a scholar of breath-stopping erudition, O'Rahilly nevertheless erred in seeing the early history of Ireland as a contest between invaders speaking languages from rival families of Celtic languages, a controversial idea in his own lifetime and one largely dismissed today.

More recent scholarship downplays the pagan origins theory in favour of the classical influences flowing from the early monasteries. Kim McCone, in the aptly titled *Pagan Past and Christian Present in Early Irish Literature* (1990), and Donnchadh Ó Corráin and others in *Sages, Saints and Storytellers* (1989) advance compelling evidence in support of their views. The strength of this interpretation is that it relies more on available texts in the Celtic languages and in Latin instead of on simulacra postulated from shards of what was once presumed to have existed. As we absorb these new insights, however, we may have to redefine the mythical roots of Celtic mythology. Not all old stories in either Irish or Welsh had comparable status in the traditions that produced them. And some parallels with classical culture are now believed to have been introduced by Christian scribes. This reverses the earlier perception that the echoes of classical culture were introduced by pagan storytellers, were coincidental or were derived from some kind of universal consciousness.

As with other mythologies, Celtic narratives have been subject to successive schools of interpretation growing out of the intellectual movements of the past 150 years. Psychological theorists discern a unified imagination that overrides culture and language and emanates from the universality of human experience. The followers of both Sigmund Freud and Carl Gustav Jung find mythology to be the product of the unconscious mind. For Freudians, mythology can be traced to stages in the predictable steps that each human must follow from birth to maturation. For Jungians mythology derives from the collective unconscious inherited by each human being, regardless of language, colour or social station.

Though the weight of his ideas has not been felt as heavily elsewhere, few theorists have been so influential on Celtic studies as has Georges Dumézil (1898–1986), an Indo-Europeanist and historian given more to Roman and German traditions. Sometimes designated the 'New Comparative Mythology', Dumézil's theories draw on the French tradition that seeks a sociological context for both religion and myth, asserting that mythology embodies a system of symbols encoding the rules of society. In Dumézil's view, early Indo-European societies, including the Celtic, were divided into three parts according to social function. These were the numerically smaller priestly and warrior classes and the larger producing class. Each group regarded itself as having been ordained to its particular class by a mythological origin. Although Dumézil himself devoted only a portion of one volume to early Ireland, *Le troisième Souverain* (1949), his ideas were brought to bear on a wide range of early Welsh and Irish tradition in Alwyn and Brinley Rees's *Celtic Heritage* (1961). The Rees brothers purport to discern an underlying unity in early Welsh and Irish social and political organization as well as in large bodies of narrative.

From the 1960s through to the beginning of the twenty-first century, one commonly sees citations to Dumézil in Celtic scholarship, but the ideas of rival theorists continue to enter discourse. These include the structuralists, notably Claude Lévi-Strauss, who emphasize the presence of a world-wide pattern of opposition between certain terms and categories, such as wilderness/village, upstream/downstream, raw/cooked, etc. Rivalling them but with more lasting influence are the formalists, Vladimir Propp and Walter Berkert, who relate both myth and folktale to biological and cultural 'programmes of action' whose incidence is, again, found world-wide.

PART ONE

Contexts

I

Names in the Dust
Searching for Celtic Deities

SCRUTINIZING THE INSCRUTABLE CELTS

Most readers of this book probably already have some background in classical mythology. They will find it handy in keeping straight allusions to Artemis, Aphrodite and Hephaestus as well as knowing that those Greek Olympians had counterparts named Diana, Venus and Vulcan among the Romans. Those names appear again and again in discussion of Celtic mythology, especially the older traditions. Yet a knowledge of classical mythology is also likely to set expectations that Celtic traditions cannot fulfil. Any student can read enough from ancient sources about, say, Artemis-Diana, that she seems to be a knowable figure. Dozens of representations in art illustrate aspects of Artemis's character, her coolness and hauteur or her athleticism. We can speak about her presumed personality the way we can about a character in fiction or dramatic literature. This is not true of the earliest Celtic figures that survive only in partially destroyed statues, badly weathered inscriptions or cryptic passages in unsympathetic classical commentaries. We get a fuller picture if a deity's cult was widespread, but often the modern reader is in the position of the palaeontologist trying to extrapolate the image of an early hominid from a piece of jawbone, a femur and a knuckle.

As for the ancient Celts of the continent and Britain, we have moved beyond the blinkered vision of the Romans. Until recently, we tended to see all their battles and enemies through Roman eyes. The imperialist cliché portrayed the Celts, like other 'barbarians', as crude, disorderly and improved by domination, whereas the Romans were seen as cosmopolitan, orderly and effective law-givers. Recent archaeological evidence prompts revision of this model. The widespread Celtic population thrived with a complex social organization of great noble houses and a system of clients and patrons, often in urban settings. Celtic standards of craftsmanship, especially in metals, equalled and surpassed those of the early Romans. Numerically superior, the Celts reached an apogee of cultural expression and political expansion just before the rise of Rome. In 390 BC the Celts sacked Rome itself, not to occupy it or make it a fiefdom but rather just as a show of aggressive force. In 279 BC they apparently sacked the Greek shrine of Delphi. But in little more than another fifty years, in 225 BC, the Romans annihilated a Gaulish army at Telamon, along the western shore on the road to Pisa, slaughtering perhaps 40,000 and taking another 10,000 prisoner. The imperial tide would be halted now and again but never reversed. Ultimately the social and cultural similarity of the Gauls to the Romans hastened the absorption of conquered peoples into the empire.

Even though they did not give us their history, our accumulated knowledge of the ancient Celts, surviving and rediscovered, now fills several fat volumes. Continental Celts divided into two cultural provinces, the eastern, centred on the Danube valley, being more influenced by Greek culture. We can place by name the domains of up to a hundred Celtic tribes and peoples. Some of those peoples may be studied in abundant detail, such as the Aedui of what is now eastern France, who were first allied with the Romans before being crushed in rebellion against them. Other names reappear on the modern map. The Swiss refer to their country as Helvetia after the ancient Helvetii of the Alps, just as the modern Belgians take their name, if not their ethnicity, from the Belgae. We have excavated large proto-cities such as Alésia and Bibracte in what is now eastern France, and Manching in southern Germany, the latter's defensive wall measuring four miles. Individual faces emerge from records, such as Abaris the Hyperborean (sixth century BC), possibly the earliest druid, who conversed with Pythagoras.

Two resisters to Roman domination, one Gaulish, the other British, have so fired the imagination of readers over the centuries that they sometimes seem more mythical than historical. Vercingetorix (from the Latin *ver*: over; *cinget*: he surrounds, i.e. warrior; *rex*: king) led a heroic but ultimately futile resistance to Julius Caesar's conquest. A prince of the Arverni people, he could not rally other nobles to his cause and instead commanded a rag-tag army of the people, who made him their king in 52 BC. His initial success led other peoples to join him until, in a fatal error, he allowed himself to be put under siege at Alésia. Forced to surrender, Vercingetorix was humiliated in display before Roman crowds, imprisoned, and eventually executed in 45 BC. Rediscovered in the Romantic nineteenth-century reinterpretation of ancient history, an aggressive, moustachioed Vercingetorix was commemorated by Napoleon III in a huge, heroic public monument at the modern village of Alise-Sainte Reine on the site of Alésia, 32 miles northwest of Dijon. Long cited in the French school curriculum as the first national hero, Vercingetorix's struggle is so widely known to most French people that it has inspired a long-running comic strip, Asterix the Gaul. His British counterpart, the tall red-haired queen Boudicca, lives on in even greater esteem. Her name, spelled many ways, Boudica, Boadicia, Bunduca, Boadicea, etc., may mean 'victory' (cf. Old Irish *búadach*: victorious; Welsh *buddagol*: victorious). After the Romans killed her husband Prasutagus, they scourged Boudicca and mistreated her daughters. Infuriated, she led her own people, the Iceni of eastern Britain, and the neighbouring Trinobantes in a brutal if short-lived rebellion, during which her forces burned the cities of Colchester and London. When her fortunes declined, she took poison rather than be taken prisoner (*c*.AD 61). Her story has always been accessible as it appears in the works of Tacitus, the well-regarded historian, to whom she was a dangerous giantess. Her persona began to be reshaped in Renaissance drama and continues to expand in contemporary popular fiction. A victorious Boudicca is commemorated in a heroic nineteenth-century statue on Westminster Bridge, London (a more maternal rendering stands in City Hall, Cardiff, Wales).

SUN AND SKY

One of the few constants across cultures and climes, the sun engenders homage in many early religions as the author of life and the patron of healing and fertility. The wheel and the swastika, ubiquitous symbols of the sun, are found with early settlements as far apart as Asia and North America. Veneration of the sun appears widely in late Stone Age and Bronze Age Europe, especially Scandinavia. The thirteenth-century BC Trundheim Chariot, found in Denmark, indicates attitudes and beliefs many generations before the advent of writing. It features a small bronze horse-drawn wagon containing a gilt sun-disc. Even without corroboration from other contemporary materials, we can infer the existence of processions and sun worship.

Close observation of the sun's apparent movement is evident in the construction of many passage-graves surviving in Celtic lands. The two best-known are Newgrange (3200 BC) at the bend of the Boyne River, near Slane, Co. Meath, Ireland, and Gavrinis (3500 BC), on a small island seven miles southwest of Vannes, Brittany. Both predate the coming of Celtic languages by almost two millennia and were built by indigenous populations whose survivors, evidence suggests, were absorbed into Celtic culture. A passage-grave consists of a large man-made mound over a stone passage leading to an interior chamber. Newgrange, now much frequented by tourists, varies between 260 ft (79 m) and 280 ft (85 m) in diameter, with a passage 62 ft (18.9 m) ending in a 20 ft (6 m) chamber measuring 17 ft by 21.5 ft (5.2 m by 6.5 m). Dark most of the year, the Newgrange passage is aligned so that the sun's rays will penetrate the mound through the 'roofbox', a special aperture over the entrance, to illuminate the chamber dramatically and briefly at sunrise on the five days of the winter solstice, 19–23 December. Some other passage-graves, however, are aligned to the moon or other celestial features.

At both Newgrange and Gavrinis, mysterious incised markings decorate many standing stones, but there is some question whether Celtic populations knew of the graves' associations with the sun. Three intertwined spirals, sometimes called the trispiral, are generally speculated to be sun symbols. The figure is widely used in contemporary

Irish art, especially jewellery, and was the logo for *Riverdance*, the popular musical review. In early Irish literary tradition, Newgrange, under the name Brug na Bóinne [hostel of the Boyne], is a residence of Angus Óg, a god of poetry, and in oral tradition it is a prominent *sídh* or fairy mound. The carvings at the smaller Gavrinis are more ornate but less open to speculation. Although once a destination of Christian pilgrimage and a frequent place name in oral tradition, Gavrinis has no folkloric associations with the sun.

Sun signs and solar imagery appear widely in early Celtic culture, but they do not necessarily support a conclusion readers might expect, that there was a single sun deity. A wheel, conventionally thought of as a sun sign, appears among the details of the Gundestrup Cauldron. Other archaeological evidence shows us that Iron Age Gauls, as well as those of the Roman occupation, cast solar-wheel models into the water as well as placing them as offerings at shrines, such as at Alésia and Lavoye in eastern France. The portrayal of a god with a wheel on a mace-head found at Willingham Fen, Cambridgeshire, implies the existence of a Romano-Celtic sun cult. Participants in some kind of sun cult wore the solar-decorated headdresses that survive at Wanborough temple in Surrey. Early Celtic coins bear sun symbols linked with horses. During Roman occupation sun symbols, such as the solar wheel, were associated with the worship of Jupiter, the Roman sky god whose cult extended to the colonies, often merging with local deities. And the sun is also implicit in the three-legged triskele so prevalent in early Celtic design, which survives, somewhat altered, as the symbol for the Isle of Man.

The earliest text suggesting Celtic sun worship comes from the *Confessio* of St Patrick (fifth century), where the saint contrasts worship of the sun, rising by the command of God, with worship of the 'Sun' who is Christ; the former leads only to pain and damnation, the latter to eternal life. While some commentators cite this as certain evidence of sun worship in pre-Christian Ireland, and by extension among all the Celts, there is no concurrent testimony in early Irish texts or physical remains. References to the sun may only have been the saint's rhetorical ploy to strengthen his case. The name of the Irish hero Lug Lámfhota [Old Irish, *Lug*: light, brightness] implies solar connections, as does that of his Welsh counterpart Lleu Llaw Gyffes, but informed commentators today reject T. F. O'Rahilly's contention that Lug's battle with Balor of the Evil Eye is an anthropomorphic corollary of a solar battle. The teasing etymology of the Irish hero's name Mac Gréine [Ir. son of the sun] may be no more indicative of a cult than Louis XIV's nickname, *Le Roi Soleil* [the sun king]. Thus Anne Ross concluded in *Pagan Celtic Britain* (1967) that there was no Celtic sun god.

Evidence for a Celtic deity of the sky is easier to come by. The Roman poet Lucan (first century AD) speaks of three great divinities in Gaul, one of whom is Taranis, known for his bloody worship. Comparative etymology implies the root of this name is *taran* [thunder] and that Taranis should be 'thunderer'. Although the figure bears no inscription, the statue of a bearded man holding a wheel in his lowered left hand and a thunderbolt in his raised right hand found at Le Châtelet in eastern France may indeed be Taranis. During Roman occupation Taranis became an epithet or cognomen of Jupiter, the Roman sky god (see pp. 38–9).

EARTH AND WATER

Like other polytheistic peoples, the Celts tended to perceive the spiritual (a view we call numinosity) in all parts of the accessible physical world. The surviving oral traditions of Ireland, Gaelic Scotland, Wales and Brittany place deities at countless, easily identifiable landforms such as caves, waterfalls, fords or conspicuous hills. In Roman Gaul prominent rivers and larger springs were either identified with or associated with nameable divinities, such the Marne (Dea Matrona), the Seine (Dea Sequana) or the Saône (Souconna). But shadowy though she may be, only one early deity appears to have transcended the local and particular from the continent to the British Isles.

Her name survives in disparate forms, among them Ana, Anu and even Anna. Ana may or may not be identified with Danu, Dana, a matter of some scholarly contention, as addressed in the next paragraph. The often unreliable tenth-century *Sanas Cormaic* [Cormac's Glossary] says that Ireland may be known as the 'land of Ana'. Although she has no narrative personality, her name is cited in several early Irish stories as well as in the Kerry place name Dá Chich Anann [the Paps of Ana], for two breast-shaped hills ten miles east of Killarney. Allusions to her suggest dual characteristics: beneficent as the patroness of Munster, Ireland's southerly province; or malevolent, contributing to the character of Áine, a deity of desire remembered at Cnoc Áine (Knockainy), near Lough Gur, a neolithic site in Co. Limerick.

The name Danu is found only in the genitive form *Danann*, inviting comparison with a similarly named patron, D—, in the title of the immortal invaders of Ireland, the Tuatha Dé Danann. It would make for harmonious simplicity if Ana and Danu were identical and the ancestral mother-goddess of Ireland was one and the same with the patroness of the gods, but that cannot be proven. Further parallels are tantalizing. The name for the Danube River, in whose valley Celtic culture flourished during the Iron Age, is based on a Celtic word, *danuv*. The root of the issue runs deep into Indo-European inheritance. A river goddess named Dānu is found in Sanskrit literature.

A Welsh counterpart of Ana is Dôn, mother-goddess of five significant children in the fourth branch of the *Mabinogi*, the historic masterpiece of medieval Welsh literature.

Epigraphic evidence points to hundreds of other shadowy minor territorial deities among the continental Gauls. Of these, Nemausus and the female Nemausicae, worshipped at Nemausus (Nîmes, southeastern France), Arausio, eponym of the town of Arausio (Orange, southern France), and Vasio, native spirit of the Roman town of Vaison-la-Romaine in the lower Rhône valley, are the best known. In the absence of a Gaulish literary tradition none of these figures is now more than a name to us.

Quite the opposite case occurs in early Ireland, where there exists an abundance of literary materials coupled with a relative paucity of physical evidence. Mór Muman [Ir. *mór*: great], the territorial goddess of early southern Ireland, with solar and sovereignty associations, was thought so beautiful that every woman in Ireland was compared to her. Medieval scribes assigned extraordinary qualities to her in an attempt to historicize her. She knew frenzy or exaltation, lived for a while under enchantment, heard voices, could fly, yet wandered Ireland in rags for two years. As would befit a territorial goddess, she is thought to have enjoyed sexual intimacy with known historical figures. One such encounter is recorded as taking place at the great limestone acropolis of Cashel, in what is today Co. Tipperary. After tricking the wife of the reigning king, Fíngein mac Áeda (d. 613) to have her husband lie with her, Mór bore him a son, Sechnesach. Hearing distant, unexplained voices, Mór flees before the child is born, and Fíngein dies shortly afterwards. Her name lived on in local oral tradition, proverbs and place names. Aspects of her persona survive in the better known Mórrígan, the 'Great Queen', one of a triad of war-goddesses who play continuing roles in early Irish tradition.

A personification of the power of the land appears as Fódla, one of three sister-goddesses, along with Banba and Ériu, who both embody and give their names to the entire island of Ireland. Members of the immortal Tuatha Dé Danann, Fódla and her sisters met the Milesians, invading mortals, in what is now Co. Limerick, according to the pseudo-history *Lebor Gabála* [Book of Invasions] (see Chapter 7). In that episode Fódla asks that Ireland be named for her, and indeed her name was once a poetic national name, notably in the poetry of Tadhg Dall Ó hUiginn (1550–91). The root of her name survives in the Scottish place name Atholl [cf. Scottish Gaelic, *Ath Fòdhla*: the next Ireland]. Atholl is at the base of the Grampian Mountains, toward the eastern edge of the cultural influence of the Gaelic-speaking invaders who came from Ireland to the Highlands about AD 500 and after. Despite her divine origins, Fódla developed something of a narrative personality in early Irish tradition and was married to the prominent warrior of the Tuatha Dé Danann, Mac Cécht.

Perceiving that water is an enhancer of fertility and a life-giver as well as a life-taker, the early Celts had many reasons to personify and venerate it. Water can move quickly, take an infinite variety of forms and seemingly catch the sun. Wells and springs arise from deep within the unfathomable earth. Rivers may carry weighty cargoes and also nourish the fields. In awe of such power the Celts, from at least the middle Bronze Age, began to show their appreciation of water through gifts of jewellery, weapons, cauldrons, armour, coins, animal and even human sacrifices. One of the great treasures of Celtic art, the bejewelled Battersea Shield, was thrown into the River Thames near London shortly after the arrival of the Romans in the first century AD. Although votive materials may be found in all bodies of water, more are found in wells, perhaps because of a presumed link to the otherworld. The attributing of powers to wells continued through Christian times, when the severed heads of saints are thought to have been placed at certain holy sites. There are abundant examples in Ireland, especially associated with St Brigid, and also in Wales; but even St Melor of Cornwall and Brittany was thought to be a patron of holy wells.

We read descriptions of the magical powers attributed to wells and streams in early Irish narrative. Connla's Well (also known as the Well of Cóelrind) and the Well of Segais are both surrounded by nine hazel trees whose nuts fall into the water, where they are eaten by eager salmon. The nuts contain inspiration, knowledge and wisdom, concepts not always defined as they would be in the modern world. Knowledge here implies an esoteric, metaphysical perception, something that can only be bestowed, not gained gradually through sustained, unaided effort. Alas, the site of these wells is never clearly established, although the Well of Segais was traditionally (but inaccurately) thought to be the common source of the Shannon and Boyne Rivers. Connla's Well may be in fabulous lands like Tír na nÓg [the land of youth], usually thought to be under the sea or more fancifully in Co. Tipperary. The identifiable pool of Linn Féic on the Boyne River in eastern Ireland or the falls of Assaroe on the Erne River in the northwest are the real-world sites where Fionn mac Cumhaill gains superior knowledge by touching the salmon with his thumb and tasting the fish when he thrusts his thumb into his mouth.

Water deities, whether associated with wells, lakes, cataracts or rivers, tend to be female. Ritona or Pritona, a name indicating passageway, was the goddess of fords and water-crossings at Trier on the Moselle River. The ford could also have been seen as a metaphor for the passage between life and death, this world and the next. Also worshipped in Trier as well as in nearby Metz, eastern France, was Icovellauna, credited with powers of healing. No images of her survive, but her name tells us something about her function, for example: *Ico*-can mean 'water'. She presides over an octagonal shrine known as Sablon, built in Romano-Celtic times. Much earlier, perhaps as early as the third century BC, is Glanis, eponym of the sacred springs at Glanum in what is today Provence, southern France. Greeks and

Romans occupied the site before the coming of the Celts. Ancient cisterns near the springs indicate that pilgrims came here to bathe. Adjacent to one of the springs there is an altar to Glanis and to the Glanicae, a brood of local mother-goddesses linked to Glanis and her healing power.

Three deities of early Britain, Brigantia, Coventina and Sulis, are better known to us from the wealth and abundance of their remains. Cults for each of the three flourished during the Roman occupation, giving the goddesses Mediterranean-influenced faces as well as Latinate names. Brigantia, probably a British counterpart of the Gaulish Brigindo, came to personify the hegemony of the powerful Brigantes confederation of warring tribes, centred in what is today West Yorkshire. The River Brent, a tributary joining the Thames at Brentford, is named for her. The Romans tended to equate her with Minerva, goddess of wisdom, but more recent commentators see links between her and Brigit, the Irish fire goddess. Coventina, in contrast, may have been represented by Graeco-Roman-influenced iconography as a nearly naked water nymph or as a triple nymph pouring water from a beaker, but was not equated with any member of the Roman pantheon. Coventina's inscriptions range as far as Galician Spain and the Gaulish Mediterranean coast at Narbonne, but her principal shrine was at Carrawborough on Hadrian's Wall in Northumberland. Excavations in 1876 at her well here, called Procolitia or Brocolitia, uncovered a cache of 14,000 ancient coins. Other items may signal motivations for her worship, such as the number of brooches, ornamental clasps or fibulae apparently given by women in hopes of safe childbirth. Figures of a horse and a dog are among the statuettes dedicated to her. Her Roman epithets *Augusta* [august, majestic] and *Sancta* [holy] underscore the esteem she enjoyed. Curiously, though, the powers of healing attributed to her cannot be supported by a contemporary analysis of the waters at Carrawborough.

The high status of Sulis or Sul can be presumed from the many altars dedicated to her in the Romano-British city of Bath, her principal shrine. Today a resort town in Avon (before 1982, Somerset), ten miles southeast of Bristol, Bath has been known for its medicinal waters since prehistoric times and is one of the oldest continually inhabited spots in Britain. The Roman city was called Aquae Sulis, enshrining the goddess, and was a destination of international pilgrims. For such a distant province, Aquae Sulis was a city rich in art, especially sculpture, architectural design and religious materials. Extensive excavation in the late twentieth century has made it one of the best known Roman settlements. During the Roman occupation Sulis became conflated with the Roman goddess of wisdom Minerva, not simply identified with her but effectively merged with her. Their names are fused, Sul-Minerva or Sulis Minerva, but as the Celtic portion is always put first we assume the native half of her persona dominated; the many surviving inscriptions encompass both Celtic and Latin forms, separately and together. Linguistically *sul-* is related to the Indo-European root for 'sun', which in turn can be linked to the heat of the natural springs. Sulis's curative waters might be used for a range of conditions, among them the problems of mothers unable to nurse. Additionally, her name was also invoked to wreak vengeance upon enemies of petitioners. A cult statue of Sul-Minerva done as a classical goddess survives to the present, though badly mutilated. The gilded bronze head, once helmeted but now violently separated from the torso, has become one of the most photographed art objects from early Britain.

Two Irish river goddesses, never given visual representation, play leading roles in early literary tradition. They are Boand (whose name may mean 'she who has white cows'), a deification of the Boyne River, and Sinann of the Shannon River. Although small by continental norms, both rivers are endowed with cultural and historical resonance far greater than the volumes of water they carry. The Boyne, about 70 miles long, runs northeast across three counties, parts of Kildare and Offaly and all of Meath; it empties into the Irish Sea at Drogheda. Ancient monuments abound in its valley, of which the most famous are the passage-graves of Newgrange, Dowth and Knowth, and the Hill of Tara, where the *ard rí* [high king] was crowned. The 224-mile Shannon nearly divides the island vertically and was difficult for early peoples to ford, the best crossing being at Athlone. The last 70 miles of the river, southwest of Limerick, widen into an expansive estuary navigable by vessels of 1,000 tons.

Imperious and lusty, Boand has such a developed character in early Irish narrative that she is credited with a lapdog, Dabilla. A considerable beauty, she is the sister of an even greater beauty, Bébinn, a patroness of childbirth. While married to Nechtan (whose name derives from the Latin Neptune), Boand has an affair with the Dagda, usually known as the 'good god', to produce Angus Óg, the god of poetry. To conceal her adultery, she asks Elcmar, a magician, to be Angus's foster-father. A confusing alternative version retells the story with the players under assumed names: Boand (now known as Eithne) is married to Elcmar when she succumbs to the charms of Eochaid Ollathair (another name for the Dagda), again producing Angus Óg.

Although the daughter of Lir the sea god, Sinann appears in fewer stories. The best-known tells of her failed attempt to seek knowledge and her associations with the Shannon River, a story strikingly similar to one told of Boand. When Sinann seeks esoteric knowledge at Connla's Well, she is denied, apparently for having violated certain protocols. In anger, the well rises up and drowns her; Sinann's body is washed up on the banks of a river, the Shannon, which is then named for her. Boand drowns in two versions. In the first, closer to the story of Sinann, Boand defies the magical powers of the well of Segais, causing the well to rise up, mutilate and drown her. The water from the well, now a river, washes her body away to the sea. In the second, Boand violates a taboo by looking into the well of Sídh Nechtain (bearing the name of her husband), which rises up and follows her as she flees toward the sea.

The third Irish river goddess, commemorated in James Joyce's *Finnegans Wake* (1939), is Anna Livia Plurabelle, the spirit of Dublin's River Liffey. Contained in the name is an allusion to Ana/Anu, the older goddess. Joyce did not invent the figure, as is commonly supposed. He did contrive the nonce word 'Plurabelle' [more than one beauty] and added it to 'Anna Livia', a popular pseudo-Latinization of *Abhainn na Life*, the River of the Liffey, the plain in which Dublin is situated. As with so many names in *Finnegans Wake*, this one contains within it several cross-linguistic puns. During the 1990s a statue and fountain of Anna Livia Plurabelle on Dublin's O'Connell Street met with public ridicule and was replaced with the Millennium Spire. An earlier name for the river was *Ruirteach* [rough, tempestuous].

BIRDS, ANIMALS, FISH

The Celts, like all humans, have seen analogues for their values and themselves in their fellow mortals, feathered, furred and finned. The impulse to view the hawk as embodying the predatory motive in humans, or the fox as incarnating the wily, is hardly unique to any culture. In the oral traditions recorded in Celtic countries during the nineteenth and twentieth centuries, virtually every creature found in Europe is assigned some human attribute or value to enrich a narrative. In many instances a hare or a cow in a Breton or Scottish Gaelic story is no different from counterparts in other European languages. Yet in other instances, such as those concerning the crane, the boar or the salmon, we can see echoes from the earliest materials: animals carved on Iron Age altars, or figures of zoomorphic gods, where animal characteristics are given to human forms. Even in ancient culture, though, not every representation is of the same value; some are divine or totemistic, others merely decorative. Our intention here is to single out the birds, animals and fish who appear continuously over the centuries.

From the earliest times, even the proto-Celtic Urnfield period, *c.*1500–800 BC, Celtic art shows a marked preference for water birds of different kinds. A cormorant appears to be drawing a chariot holding the sun. Other water birds pull a chariot in which idols are seated. Ducks are shown beside a solar wheel or forming the prow and stern of a boat carrying the sun-disc. Swans and cygnets, together with the non-aquatic ravens, decorate a horse-prod or flesh fork from Iron Age Ireland, found at Dunaverney. Some commentators see in these examples associations with a cult of the sun in its healing powers.

More significant are the long-legged wading birds, the egret and the crane, which can resemble one another in badly worn 3,000-year-old icons. The egret, distinguished by long white tail-feathers, appears in Urnfield icons and most prominently in triplet form at a temple of the Gaulish god Esus. A common pairing puts an egret on the back of a bull, an important cult animal, as we shall see. But the egret does not survive so visibly in later vernacular tradition.

The crane, with its long bill, fared better, perhaps because of the perception that the bird was a transformed human. Julius Caesar (first century BC) reported that the ancient Britons refused to eat the crane's flesh under the impression cranes had been human in a previous life. Giraldus Cambrensis (twelfth century) reported the same taboo in Ireland. The crane is also found in Urnfield iconography, at the temple of Esus, and may also be paired with bulls, but it appears dozens of times in vernacular, especially Irish, narrative, often metamorphosed and magical. One Aífe, lover of Ilbrec, was transformed into a crane by Iuchra, a jealous rival. Living as an amphibian for 200 years, she inhabited the realm of Manannán mac Lir, the sea god, sometimes seen as her 'husband'. When she died, Manannán made her skin into the renowned crane bag, containing marvellous artistic treasures.

Known in Irish as the *corrbolg*, the crane bag is at once one of the most mysterious and most commented-upon artefacts in early Irish tradition. Two heroes were thought to have owned it at different times: Lug Lámfhota and Fionn mac Cumhaill. Some modern commentators see the crane bag as part of an origin myth of language and consequently of poetry. Initially Manannán filled the crane bag with items peculiarly precious to him: his own knife and shirt, the king of Scotland's shears, the king of Lochlainn's helmet, the bones of Assal's swine and the girdle of the great whale's back. The substance and contents of the bag imply to some modern readers that it should also have contained the letters of the ogham alphabet. Used for inscriptions before the introduction of Christianity, ogham employs stick-like ciphers, each of them the counterpart of a letter of the Roman alphabet, as suggested by the legs of flying cranes. This association of the crane and the crane bag with writing became more widely known during the era of the influential Irish literary journal, *The Crane Bag*, 1977–81, which reprinted the story in each issue.

The crane is not always benign, however. In ancient belief, those cranes who were not transformed humans were thought stingy and disagreeable. A soldier passing such a crane on his way to battle was doomed. Linked with this perception is the medieval Irish portrait of *glám dícenn* [poet's execration]. A poet used this as a verbal weapon of war, by standing like a crane on one leg, with one eye closed and one arm extended. A victim of *glám dícenn* might have his face blistered or lose his life.

The swan, a symbol of beauty, good luck, and travel to a world beyond the physical, appears even more frequently than the crane in both ancient culture and later narrative tradition. Somewhat contradictorily, the swan may represent both purity and sexual energy, the latter based on its long, phallic neck and observed proclivity for frequent coitus. Again found in Urnfield and Hallstatt (800–600 BC) cultures, the swan is represented in art surviving all over Europe. Swans draw a wheeled cauldron (seventh–sixth centuries BC) found at Orastie, Romania. At Alésia in eastern France, three mothers appear in a sculpture with three children, while a fourth child is seated in a boat and accompanied by a swan.

The best-known Irish swan narrative is *Oidheadh Chlainne Lir* [The Tragic Story of the Children of Lir] in which the four fostered children, Áed, Finnguala, Fiachra and Conn, are put under a spell by their cruel stepmother Aífe. They must live as swans in three exiles, each of 300 years' duration. In other Irish literary cycles, a flock of destructive swans ravages the area around Emain Macha, Co. Armagh, at the time of the hero Cúchulainn's conception. These swans wear chains of gold and silver, as does Cáer Ibormeith, beloved of Angus Óg in *Aislinge Oenguso* [The Dream of Angus], when she is metamorphosed into a swan. Men as well as women may in these tales take swan form, as Mongán of the Irish Cycles of the Kings does. So does the otherworldly Midir in the third part of the ninth-century Irish story, *Tochmarc Étaíne* [The Wooing of Étaín], after he wins an amorous embrace from the beautiful Étaín and takes swan form to fly through the smoke hole in the roof.

The boar, declares Anne Ross in her authoritative *Pagan Celtic Britain* (1967), 'is, without doubt, the cult animal *par excellence* of the Celts'. Citations abound in every aspect of Celtic culture, from the eleventh century BC to the present. On one of the greatest treasures of Celtic religion, the Gundestrup Cauldron found in Denmark, we may see two warriors with boar-crests on their helmets while two demi-gods hold small boars aloft. A British tribe of Roman times called themselves the Orci or 'people of the boar'. The boar was found all over Europe in early times and was, along with the bear, the most aggressive and ferocious animal a person was likely to encounter. Esteemed for its physical strength and heroic defence when cornered, the boar was a prize prey for hunters. The meat of the boar, called 'the hero's portion', was given prestige at banquets – thus the animal could link war and hunting as well as feasting and hospitality. The boar's skin was thought appropriate dress for a warrior, and a boar's head appears on the crest of the Clan MacKinnon from Gaelic Scotland.

Deification and personification of the boar would follow. A Gaulish god named Moccus, equated by the Romans with Mercury, epitomized the power of the boar. Yet there was also a Romano-Gaulish sow deity named Arduinna, associated with the Ardennes Forest. Neither of these attracted huge cults and both seem pale compared to the boar figures in vernacular tradition, even in Ireland where the boar became extinct as early as the twelfth century. An encounter with a boar kills the hero of the Irish Fenian Cycle, Diarmait Ua Duibne, an episode echoing Adonis's fatal boar hunt in classical mythology. Diarmait's boar is his own half-brother; Diarmait's father Donn had killed a bastard son whose spirit was transformed into the animal. Orc Triath was an otherworldly boar or pig in Irish tradition; and the similar-sounding Torc Triath was king of the boars in the pseudo-history *Lebor Gabála* [Book of Invasions]. Elsewhere in the *Lebor Gabála*, the purported narrator of the story, the survivor Tuan mac Cairill, who tells of the different invasions to St Finnian of Moville, is transformed into a boar, among other things. Otherworldly boars are found as well in Welsh tradition under the name of Twrch Trwyth and in Brittany as Tourtain. Boars are also featured prominently in the *Mabinogi*, the exemplar of medieval Welsh literature. In the third branch, *Manawydan*, a gleaming white boar leads Pryderi, the blameless hero who appears in all four branches, into an enclosure from which he cannot escape. In the fourth branch, *Math*, the magician Gwydion takes the form of a boar and his brother Gilfaethwy a sow so that together they may produce the tall piglet, Hychdwn Hir.

Figuring even more prominently than the boar on the Gundestrup Cauldron is an antlered zoomorphic figure, squatting in a position which resembles the half lotus in yoga. We call this figure, rather glibly, Cernunnos [the horned one], as his name is known from only one inscription, but his physical representation is so widespread that he was surely an important god of the continental Celts, or, on the assertion of some commentators, the principal god. With a man's body and the horns of a stag, he is the lord of nature, animals, fruit, grain and prosperity. Representations of Cernunnos are found from pre-Roman times but are even more frequent during Roman occupation, especially in north-central Gaul. He is always shown with the torc or neck ring, a common artefact of Celtic religion also found around the neck of the warrior depicted in the statue of the Dying Gaul (third century BC). He may or may not be bearded and is often accompanied by ram-headed serpents. Then again, our knowledge of Cernunnos is so tenuous that he may not be a divinity at all but rather a shaman-like priest with antlers affixed to his head.

Both the stag and the hornless deer, stag or doe, were important cult animals. As monarch of the northern forests, the stag was admired for its speed, grace and sexual prowess during the rutting season. Shed in autumn and growing again in spring, the antlers re-enact the growing season. Their hardness evokes erect male genitalia; carved antlers were used to make phallic amulets. Carvings in the Camonica Valley of the Italian Alps link the stag with sun imagery. In early Irish tradition stags might also be associated with women. Flidais, the Diana-like early goddess of wild things, is also mistress of stags. The war-goddess Mórrígan might also take the form of the stag. In Gaelic Scotland, where deer were and continue to be prevalent, there are indications of deer worship in the Lochaber region. The *sianach* is a deer-monster in Scottish Gaelic oral tradition.

In early Irish and Welsh narratives, deer appear most often in two modes, as enticers of mortals to the otherworld and as transformed beings. The great Irish hero Fionn mac Cumhaill often hunts an enchanted stag who is the metamorphosed god Donn. With the coming of Christianity, the stag became a guide for souls seeking heaven and was so represented in cemeteries. As for transformation, both mortals and fairies might become deer, willingly or unwillingly. One Irish story depicts a jealous woman turning one hundred girls into deer. Perhaps the strangest of these transformations comes in a poem attributed to St Patrick (fifth century) titled in English 'The Deer's Cry' or 'St Patrick's Breastplate'. The saint uses a power called *féth fiada* to turn himself and a companion named Benén into wild deer so that they may escape ambush while on their way to evangelize Tara, the royal hill in the Boyne Valley. Their adversaries see only a deer with a fawn.

Some fawns, on the other hand, may be warlike, like the Irish Fenian hero Oisín, the principal son of Fionn mac Cumhaill. To conceive him, Fionn sleeps with the deer-woman, Sadb, thus explaining Oisín's name, the diminutive of *os* [deer], meaning 'little deer' or fawn. Within the bulk of Fenian narratives the character of Oisín manifests no hints of zoomorphism, but in later tales he is the one invited to enjoy a 300-year love affair with a beautiful damsel, Niam, in the otherworld, as in Micheál Coimín's *Laoi Oisín i dTír na nÓg* [The Lay of Oisín in the Land of Youth], *c.* 1750. The persona of Oisín was also the basis for James Macpherson's creation Ossian in the *Poems of Ossian* (1760–63).

The name of the horse goddess Epona has long had a certain cachet and is likely to be among the first a beginning reader would encounter in discussions of the Celtic world. That arises in part from her popular but unsupported association with the superb Uffington White Horse in Oxfordshire, one of the earth's largest pictorial works of art. With a distinctive taut, curvilinear style, the figure, 364 ft long, was cut through the sod to the underlying layer of white chalk about 50 BC. Unfortunately, surviving evidence suggests that the cult of Epona did not arrive in Britain until after the coming of the Romans almost 100 years later in AD 43. Epona's cult originated in eastern Gaul near Alésia prior to its spread to Britain; inscriptions and statues commemorating her are more numerous than for any other goddess. She is usually shown on horseback, sometimes sidesaddle, often clothed but occasionally nude and nymph-like. Her name is sometimes given in plural form, Eponabus, perhaps explained by the triplication of her form as found at Hogonange in the Moselle Valley. Roman commentators noted her popularity with the cavalry, who erected her statue in stables. She was the only Celtic deity ever placed in the Roman pantheon, where she was remembered on 18 December.

The horse, not native to Europe, was introduced about the eighth century BC in the Iron Age and quickly became associated with the aristocratic warrior elite. Horses were seen in continental Celtic culture only a short time before they began to be employed in sacrifices and ritual practices, as when drawing their funerary chariots, and sometimes interred with humans. Not surprisingly, then, the horse may be linked with deities other than Epona, such as the Gaulish Rudiobus, who is honoured with a beautifully preserved bronze statue (first century BC) found in the Loire Valley, western France. Rudiobus may be an aspect of Gaulish Mars (see Chapter 2) rather than a native god. Celtic Jupiter and Celtic Apollo also had associations with the horse, the former in huge columns where the sky god and sun god would appear on horseback. Horse figurines appear as votive offerings at the healing springs of Celtic Apollo (also worshipped as Belenus).

Owning horses may have been an uncommon luxury in the remote British Isles after the fall of the Roman empire, one of the reasons the horse is conspicuously absent in the heroic tales of Fionn mac Cumhaill, for example. The horse, nevertheless, remained in high esteem. As the swiftest of terrestrial travellers, it could be associated with the courses of the heavens of the sun. The Irish hero Cúchulainn has two prized horses, Liath Macha and Dubh Sainglenn or Saingliu. The second most common man's name in early Ireland, Eochaid/ Eochu, means something like 'horse rider' or 'fighter on horseback'. According to Giraldus Cambrensis's twelfth-century *Topographia Hibernia*, a medieval Irish ritual required the slaughter of a white mare and the would-be king's supposed sexual union with it, an act that would assure his achievement of sovereignty (see Chapter 3). In early Irish and Welsh narrative the pairing of the horse with different women rings with sexual resonance. At the beginning of the action of the epic *Táin Bó Cuailnge* [The Cattle Raid of Cooley], the pregnant Macha (one of three women to bear this name) is forced to run a humiliating footrace with the horses of King Conchobar mac Nessa. At issue is her husband Crunniuc's boast that she can outrun any steed. Breathlessly, she does cross the finish line first, and then collapses in mortal agony, giving birth to twins, cursing all the men of Ulster to suffer the pangs of childbirth (Ir. *ces noínden Ulad*) for five days and four nights at the time of their greatest difficulty (see Chapter 9).

Echoes of Epona and the shadowy early British goddess Rigantona survive in the sonorously named Rhiannon, one of the major female characters in the Welsh *Mabinogi*, appearing in the first and third branches. When Rhiannon rides by on a white horse, Pwyll, prince of Dyfed (southern Wales) is so bedazzled by her that he resolves to make her his wife. When Rhiannon after a few years of marriage produces a son, the infant is stolen on the night of his birth, May Eve, a fateful day on the Celtic calendar. She is falsely accused of the child's murder and is forced into a mortifying but telling public penance: she must sit by the horse block outside the palace gate for seven years, offering all visitors a ride on her back. In time, the son is found, identified and returned to her, after which she gives him the name Pryderi. In the third branch of the *Mabinogi*, Pryderi, risen to power, promises his still beautiful mother, Rhiannon, to a powerful comrade-in-arms, Manawydan. Rhiannon and Pryderi are some of the few to survive a deadly mist that devastates Dyfed.

As both continental and insular Celts were cattle-raising and cattle-driving peoples, their ready use of bovine imagery bespeaks profound veneration and reverence. In this they were not unlike other early Europeans. Prehistoric cave paintings at Lascaux in France and Bronze Age mosaics in Crete long predate Celtic artistic expression. A small bronze figurine of a bull with extended, implicitly aggressive horns was found at Hallstatt (seventh century BC), and comparable figures appear in different parts of the Celtic world over the next several centuries. The Gundestrup Cauldron features two images of bulls, one of a slain carcass on the base plate, and another in which three sword-wielding warriors assault three larger-than-life bulls, their inflated stature implying supernatural rank. Abundant evidence of bull sacrifice survives in Iron Age graves and is later testified to by Pliny the Elder in *Natural History* (first century AD). Romanized Gauls worshipped a three-horned bull named Tarvos Trigaranus, examples of which survive in Trier, Germany, and at the Cluny Museum in Paris. Forty other figures of triple-horned bulls survive at such well-known sites as Glanum in Provence and the ringfort of Maiden Castle in Dorset. Figures of bulls are carved in stone near Burghead, north-eastern Scotland.

Bulls were used in divination ceremonies in both Ireland and Scotland. The best-known of these was the *tarbfheis* [bull-feast or bull-sleep] at Tara, in which a new king was chosen by having a man, not the candidate for kingship, feast upon a slaughtered bull, lie under an incantation from druids, and then know the identity of the new king in a dream. Further discussion of early kingship appears in Chapter 3. A comparable ritual in Gaelic Scotland was the *taghairm*, which required a person seeking the answer to an important question about the future to wrap himself in the steaming hide of a newly slain bull in a remote place, preferably near a waterfall. The supplicant would then learn the answer to his question while in a trance.

The most celebrated bulls in all of Celtic literature are Donn Cuailnge, the Brown Bull of Ulster, and Finnbennach, the White-horned Bull of Connacht, in the great epic of early Ireland, *Táin Bó Cuailnge* [The Cattle Raid of Cooley]. Although never anthropomorphized, the two bulls carry with them the fortunes of their respective provinces. The conflict between them is a constant theme in the narrative, and their final battle, won by Donn Cuailnge, is the climax of the action. Many commentators have observed that the bulls appear to be of divine origin. And in later oral tradition, threatening supernatural bulls are thought to inhabit certain waterways, such as the Scottish Gaelic *tarbh uisge* and the Manx *taroo ushtey*. A distant echo of the *Táin* narrative may be indicated by carvings on the stone known as Cloch nan Tarbh near Loch Lomond, in which a Scottish bull is depicted as defeating an English one.

Not being maritime peoples, the ancient Celts made relatively slight iconographic use of marine creatures. The dolphin appears widely in religious art, and a prominent dolphin on the Gundestrup Cauldron is ridden by a small male figure, perhaps a godling. Unidentifiable fish, possibly salmon, are portrayed on certain Gallo-Roman altars. Nodons, ancient god of the Severn in western England, is shown hooking a salmon. But it is not until we approach the vernacular tradition that we find extensive references to marine life, especially that living in fresh waters, the eel, the trout and, most conspicuously, the salmon.

In early Irish and Welsh traditions salmon are the repositories of otherworldly wisdom, esoteric knowledge that they have gained by eating hazelnuts fallen into pools at the headwaters of important rivers. As salmon swim from salt to fresh water, they may have been seen as travellers between worlds. Their ability to swim against the current and up cataracts easily excites human imagination, and their pink flesh may have evoked human flesh. Two salmon of wisdom are cited in Fenian stories, both touched by the hero Fionn mac Cumhaill, one at the pool of Linn Féic along the Boyne River and the second at the Falls of Assaroe on the Erne waterway. In the former, better known story, the bard Finnéces (whose name can be confused with Fionn's, often

Finn in Old Irish) has been fishing for the salmon for seven years when the youthful hero happens along. Finnéces thinks his patience has been rewarded when he finally catches the fish and begins cooking it over a fire. But Fionn touches the cooking salmon with his thumb, burning it, and thrusts it into his mouth, thus giving himself the otherworldly wisdom Finnéces had sought. A comparable Welsh salmon swims under the name Llyn Llyw in the Severn and is the 'wisest of forty animals' and 'the oldest of living creatures'; it tells the hero Culhwch where the youthful Mabon is being held prisoner.

Human interactions with salmon take many forms. Like the Norse god Loki who took the form of a salmon to escape detection, several personages are wholly or partly transformed into salmon, such as the poet Amairgin of the Milesians, Fintan mac Bóchra who survived the Biblical flood, and Taliesin the Welsh poet. Tuan mac Cairill, putative narrator of the pseudo-history *Lebor Gabála* [Book of Invasions], tells the story of being changed into a salmon and eaten by a woman who gives birth to him under his own form so that he might tell the history of Ireland. The beautiful Lí Ban of Lough Neagh in Northern Ireland becomes a salmon except for her head. The motif migrated easily into early Christian narrative, as in the story of Saint Fínán Cam's mother who was impregnated by a salmon when she went swimming after dark. Saint Kentigern (d. 603) is reported to have found a ring in a salmon, a story which explains the seal of the City of Glasgow, of which Kentigern is a patron. The motif of the ring thrown into the water to be caught by a salmon bears the Aarne-Thompson international catalogue number of 736A, meaning the same episode is also found in other traditional literatures, without our having a clear explanation why it should be so widespread. In an Irish variant of 736A, Ailill (one of dozens bearing this name) casts the ring into a stream, and much later the Irish hero Fráech discovers it in a salmon's belly.

2

Remnants of Celtic Religion

DRUIDS

'Druid' is a troublesome word for readers of Celtic myth. As one of the few concepts from early Celtic culture to have migrated into popular usage, any mention of a 'druid' now conjures up a fog of associations and connotations that cannot be supported by texts written in any language before AD 1500. 'Druidism', for example, will not work as a synonym for Celtic religion or Celtic culture as a whole, although such implications still exist in print. Further, the druids did not build the surviving ancient monuments in Western Europe once attributed to them, such as Stonehenge in England or Carnac in Brittany, both constructed well before Celtic languages were spoken in those areas. What little we know about the druids comes primarily from ancient sources, Greek and Roman, augmented by early Irish and Welsh documents. There is even some argument about what the root meaning of the word 'druid' might be.

One of the reasons we know so little about what druids thought or practised is that their learning was oral and secret, judged too sacred to be written down where it could be seized upon by the uninitiated or the profane. Such practice has many parallels in other religions, starting with the mystery cults of later Greece. The claim by modern druids to be in possession of esoteric wisdom that has survived in secret from ancient times is not supported by scholars outside their religious community.

The druids were a religious order among the Celtic peoples of ancient Britain, where, perhaps, the order originated, and Gaul and Ireland. One commentator calls them priest-philosophers, another magician-sages. They might fulfil many roles for the society they served: judges, diviners, intellectuals, mediators with the gods. The druids of Gaul had authority over divine worship, officiated at sacrifices (including, perhaps, human sacrifices), exercised supreme authority over legislative and judicial matters, and educated elite youth along with aspirants to their order. As members of a privileged learned class, they did not have to pay taxes or serve in the military. Ancient commentators classified them in three strata, a categorization supported by early Irish records. Highest in status are the philosophers and theologians, who bear the name druid without modification. They were not the only persons of elevated rank. Below them are the diviners and seers, also known as *vates* or *manteis*. Third are the panegyric poets or *bardi*. The Irish *filid* (sing. *fili*) is an exact cognate of *vates*, and the Welsh *gwawd* is a near cognate. Bards, as we use the term in English, also existed in Ireland and Wales. Both women and men served as druids according to Irish sources, but the evidence for female druids among the ancient continental Celts is more ambiguous. In an oft-cited passage in Tacitus' *Annals* (first century AD), the Roman general Suetonius Paulinus was greeted on the island of Anglesey in northwest Wales by druids and also by black-robed women with dishevelled hair like furies, who stood beside but apparently separate from the druids. Several scholars have recently argued convincingly that although classical sources do not name female druids, the presence of women as magicians, warriors and commanders in battle (see Chapter 4) implies the likelihood of women as druids in ancient times.

Put another way, even the most reliable of classical sources were still subject to their own prejudices and may be interpreted with reference to knowledge come to light in the last century. The oldest text referring to the druids comes from an anonymous Greek from *c.*200 BC who spoke of certain 'philosophers' among the barbarian Celts. Julius Caesar's seven-volume *Gallic War* (first century BC) has long been the most frequently cited source, although we recognize today that many of his observations are taken from subordinates as well as from the stoic philosopher Posidonius (*c.*135–*c.*51 BC). In Caesar's disdainful view, druids were one of two groups of men who held honour among the Gauls, the other being the nobles (*equites*). In contrast to the nobles, the druids were a highly organized inter-tribal brotherhood. If anyone were to disobey their decrees, the druids would give him the severest of punishments: to be barred from sacrifices. One druid was to be made chief over the others, and upon his death another would be appointed. If there were several candidates of equal merit, an assembly of druids would vote for the successor. This was not always orderly, as armed conflict was known to break out among disappointed candidates and their supporters. Once each year the druids would assemble at a sacred place in the land of the Carnutes, between the Seine and Loire Rivers, thought to be the centre of all Gaul, at which time druids would rule on all the disputes of the preceding year.

Caesar speaks of a druidical religious belief that human souls do not cease at the death of the body but are reborn in different forms. In classical times such a belief would be known as a variation of metempsychosis, a doctrine espoused by sixth-century BC mathematician and philosopher Pythagoras. Today we are more likely to speak of it as reincarnation, an idea found in Eastern religion and advanced by any number of modern mystics and prophets. Thus many informed commentators see the druids as Celtic counterparts of the Roman *flāmines* or the brahmins of India. There is no reliable documentation, however, to support the speculation that the druid was a Celtic equivalent of the shaman of north Asia and among native North Americans. The shaman is a healer with magical powers who serves as a medium to the spiritual world to bring about good or evil; the shaman becomes a medium in an ecstatic trance, sometimes assisted by natural hallucinogens. The only shard of evidence for a link with shamanism is the pierced antler, perhaps used as a headdress, found at a fourth-century AD Roman bath-site in what is now Hertfordshire.

Augmenting Caesar's view of druidical religion is the description of a ceremony in Pliny the Elder's *Natural History* (first century AD). During a festival of the sixth day of the moon, white-robed druids climb an oak tree, cut with a golden sickle the mistletoe growing there, and sacrifice two white bulls as part of a fertility rite. European mistletoe, unlike its North American counterpart, grows in nest-like balls, a parasite high on the limbs of trees such as the oak and the apple. What is implied by this procedure has been the subject of enormous commentary, including that in Sir James Frazer's *Golden*

Bough, whose title is a translation of Virgil's name for mistletoe. Informed opinion today asserts that the druids felt mistletoe mixed in drink could cure barrenness. The analogy is to the plant's flourishing in winter when the oak supporting it is barren and apparently dead. But even more powers may be implied. When Lindow Man, the second-century BC British murder victim, was exhumed in 1984, the analysis of his stomach revealed he had eaten mistletoe pollen prior to his death.

More troublesome are the druidical associations with the oak tree. Contemporary informed opinion now rejects the etymology of the word 'druid' as derived from the speculative root *dervo-vidos*: 'knowledge of the oak'. The English word 'druid' is not borrowed from any Celtic language and derives instead from the Latin *druidae*, *druides* via the French *druide*. Both Latin and Greek (*druidai*) forms are plural, presupposing a Gaulish root, *druvis*, from *druvids*, which has yet to be found in any inscription. Celtic languages offer tantalizing cognates. The Old Irish *druí* is sometimes translated as 'druid' but may also mean magician, wizard, diviner, poet or learned man. The Welsh *dryw* [seer] is probably a cognate of the Irish. From these Kenneth H. Jackson hypothesizes a Gaulish original of *druwids*, meaning 'wise man of the woods' or 'very wise man'. These seem unrelated to the several Celtic words for oak, Old Irish *dair*, etc. But the Greek root for oak, *dru-*, is implicit in the name of the sanctuary Drunemeton among the Galatians of Anatolia, which the geographer Strabo (first century AD) tells us was filled with oak trees.

Whether Lindow Man was a druidical sacrifice is impossible to say on the evidence, but plentiful classical testimony speaks of the druids' role in other human sacrifice. With some disgust, Caesar speculated that the druids felt supernatural powers could be controlled only if one human life were exchanged for another, so that victims would be slaughtered as a kind of compensation for men falling in battle. Criminals and social outcasts would be favoured for this role but, lacking them, any helpless innocent would do. Strabo supplies vivid details. The Cimbri people of Gaul (who may or may not have been Celts) liked to collect the blood from the slashed necks of victims in cauldrons with the expectation it might aid in divination. The death-throes of stabbing victims were also thought to portend the future. Other victims might be imprisoned for five years, shot with arrows, impaled, or, most memorably, burned alive in a huge wicker figure of a man. This last image has been drawn by several artists over the centuries and was the premise of a 1973 British cult movie *The Wicker Man*. Tacitus describes druidical altars on the island of Anglesey as being drenched with blood and human entrails.

Roman contempt for the druids became the pretext for their suppression. Druidical practice was judged 'seditious' in occupied Gaul. Inscriptions on Gallo-Roman altars and shrines, however, indicate that elements of the older cults continued all through the Pagan period. The end of native tradition came more abruptly in Roman Britain, in AD 61, when imperial troops pursued the druids to Anglesey and slaughtered them.

Early Irish literary record cites the names of hundreds of druids, always in prominent positions in the courts of powerful rulers. In the *Lebor Gabála* the druid Mide, eponym of the province of Mide (coextensive with Co. Meath and parts of six other counties), lights the first fire in Ireland, which lasts for seven years and from which every other fire is lit. Instead of oak, the druids of Ireland favoured the wood of the yew tree, hawthorn and rowan, especially for use in wands. Such wands might be carved with the figures of the ogham alphabet. Druids watched flame and smoke for telling signs and chewed raw flesh to induce visions. As masters of divination, they possessed three powers that would later be attributed to poets and heroes. Those powers were *díchetal do chennaib* or extempore incantation, perhaps a kind of clairvoyance or psychometry in which the seer conveys his message in quatrain or verse; *imbas forosnai* or poetic talent that illuminates, which comes to the seer only after he/she chews on a piece of red meat from a pig, dog or cat; and *teinm laida*, breaking open of the pith, most mysterious of the three, which the hero Fionn could gain by gnawing his magical thumb and chanting. With the coming of Christianity, druids were portrayed as disputing unsuccessfully with Saint Patrick and Colum Cille.

Druidism may not simply have been snuffed out with the coming of Christianity, but any argument that it has survived in some form to modern times gets no hearing from Celtic scholars in leading universities. Nonetheless, the popular press reports that people calling themselves 'druids' appear from time to time at the ancient monuments of Great Britain and Ireland, especially at the time of the summer solstice. For the true believers, their faith has survived in secret through centuries of Christian hegemony. Sceptics, including nearly all academics, trace modern druidism to seventeenth- and eighteenth-century antiquarians in England, France and Germany, beginning with John Aubrey (1616–97) and William Stukeley (1687–1765), the latter of whom took the pseudonym Chyndonax, after an ancient druid allegedly named in an inscription found at Dijon, France. In their view druids had migrated to Europe from India but were nonetheless linked to aboriginal North Americans. Virtually every prehistoric monument was attributed to druidical religious practice, most prominently Stonehenge on Salisbury Plain in Wiltshire. The phrases 'druids' table' and 'druidical circles' were applied to megalithic structures today called dolmens or portal tombs as well as to stone circles. Stukeley may have founded the Order of Druids in 1717, a claim that is disputed, but documents support Henry Hurle's establishment of the Ancient Order of Druids, a quasi-masonic society, in 1781. A doctrinal dispute created the breakaway United Order of Druids in 1839. Under the banner of neo-druidism the Welshman Iolo Morganwg (né Edward Williams, 1747–1826) launched the national cultural society called Gorsedd Beirdd Ynys Prydain [Throne/Assembly of the Bards of the Isle of Britain] in 1792, which fostered a revival of interest in the Welsh national heritage.

ROMAN INTERPRETATION AND CELTIC ACCOMMODATION

The Romans in Gaul, like subsequent imperialists, were indifferent students of the culture and language of conquered peoples. They were not incipient anthropologists ready to make close observation of outlandish and multiform religious practice. As well as being reluctant to record much detail about native religion, the Romans assumed that strange Gaulish deities were actually new guises of the gods they had worshipped in Rome. The artefacts and modes of worship might be entirely different, but the Romans sensed that there was something in the portrayal of or the powers attributed to a god, that made him identical to, say, Mercury or Jupiter. At Bath in Roman Britain, the indigenous healing deity Sulis was merged with the Roman Minerva, as mentioned previously, so that she became known as Sulis Minerva or Sul-Minerva. The phrase for this view, *interpretatio Romana*, comes from Tacitus' *Germania*, but the mindset was shared by all Romans. Again it is Julius Caesar's *Gallic War* that focuses what the Roman commentators observed. Drawing on classical records, we now speak of Gaulish Mercury, Gaulish Apollo, and Gaulish Minerva because we lack fuller information on native names for the deities. Gaulish Mars, then, is not a local copy of a Roman god but rather the name we must now ascribe to a Celtic deity whose cult or possible iconography we cannot know.

A systemization so patronizing and short-sighted has two severe shortcomings that are probably immediately apparent to the reader. First, Caesar attributes spheres and functions to the Gaulish gods analogous with a Roman model that may never have existed in the Gaulish context. Second, Caesar implies a Roman-style pantheon of Gaulish gods worshipped throughout the culture, whereas other evidence does not corroborate that there was ever such an ordering or that any gods were worshipped universally.

Before we disparage Caesar's efforts further, we should acknowledge that his point of view is not alien to that of most modern readers. Our education, our sense of order and logic, derive from classical culture as reinterpreted over the centuries. Further, modern readers are likely to have studied classical mythology, Greek as well as Roman, before investigating the Celtic, as mentioned earlier. If one does not expect that the Celtic god is a duplicate of Apollo or Mars, a modern reader can be forgiven for thinking the Celtic god might be portrayed in some of the same ways, for example to be pictured in sculptures or carvings, venerated in sacred hymns or characterized in sacred narratives. Such corroboration is, alas, hard to come by.

Edward Anwyl noted as long ago as 1906 in *Celtic Religion in Pre-Christian Times* that of the 374 deity names known at the time from inscriptions and other records, 305 occur only once. Texts in the Gaulish language are disappointingly skimpy. One of the longest, the Larzac Inscription, found in a cave in southern France in 1983, employs only 160 Gaulish words in Latin cursive script, none of them portraying divine figures in narrative.

The multiplicity of names does not necessarily mean that each name refers to a single divinity. We know from Greek tradition that important deities may be known by more than one name. Apollo, for example, is also known as Phoebus, his preferred name in the *Iliad*, just as Athena may be known as Pallas. In later Irish tradition, one name may indicate a trio of deities who are grouped together, such as Mórrígna, which includes the Mórrígan, Badb and Macha. Again among the Irish, one name may also indicate three distinct persons, as there are three discrete Machas, only one of whom is included under Mórrígna (see triplism, pp. 44–6 below). Gods may also be known under pious circumlocutions, such as 'the god of our people', or as Christians say, 'Our Lord'. Joseph Vendryes (1948) reminds us that the Gaulish god called Teutates cited by Lucan (first century AD) appears to derive his name from the word for 'tribe', *teutā* (cf. Old Irish *tuath*), so that his name might very well mean 'the god of the tribe'.

An untold number among the multiplicity of Gaulish names undoubtedly indicate local deities, unknown a half hour's walk from their presumed demesne. The Gauls may well have anticipated later oral tradition in Ireland, Gaelic Scotland, Wales and Brittany that assigns a spirit, spectre or even 'fairy' to most prominent caves, promontories, waterfalls, heaths or crossroads. Such phenomena are unlikely to be called 'gods' by English observers, as centuries of education in classical models give us more demanding expectations, such as that a 'god' be something like an Olympian. We recognize that such creatures as the menacing Scottish kelpie, a 'water horse', or the spectral Breton *yannig*, a maritime demon, are of a lesser order, even if we are uncertain about which rubric might contain them. An isolated Gaulish inscription or a cryptic reference in a Roman text does not allow us to know the status of the supernatural figure in that long-extinct culture.

Overlying all these questions is the process modern scholars have named *interpretatio Celtica*, apparently initiated by indigenous populations. When Romans built temples to the gods of their pantheon in occupied territories, resident Gauls and Britons appear to have fused some of their gods with those of the conqueror. The merging (or confusion) of cults is commonplace elsewhere in the ancient world. The cult of the old earth mother Ge (also Gaia, Gaea) was so closely associated with that of her daughter Themis, consort of Zeus, that the two are sometimes seen as one and called Ge-Themis in modern texts. Among the great world religions the process is called syncretism, as when, for example, the evangelism of Christian missionaries in Guatemala becomes riddled with native animist cults. This appears to be what happened in the name of Mars Vesontius in what is today Besançon in eastern France. Joseph Vendryes argues that the local god was equated with and merged into Mars, displacing the earlier interpretation so that the dedication simply linked Mars to the location (Vesontius/Besançon). So it is with Apollo Grannus of Gaul, Jupiter Parthinus of Dalmatia or Mars Rigonemetis of Lincolnshire, whose name incorporates *nemeton*, the Celtic word for sacred grove. Not all fusions are complete, however. Some other native deities may be merged with the Roman pantheon, as Mars Olloudius or Mars Teutates, or their inscriptions may appear by themselves, as Olloudius or Teutates.

Caesar speaks of six gods among the Gauls and ranks them in order of his perception of their importance: Mercury, Apollo, Mars, Jupiter, Minerva and Dis Pater (or Pluto). His placement of Mercury as first among the divinities is supported by the observation that he was most honoured among the Gauls, which is additionally confirmed by modern archaeology. There is a brief moment of reassurance here as the Roman Mercury, divine messenger and god of borders, ranks in the lower middle of the pantheon while Jupiter (or Jove), of course, is the supreme Roman deity. Caesar, whom we recognize as something of an agnostic in private, allowed his observations to re-order what he had brought with him.

Gaulish Mercury, according to Caesar, was the inventor of all the arts, a guide on roads and on journeys, and the most influential in commerce and money-making. Unlike his Roman counterpart, his patronage of arts extended to those of war. Iconographic images often represent him much like the classical Mercury: youthful, beardless and equipped with the caduceus (snake-entwined traveller's wand), the petasus (winged hat) and the purse of plenty; yet in other instances he could be bearded and dressed in Gaulish costume. In some representations he is triple-faced, and in others triple-phallused. His cult partner might be Maia, whom the Romans identified with an old Italian goddess of the springs, or Rosmerta, a native deity associated with prosperity, fertility and motherhood. In inscriptions he is assigned at least forty-five epithets or cognomens, including Mercury Moccus, from the Gaulish word for 'pig', implying an association with hunting.

While the Romans never bothered to record a native name for Gaulish Mercury, modern scholars discern two. The favoured is Lugos or Lugus, found in many inscriptions and implicit in the Roman town name Lug(u)dunum, which is itself the root of the modern place names Lyon, Laon, Loudon, Leiden, Liegnitz, etc. Lugos/Lugus also looks like an anticipation of the Irish hero Lug Lámfhota, whose epithet *Samildánach* means 'possessing many arts, crafts, trades', the Welsh Lleu Llaw Gyffes and the calendar feast of Lughnasa. Attractive as this argument is for the continuity of continental and insular Celtic culture, other commentators suggest the name Erriapus for Gaulish Mercury on the evidence of a carved head found in the Garonne region of southern France.

Apollo's name is immediately associated with poetry, music and the civilizing benefits of culture in modern reference, but his realm was wider in the ancient world. As the only deity of the Roman pantheon borrowed whole and entire from the Greeks, not merely adapted or fashioned into a counterpart, as Mercury was, Apollo's cult nonetheless underwent a sea change in the journey from Delphi to the banks of the Tiber. The Roman populace favoured Apollo's healing powers, which they linked to his association with the sun. Modern handbooks of mythology are more likely to shift this power to Apollo's adopted 'son', Asclepius or Aesculapius. Yet it is the power of healing, especially at thermal springs (warmth presuming the power of the sun), that Caesar cites in distinguishing Gaulish Apollo. He is sometimes assigned one of two consorts, Damona in northeastern Gaul and Sirona, whose cult extended from what is now Hungary to Brittany. Gaulish Apollo had as many as fifteen epithets, of which the most conspicuous were Belenus, Citharoedus, Grannus, Moritasgus and Vindonnus, each of them worshipped at healing springs.

Once again, the Romans gave no thought to a Gaulish name for

Gaulish Apollo but they inadvertently preserved evidence to allow us to decipher several native identities. Among the most resonant of these is the cognomen Belenus, as it is indeed also the name of a deity who was worshipped from the Adriatic to Scotland and as late as the beginning of the third century AD in the eastern Alps. The Celtic root *bel-* (Gaulish: bright [?], brilliant [?]) also appears in the Irish Beltaine and the Scottish Gaelic Bealltuinn, names for May Day, one of four principal holidays on the Celtic calendar. Belenus, then, must have been a solar character like Roman Apollo. Such wisps of information hardly give us the full identity of Gaulish Apollo but they hint at shadowy but sure outlines just beyond our grasp.

Gaulish Apollo's sometime consort Damona is the more usual cult partner of Borvo (also Bormanus and Bormo), a healing god of Gaul with shrines scattered from Bourbonne-les-Bains in the upper Marne valley to Galicia in northwestern Spain. At Vichy he is seen seated with a warrior's helmet and shield, a horned serpent rearing up against him. If these accoutrements signal a patronage of the arts of war, then Borvo too may be Gaulish Apollo.

More tenuous but even more intriguing is Gaulish Apollo's possible identification with Maponos, the Divine Youth, whose cult flourished in the north of Britain but was also found in Gaul. Like the others, Maponos's name is found at healing springs, at least in Gaul. In Britain he is equated with Apollo Citharoedus (the harper/cithern player) and attributed with skill in the art of music; this latter talent, of course, was an attribute of Apollo in Greece and Rome. Maponos, most commentators now agree, contributes to the conception of the Welsh divine hero Mabon. Linguist Eric Hamp argues further that an accurate gloss of the title *Mabinogi*, for the four related narratives of medieval Welsh literature, would be 'the (collective) material pertaining to the god Maponos' (see Chapter 13). If Maponos is indeed a divine persona behind Gaulish Apollo, the shadow he cast was long. The British divinity is additionally the counterpart of the Irish Angus Óg, god of youth, beauty and (qualifiedly) love, especially when he is referred to by one of the many forms of his patronymic, Mac Óc, Mac-ind-Óc, etc.

The Roman deity Mars, like the Roman Apollo, was attributed spheres and functions not always accounted for in tidy, modern handbook accounts of him. Certainly he was the principal god of war, patron of the Roman army, ranking second only to Jupiter in the pantheon; his very name gives us the English word 'martial'. Among the Roman populace more generally, however, including emigrants to conquered colonies of Gaul and Britain, Mars retained qualities of Mamers, his anticipation among the Sabines and Oscans as well as the Italianate Mavers or Mavors. Such a deity was a pacific defender of fields and borders, thus a tribal or territorial entity as well as a healer. For these reasons Roman observers attributed to Gaulish Mars diverse powers in addition to those of combat. In shrines at Movilly, now in Burgundy, eastern France, and at Trier, he is not a warrior on the Roman model but rather he fights and protects against bad health and infertility. One explanation for this may be that once Gaul became an occupied province, Mars was more likely to re-enact the powers of his earlier manifestations and to shake off (though not completely) the more bellicose persona, linked to Greek Ares, of conquering armies or the imperial capital. And so it was that Gaulish Mars was more likely to be aligned with healing gods; Mars Vorocius, dressed as a Celtic soldier, was thought to heal ailments of the eye at what is today Vichy, central Gaul. Afflictions of the eye might also be taken to Mars Mullo (cf. L. *mullo*: mule), worshipped widely in northwestern Gaul in what is today Normandy and Brittany. Mars Nabelcus was a protective local deity in Provence. The cult of the great healer-god Mars Lenus attracted huge numbers of worshippers among the Traveri of the Moselle valley, centring on the Roman city of Trier. Such associations extended to Roman-occupied Britain. Mars Loucetious was commemorated on the altar of the healing temple at Bath. And Mars is equated with the British god Nodons, whose third-century AD healing sanctuary at Lydney Park on the River Severn, Gloucestershire, is one of the most substantial surviving monuments from Roman Britain.

Such worship did not, however, drive out all the warlike manifestations associated with Gaulish Mars. His sometime epithet 'Caturis' means 'king of combat' or 'master of fighting'. Mars was linked with Segomo, whose name means 'victorious', in both Gaul and Britain. Mars Corotiacus in Britain is depicted as a cavalryman trampling an adversary beneath his hoofs. As Mars Camulos, in Britain he began to absorb the important native war god whose name was recorded in the Roman place-name Camulodunum, ancestor of modern Colchester.

Of these local associations of Gaulish Mars, the one attracting the most interest is Mars Toutatis, found only at Barkway, Hertfordshire. On one hand, this may only mean that Mars was the god of the local tribe, *teutā*, as Vendryes has argued (see above). Or it may mean that Gaulish Mars is ultimately identified with the war god named Teutates, described by Roman poet Lucan in *Pharsalia* (first century AD). Our only other evidence for Mars = Teutates comes from the anonymous ninth-century AD author of the Berne Commentaries on Lucan (*Scholia Bernensia*) who forthrightly equates the two. Other sources identify Teutates with Gaulish Mercury, whose functions, we have said, often overlap with those of Mars.

Teutates, Taranis and Esus, according to Lucan and others (not Caesar), were the three principal native gods of Gaul. Their names are often cited together, Teutates appearing first, but they do not appear to have formed a triad. Despite many inscriptions to Teutates in Gaul and Britain, he remains a shadowy figure, perhaps because what we think of as his name may be only the designation 'god of our tribe' (*teutā*). Lucan records that Teutates was propitiated with human sacrifice; later commentators would specify that drowning was the favoured mode of execution, especially on 1 November, the feast known as Samain on the Old Irish calendar. Modern commentators profess to see Teutates as the figure plunging victims into a vat of water on the Gundestrup Cauldron (fourth–third centuries BC).

Taranis, conventionally called 'the thunderer', was, in Lucan's view, an even crueller god, for his worship demanded that victims be burned alive in wooden vessels. Indeed, Taranis's worship was more brutal and heartless than that of the Scythian Diana (north of the Black Sea), a ghoulish standard of comparison. Modern commentators have speculated that the well-born man executed near Lindow Bog in the fourth century BC may have been sacrificed to Taranis or Teutates. Worship of Taranis may indeed have been bloodier than that of Teutates, but it appears less widely spread. His name survives on only seven altars, many of them modest affairs, from Britain to the Balkans. The ninth-century Berne Commentaries call Taranis a 'master of war' but link him to Jupiter rather than to Mars; the same source also allows an identification of Taranis with Dis Pater (see below). Supporting the first Berne assertion, Taranis is often paired with the wheel symbol, evoking the sun, also associated with Jupiter. But Taranis was only an embodiment of thunder as a natural force, and his cult gives no evidence of the anthropomorphized complexity of the Roman sky god. An echo of Taranis's name persists in the Welsh hero Taran (Welsh *taran*: thunder), who survives the epic battle between kings Bendigeidfran and Matholwch in the *Mabinogi*.

Esus, linked to both Mars and Mercury, was worshipped in many places in Gaul and appears to have been the eponymous god of the Esuvii of the northwest, in what is today Normandy. Hardly less demanding than the other two, he was, to Lucan, 'uncouth Esus of the barbarous altars'. Human sacrifices were suspended from trees and ritually tortured, so that priests might read omens from the direction blood took in running from the wounds. Temple depictions link Esus with the crane and also with three symbolic egrets, birds later associated with the Irish hero Cúchulainn. As Esus was also sometimes seen as a woodcutter, an occasional role for Cúchulainn, learned speculation once asserted a link between Esus and the Irish hero that a more cold-eyed reading of the evidence has rejected.

Gaulish Jupiter, as mentioned, ranked fourth in Caesar's roster of the native gods. This would imply that the Celtic god or gods he observed were not distinguished by their primacy over the rest of the divines or patriarchy of the divine families. Roman Jupiter's other powers, over the sun and sky, as well as thunder, lightning and oak trees, offer analogues to what Caesar might have perceived in indigenous religion. As we have said, Taranis 'the thunderer' is frequently equated with Jupiter as well as with Mars. In an inscription found near Paris, the name Jupiter is associated with 'Cernenus', which may be a variant for Cernunnos, the antlered god. This would not identify Jupiter absolutely with Cernunnos, only associate the two. Anne Ross argues that the large, bearded, bare-chested figure on the Gundestrup Cauldron, holding a wheel symbol in his right hand, is Gaulish Jupiter, while the horned Cernunnos sits nearby. The wheel and the beard also appear on the bronze figure (first–second centuries AD) found at Le Châtelet, previously speculated to be Taranis, in the upper Marne valley; the stylized lightning flash and thunderbolt are similar to what is found in classical iconography but the wheel is distinctly Celtic.

Simultaneous with the cults of the god or gods the Romans called

Gaulish Jupiter, the Romans imported the worship of their own god Jupiter. Gradually the Roman cult absorbed those of indigenous gods worshipped high in mountain elevations. In the Alps around Great Saint Bernard's Pass lay the sanctuary of Jupiter Poeninus, in Austria Jupiter Uxellinus, and in the Pyrenees Jupiter Beissirissa. Influence from the Mediterranean seems to have prompted the building of the 150-plus Jupiter columns or Jupiter-Giant columns, some standing 45 feet (14 m) high, found primarily near the borders of what are today Germany and France, the Rhine and Moselle Rivers, with a few in Britain. They are four- and eight-sided stone plinths, some copying oak trees but often with Corinthian capitals that honour the Celtic sky god. Roman motifs include inscriptions to Jupiter and Juno as well as trampled serpentine monsters, probable counterparts to the Giants of the Earth defeated by Jupiter. But the deity of the columns is often depicted with the Celtic sun wheel and may be seen as a horseman, as the Roman god never is.

The Roman Minerva, like her Greek counterpart Athena, was primarily a goddess of wisdom, invention and the martial arts; only secondarily was she a patroness of domesticity and crafts. The Gaulish Minerva, however, Caesar tells us, taught the first principles of the arts and crafts. Her worship was widespread in Gaul and also extended to Britain where, as the geographer Solinus (second century AD) describes, her sanctuary possessed a perpetual fire, earning her the epithet *Belisama* [most brilliant]. In Britain too the cult of Minerva became thoroughly conflated with the native healing goddess Sulis at the shrine of Bath, known as Aquae Sulis in Roman times. Their merger is often cited as the archetypal example of *interpretatio Romana*. In inscriptions the name of the indigenous goddess always goes first: Sulis-Minerva or Sul-Minerva. The much-photographed large bronze head of Sulis-Minerva, ripped from its torso with helmet severed, indicates that the goddess at Bath was portrayed in classical dress. Elsewhere Minerva's sometime epithet Sulevia links her with the triad of mother-goddesses, Suleviae, known in many parts of the Roman-occupied Celtic world and in Rome itself. Minerva may also be identified with the tribal goddess Brigantia, worshipped in what is now Yorkshire.

The motif of her perpetual fire in Britain as well as her links to

Brigantia may signal that Gaulish Minerva is identical with the pre-Christian Irish fire goddess Brigit, a patroness of smithing, fertility, cattle, crops and poetry. Although much associated with Co. Kildare, Brigit was probably worshipped at Corleck Hill, near Drumeague, Co. Cavan, where a stone head thought to be hers once stood. She is honoured in one of the four seasonal feasts of early Ireland, Imbolc, 1 February on the Gregorian calendar. Brigit, in turn, contributes much to the persona of St Brigid of Kildare (d. 525), still argued to be an historical personage by Church authorities, whose feast day is also 1 February (see Chapter 5).

Dis Pater, Dispater or simply Dis is a name Caesar and other Romans preferred for the god we call Pluto or Hades, deity of the nether world, ruler of the dead. The preference for 'Dis Pater' was not simply a euphemism for dreaded Pluto, whose name actually translates as 'giver of wealth'. Dis, from the Latin *dives*, also implies wealth, as in the riches of the earth or the numbers who attend or accompany; *Dis Pater*, therefore, could be translated as 'Rich Father'. Caesar reports the druids as preaching that all Gauls were descended from this divine ancestor, a congruent faith for the 'rich father', even if he ruled the dead. While the notion of a common ancestor clearly struck Caesar as peculiar, it has many parallels in Indo-European tradition, as far away as India, as well as in medieval Ireland. Scattered groups in early Irish society claimed descent from the hero Lug Lámfhota, as later great dynasties were thought to flow from the loins of Conn Cétchathach [of the Hundred Battles] and Niall Noígiallach [of the Nine Hostages], the latter extending into Gaelic Scotland. Put another way, Caesar may simply have ascribed the name of Dis Pater to one or a series of ancestor cults. Then again the name Dis Pater is found in inscriptions and his persona is given icons. On an upright stone at Varhély in what is today Romania, Dis Pater is accompanied by a three-headed dog, perhaps a local variant of Cerberus of classical tradition. Elsewhere in the Balkans and in southern Germany, Dis Pater is portrayed holding a scroll, perhaps a roster for the day of reckoning; accompanying him is the apparent consort Aericura, a Celto-Germanic goddess.

If Dis Pater may indeed be identified with a native deity, nominations have not been lacking. The ninth-century Berne Commentaries assert that Taranis is the Gaulish god behind Dis Pater as well as behind

Jupiter, a notion not supported by later commentators or archaeological evidence. A better case can be made for Sucellus [L. the good striker, he who strikes to good effect], who is always seen with a long-shafted mallet or hammer, whose significance – weapon or tool – is not known. A very masculine figure with curling hair and beard, Sucellus is always seen with his cult partner Nantosuelta. He is often seen with a dog (another Cerberus?), a cask and a drinking jar. His worship was widespread in Gaul but also known in Britain. Anne Ross in *Pagan Celtic Britain* (1967) argues that the horned Cernunnos provided the ultimate identity for Dis Pater, as he was a god of wealth, underground regions and fecundity; further, his widespread worship implies that Cernunnos was the ancestor deity of the Gauls. Still other commentators see a parallel to Gaulish Dis Pater in the pre-Christian Irish god Donn, who was thought to reside at Tech Duinn [the House of Donn], a rocky islet near Dursey Island at the extreme western end of the Beare Peninsula, Co. Cork, in the southernmost reaches of the province of Munster. Donn, seen as aloof, preferring to live away from other gods, was unquestionably the ruler of the dead; the dead live with him on Tech Duinn. But he is also an ancestor deity. He became confused with Donn mac Míled, son of Míl Espáine in the pseudo-history *Lebor Gabála* [Book of Invasions], who went to live on the same rocky islet after he offended the goddess Ériu. In early Christian commentary, the souls of the damned were thought to linger in Tech Duinn on their way to hell. Pious folklore borrowed aspects of Donn to describe the devil. Later oral tradition ascribed to Donn the power to cause storms and shipwrecks.

Caesar's half-dozen do not constitute a Gaulish pantheon, as we have said, and neither do they exhaust *interpretatio Romana*. Other classical observers perceived yet two more Gaulish deities in Roman guise, a god of eloquence whom they identified with Hercules, and a craft god, Gaulish Vulcan. A key informant here is Lucian (second century AD), a witty Greek born in Syria whose *Dialogues* often treat the gods lightly.

Lucian learned from a Gaulish informant that the Gauls associated polished speech with Hercules because of his great strength rather than with Hermes (Greek counterpart to Mercury), as the Greeks did. Hercules, called Heracles by the Greeks, was initially portrayed as the heroic but mortal son of Zeus from a dalliance with Alcmene, and came to be worshipped as a god after his self-immolation in honour of his divine father. Lucian's informant further advised him that the Gaulish name for Hercules is Ogmios. While in Gallia Narbonensis (now southern France), Lucian encountered a startling picture of the indigenous god. He bore some of the attributes of Hercules, such as the club and the bow, but he appeared older: bald and sunburned. His eloquence appeared to enslave. Thin gold chains came from the tip of his tongue to the ears of an otherwise happy-looking band of men who tagged along behind him. This portrayal of Ogmios was later re-imagined by the German Renaissance painter Albrecht Dürer (1471–1528). In the ancient world there was scant physical evidence to support Lucian's story, only two lead curse tablets found at Bregenz, Austria, on the shore of Lake Constance; both invoke Ogmios's name, one in a curse on an infertile woman, that she never marry.

The later, insular personage who appears to bear the closest resemblance to Ogmios is Ogma, the Irish orator-warrior of the Tuatha Dé Danann, one of the three principal champions of his people, along with Lug Lámfhota and the Dagda. He was the patron of poetry and eloquence and was also the fabled inventor of the ogham alphabet, a philological cognate of his name. Ogham was the earliest form of written Irish in which the Latin alphabet was adapted to twenty 'letters' of straight lines and notches. Like Gaulish Hercules, Ogma was conventionally known as a 'strong man'. Compelling as the Ogmios–Ogma link may appear, authoritative scholars including Rudolf Thurneysen and Anton van Hamel long ago disputed that the names are cognate. More recent commentators have asserted that the Irish god's name may still be derived from Ogmios, even through intermediaries, if not actually from the same root or direct contact.

Neither Julius Caesar nor other Roman commentators speak of a Gaulish Vulcan, and references to Vulcan in Roman-occupied territories are rare, existing only on silver plaques found at Barkway, Hertfordshire. It is archaeological evidence alone that points to the cult of a smith god among the ancient Celts, with most remains in the north of Roman Britain. Among the complete survivals is a second-century AD earthenware vessel found at Corbridge, Northumberland, depicting a bearded figure dressed in a smith's costume: a conical cap and a belted tunic leaving the left shoulder uncovered. He stands over an anvil clasping an ingot in one hand and a pair of tongs in the other. Appliqués of conventional smith's tools, anvils, hammers and tongs, appear on rough, grey ceramic potsherds found in Durham, North Yorkshire and Northumberland. A bronze figure of a smith has been found in Lyon, France, very similar to one in Sunderland. Collectively, these examples do not prove a Celtic counterpart to Vulcan – no lameness, for example – but they do imply a native divinity parallel in many respects to the Roman god.

Smiths and other craftsmen enjoy a high regard, a reverence, even a sense of awe for their apparently magical powers, in many pre-technological societies. For the observer without a knowledge of ele-mentary physics, the sight of a man who can yield a stream of brilliant liquid metal from the firing of a certain rough rock evokes a practical wizardry. In early Gaelic Scotland a smith need only hold his hammer over the sick or infirm in order to drive away illness.

Not surprisingly, then, early Ireland, Wales, Scotland and the Isle of Man provide us with more than half a dozen divine or superhuman smiths, of which the most memorable are the Irish Goibniu and his popular counterparts, the Gobbán Saor and the Welsh Gofannon and Glwyddyn Saer. All four of these names relate to a word meaning 'smith', Old Irish *gobae* and Welsh *gof, gofan*, and indeed all four personae may have derived from the same divinity. Goibniu was the smith of the divine family, Tuatha Dé Danann, and part of the triad of craft gods, *na trí dé dána*, along with Credne, the bronze artificer, and Luchta, the carpenter or wright. Goibniu is a tireless armourer in *Cath Maige Tuired* [The (Second) Battle of Mag Tuired], where he fashions for the hero Lug Lámfhota the spear that penetrates Balor's eye. His keen arrow and spear tips are always lethal. He might also be a fighter himself, as when he slays the spy Rúadán who had impaled the smith with one of his own spears. Like so many Celtic divinities, Goibniu could be a healer: an Old Irish charm cites his name to aid removal of a thorn. More pertinently, he hosts the otherworldly feast *Fled Goibnenn* [Goibniu's feast], where guests imbibe great quantities of an intoxicating drink, now thought to be ale. Instead of merely getting drunk, guests are protected from old age and decay. His delivery of splendid drinks points to a link with Hephaestus, Greek counterpart to Vulcan, who provides a comparable service to the gods in the *Iliad*.

The folk figure Gobbán Saor [Ir. *saor*: smith, wright], known in both Irish and Scottish Gaelic traditions, clearly derives from Goibniu, although many storytellers thought he was historical. He was credited with assisting workmen in the construction of early monasteries and round towers. Both Goibniu and Gobbán appear to have contributed to the shadowy Welsh figure Glwyddyn Saer, perhaps derived from the many Irish incursions and settlements in Wales. Standing much taller in myth is the Welsh divine smith Gofannon, one of the children of Dôn, who also appears in the celebrated eleventh-century story *Culhwch and Olwen*. For this third task, Culhwch was asked to get Gofannon to sharpen the plough of Amaethon, the divine ploughman and magician. Gofannon's murder of his nephew Dylan signals to many commentators a parallel with Goibniu's slaying of Rúadán.

TRIPLISM

The early Celts, like other Indo-Europeans, attached symbolic significance to most frequently used numbers, but gave the greatest to the number three. Artistic expression dating from all periods of Celtic history underscores this penchant. A shorn skull with three separate faces, dating from the early Iron Age, was found at Corleck, Co. Cavan, Ireland. A curly-haired, curly-bearded, three-faced personage peers out from a terracotta vase found at Bavay, France. Other three-headed or tricephalic figures survive at Reims, France, in Germany, the Channel Islands, Scotland, and elsewhere in Ireland. Swirling La Tène art often resolves in figures with three cusps. Gaulish Mercury, as cited earlier, displays three faces and three phalluses. The traditional symbol of the Isle of Man is the three-legged triskele just as Brittany is represented by the trefoil.

No explanation of the power of three is given in any Celtic-language text, even though traditional learning was often formulated into the triad in both Ireland and Wales. The extensive Welsh Triads, *Trioedd Ynys Prydain*, brought together in the twelfth century, deal with such diverse matters as native learning, poetry, law and medicine. But other commentators have had much to say about the power of three in the larger European context. Pythagoras (sixth century BC) cites three as the perfect number, signalling beginning, middle and end. The stool of the pythia or soothsaying priestess at the oracle of Delphi always had three legs, a tripod; it was stable and would not rock. In many religions three may represent life: male, female and progeny. Three may also represent the visible world: sky, earth and underground; or space: before, after and right here, or above, below and this world, one explanation of the universal cross. The influential myth theorist Georges Dumézil argued that three became such a significant number on analogy with the tripartite division of early European society: farmers, warriors and clergy.

Writing in 1952, Joseph Vendryes pointed out that triune figures often have one dominant personality and two lesser ones, which are virtual ciphers. It may be, he argued, that there was initially only one dominating figure who was then doubled twice. Early Irish dynastic records support this contention as when they cite important figures' names in triplicate. A prime example of his thesis in narrative literature appears in the Deirdre story (see Chapter 4). The tragic princess flees with her lover Noíse, who has a developed dramatic personality, and the fugitive couple are accompanied by his two brothers Ardan and Ainnle, who are distinguished only by the sounds of their voices. At the same time, other early Irish texts also offer a refutation of Vendryes' thesis. Of the trio of war-goddesses known as Mórrígna [Ir. great queens], Badb, the Mórrígan and Macha, each has a distinctive personality and takes a different role in an assortment of narratives; see Chapter 4. Badb, the crow goddess, visits places of battle both before and after conflict. The ferocious Mórrígan does not take part in battle but can stampede whole armies with her frightful appearance. Macha, one of three queens with this name, is the eponymous founder of Emain Macha, the eighteen-acre hillfort in Co. Armagh, Northern Ireland.

Triple divinities are easy enough to find elsewhere in European tradition, but often there is but one divine trio prominent in a single culture. For the Greeks the 'triple goddess' consists of Selene (above the earth), Hecate (below the earth) and Artemis (open places, hunting, athletic competition). Among the Celts there are dozens, more than we have names to assign to them. In both Gaul and Britain we find remains of triple mother-figures, cited earlier as the Matres. Distinctive hooded figures, the Genii Cucullati [L. hooded guardian spirits], are depicted in outdoor garments, and found as far apart as contemporary Austria and Britain. In Britain they appear as three dwarfs and are found in clusters near Hadrian's Wall in the north and in the Cotswolds in Gloucestershire. The hooded figures anticipate the appearance of Christian monks, with important exceptions; one ancient figure appears with an extended phallus, perhaps intended as a candle-holder. The spring sacred to the territorial goddess Coventina, herself a single persona, is presided over by figures of three goddesses. And, as mentioned before, Lucan (first century AD) cites the Gaulish gods Teutates, Taranis and Esus in close proximity to one another, implying a triad.

Continuity is unmistakable in insular tradition. There are three personifications of Ireland, Ériu, Banba and Fódla. Three gods patronize the crafts: Goibniu, Credne and Luchta. According to the tenth-century *Sanas Cormaic* [Cormac's Glossary], there are three Brigits, the pre-Christian fire-goddess and two lesser Brigits about whom details are not provided. The sorceress Tlachtga was raped by the three sons of Simon Magus and gave birth to triplets on a hill in Co. Meath, where a festival was long celebrated in her honour. Finn Emna, also known as the Three Finns of Emain Macha, were the triplet sons attributed to king Eochaid Feidlech who joined their mother in a rebellion against their father. The three Fothads do field battle with Fionn mac Cumhaill and his men. The Three Collas, Colla Uais, Colla Menn and Colla Fo Chríth, eliminate Emain Macha as a centre of power and establish the kingdom of Airgialla in what are today Counties Armagh, Monaghan and parts of Louth and Tyrone. In Wales there are Three Exalted Prisoners and Three Generous Men of the Isle of Britain. Branwen of the *Mabinogi* is one of three matriarchs.

SUMMARY

From the ancient sources, written and material, we have gathered only shards of what was once a great edifice. Anthropomorphized gods and goddesses, as well as cults, heroes and heroines once existed among the peoples we call Celts. Comparable elements among the Sumerians,

Babylonians, Egyptians, Greeks and Romans gave rise to those stories in which some characters are gods that we call 'mythology' in English. Tantalizing wisps of narrative, like the portrait of Ogmios pulling a band of men with chains strung from the tip of his tongue, lead us to imagine that a larger body of narrative once existed, defining relationships between deities and heroes, attributing dramatic personalities to names we know only from survivals.

The continuity of the Celtic languages from continental Europe to the British Isles does not imply an ethnic continuum from Hallstatt to the Hebrides and the Aran Islands, as we have said. By analogy, Castilian aristocrats and Bolivian tin-miners might both speak Spanish, but they are not the same people. A shared language, however, even a shared family of languages, means a continuity of concept. If the sun and the sky are named in comparable words, they may be conceived in comparable ways, and so with birds, animals and fish. The druid of ancient tradition stands comparison with the druid of insular tradition. The magic accorded the number three, hardly unique to the Celtic peoples, certainly appears to be a conceptual continuity. The nearly obscured names of Gaulish gods, such as Lugus/Lugos, show up in heroes from Irish and Welsh tradition, Lug and Lleu. For these and other reasons we benefit from examining the ancient survivals side by side with the greater body of tradition arising among the insular Celts centuries after the end of ancient learning.

3

Sacred Kingship in Early Ireland

WHO COULD BE KING

Early Ireland was not a kingdom, but it had many kings. It follows, then, that the boast of many Irish persons that they are descended from ancient kings is not entirely groundless. F. J. Byrne (2001) estimates that there were never fewer than 150 kings in Ireland from the fifth to the twelfth centuries, when the population was under half a million. Such a 'king' is not the counterpart of the chief executives of early modern nation states, like Henry VIII or Louis XIV. In one sense the terms 'petty king' or 'chieftain' might seem more accurate to describe the office. Yet the Old Irish word for king, *rí* (later *ríg, rígh*), appears in early texts as a translation of the Latin *rex*. Scribes who write of the *rí* appeared to be implying a king as he would have been understood in classical culture. These same early scribes write of the *rí* as the embodiment of the luck and prosperity of his people. His initiation called for profound and mysterious ritual that signalled a spiritual and physical intimacy with sovereignty. He was sacred because he could perform functions denied to ordinary mortals as well as to such elevated figures as druids and poets. Several formidable figures designated as *rí* loom large in early Irish narrative, such as Niall Noígiallach [of the Nine Hostages], Conn Cétchathach [of the Hundred Battles] and Brian Bórama (Boru), often dominating epochs rather than mere households or precincts. These are grounds for using the English 'king' for *rí* without prefix or qualifier.

Few generally educated readers know very much about Ireland from the fifth to twelfth centuries, in part because things Irish are rarely taught in English-speaking schools. Paradoxically, there is an enormous amount to know. From genealogies alone we can cite the names of more than 12,000 persons living in Ireland from before AD 1100, compared to a few hundred names from early Anglo-Saxon records and even fewer from the Germanic kingdoms of the continent. Beginners may find the names onomastically intimidating, like Fiachu ba hAiccid or Tipraite mac Taide, which do not appear to have ready counterparts in English or other European languages. Beyond this lies a society whose concepts of family, property and law are radically different from what we know from modern culture or even Europe of the high Middle Ages. There is not the space here to address this lack, but some salient observations are essential in reading this and later chapters.

The Romans visited Ireland but did not conquer it. This brush with Roman civilization introduced Christianity and written records to the island but not Roman law. The Irish maintained their own legal system, the Brehon Laws, until they were displaced at the end of the twelfth century. Early Ireland was dominated by warring dynasties, of which the most important was the Uí Néill, initially based in the north but eventually extending over much of the land, dividing into different factions. Norsemen or 'Vikings' raided monastic centres, established the first cities such as Dublin and Limerick, settled into the population but found their power curtailed after their defeat at the Battle of Clontarf, 1014. Writing was the franchise of clerics we today call Irish monks, to distinguish them from the great continental orders, the Benedictines, Augustinians and Cistercians. The Christianity they practised we call 'Celtic Christianity' because it differed in discipline and artistic expression from the Roman (or Rome-based) Church. The native religious tradition came to an end in 1169–70, when Henry II of England, sanctioned by Pope Adrian IV, brought Ireland closer to Roman discipline. In Henry II's time and after came the Anglo-Normans, French-speaking nobles from Britain who displaced many native landowners and made French the language of privilege and law. In time, these families, sometimes referred to as the 'Old English' (as opposed to post-Elizabethan settlers), integrated into the rest of the population and were described as more Irish than the Irish themselves, in effect Hiberno-Normans.

In chronological summary:

432	Traditional, perhaps contrived date for the arrival of St Patrick and the beginnings of Christian Ireland.
516	Uí Néill extend power to Leinster in eastern Ireland.
593/597	Death of St Colum Cille, member of Uí Néill, who had participated in first Christian initiation of an Irish king.
794	Vikings begin raids on the British Isles.
804	Founding of monastery at Kells, home of *The Book of Kells*, masterpiece of Celtic Christian art, probably created at Iona in the Hebrides.
837	First Viking fleets on Irish inland waterways.
849	Danes begin to settle in Ireland.
1014	Irish defeat Norseman; Irish king Brian Bórama killed.
1169	Arrival of Anglo-Normans in Ireland
1198	Death of Ruaidrí Ua Conchobair (Rory O'Connor), the last *ard rí* (high king).

The early Irish did not practise primogeniture, the ruthlessly clear rule that mandates passage of a title from an older male to his firstborn son, regardless of that son's fitness or favour with his father. The new Irish king did not necessarily come from an old king's *fine* [family or kindred] but rather his *derbfhine* [certain kin], the descendants of a common great-grandfather over four generations. According to an old law tract, *Cóic Conairi Fuigill* [The Five Paths of Judgement], a prospective king must be the son of a king and the grandson of a king. He should be physically unblemished, a man of property, of good legal standing and not guilty of theft. Other requirements underscore how differently the family was conceived in early Ireland as compared with later Christian times. The would-be king should be the son of a principal wife (*cétmuinter*) when possible, or, failing that, the son of a legitimate second wife. If that were not possible he might be the son of a concubine, or, in a worst case, the son from a list of other female partners. An oldest son might expect to succeed his father, but a younger son might also rise to power.

To be more specific about the names for different steps in the process is to enter scholarly contention. The dominant informed view of the last century was formulated by one of the first great modern Celticists, Eoin MacNeill, in his *Celtic Ireland* (1921). In his analysis, a person eligible to succeed to a kingship (*rígdomna*) should belong to the same *derbfhine* as the king who has already reigned. An election, test or contest then determined the succession from the full four generations of potential candidates. Put another way, any male descendant of a kingly paternal great-grandfather could at least be considered for succession to kingship, even though the king immediately before him might only have been his second cousin. This was not a system that encouraged domestic tranquillity.

According to the seventh-century *Audacht Morainn* [Testament of Morann], advice given by the legendary Morann to a young king, a true and good ruler will have *fir flathemon* [truth of the ruler], meaning that he will be righteous, will enjoy a character above reproach, will descend from high ancestry and will be capable of heroic action. He should ensure peace and justice, security of his *tuath*'s borders and all the prosperity of bountiful harvests and rivers teeming with fish.

Complicating our vision of kingly succession is the concept of the 'tanist', a word which has made an unlikely migration from early Ireland to modern intellectual discourse in entirely different contexts, changing definitions along the way. The Old Irish words *tánaise*, *tánaiste*, according to the *Royal Irish Academy Dictionary of the Irish Language* or *DIL* (1913–83), mean 'second', 'next', or 'second in rank or dignity, heir apparent'. This older definition continues in the Modern Irish word used for the deputy prime minister of the Republic of Ireland, *Tánaiste*. Under the influence of Sir James Frazer of *Golden Bough* fame, of the 'Cambridge School' of early twentieth-century mythology interpretation, and especially of theoretical maverick Robert Graves (1895–1985), the Irish-derived English word 'tanist' came to mean something entirely new. Surrounding this definition is the theory that ancient sacred kings in the Mediterranean and elsewhere were ritually slaughtered in imitation of the vegetation cycle, or 'harvested' before they began to decline. The tanist here is the presumptive heir apparent to the reigning sacred king who replaces the older man after his sacrifice. Always seen as younger than the sacrificial king, this tanist may be seen as a rival to the older king, and he may also serve as executioner in the death ritual. Central to this conception is the certainty of the tanist that he is going to succeed the sacred king before the sacrifice and then his actual later assumption of the role.

Early Irish records do not testify that any such transaction ever took place, neither ritual slaughter nor transfer of power to the slayer. There is, however, a familiar phrase in the annals, *a suis* [killed by his own] that testifies to much internecine conflict, but nothing that prescribes ritual murder for the *tánaise ríg*'s ascension to power. In *Celtic Ireland* Eoin MacNeill argues that there is no evidence the Irish had a preliminary selection of a king's successor before the office was vacant until after the coming of the Anglo-Normans and feudalism (1169–70). In pre-Norman times the usual term for a person eligible to succeed to the kingship, *rígdomna*, and *tánaise* or *tánaise ríg*, existed side by side and were mutually exclusive. As Dáibhí Ó Cróinín points out in *Early Medieval Ireland* (1995), the term *tánaise ríg* appears in the annals earlier, AD 848, but in reference to a Viking leader, whereas *rígdomna* would not first appear for another nineteen years, in AD 867. Both of these dates are relatively late, compared to other terms pertaining to kingship. The distinction was that the entire tribe looked forward to the *tánaise ríg* becoming king without facing dispute. In the general run of things the *tánaise ríg* did succeed, whereas the *rígdomna* did not in every instance. Two routes to kingship could have existed side by side, although neither is the one asserted by Sir James Frazer and Robert Graves.

HIGH KINGS AND TARA

Having become a popular woman's given name, Tara is one of the few place names from early Ireland that most readers will recognize easily. The idea that Ireland once had a high king or *ard rí* is so familiar and resonant that the terms appear in the titles of popular novels, even as the names of gift shops. Characteristic of the romantic and imaginative reshaping of the distant past is Thomas Moore's heroic poem 'The Harp That Once Through Tara's Halls' in his *Irish Melodies* (1808), widely anthologized over the next century. Admittedly, Tara appears as the seat of a kingship in early Irish heroic narratives from the Ulster Cycle, but the nineteenth-century imagination aspired to see Tara as a magnificent palace, a Hibernian Windsor or Fontainebleau, if smaller. Margaret Mitchell's naming of the O'Hara mansion Tara in her American Civil War epic *Gone with the Wind* (1936, filmed 1939) put the notion into everyday speech in the English-speaking world.

A tourist's visit to the hill of Tara (507 ft, 155 m) in Co. Meath, six miles southeast of Navan, sharpens perspective. From a distance there appears to be no hill at all, only a slightly rising gradient on the approaching road. Arriving at the designated site, one can see for a great distance, rumoured to be more than a third of all of Ireland, a prospect that surely delighted ancient visitors. Undulating mounds and earthworks, easier to perceive from aerial photographs, bear grandiose names – the Banqueting Hall, the Rath of the Synods, the Mound of the Hostages, etc. There is also a phallic shaft of weathered granite known as Lia Fáil [stone of destiny], put up in modern times to commemorate the martyrs of the 1798 rebellion and to remind visitors of the original stone. There is no evidence to support the contention that this is the original site, nor is there any against. Nonetheless, continuous archaeological investigation of the site reveals that the ancient Tara was the favoured venue of extraordinary activity over many centuries. The famous Tara Brooch, much copied, was not found on the site, however; its exalted craftsmanship led observers to assume it was made for a high king, even though it was found on the beach at Bettystown near Drogheda, Co. Louth. A king initiated at Tara would have distinctions to raise him apart from the 150 or so other contemporary kings.

The realm of the *rí* was the *tuath*. An early Irish law text decrees that 'there is no *tuath* which has no clerical scholar, no church, no poets, no king to extend contracts and treaties to other *tuatha*' (pl.). A king of the *tuath*, or *rí tuaithe* (gen.), had no army, only a bodyguard of mercenaries, a retinue of noble clients and a steward to collect revenues. The definition of *tuath* would change over the centuries, but it did not always have territorial specifications. The entity was bound together by intimate relations that prevented it from evolving into a state.

The political structure of early Ireland was based in large part on what we would call today 'clientship'. Ordinary people living in the realm of the king were not citizens in the modern sense, nor were they subjects as people were in the days of powerful kings of nation states, or as they would have been in early modern times. Instead, the ordinary person had an agreement or pledge with a king as the king might have with kings more powerful than he was. In Eoin MacNeill's depiction of the well-ordered *tuath*, a king was a war leader and president of his assembly. D. A. Binchy (1970) argued that in earliest times the king had been a priest and a judge as well as a war leader. Although commentators often use the word brehon (*breithem*) to denote what we would call a judge in something approaching the modern concept of judge as an interpreter of state-written codes, an early Irish king might rule with the counsel of a brehon on land disputes.

A king could be classed in several kinds of hierarchies. The old tract titled *Críth Gablach*, probably the most widely known we have, gave fanciful names for three grades of king: (i) *rí benn* [king of peaks or 'horns'] because of the high demand of his honour; (ii) *rí buiden* [king of bands] for his prowess in leading men and taking hostages; or (iii) *rí bunaid cach cinn* [ultimate king of every individual] for his ability to extend his control and coercive authority. Clusters of local kings [*rí tuaithe*] might be dominated by a greater king who ruled through his personal or dynastic connections, or perhaps by his commanding physical presence. Such an over-king might be called simply *ruirí* [great or over-king] if he dominated as few as four local kings, *fuiríg* [sub-king]; or he might be called *rí cóicid* [provincial king], or most exalted of all, *rí ruirech* [king of over-kings]. He was not, however, called the *ard rí* [high king] in earlier texts.

From a very early date a king might acquire the title *rí Temro* or *Temrach*, literally 'king of Tara', which implied dominance over other kings, as Edel Bhreathnach and Conor Newman (1995) point out, but it did not necessarily imply a territorial claim over the whole island. Successive rulers crowned at Tara would enlarge the expectations of the office.

The title *ard rí*, as F. J. Byrne has pointed out, is not very old, nor is it found in legal texts. It lacks precise significance and does not necessarily imply sovereignty over Ireland. The *DIL* does not contain an entry for *ard rí*, implying at the very least that its usage was not widespread in any early texts. At its first appearance it denoted an important king of a region or province, such as Ulster, *ard rí Ulad*, and in poetry it could be used figuratively for any over-king, a gesture of flattery. Much of what we read about in later Irish literature, including the Ulster Cycle, was quite simply invented and then accepted as fact. The polite name we have for such a document is pseudo-history, as it was given more credence than those narratives we call legend.

A cynic could charge that much of what we call history is really pseudo-history, especially when history is edited to flatter powerful conquerors. Indeed, much of record-keeping in early Ireland is patently arranged to flatter the most powerful family, actually a federation of dynasties, the Uí Néill. But the most celebrated of Irish pseudo-histories, the *Lebor Gabála* [Book of Invasions] (see Chapter 7) appears to have been a sincere if misguided attempt to harmonize irreconcilable sources.

The first documented claimant to the status of high king was Máel Sechnaill (d. 862), later romantically known as 'Malachy I'. The creation of his title was, as F. J. Byrne argues, political propaganda by the Uí Néill on behalf of the Tara dynasty, which it controlled. Some kind of sacral kingship, however, may have existed at Tara from much earlier times. From the mid-800s perspective, the pseudo-history claimed that high kingship had begun centuries earlier and had included Diarmait mac Cerbaill (d. 565), the last important pre-Christian monarch. Once established, the high kingship continued for another 300 years. Although the title of high king might link a ruler to Tara, his actual seat of power, the one that allowed him to be eligible for the honour, might be far distant. The last high king was Ruaidrí Ua Conchobair [Rory O'Connor] of Connacht, who remained in power up to the time of the Anglo-Norman conquest, 1169.

Two unique tests determined the suitability of a candidate to be high king at Tara, the first employing stones and instruments, the second the ritual killing of a bull. In the first he would be asked to ride in a royal chariot, and if it rejected him he was clearly unworthy. He would try to put on a royal mantle that was too big for the unworthy. He was asked to drive his chariot between two stones, only a hand's breadth apart, to see if they would move apart to accommodate his wheels. And last he would be asked to come into contact with the Lia Fáil [stone of destiny], the stone penis, which would cry out at the touch of the right man. *Fál* (gen. *Fáil*) by itself is also a poetic name for Ireland, which also may be known as *Inis Fáil* [island of destiny]. Semantically, this suggests that the high king at Tara was a king of all

Ireland, as the Uí Néill no doubt wished to imply, but such a role is not supported in law texts.

The second ceremony at Tara by which the high king (that is, of all Ireland) might be chosen was the *tarbfheis* or bull-feast, which began with the slaughter of the innocent animal. To select a candidate for kingship a man taken at random first ate his fill of the bull's flesh, drank a broth made from the bull's blood and then lay down to sleep in the bull's hide. Four druids would then chant an incantation over him, during which time he must see in his sleep the right person to be king. The word *feis* is usually translated as 'feast', but it originated as the verbal noun *fo-aid*, meaning 'to spend the night with' or 'to sleep with'. King Conaire participates in such a *tarbfheis* in the eleventh-century narrative *Togail Bruidne Da Derga* [Destruction of Da Derga's Hostel], a story of the innocent Conaire's struggle with relentless fate. The bull, additionally, was used in divination rites elsewhere in the Celtic world. In early Scotland a man seeking the answer to an important question might spend the night inside the still-steaming carcass of a newly killed bull.

A burial site as early as the third millennium BC, Tara had long been a centre of religious ceremony. It had once been sacred to Medb of Connacht, later an important figure in the Ulster Cycle and the *Táin Bó Cuailnge*, while she was still considered to be a goddess; her double, Medb Lethderg, ruled the hilltop. The Uí Néill, whose first homeland was in the north, seized Tara from the Leinstermen of the east in the fifth century, before Christianization. The first kings of Tara were important local rulers whose prestige was enhanced by their initiation on such hallowed ground. With the coming of the high king, Tara became the generator of its own myth. In dozens of early Irish narratives it became the royal residence of a succession of dominating rulers. In the stories of legendary king Conaire Mór, Tara appears to be a magical kingdom. It is to the court at Tara of Arthur-like Cormac mac Airt that the youthful hero Fionn mac Cumhaill proves himself by slaying the fiery Aillén mac Midgna, who had been preying upon the 'palace' every year on the eve of Samain (1 November).

Even after Tara was abandoned as a place for religious ritual and became overgrown with weeds and bushes, it remained the site of one of the largest fairs held in medieval times and was the scene of an engagement by the United Irishmen in the rebellion of 1798. As late as 1843, the patriot and parliamentarian Daniel O'Connell held 'monster rallies' at Tara, urging thousands of his impoverished countrymen to demand their rights.

It was not only the Uí Néill who wished to create their own history to enhance Tara. Christian ecclesiastics invented the story of Saint Rúadán, supposed to have lived in the sixth century, who put a curse upon Tara because king Diarmait mac Cerbaill insulted him in a Church/state dispute. In the greatest pseudo-history of Ireland, the *Lebor Gabála*, much of it compiled by ecclesiastics of later centuries, the victorious Milesians (that is, real mortals or the Gaels themselves) named the hilltop Temair after their queen, Téa. Temair is, in fact, one of several Irish spellings for the site; the anglicized Tara derives from its genitive form, *Teamhrach*. Its etymological root is not clear, perhaps 'dark one', 'spectacle', 'elevated place' or 'assembly hall'.

INITIATION OF KINGS

Bad press dies hard. A slander uttered once can have the permanence of granite. A hundred truthful corrections frequently cannot erase the lasting effects of one defamation, especially if it is inflammatory. In early Ireland there was no more antagonistic reporter than the well-born Welsh cleric Gerald de Berri (*c.*1146–1223), usually known as Giraldus Cambrensis or Gerald of Wales, who supported the disdainful view the Anglo-Normans held of the native Irish. Gerald first visited Ireland in 1183 and later returned in the entourage of Henry II. His detailed, mostly first-hand observations of the Ireland he visited are found in two texts, the earlier *Expugnatio Hibernica* [The Conquest of Ireland] and the more informative *Topographia Hibernica* [Topography of Ireland] (*c.*1185). Useful observations not found elsewhere abound in *Topographia*, but they are often interleaved with heated diatribes against what the author perceives to be the unspeakable savagery of the natives. Late in his account is the horrified description of the confirming of a new king that has echoed down eight centuries and remains in print in inexpensive paperback editions in our own time. Giraldus begins the passage with an apology, allowing that '. . . the austere discipline of history spares neither truth nor modesty'.

There is in the northern and farther part of Ulster, namely in Kenelcunill [i.e. Cenél Conaill, Tyrconnell, Co. Donegal], a certain people which is accustomed to appoint its king with a rite altogether outlandish and abominable. When the whole people of that land has been gathered together in one place, a white mare is brought forward into the middle of the assembly. He who is to be inaugurated, not as chief, but as beast, not as king, but as an outlaw, has bestial intercourse with her before all, professing himself to be a beast also. The mare is then killed immediately, cut up into pieces, and boiled in water. He sits in the bath surrounded by all his people, and all, he and they, eat of the meat of the mare which is brought to them. He quaffs and drinks of the broth in which he is bathed, not in any cup, or using his hand, but just dipping his mouth into it round him. When this unrighteous rite has been carried out, his kingdom and dominion have been conferred.

(Cambrensis, 1984: 110)

The experienced reader of modern propaganda will notice tell-tale signals undermining Giraldus's credibility. He does not speak from personal observation, as he does elsewhere in the *Topographia*, and he places the outrage in the remotest part of the island where the invaders had yet to set foot. More tellingly, Giraldus was an interested observer: he and members of his family were part of the body of conquistadors who were sworn to bring the barbarous and semi-pagan Irish back into the embrace of the holy mother Church in Rome. Yet this is not to say that Giraldus wilfully invented the entire episode out of thin air. Informed commentators on early Ireland have admitted that the horse is often sacrificed as part of kingship rituals among many Indo-European peoples. F. J. Byrne points out that there are obvious parallels, from distant ancient India and from pre-medieval Norway, where the king and his people were obliged to eat horse flesh together; even an early Christian king such as Haakon the Good (*c*.914–961) submitted to the apparently pagan rite.

Giraldus's portrayal of the bath of broth is certainly precedented in early Irish heroic narrative. One common motif portrays a wounded hero cured and restored in a broth containing pieces of meat. Fráech, a mortal hero, son of an otherworldly mother, in the eighth-century

Táin Bó Fraích [Cattle Raid of Fráech], is resuscitated in a broth-bath after having been treacherously induced to enter a pool and attacked by a water monster. This story is linked to the explanation of the place name of the historic mound Carn Froích (Carnfree, Co. Roscommon), where the Ó Conchobhairs (O'Connors) were inaugurated as late as the fifteenth century, and Carn Froích is but three miles from Cruachain, fabled home of Queen Medb, where the kings of Connacht were crowned. Following this, F. J. Byrne has asserted that there is a confused tradition connecting the broth-bath with a royal inauguration site. Further, it is reasonable to suppose that Giraldus picked up from the Irish or Norse of the southeast of Ireland a more primitive account of an obsolete pagan rite, which he then libellously asserted to be still in force among an unvisited tribe in remote Donegal.

As for the implication that the new king must perform an act of coitus as a part of his initiation, the early Irish record is rife with sexual metaphors. The sacral king is the spouse of his *tuath*, and his initiation until the time of Diarmait mac Cerbaill (d. 565) was called the *banais ríghe*, or, literally, 'the wedding feast of kingship'. *Banais*, the normal Irish word for marriage, incorporates as a prefix the word *ban*, meaning 'woman'. We have no first-person accounts of the *banais ríghe*, but we can deduce that the ceremony comprised two elements: (a) a libation or ceremonial drink offered by the 'bride', and (b) the sexual intercourse between the new king and the sovereignty of Ireland. Alas, no document survives to tell us how this 'bride' was portrayed – an actual person playing a role, an icon of some kind or a decorated simulacrum meant to signify a person. Recent commentators have shown that the motif of sexual union between king and goddess persisted until the later Middle Ages in literature and possibly also in ritual. At Tara the ceremony was known as *feis Temrach* or *feis Temro*, employing a different word for the sex act, *feis*, as considered above. The great Geoffrey Keating, the father of Irish historiography in his *Foras Feasa ar Éirinn* (1629–31), describes the *feis Temrach* as an annual event in which the high king reaffirms his legitimacy. A more recent examination of the evidence suggests that the *feis Temrach* was held only intermittently and at 'seed time' rather than at Beltaine (May Day) because it was the supreme fertility ritual, designed to secure that man and beast and earth shall be fruitful throughout the king's dominions. Although any explanation of the *banais ríghe* would no doubt have further disgusted Giraldus Cambrensis and might also raise the eyebrows of contemporary readers, the concept of the king 'marrying' his kingdom is by no means uniquely Irish or Celtic. Parallel examples may be found as far afield as the early cultures of India and the Semitic peoples of the Middle East.

SOVEREIGNTY

Kingship is male; sovereignty is female. Specifics of early Irish kingship can be documented in space and time. Our knowledge of sovereignty figures comes from traditional narratives, some of which we today call 'myths'. Although the notion leaves scant legacy in the modern imagination, the early Irish were by no means the first people to envision a female embodiment of power and authority. Further, this creature, sometimes enticing, sometimes loathsome, must be won sexually by an aspiring king. The Greek word for the king's intimate union with the embodiment of sovereignty is *hierogamy*, for sacred [*hieros*] marriage [*gamos*], although the concept is certainly much older than the heydays of Cnossos and Mycenae. In the Sumerian myths of the Tigris–Euphrates valley (second millennium BC), the aspiring king must mate with Inanna, queen of heaven and goddess of love and fertility, on New Year's Day in her residence. The king is portrayed in a hymn as an incarnation of Dumuzi, a shepherd-king and husband of Inanna, who appears in a rite of hierogamy which culminates in their ecstatic sexual union. This may have been acted out in life with one of Inanna's temple prostitutes. Early Indo-European tradition evidences correlatives and echoes of a kind of spiritual and/ or physical sexual union between the male king and divine female sovereignty figure, even as far away as the instances of Vishnu and Sri-Lakshmi in India.

Sovereignty figures – perhaps goddesses – in early Ireland may wear different faces. Not only are her identities fluid, but she may veer from being an alluring young beauty of promiscuous appetite to being a frightful, demanding crone. This pattern contrasts with the iconography of early Gaul and pre-Roman Britain where representations of divine couples usually show the female half as a personification of plenty and the earth's abundance. Rosmerta, to take but one example, was worshipped from what is today Germany, across France and the Low Countries to Britain; she was frequently seen as the cult partner of Gaulish Mercury. We not only know her name but we know how she was propitiated. In Ireland, there are no clearly identifiable icons, only shadowy, sometimes nameless figures from early narratives. Sovereignty may be a goddess of the land or a personification of Ireland itself, who blesses fertility, fortunes and prosperity. In the earliest narratives, the goddess of sovereignty has primacy that a mortal king must approach with timidity; in later tradition the king has a primacy that the sovereignty may threaten to disrupt.

One of several early sovereignty goddesses is Mór Muman, whose name means literally 'Great of Munster', the southernmost of Ireland's five ancient provinces. Originally a goddess of the Érainn people who migrated to Ireland in late prehistoric times, Mór had associations with the powers of the sun and eventually came to be worshipped all across southern Ireland or Munster. She was thought so beautiful that every woman in Ireland was compared with her. In an attempt to historicize her, medieval scribes assigned extraordinary powers to her such as exaltation and frenzy and the ability to fly; nevertheless, she was thought to have wandered Ireland for two years in rags. She was also ascribed sexual intimacies with known historical figures, such as Fíngein mac Áeda (d. 613) of Cashel, Co. Tipperary. She conceived a son by him but, hearing voices, fled before the child, Sechnesach, was born. Fíngein died soon after. Her name survives in more than a dozen place names, notably Tígh Mhóire [the House of Mór] in the parish of Dunquin, Co. Kerry. Aspects of her persona drifted into other figures, such as Medb, the warrior queen of Connacht, Mórrígan, the goddess of war fury, and the Cailleach Bhéirre or Hag of Beare, the mythic frightful old woman of the Beare Peninsula between the Kenmare estuary and Bantry Bay (see Chapter 4).

The three most frequently cited sovereignty deities, Banba, Fódla and Ériu, appear in the pages of the pseudo-history *Lebor Gabála* [Book of Invasions], which is discussed at greater length in Chapter 7. Their entrance comes shortly after the arrival of the last of the invaders, the Milesians, equivalent both of mortal human beings and the Gaels of early Ireland themselves. At first all three oppose the invaders and only change their minds when they can demand favours. Banba meets the Milesians at a mountain called Slieve Mish on the Dingle Peninsula of Co. Kerry, where she asks that they take her name for all of Ireland. Although she is ascribed a father named Cian and a husband named Mac Cuill, her name appears to have once applied to south Leinster, Ireland's easternmost province, or the plain in Co. Meath that contains Tara. Fódla appears before the Milesians at Slieve Felim in Co. Limerick, and she too asks that her name be given to the whole of Ireland. Personifying the power of the land, Fódla is also ascribed a family, and echoes of her name are found in both Irish and Scottish Gaelic place names. The Milesians allow the three names to be used for Ireland, but Amairgin rules that Ériu's will be the chief name, while the others persist as poetic alternatives. Of more lasting effect is the meeting with Ériu at the hill of Uisnech in what is today Co. Westmeath, often cited as the centre or omphalos [navel], of Ireland. She is portrayed wearing circlets and rings, prompting some commentators to suggest that she has an identification with the powers of the sun. After Ériu tells the Milesians that Ireland is the fairest of all lands under the sun and that the Milesians are the most perfect race the world has ever seen, the poet Amairgin promises her that the country will bear her name. Indeed, the Modern Irish name for the Republic of Ireland, Éire, is derived from Ériu, as is the anglicization Erin. An annual fair at Uisnech that continued into early modern times was attributed to Ériu.

Ériu appears to be portrayed in stories with conscious political motivation, such as the pre-eleventh-century *Baile in Scáil* [Ir. The Phantom's Frenzy]. In this the shadowy king of pre-history Conn Cétchathach [Ir. of the Hundred Battles] and his men set out from Tara and are enveloped in mist so that they lose their way. A horseman invites them to a house 30 feet (9 m) long with a ridgepole of white gold. In a room full of gold, they find a damsel seated on a chair of crystal and wearing a crown of gold. Upon a throne they see a Phantom, whose like had not been known at Tara. He reveals himself as the godly Lug Lámfhota, and the damsel as Sovereignty of Ireland, Lug's wife, who then serves Conn with enormous portions of meat. Though she is not identified in the text, commentators identify the 'wife' with

Ériu. Next to her are a silver vat, a gold vessel and a gold cup. She asks to whom she should serve the red ale therein contained. The Irish for red ale, *derg-fhlaith*, contains a pun on *laith* [ale, liquor] and *flaith* [sovereignty]. Lug answers by naming every prince from the time of Conn onward, although none of these names appears in historical records. Lug and the house disappear, but the gold cup and other vessels remain with Conn. The offering of a reddish drink signifying sovereignty, with unmistakable sexual connotations, also appears in other early Irish stories.

In addition to being described as sovereignty figures, Banba, Fódla and Ériu are also described as tutelary goddesses, meaning they are patronesses or guardians of the land. Many Celtic deities have the power of shaping, taking different forms, a capacity shared by the Greek divinities as described by Homer in the *Iliad*. Among the shapes they could take was that of an ugly old woman, but one still seeking sexual favours. There are two views on why sovereignty should sometimes be seen as physically repulsive. One is that the sovereignty figure can also be a bringer of death or the deliverer of a curse. The second is allegorical, on the perceptions of a young prince reaching maturity: that the responsibilities of sovereignty are ugly and frightening until they are embraced.

A model of this motif is found in the eleventh-century *Echtra Mac nEchach Muigmedóin* [The Adventure of the Sons of Eochaid Mugmedón], a story that promotes the authority of the Uí Néill, that powerful dynasty of early Ireland. The key figure is Niall Noígiallach [of the Nine Hostages], the possibly historical fifth-century founder of the Uí Néill dynasty. Before he has reached his maturity, Niall and his four brothers go hunting, stopping in a forest to cook a meal. One, Fergus, while looking for water, finds a horrible hag, black as coal, with hair like the tail of a wild horse, smoky eyes, a crooked nose, green teeth that can cut oak and green nails; worse, she is covered with pustules. She wants a kiss; otherwise, no water. Three brothers refuse, and one, Fiachra, gives her a small kiss, allowing him to see Tara and later to found a royal line in another part of Ireland. Niall agrees to kiss the loathly lady, volunteers to lie with her, and then throws himself upon her, giving her a most passionate kiss. At this the hag is transformed into a wondrous beauty, clad all in royal purple, with bronze slippers on her white feet. She reveals herself as Flaithius, the sovereignty of Ireland, and grants Niall the water, kingship and domination over the country for succeeding generations. She also advises Niall to refuse to give water to his brothers until they grant him seniority over them and agree that he might raise his weapon a hand's breadth above theirs.

Although she has many counterparts in Ireland as well as in Gaelic Scotland and the Isle of Man, the most widely known hag of sovereignty is the Cailleach Bhéirre or Hag of Beare. While her name identifies her with the Beare Peninsula in Counties Cork and Kerry, she is also linked to several other locations in Munster. The Cailleach speaks in her own voice in an early, perhaps ninth-century dramatic monologue, translated under different titles. She declares that she is not the king's but the poet's mistress, and that she has a special liking for the plain of Femen in Co. Tipperary. As with the hag who made love to Niall Noígiallach, she will appear to a hero or warrior as an old woman asking to be loved. When she receives love, she becomes a beautiful young maiden. The Cailleach Bhéirre passes through at least seven periods of youth so that each husband passes from her to death of old age. She has fifty foster-children in Beare, and her grandchildren and great-grandchildren are the people and races of Ireland.

Just as aspects of the old territorial goddess Mór Muman migrated to the Cailleach Bhéirre, so too aspects of the Cailleach can be found in the eighteenth-century poetic personification of Ireland, the Seanbhean Bhocht [the poor old woman]. An anglicization of this name, Shan Van Vocht, was used as the title of a song sung by the United Irishmen in their rebellion of 1798, sometimes dubbed 'the *Marseillaise* of Ireland'.

The story of the aspiring young male who semi-willingly has intimacies with a loathly lady, transforming her into a great beauty with his lovemaking, has striking parallels in the literatures of other countries in Europe. The most prominent is 'The Wife of Bath's Tale' of Geoffrey Chaucer's *Canterbury Tales* (c.1390). At one time commentators argued that because the Irish stories were older, and perhaps also because they were less well known in scholarship, they must have been the models for the English ones. Our greater knowledge today suggests that the relationship between the Irish and English stories is not so simple. Instead, the transformed loathly lady episode is so widespread in world literature as to merit its own international folk motif number of D732. Like many things Celtic, it is a part of European and international culture.

4

Goddesses, Warrior Queens
and Saints

IN LIFE

The boom in popular and academic interest in the early Celts that followed the publication of Anne Ross's *Pagan Celtic Britain* (1967) and Proinsias MacCana's *Celtic Mythology* (1970) coincided with the rise of modern feminism as a cultural, political and scholarly force. Formerly the domain only of linguists and mythographers, Celtic narratives now served up allusive references in popular culture; Rhiannon became a figure in a rock song as well as a character in the medieval Welsh text of the *Mabinogi*. The Celts themselves may have been an archaic people, removed from the centres of European innovation, but they seemed 'new' because they were perceived (wrongly) to be apart from the patriarchal culture that has dominated the West since the Renaissance. True, the world of early Irish and Welsh literature was characterized by aristocratic warriors in pursuit of martial honour, but there were also stories of female personae in roles beyond the familiar ones of spouse, mother, nurturer and focus of male desire. The enticing and dangerous sovereignty figures, as cited in the previous chapter, presented active, seemingly libidinous women. Deirdre, the Irish tragic lover whose reawakened literary prestige began in the generation of Lady Gregory (1852–1932) and J. M. Synge (1871–1909), became so well known that her name was revived under different spellings in the younger generation. Many feminists delighted in the abundance of assertive women in early narratives, such as Queen Medb (anglicized Maeve, Modern Irish Medhbh, etc.), who led armies into battle even as men swooned at her beauty. The historical warrior queen Boudicca, cast in bronze on the Thames embankment as an emblem of Victorian imperialism in 1902, was still on public display, now outlined with a corona of new resonance. By the early twenty-first century, there were more than a dozen volumes examining the roles of women in early Celtic religion, lore and epic, some of them polemical, drawing on different sources and arriving at contradictory conclusions.

The strong women portrayed in early Celtic tradition should not imply that the everyday life of Gaulish, British or Irish women was a feminist Arcadia. Male dominance approximating polygamy was commonplace, with a powerful man impregnating plural wives, concubines and household servants, a behaviour persisting after the advent of Christianity. Nevertheless, physical and written evidence asserts that Celtic women were indeed seen as much more than servants and consorts. In early Celtic iconography, men and women are portrayed as of roughly the same size and stature. Celtic women in life assumed roles denied them in Mediterranean societies. In accounts other than those of Julius Caesar (first century BC), we read of female druids, who also appear in later Irish narratives. Flavius Vopiscus (*fl.* AD 300) lauds the prophetic power of druidesses, a capacity they also retain in Irish traditions. The ancients also perceived Celtic women to be sexually independent. The geographer Strabo (first century AD) reports on an island near the mouth of the Loire on the west coast of Gaul where the women of the Samnitae excluded men from their society, going ashore occasionally so that they might have intercourse with men of their choosing, thus perpetuating their kind (*Geographia*, IV). Celtic women might make war as well as love. Several classical commentators describe women appearing on the battlefield alongside their men. Diodorus Siculus, a contemporary of Caesar, observes that Gaulish women were as large, powerful and brave as male warriors. The last great Roman historian, Ammianus Marcellinus (fourth century AD) depicts fighting women more furious than the men, huge creatures with bulging necks who frightened the Romans with their white skin and piercing blue eyes. Some modern commentators have suggested that these and other portrayals of Gaulish amazons are but another slur against the barbaric Celts, but indigenous expression argues otherwise. Two of the oldest Celtic artefacts associate the female with battle. A pot found in a seventh-century BC grave in what is now Sopron-Varhély, Hungary, bears the incised form of a goddess with warriors on horseback. More impressive is the bronze model cult-wagon dating from the same period, found at Strettweg, Austria. The wagon consists of four wheels supporting a platform on which an artist has depicted a ceremonial scene. A female figure with prominent breasts, perhaps a divine huntress, appears with stags and armed men, hunters or warriors, both mounted and on foot. Such portrayals are complemented by the helmeted goddess on the much-studied Gundestrup Cauldron, the bronze figure of a female warrior found at Dinéault, Brittany, and others. Amazonian women also appear in the early literatures of Ireland and Wales, the best known being Scáthach of the Isle of Skye, the martial tutor of the Irish hero Cúchulainn.

The early Irish and Welsh tell us much about the conduct of daily life in their laws, which derive from native tradition rather than Roman law as in the rest of Western Europe. Those in Ireland are known as the Brehon Laws, named for the *breithem*, the judge or arbiter before the Norman invasion; some precedents date from as early as the sixth century. Welsh native law was codified by king Hywel Dda or Hywel the Good (d. 950). Brehon law allowed for nine forms of marriage, of which the primary was one in which both partners entered with equal financial resources. A second form of marriage was one in which the wife contributed little or no property, and a third was one in which the wife was better off financially. A woman might marry by choosing to elope without the consent of her family. Property a woman brought into a marriage remained hers. She could initiate a divorce from her husband for violence, adultery or impotency, or for his being homosexual. Sexual harassment was punished. In other respects, women did not fare so well under Brehon law. A husband might take a concubine; during the first three nights the concubine was in the household, the first wife was free of liability for any violence she committed short of murder. The concubine, in turn, was allowed to inflict whatever damage on the first wife she could accomplish with her fingernails, such as scratching, hair-tearing and minor injuries in general.

The laws of Hywel Dda allowed for fewer forms of marriage but are in many ways comparable in male–female relations. A wife could be compensated for physical abuse from her husband, but only a husband in Welsh law could retain property after a divorce. Welsh law proposed a complex formula for custody rights in divorce: after seven years of marriage a husband would retain the oldest and youngest child while the wife would be assigned all the middle children.

The end of the Celtic Church in Ireland, 1169/70, and the closer union with Rome, rescinded the rights women enjoyed under the Brehon Laws, just as Edward I's conquest of Wales, 1276–84, replaced the laws of Hywel Dda with those of Rome. The extension of Roman law, with its explicit patriarchy, into the Celtic fringe of the British Isles meant the extinction of women's rights to their own property, rights for compensation from abusive husbands and freedom to initiate divorce. This vivid and demonstrable contrast between the suppressed and nearly lost Celts as against the rigours of 'civilizing' English rule and religious orthodoxy prompts some modern commentators to wish aloud for a society that never existed.

Instead of presenting us with inviting milieus for post-Enlightenment views of gender and sexuality, medieval Celtic Europe gives us representations of women's bodies we are not sure we can understand. Among the most studied and contentious of these are the provocative, possibly obscene statues known as Sheela-na-gigs. The Irish phrase is *Sile na gCioch*, or Sheila (Cecilia) of the breasts, but usage has favoured the anglicized sheela- (or sheila-) na-gig. These stone carvings from medieval Ireland, Wales and Scotland depict a naked woman smiling grotesquely, her legs apart, with her hands spreading her genitalia. Faces and bodies are unerotically crude and cartoonlike, but the Sheela pose may be found in modern pornography. A recent guidebook numbered more than 144 examples, most of them found originally in churches, where they were once displayed prominently. An agreed origin and date for the statues has not been determined, although speculation has not been wanting. They may be borrowed from French Romanesque depictions of the sin of lust, meant as a warning to the faithful. Such a portrayal would be congruent with a dictum of the early Christian theologian Tertullian (second–third century) that the entrance to hell lies between the legs of a woman. Or the Sheelas may have been fertility figures, used as cures for barrenness. Recent feminist commentators have asserted that the Sheela-na-gigs are reminders of the primal earth mother whose role over life and death predated Christianity. Whatever their meaning, their survival testifies that the scribes and storytellers who kept medieval Irish and Welsh narratives alive, as well as the audiences for them, were exposed to images of the feminine that were not of mothers, consorts, virgins, saints or martyrs.

MOTHERS, PARTNERS AND HEALERS

Marija Gimbutas in *Goddesses and Gods of Old Europe* (1974, 1982) posits the existence of a Neolithic mother goddess, whose persona reappears in later tradition. Readers of classical mythology encounter names for the great mothers early in their study. Hesiod's story of the origin of the cosmos (*c.*700 BC) begins with a female deity, Ge (or Gaia, Gaea), whose cult all but merges with that of another earthly mother Themis. Ge or Ge-Themis is then succeeded by Rhea the Titaness, and Rhea by Hera the Olympian. Each of these remains maternal while initiating momentous action. Ge, for example, creates her own consort, Uranus, the sky deity, and later conspires with her son Cronus to overthrow Uranus, allowing Cronus to become ruler of the Titans.

The surviving evidence does not suggest there was ever a Celtic deity of such magnitude. Instead of one mother, there were many. In Britain alone at least fifty dedicatory inscriptions and images relating to a mother-goddess cult have been uncovered, with even more examples from what is today Burgundy in eastern France and the Rhineland of Germany. Mother deities are depicted in statues both singly and in triads, usually seated, accompanied by a child, often a male child nursing. They may also be associated with symbols of abundance such as animals, fruit, bread or cornucopias. Such early divinities rarely have names. The Matroniae Aufuniae (second century AD), seen with baskets of fruit, are found at what is now Bonn, Germany. The goddess of the Marne, Matrona (see Chapter 1), has maternal associations as her name suggests. She was also worshipped in Britain where Marnian immigrants settled. Matrona is the apparent source for the Welsh Modron, mother of the abducted child Mabon in the eleventh-century Welsh story of *Culhwch and Olwen* (see Chapter 13). Modron may have been transformed into the early Christian Saint Modrun, patroness of churches in Wales, Cornwall and Brittany, conventionally represented as a fleeing woman with a small child in her arms.

Neither is there a Ge, Rhea or Hera from early Irish and Welsh narrative. As mentioned in Chapter 1, the goddess Danu, known only from the genitive form of her name in Tuatha Dé Danann [people of the goddess Danu], has no dramatic character of her own. She is tantalizingly close to Ana/Anu, a leading goddess of pre-Christian Ireland whose name appears to be commemorated in Kerry's breast-shaped hills, Dá Chich Anann [the Paps of Ana], an identification that cannot be proved. The Welsh counterpart of Ana and Danu is Dôn, whose name is alluded to frequently in the Fourth Branch of the *Mabinogi* (see Chapter 13). She is married to the ancestor deity Beli Mawr, whose name is less often cited than hers. Her five children, Arianrhod, Gwydion, Gilfaethwy, Gofannon and Amaethon, embody the forces of light and good in their conflict with the more malevolent Children of Llŷr. But Dôn only influences rather than dominates action.

There is no Celtic patroness of marriage, ancient or medieval, and there is no indication of there ever having been a cosmic marriage between earth and sky as one finds in Greece and Egypt. Something approaching a figurative divine marriage arises with the numerous ancient goddesses who are always seen with male cult-partners of comparable stature. Their portrayal does not pretend the semblance of a domestic life, and the divine couples often lack attributed offspring. Miranda Green has observed (1995) that many of these divine pairings follow a cultural pattern: an intrusive Roman god marries an indigenous deity with Celtic attributes. The Gaulish goddess known by the Latin name Rosmerta [good purveyor, great provider], whose cult stretched from what is today Germany to Britain, is usually linked with Gaulish Mercury. Images of fertility and prosperity, possibly including a bucket for dairy products, adorn her statues. She may also be a patroness of fertility and motherhood. Even though her iconography often resembles that of the Roman goddess Fortuna, and she sometimes assumes aspects of Mercury himself, Rosmerta's worship indicates she is an indigenous deity whose name alone is Roman. Her cult partner, Gaulish Mercury, another native god given a conqueror's name (see Chapter 2), adopts the caduceus and purse of Roman Mercury and looks like his Roman namesake; Roman Mercury, however, never had a cult partner.

Nantosuelta and Sucellus are two more Gaulish deities with Romanized names; hers means 'meandering stream' and his 'good striker'. They are often seen together, the best known example being a stone relief found at Sarrebourg, near Metz, France. As tall as her mate, with long flowing hair adorned with a diadem, Nantosuelta is fair of face and noticeably younger than Sucellus. In her right hand she holds a dish over an altar, while with her upraised left she grasps a long pole on which is perched what looks like a small house. What all these might signify is not clear, just as there is little agreement about what is implied in the long-handled hammer in Sucellus's left upraised arm. Although they are commonly associated, sometimes accompanied by motifs of ravens and beehives, both Nantosuelta and Sucellus might also appear singly in shrines in both Gaul and Britain.

Other surviving votive figures of divine couples do not always carry names or distinguishing iconographic motifs. Among those we can name is the Gaulish healing goddess Sirona [divine star(?)], often paired with Apollo in his guise as the spring deity Apollo Grannus. Sirona usually bears reminders of fertility, such as eggs, fruit and edible grain; she may have a serpent circling her arm and a diadem upon her head. Another Gaulish healing goddess Damona ['great' or 'divine cow'], also portrayed with edible grain and a serpent circling her hand, is usually seen with a male healer, Borvo. Worshipped very widely, Borvo is also known as Bormo and Bormanus; when he is known as Bormanus (indicative of bubbling water), his cult partner bears a doublet of his own name, Bormana. The polyandrous Damona, meanwhile, may also be seen with Apollo Moritasgus, or Apollo seen as a healer at Alésia in what is now Burgundy, eastern France.

Burgundy was also the realm of Sequana, the healing goddess, the personification of the River Seine, who was worshipped at the river's source, *Fontes Sequanae* [Springs of Sequana], in a valley near the modern city of Dijon. Of the many curative spring deities in Gaul and Britain, Sequana is one of the few with an iconographic presence. While not a creature of narrative, Sequana's many representations and artefacts associated with her worship suggest a developed if static persona. She was a benign goddess. Pilgrims seeking cures left behind images of themselves with depictions of eye ailments, problems of the head, limbs and internal organs. Votive models of breasts and genitalia imply the power to deal with women's disorders, although men appear to have sought aid here as well. Nevertheless, Sequana's attention to procreation and the nursing mother establish a link with fertility and motherhood, pertinent to the question of why healing should have been attributed to a female deity.

In Mediterranean culture, the power to heal was thought to be male, attributed first to Apollo, and later to his reputed son, Asclepius of Epidaurus (Aesculapius to the Romans). But early Celtic divine healers, both unnamed and named, are female. They possess generative as well as curative powers. Mother-goddesses, further, are often venerated at spring shrines. The feminization of the power of healing may have been an extension of the worship of the nurturing mother, or it may have been a reflection of everyday practice. A funerary stone (first century AD) erected in what is now Metz in eastern Gaul depicts a female figure with a doctor's accoutrements. How many women actually served in this role is not known.

Two spring goddesses attracted extensive cults in Roman Britain – Sulis and Coventina. With worship centred at Bath, Sulis was a native deity whose cult merged with that of the Roman Minerva, a process described in Chapter 2. Although some scholars have asserted that Sulis was originally male, she is referred to as *dea* [goddess] in Roman commentaries, and the much-photographed surviving bronze head of Sulis depicts an unmistakably female face. As with Coventina, Sulis patronized both eye ailments and female disorders. The model bronze and ivory breasts found at Bath may have been worn as amulets by mothers until their infants were weaned and then given in thanksgiving to Sulis for having encouraged lactation. But Sulis was also a scold. Found at her shrine are 130 *defixiones* or curse tablets. These are sheets of pewter or lead inscribed with messages to the goddess filled with complaints against bullies and perceived enemies with requests for retribution. Such curse tablets also exist in the Mediterranean world, but here they beseech a healing goddess to invert her beneficent powers.

Like Sulis, Coventina's worship was focused on one particular site, namely what is now Carrawburgh on Hadrian's Wall, although evidence of her cult can be found as far afield as southern Gaul and northwestern Spain. A well-preserved stone relief portrays her flanked by two nymphs, which may be a triple image of the goddess herself, as she is also nymphlike. Precious tributes are found at her shrine, including 16,000 coins, finger rings, brooches and decorative pins, such as appear at sites of other healing deities, including Aesculapius or Asclepius. There is little direct evidence, however, to prove she was a healing goddess and she may have been what Lindsay Allason-Jones (1989) calls an 'all-rounder' goddess, a kind and generous protector against all the evils afflicting mankind.

HAGS

A woman's beauty can be counted on to catch the eye of the beholder. So will a woman's ugliness. During most of modern literature, beginning at least with Provençal troubadours of the twelfth and thirteenth centuries, the reader has become used to the simple equation that beauty equals desirability and that ugliness invites disdain and rejection. Early Irish and Welsh narrative tradition presents more complex portraits. Men still prefer the company of beautiful women, but a woman's role within a story is not complete with a mere assessment of her appearance. The ill-favoured hags of the sovereignty stories, cited in Chapter 3, reward most generously the prospective kings who make love to them. Similarly, the gorgeous Welsh Blodeuedd (whose name means 'flower face', Chapter 13) turns out to be a catastrophic mate, filled with deceit and treachery. We cannot know the implications of a pretty or an ugsome face, whether benign or malevolent, until we see how the persona behind it completes her role in the narrative.

A woman's ugliness can contribute to her arresting dramatic entrance, such as that of the seer Cailb in the pre-eleventh-century story *Togail Bruidne Da Derga* [The Destruction of Da Derga's Hostel]. Da Derga, Conaire and all the guests are seated when, after sunset, a lone woman asks to be let in. The narrator then pauses for a paragraph on her surreal hideousness: shins as dark as a stag beetle and as long as a weaver's beam; her 'lower hair' reaches to her knees and her lips are on one side of her head. Entering and proclaiming herself Cailb the seer, she rebuffs a challenge to the apparent meaninglessness of her name by standing on one foot, holding up one hand and chanting in one breath the thirty-two different names she can bear, including Badb. Her appearance, the assembly learns, foreshadows the fearsomeness of her prophecy that all present will be destroyed except for what the birds can carry off in their claws.

The Irish hero Cúchulainn usually has an easy time with prominent beauties but encounters mighty adversaries among the ugly. The Scottish druidess Dornoll takes Cúchulainn as student in her martial instruction and falls deeply in love with him. His resistance to her wins her continuing enmity. Cúchulainn takes instruction with the amazonian Scáthach on the Isle of Skye, after which he encounters a grotesque one-eyed hag while travelling along a narrow ridge. She is Éis Énchenn, who first commands and then begs that he get out of her way. When he complies, clinging only by his toes, she strikes him, trying to knock him down the cliff. He counters with his thrusting salmon leap, severing her head.

The hero Fionn mac Cumhaill also faces frightful female adversaries. The three ugly daughters of Conarán try to punish Fionn and some companions for violating the taboo of hunting without permission, by entrapping them in a cave. Fionn's former enemy Goll mac Morna saves them by killing the three sisters.

Ugly women in early Welsh narrative also appear formidable initially, but, like their Irish sisters, they are bested by male figures. The women often gain control of fantastic cauldrons. The myth of the cauldron runs very deep in Celtic culture, beginning with the great treasures from the ancient world. The extensively studied Gundestrup Cauldron, recovered in Denmark (see pp. xix–xx, 38), is covered with artistic decoration that provides a kind of Rosetta Stone for the interpretation of early religion. Numerous cauldrons appear in both Welsh and Irish narrative, always with magical properties, such as bubbling inexhaustibly or offering unique powers; they are probably ancestors of the Arthurian Grail. The haggish Ceridwen, a shape-shifting witch, keeps a cauldron of knowledge at the bottom of Bala Lake in north Wales, hoping to reserve its powers for her children, the fair-faced daughter Creirwy or the hideous son Morfran. Three savoury drops intended for Morfran fall instead to Gwion Bach, granting to him unique powers of insight and superhuman wisdom. Ceridwen then pursues Gwion Bach and the two shift shapes until she at last consumes him as a grain of wheat. The grain impregnates Ceridwen, and nine months later she gives birth to Taliesin, the divinely inspired poet (see Chapter 13).

In *Branwen*, the Second Branch of the *Mabinogi*, the ill-featured giantess Cymidei Cymeinfoll [W. bloated with war] becomes a personification of a cauldron of regeneration. Just as the cauldron could bring alive dead warriors, so she could create them by becoming pregnant and giving birth to fully armed soldiers every six weeks. The hero Matholwch incarcerates Cymidei and her husband Llassar Llaes Gyfnewid in an iron house, which he then burns. The couple escape and give the cauldron to Brân/Bendigeidfran, the deity later described as the 'king of Britain'.

Of all the females with ill-favoured visages, the one who generates the most extensive lore is Cailleach Bhéirre, known in English as the Hag of Beare, cited as a sovereignty figure at the end of Chapter 3. Named for the Beare Peninsula between Bantry Bay and the Kenmare River in west Co. Cork, she is linked to several locations in the south and west of Ireland and has similarly named counterparts in Gaelic Scotland and the Isle of Man. Undoubtedly first a goddess, she is featured in a poem of AD 900, where she is an old woman lamenting the loss of her youth, and she remained celebrated in both written and oral tradition up through the twentieth century. Somewhat sinister but wise, she came to be thought of as a nun in early Christian times; the word *cailleach* comes from the Latin for a veil, *pallium*. But she also speaks of having had many lovers, children, foster-children, as well as grandchildren and great-grandchildren; she never relates Christian wisdom.

Her physical unattractiveness, rooted in her early associations with sovereignty, never contributes to a sense of villainy for the Cailleach Bhéirre. In the earliest traditions, she is thought to have taken many lovers while young, including the ferocious Fenian warrior Fothad Conainne. Later she was linked to landforms and attributed with powers that transformed animals into the standing stones surviving from Neolithic times. In Gaelic Scotland, where she was known as Cailleach Bheur, she had a blue face as the daughter of the pale winter sun and became a female spirit of the wilderness and the protectress of wild animals. In Scotland also she took a watery form known as Muileartach. In Ireland citations of her age became proverbial so that when people reached very advanced years they were said to be 'as old as the Cailleach Bhéirre'. In her lamented lost loves, her crabbed promises of sovereignty to fearful but aspiring princes and her extreme longevity, she became an embodiment of human disappointment, like us in everything except mortality.

BEAUTIES

Narrators of early Irish and Welsh literature had different expectations for beauty. It may be a transient quality, like youth, but we do not all share in it. Young heroes stand in awe of female beauty, sometimes in fear of it. Yet in some Celtic narratives are beautiful women who are much more than the apogee of male wish.

There are, admittedly, some women who are little more than a pretty face, such as Olwen, focus of the quest by young Culhwch in the eleventh-century Welsh narrative in Arthurian setting, *Culhwch and Olwen*. The hero falls in love with Olwen without so much as seeing her; her name means 'flower track', because four white clovers spring up wherever she steps. To find her Culhwch must endure an exhausting quest and, after they meet, he must satisfy her father, the giant Ysbaddaden, by completing forty herculean tasks, culminating in the chaining of the great boar Twrch Trwyth. Meanwhile, the narrative offers few details about Olwen to suggest she will have much to share with Culhwch once he succeeds in winning her.

What feminists call 'the male gaze' is often in evidence, as it is elsewhere in Western culture. Consider the lip-smacking delight in the description of Étaín (also Éodoin, anglicized as Aideen), who is the living standard by which every other beauty is judged. It appears in the eighth- to ninth-century narrative *Tochmarc Étaíne* [The Wooing of Étaín], which will be considered at length in Chapter 8.

As white as the snow of one night was each of her two arms, and as red as the foxglove of the mountain was each of her two cheeks. As blue as the hyacinth was each of her two eyes; delicately red her lips; very high, soft and white her two shoulders. Tender, smooth and white were her two wrists; her fingers long and very white; her nails pink and beautiful. As white as snow or as the foam of a wave was her side, slender, long and soft as silk. Soft, smooth and white were her thighs; round and small and firm and white were her two knees; as straight as a rule were her two ankles; slim and foam-white were her two feet. Fair and beautiful were her two eyes; her eyebrows blackish blue like the shell of a beetle. It was she the maiden who was the fairest and the most beautiful that the eyes of man had ever seen . . .

(Cross and Slover, 1936: 83)

Étaín's way in love is not easy. She is pursued by Midir, who already has a wife, the jealous Fuamnach. She transforms Étaín into an insect only for her to be born again as a younger Étaín more than 1,000 years later.

A woman's beauty is never a static or indifferent property. Mugain, the strumpet wife of Conchobar mac Nessa, king of Ulster, bares her breasts to effect change in a warrior's behaviour. She and her maidens reveal themselves to Cúchulainn, the Ulster champion, ostensibly to stifle his battle fury. Instead he is so startled and embarrassed, or, alternatively, consumed with passion, upon seeing the women that it requires three vats of icy water to cool him down. Countless warriors, especially in the Fenian Cycle, are lured by beautiful women who are later revealed to be transformed animals, especially deer, or lead the warriors to enchanted residences [bruidne in Irish] in which they become entrapped. The golden-haired Niam (Modern Irish: Niamh) leads the Fenian hero Oisín to Tír na nÓg, the land of eternal youth, where he feels he has made only a short sojourn but returns to the land of mortals greatly aged (see Chapter 11).

Beauty implies more than romantic invitation or sexual promise. In *Serglige Con Culainn* [The Sickbed of Cúchulainn] the hero, while sleeping next to a pillar stone, dreams of two beautiful women, one dressed in green, the other in red. Laughing all the while, the two women begin to whip him, at first playfully and then so severely that the strength drains from his body, thus the 'sickbed' of the title. After a year passes, they are revealed to be two sisters, Lí Ban [paragon of women] and Fand [tear], both already married to powerful husbands. Lí Ban says she means no further harm and only wishes Cúchulainn's friendship, but also his assistance in fighting her husband's enemies. After the hero sends his charioteer, Láeg, to go with Lí Ban to investigate the invitation, he agrees and makes short work of three monstrous villains. Later, however, he spends an extended period of lovemaking with Fand, bringing him into conflict with his own wife, Emer (see pp. 212–15).

Writing in the early twentieth century, Rudolf Thurneysen remarked that whereas men had a choice of routes to high reputation and honour, the inescapable conclusion to be derived from the reading of early Irish literature is that the honour of women was conceived of primarily as sexual. A woman may boast of her chastity or fidelity, whereas a man never does. Similarly, a woman's unfaithfulness, the possibility that she may love someone other than her mate or bear the child of a man not her husband, was a subject of deep regret or horror, rather than of mere scandal as it would be in later centuries.

So it is with the two Welsh beauties whose stories appear in the context of the *Mabinogi* (see pp. 271–83), Rhiannon and Blodeuedd. Perhaps because it falls so euphoniously on the ears of English-speakers, Rhiannon is among the best known names of early Celtic tradition but knowledge of who she is does not seem widely dispersed, even among women bearing the name in contemporary society. By no means a witch, she is one of the main female characters in the first, *Pwyll*, and third, *Manawydan*, branches of the *Mabinogi*.

Rhiannon's persona is much older than the medieval text, however. She appears to be derived from the pre-Christian goddess hypothesized as Rigantona and also Epona, the horse goddess. Her pedigree within the *Mabinogi* also implies supernatural status as she is thought to be the daughter of the king of Annwfn, the otherworld; her name may mean maid of Annwfn. Rhiannon's first appearance in the narrative is almost cinematic, when she rides in on a white horse, dazzling Pwyll [sense, wisdom, discretion], prince of Dyfed, who instantly falls in love with her. After some confusion about whom she should marry, made worse by Pwyll's feckless behaviour, they are wed, after which she dispenses precious gifts, evoking her divine origin as a bountiful deity.

When she produces a son on May Eve (see Chapter 5), he is stolen, and Rhiannon is falsely accused of the infant's murder. Her punishment is public penance for seven years, during which time she must sit by the horse-block near the palace gate, offering all visitors a ride on her back. Later she is proved innocent, and the child, now called Pryderi [care, anxiety], is returned to her. When he is full grown, in the Third Branch, Pryderi promises his mother to his comrade-in-arms, Manawydan. A magical mist then lays waste the kingdom, leaving alive only Pryderi and his wife and Rhiannon and her husband. This evil work is revealed to have come from an enchanter, Llwyd, an ally of one of Rhiannon's former disappointed suitors. Llwyd is then forced to restore Dyfed to its verdancy. At the end of her story, Rhiannon is still a queen. Despite the false accusations against her, humiliations and other misuse, she always retains her sexual honour.

In that regard her opposite number is Blodeuedd, wife and betrayer of Lleu Llaw Gyffes in *Math*, the Fourth Branch of the *Mabinogi*. After his mother Arianrhod said he should have no wife of any race, Lleu's cohorts, the magician Gwydion (secretly Lleu's own father) and his great-uncle Math, contrive a gorgeous female figure from the flowers of oak, broom and meadowsweet. Her name is Blodeuedd, literally 'Flower Face'. She brings her husband little pleasure, however. While Lleu is absent she falls in love with a passing hunter, Gronw Pebyr, with whom she plots to kill her husband. As Lleu is invulnerable under normal circumstances, Blodeuedd must find secret means by which he might be taken. She tricks Lleu into a position that exposes him to Gronw, who tries unsuccessfully to kill him. Learning of her treachery and betrayal, Gwydion transforms Blodeuedd into an owl, ominous bird of the night.

Two beautiful young Irish women escape from dominating men and pay heavy prices for their independence, but their narratives take a different tone from those in the *Mabinogi*. They flee the ageing, powerful men to whom they were betrothed and assert their own form of honour by cleaving to younger lovers they select for themselves. They are Deirdre (or Derdriu, etc.) from the Ulster Cycle and Gráinne from the Fenian Cycle (see pp. 234–7). While their tales share striking parallels, they are also separated by profound differences that depict Deirdre as the more attractive personality. Certainly her adventures and subsequent downfall have been portrayed more often in English-language adaption since 1870, in poetry, drama, fiction, even opera, so that Deirdre is now popularly the best known name of any from early Celtic traditions.

Deirdre's story was widely known over many centuries. It is found in two medieval versions, a third from the early nineteenth century and several folk variants from both Ireland and Gaelic Scotland. It was also seen as a fore-tale of the great Irish epic, *Táin Bó Cuailnge* [The Cattle Raid of Cooley].

Fedlimid, the chief bard of Ulster at the court of King Conchobar mac Nessa, becomes the father of a baby girl, Deirdre. Even before her birth, the court druid Cathbad prophesies that the girl-child will grow to be a woman of wonderful beauty, but that she will also cause great enmity, leading to the destruction of Ulster. On hearing the druid's words, several courtiers demand that she be killed, but Conchobar (anglicized Conor) does not wish this. Instead, he fosters her secretly until she is of marriageable age so that he might then take her as his wife.

The girl is raised in isolation from society, with only the company of a few women, notably Leborcham, a poet and confidante. One day the two of them observe a visiting Conchobar skinning a recently killed calf in the snow. A raven perches nearby, drinking the calf's blood. Deirdre exclaims at the juxtaposition of the three colours, white snow, red blood and black raven. She declares that the man she marries will have this colouring, and Leborcham responds that such a man exists: with white skin, red cheeks and black hair. He lives nearby, Noíse (also Naoise, etc.), a nephew of Conchobar and a son of Uisnech.

After Leborcham arranges a meeting between the two, Noíse remarks, 'Fair is the heifer that goes past me.' Deirdre responds, 'Heifers are wont to be big where there is no bull.' To which Noíse replies, 'You have the bull of the province, the king of Ulster.' And then Deirdre admits, 'I will choose between the two of you, and I will choose a young bull like you.' Shortly thereafter Deirdre and Noíse elope, fleeing first across Ireland with Conchobar in pursuit and later to Scotland. Noíse's brothers Ardan and Ainnle go with them, thus the title of the best known version in Irish, *Longas* (or *Longes*) *mac nUislenn* [The Exile of the Sons of Uisnech]. It is a *remscél* or prologue of the *Táin Bó Cuailnge* and is usually found with the epic. When a host king in Scotland begins to lust after Deirdre, the party flees. Soon news of pardon from Conchobar reaches them. Wanting the young people back in the Ulster capital of Emain Macha, he sends the hero Fergus mac Róich with pledges of good faith to the fugitives. The brothers are willing to accept the invitation to return, but Deirdre perceives the falsity in the offer and fears Conchobar's treachery. Deirdre sings the verses of 'Farewell to Alba' [Scotland], before joining the others in the boat.

When they land in Ulster, Conchobar employs a ruse to separate Fergus from Deirdre and the brothers. The king's men, led by Eógan mac Durthacht, then attack quickly, killing all but Deirdre. For the next year she lives subject to Conchobar, never smiling, frequently berating him for killing what was dear to her. No longer wishing to mate with her himself, Conchobar contrives to increase Deirdre's humiliation by having her marry the hated Eógan, Noíse's murderer, and possibly also a member of a lower social order. To exacerbate her predicament, Conchobar makes Deirdre the butt of a crude sexual joke. Deirdre then commits suicide. In the earlier of the medieval texts she does this by throwing herself against a stone and smashing her head into fragments. This occurs outside her residence but before she reaches the assembly of Emain Macha, where her treatment by Conchobar and Eógan would have invited more shame and ridicule. Like a male hero, she chooses death before dishonour. The later medieval version, *Oided Mac nUisnig* [Death of the Sons of Uisnech], provides details preferred in modern retellings of the story. Here she falls from the chariot into the sea, dashing her head upon a rock, her blood leaving a red streak on the foam. The last Irish language version, perhaps influenced by Christianity to be uneasy about suicide, has her falling upon her lover's grave, overcome by grief.*

In the Fenian parallel story of Gráinne, retold in Chapter 11, the young beauty runs off with the handsome Diarmait, who is killed in a boar hunt. At the end of that tale, Gráinne is reunited with old Fionn mac Cumhaill, to whom she had been betrothed at the beginning of the action.

* See the Scottish Gaelic variant on the death of Deirdre, linking her to the Milky Way Galaxy, p. 292.

The Deirdre story in different texts is often classed as one of the 'Three Sorrows of Storytelling', along with *Oidheadh Chlainne Tuireann* [The Tragic Story of the Children of Tuireann] (see pp. 153–5), and *Oidheadh Chlainne Lir* [The Tragic Story of the Children of Lir] (see pp. 163–5).

WARRIOR GODDESSES AND QUEENS

As mentioned earlier in this chapter, classical commentators such as Diodorus Siculus and Ammianus Marcellinus describe Gaulish women participating in battle alongside the men in their society. Dio Cassius speaks of the early British war goddess Andraste, the only such native goddess whose name we are sure about, who was venerated by the celebrated early female warrior Boudicca and her people, the Iceni. There certainly were others. One may have been Nemetona, shadowy Gaulish and British goddess of the sacred grove, whose name is found on inscriptions from what is now Germany to Bath in Britain. As she often paired with Mars, Roman god of war, her cult probably had martial implications. Further, her name appears to have an echo in the Irish war goddess Nemain [battle-fury, war-like frenzy]. The fullness of Nemain's identity is not entirely clear either. She is usually cited as the consort of Néit, an Irish god of war, along with Badb, whose identity she may share. As mentioned in Chapter 1, Badb (also Baobh, anglicized Bave) is one of three Irish goddesses of war, known collectively as Mórrígna, along with Macha and Mórrígan. When the name of Nemain is substituted for either Badb or Mórrígan, commentators are inclined to see her as an aspect of those deities rather than a discrete entity in and of herself.

Of the war-goddesses known as Mórrígna, however, there is more to tell. The name in Irish means 'great queens', a plural form of the name of one of the trio, Mórrígan, often referred to in translation with the definite article, 'the Mórrígan'. Some commentators have suggested that Mórrígna is identical with the Mórrígan and that Badb, Macha and Nemain are but aspects of her. Both the collective Mórrígna and the individual Mórrígan derive aspects from the territorial goddess Mór Muman, whose sometimes lusty exploits are cited in Chapter 3. Despite continuing parallels in their stories, the Mórrígan, Macha and Badb develop differing narrative personae in early Irish tradition.

Badb is often a scourge and a torment for warriors, and she delights in slaughter. Her name means hooded crow or scald crow, and she may also be known as Badb Catha, which means crow of battle, a scavenger of carrion. She may be related to the Gaulish battle-goddess whose name is reported as Bodua, Catobodua or Cauth Bova. As a haunter of battlefields, she has much in common with later figures from folklore such as the *badhbh chaointe* [Ir. weeping crow], the mournful scavenger, and also with the famous banshee, who foretells death, if she does not actually cause it.

Personae ascribed to the Mórrígan and Macha are much more complex because both are tri-functional, each a sovereign ruler, war-goddess and promoter of fertility. Like several unnamed sovereignty figures, both the Mórrígan and Macha demonstrate robust sexual appetites, often asserting their energies on warriors and heroes as well as other deities. In an oft-cited episode, the Mórrígan copulates with Dagda, the so-called 'good god', a leader of the divine race of the Tuatha Dé Danann, and one of the principal immortals of early Ireland. This occurs while the Mórrígan is straddling the river Unshin, near the village of Collooney in what is now Co. Sligo. After their lovemaking, the Mórrígan advises the Dagda that the evil Fomorians will soon be attacking in the epochal Second Battle of Mag Tuired (anglicized Moytura), described in Chapter 7. In the Irish epic *Táin Bó Cuailnge*, the Mórrígan takes on the guise of a lovely young girl in approaching the hero Cúchulainn, clearly wanting him to pay amorous attention to her. He crudely rebuffs her, saying he does 'not have time for a woman's backside'. She then approaches him under different forms, as an eel, a wolf, and a hornless red heifer, all to no avail. Later, when she sees him in combat she becomes an old milch cow; on his request for a drink she allows suckling from each of her three teats. Later she correctly predicts his death, breaks his chariot wheels and appears as a hooded crow on the shoulder of his corpse.

Macha, while a member of the Mórrígan trio, is herself a goddess with three identities. Perhaps the three are separate for purposes of storytelling. They may share a core identity: all three are born of the same mother, Ernmass. Georges Dumézil (1954) has argued that Macha provides the model for triplism in Celtic tradition. In each of her manifestations she gives her name to Emain Macha, the 18-acre hill fort in Co. Armagh, now known as Navan Fort, that is seen as the royal seat or capital of Ulster in stories of the Ulster Cycle. One of the Machas is the wife of the invader Nemed in the *Lebor Gabála* (see Chapter 7). The second Macha, sometimes known as Mong Ruadh [Ir. red-haired], the widow of an Ulster king, travels in disguise as a leper to the western and rival province of Connacht. While there, she comes upon the sons of her rival, Cimbáeth, roasting a pig. Luring the sons into the forest on the ruse of lying with her, she instead overpowers each one of them and drags them back to Ulster, where she sets them to building a noble fortress in her honor, Emain Macha. The best-known Macha is the wife of Crunniuc mac Agnomain, who gives birth during a horse race and brings the *noínden* [Ir. debility/birth pangs] to Ulster warriors. Against her wishes, Macha's husband Crunniuc boasts that she can outrun any horse in the land. When called upon to prove this claim, Macha protests that she is pregnant and pledges that perpetual evil will fall upon Ulster because of this affair. She indeed outpaces all the horses quite easily but cries out in pain as she crosses the finish line, immediately giving birth to twins, thus naming the spot Emain Macha. The word *emain* may mean either brooch or twins in Irish. She curses all who can hear her, and their descendants to nine times nine generations, that they suffer the pangs of childbirth for five days and four nights at the time of greatest difficulty. Small boys, women, and the hero Cúchulainn were excepted (see Chapter 9).

Like Macha, Queen Medb could outrun a horse. Like the Mórrígan, Medb appears to derive some of her persona from Mór Muman, the territorial goddess. As one of the protagonists of the Irish epic *Táin Bó Cuailnge*, Medb the warrior queen of Connacht is the culmination of even more forces of territory, fertility and sovereignty. In the *Táin* alone there is justification to argue that she is the most vibrant female personality in all of Celtic mythology, and there is further testimony to her allure and power in stories composed before the epic as well as those that came after. Her name in Irish means 'she who intoxicates', linguistically related to the Greek *methu* [wine]. Like a Gaulish mother-goddess, she is often portrayed with creatures, a bird and a squirrel, on her shoulder. She is always seen as a beautiful young woman, regardless of the chronology of the story. By literary convention she is pale, long-faced, with long flowing hair, wearing a red cloak and carrying a spear that may be flaming. The sight of her is enough to deprive men of two-thirds of their strength. Medb dominates men, both by the force of her personality and through her own sexuality. Called 'Medb of the friendly thighs' by translators, she claims that it takes thirty-two men to satisfy her sexually. She boasts of having any lover she wishes, 'each man in another man's shadow'. Many men are named as her 'husbands', but the lusty and potent Fergus mac Róich is her favourite lover.

The sovereignty goddess of Tara, or 'queen' of Leinster (eastern Ireland), known as Medb Lethderg [red-side, half-red], may be an anticipation or double of Medb of Connacht. Or Medb of Connacht may be only an emanation from Medb Lethderg as the goddess of Tara is certainly the older of the two. With her own pedigree, Medb Lethderg is thought to be the wife of nine successive kings of Ireland, including the father of the heroic Conn Cétchathach [of the Hundred Battles]. The esteemed monarch Cormac mac Airt, grandson of Conn, could not be considered king until he had slept with Medb Lethderg.

In historicizing Medb of Connacht, medieval scribes constructed a detailed biography. Her father, for example, is thought to be one of the most important pre-Patrician kings, Eochaid Feidlech. Her mother is sometimes named Cruacha, for whom the fortress of Cruachain in Co. Roscommon, Medb's residence, is named. She has four sisters, all of whom are at one time 'married' to Conchobar mac Nessa, king of Emain Macha in Ulster, ultimately one of Medb's great enemies. Medb kills her sister Clothra who is pregnant with Conchobar's child, treachery that will later bring about her own death. The order and number of Medb's husbands is not certain. Conchobar may have been the first, but through 'pride of mind' she departed from his company; he still lusts for her and later violates her while she is bathing in the Boyne River. Three later husbands become kings of Connacht. She is led to her husband of the *Táin*, Ailill mac Máta, by a 'water worm' who becomes Finnbennach, the White-horned Bull of Connacht who contends in the epic with Donn Cuailnge, the Brown Bull of Ulster.

For a woman with such a demanding military and administrative career, Medb is often pregnant herself. She gives the name Maine to seven sons she bears to Ailill, under the misreading of a druid's prophecy that a son with that name will kill Conchobar. Two of her love-children fathered by Fergus mac Róich give their names to the land; Ciar is the eponym of Ciarraí, or Kerry in English, and Conmac is the eponym of Conmaicne Mara, or Connemara, the region that cradles legend in west Galway.

The most coherent portrait of Medb as alluring schemer derives from four stories in the Ulster Cycle. In three of them, *Fled Bricrenn* [Briccriu's Feast], *Echtra Nerai* [The Adventure of Nera] and *Scéla mucce Meic Dathó* [The Story of Mac Da Thó's Pig], she is only a strident supporting player. In the *Táin* (related more fully in Chapter 10) she leads the action, beginning with her bickering pillow-talk with husband Ailill in the opening scenes over who possesses the greater wealth; he claims that ownership of Finnbennach, the White-horned Bull, gives him supremacy. Sensing that she has greater determination than her husband, she takes command of her armies and her allies so that she can seize the Donn Cuailnge, the Brown Bull of Ulster, and thus best Ailill. Her judgement is not always prudent, and she is constantly diverted by her adultery with Fergus.

The Ulster champion Cúchulainn becomes her most formidable opponent and their rivalry supplies continuing conflict in a somewhat diffuse narrative. Initially she thinks she can dismiss him but she comes to see him as a worthy adversary. Attempts to entrap him are thwarted, but her scheme to pit Cúchulainn against his friend Ferdiad leads to their duel at the ford, the single most dramatic moment in the epic. The Ulster hero triumphs, further hampering the Connacht queen. In face-to-face encounter Cúchulainn taunts and humiliates her, once shooting a pet bird from her shoulder. Later, when he comes upon her alone during her menstruation, she has to plead with him to be spared. In sneering condescension he says that he will not be a killer of women and so departs. She finds revenge by setting the horrible children of Cailitin against Cúchulainn, beginning a series of events that will lead to his downfall.

Medb's bizarre death is related in a tale composed much later than the *Táin*. When Medb kills her pregnant sister Clothra, the child cut from the dying woman's womb, Furbaide Ferbend, survives and lives on an island in Lough Ree, Co. Roscommon. Unaccountably, Medb chooses to live on the same island, where she goes bathing each morning. Learning the identity of the bather, his mother's killer, Furbaide takes a hardened piece of cheese he has been eating, places it in his sling, and shoots it, hitting Medb squarely in the forehead and killing her. Old as this story is, it has left a trace in oral tradition. The island where Medb was slain is today known in English as Quaker's Island, but its traditional name is Inchcleraun or, in Irish, Inis Clothrand, Clothra's Island. The highest point on the island, known in English as Greenan Hill, derived from the Irish *Grianán Meidbe* or Medb's Sun Porch.

Although Medb did not inspire a rich body of literature from oral tradition, she is sometimes described as the 'queen of the fairies'. Her name lives on in dozens of place names, the best known of which is the cairn atop Knocknarea, Co. Sligo, a favourite locale of W. B. Yeats. It is Miscaun Maeve, or in Irish *Miosgán Méabha* [Medb's Lump]. Many commentators, perhaps wishfully, assume she is an antecedent of Shakespeare's Queen Mab (*Romeo and Juliet*, I, iv), the fairies' midwife who delivers man's brain of dreams, and who appears elsewhere in the work of sixteenth- and seventeenth-century English writers.

TRANSIT TO SAINTHOOD

It takes more to become a saint than simply to be called one. In modern times canonization is an exacting process, in which evidence and testimonials are scrutinized closely, but it was not always so. During the slow European adaptation of the Christian worldview between the end of the Roman empire and the rise of monasticism and feudalism, countless petty deities and numinous figures received what amounted to baptism. Honoured by the faithful during pre-Christian times, they continued to be venerated and invoked after the spread and acceptance of the Gospels but came to be called saints. Many are associated with holy wells in the Celtic countries. In addition, lives of saints written centuries after the supposed death of the holy person, especially in Ireland, appear to assert the territorial and property claims of rival monasteries. The sanctity of a worthy saint might confer rights on his or her monastery. Confusing the matter further are the many saints' legends, both popular and learned, composed during the Middle Ages, filled with astonishing and often fanciful adventures, pious counterparts to the secular romances that flourished about the same time. One of the great tasks of Christian scholarship has been to winnow out the reliable data from fabulous tales, an on-going labour in Celtic countries as well as in other parts of Europe. The Roman Catholic Church signalled its concern that some early claims to sainthood were not supported by trustworthy evidence when it struck many familiar names from the official calendar in 1961. Many of the desanctified were shadowy forgotten figures, but the loss of the former saints Christopher and Philomena dismayed many of the devoted.

The lives of male saints are often characterized by heroic resistance to malign forces, whether animal or human. Many male saints may bring the light of the Gospels, usually at great danger to themselves, into the dark world of paganism. We see manly saints portrayed at birth and in childhood as well as in adulthood. The lives of female saints, however, often have a sharper focus. Elissa R. Henken has observed that the lives of Welsh saints usually turn on the women's response to unwanted male sexual attention. One unwelcome act of aggression is enough to drive a holy woman to withdraw from society and take up the celibate life of a pious recluse. As in the secular tales of royal wives and heroic beauties, a woman's honour is once again defined by her sexual behaviour.

Of all the Christian personages with possible Celtic pre-Christian antecedents, none has inspired more commentary than St Brigid or Brigit of Kildare, the best known of fifteen Irish saints bearing this name. *The New Catholic Encyclopedia* gives her vital dates as *c.*460–*c.*528, and outlines her biography:

Her mother was a slave-girl; but the child was acknowledged by her father and given to a foster mother to rear. Having been instructed in letters and the accomplishments of embroidery and household duties, she was sought in marriage by an eager suitor whom she rejected on the ground that she had vowed 'her virginity to the Lord.' After paternal objections were overcome she took the veil, the symbol of the religious state; she founded in the Liffey plain a church called Cill Dara (Kildare – 'the church of the oak') and associated herself with the pious hermit, Conleth, who lived alone in nearby solitude.

(*New Catholic Encyclopedia*, 2003: 617)

Conventionally known as the 'Mary of the Gael', St Brigid has long been venerated as one of the three patron saints of Ireland, along with Patrick and Colum Cille (or Columba). Her feast day, 1 February, is celebrated today in Ireland, in Gaelic Scotland and the Isle of Man, as well as in several British Commonwealth countries. St Bride's Church, Fleet Street, London, is dedicated to her. The *New Catholic Encyclopedia* takes no note of the Celtic goddess of virtually the same name, Brigit, the patroness of fire, poetic arts, crafts, healing, smithing, prophecy, divination, cattle and crops. As multiple spellings are available for both figures (Bríd, Bride, Brighid, etc.), it may save confusion here to follow the *Oxford Dictionary of Celtic Mythology* to cite the Celtic goddess as Brigi*t* and the Christian saint as Brigi*d*.

The often enigmatic tenth-century Glossary of Cormac mac Cuilennáin implies that Brigit is the name of three different goddesses, without giving details of the other two. The prime Brigit is the tutelary goddess of Leinster, eastern Ireland. Often compared with the Roman goddess of wisdom, Minerva, Brigit is probably identical with the British goddess Brigantia, worshipped in what is now Yorkshire, and the Gaulish Brigando. Several rivers in Britain and Ireland are named for her. According to separate Irish traditions, Brigit is the daughter of Dagda, a leader of the Tuatha Dé Danann, and wife of Senchán Torpéist, a purported author of the epic *Táin Bó Cuailnge*. Other romantic and sexual adventures are attributed to her, including mating with handsome but villainous Bres, a leading figure of the struggle of the gods, *Cath Maige Tuired* [The (Second) Battle of Mag Tuired]. She was probably worshipped at Corleck Hill, near Drumeague, Co. Cavan, where a stone head thought to be hers once stood. Her feast day, Imbolc (also Óimelc, etc.), 1 February, the day ewes were thought to produce the spring's first milk, was a major Celtic calendar feast (see Chapter 5).

Commentators on early Ireland, such as the influential Proinsias MacCana, assume that the Christian saint is merely a personification of the Celtic goddess, but the Vatican saw no reason to desanctify her along with the others in 1961. The earliest Christian sources on the life of St Brigid date from no earlier than the seventh century, or more than a hundred years after her death. One Broccan is credited with a Latin hymn celebrating her life, and Cogitosus, a member of the Brigidine community at Kildare, wrote a prose *Life of Brigid*, transmitting what had been handed down about her. According to Cogitosus, she founded a sexually segregated religious community, the male half presided over by a bishop, the female by an abbess, who shared a partitioned timber chapel. Cogitosus does not comment on the origin of the name *cill dara*, 'church of the oak', although the oak tree took a prominent place in druidical worship. Neither does he acknowledge that Cill Dara was five miles from Knockaulin, the extensive Iron Age earthworks that had been a pagan sanctuary.

Cogitosus describes Brigid as a radiant beauty, who was never in want of suitors. Withdrawing from the world, she consecrated herself to Christ along with seven other virgins, eventually returning to her father's lands in Kildare, where her monastic community flourished. In the *Life of Brigid* are cited her many miracles of plenty, such as dispensing butter that is immediately replenished. She could perform triple milkings and could change water into ale and stone into salt.

Early tradition outside Cogitosus links Brigid with Faughart, two miles north of Dundalk, Co. Louth, her reputed birthplace. Site of a stream and a holy well, Faughart had been a place of pilgrimage in pre-Christian times. Nearby are megalithic tombs, underground passages, forts and antiquarian artefacts.

A modern explanation of the relationship of Brigit and Brigid, entirely speculative, is that the historical saint was an early convert to Christianity who consciously modelled her life on aspects of the fire goddess. Her purpose would have been to lead people to the Gospels by seeing that traditions of worship in the old faith could be transferred to the new.

The Welsh traveller Giraldus Cambrensis reported in 1184 that a company of nuns tended an 'inextinguishable fire' at Kildare in St Brigid's honour. Although it had been kept burning for 500 years, it had produced no ash; men were not allowed to go near the fire. In 1993 the Brigidine Sisters rekindled Saint Brigid's fire in Kildare Town.

Because of her primacy in Irish tradition, Brigid attracted volumes of lore. One of the most enduring of these legends is that she converted a pagan on his deathbed while holding a cross plaited from rushes on the floor. At one time a folk drama commemorated this moment. In it a young girl, honorifically if not actually named Brigid, knocked on the door three times, seeking admittance, asking that all within go down on their knees and do homage. On the third knock, those within would welcome her. In some areas remnants of the rushes were gathered up and woven into spancels for cattle and sheep, girdles and crosses; others could be made into mattresses. These protected the believers from natural calamities, such as fire, storm and lightning. Closer to the body, Brigid's artefacts had curative powers, especially for the illnesses of childbirth and in countering barrenness. A survival of this ceremony is the Brigid's Cross, a distinctive design in which four stalks of rushes extend from a square. It is still one of the most common folk items on sale for tourists in Ireland.

Popular tradition has unwittingly attributed to St Brigid many of the powers once held by Brigit the goddess – the spring rite, the rebirth of nature, as well as fertility and guardianship of the land.

5

Calendar Feasts

SUN, MOON AND TIME

Hallowe'en does not stand tall among our holidays. Banks remain open, and the post is still delivered. Small children gorge themselves on sweets while their older siblings practise mischief. October 31 signals no marker in the solar or lunar cycles. The day has no political significance, and its only place in Christian reckoning is that it anticipates the holy day of All Saints, 1 November. In America in recent years Christian fundamentalists have objected to Hallowe'en celebrations in public schools because of its purported pagan origin. Meanwhile, self-styled neo-pagans have come to look upon the day, and especially its evening, as the major feast of the year. Discussions of Hallowe'en on television and in the popular press are the most likely places in everyday discourse where one will encounter the word 'Celtic'.

What we call Hallowe'en (short for All Hallow E'en or Evening) is indeed a much-changed survival from the ancient Celtic calendar. Together with its spring counterpart six months later, May Eve, the two celebrations are the most vivid remnants in industrial, secular English-speaking society of what was once the Celtic worldview. Two other days were once prominent, 1 February, still known as Saint Brigid's Day in Ireland and parts of the British Isles and Commonwealth, and the August holiday, or Lammas Day, which survives as the very secular August Bank Holiday in Britain and Ireland.

The perception of predictable movements of the sun and moon precedes the beginning of written records by many centuries. The builders of Newgrange (3200 BC), to take a prominent example, knew

93

that a shaft of sunlight would extend the length of a 68-foot passage on the winter solstice. Details in the construction of the pyramids a few centuries later reveal a comparable knowledge of earth–sun relationships in the eastern Mediterranean. The sun alone, however, would not be the sole determinant in the measurement of time.

The calculations of time that came with written records in widely separated parts of the world are based on three predictable phenomena in nature: the moon, the sun and the change of seasons. Basing time on the phases of the moon, the lunar calendar, gives us the concept of months; we can hear an echo of the word 'moon' in the English word 'month'. The lunar month is only 29.5 days, however, or 354 for the year, more than eleven short of the 365.2422 days on the solar calendar. A fixed day on the lunar calendar, such as the sixth day of the third moon, would fall eleven days earlier in the following year by solar calculations, unless allowances and adjustments were made. Our calendar, the Gregorian, first adopted in 1582, is lunisolar, a synchronization of lunar and solar. Our determination of the seasons has come to follow moon and sun movements, the two solstices and the two equinoxes, which we observe with expensive, very precise instruments. The ancients relied on evidence closer at hand, such as vegetation cycles, the breeding patterns of domesticated animals, and, especially among the Celts, the driving of cattle to different seasonal grazing grounds, called transhumance.

The Celtic calendar feasts harmonize the seasons with cycles of the moon. The autumn feast that anticipates Hallowe'en was originally the first day of the eleventh month, but Christian influence, as we shall see, moved it back to the last day of the tenth month, what we now designate as 31 October. Similarly, the other holidays fell on the first days of the second, fifth and eighth months, which we now equate with February, May and August. The four holidays have no calculation in the sun's cycle, that is, they are not a fixed number of days before or after a solstice. Surprisingly, considering the importance of the winter solstice at Newgrange and at Gavrinis, a similar passage-grave in Brittany, sun cycles do not appear to have inspired any holidays in the ancient Celtic calendar. Then again, both were constructed long before the arrival of the Celts even though they survived in Celtic lands. Celebrations by neo-druids and neo-Celts at places such as Britain's Stonehenge (c.1700

BC), also built before the arrival of the Celtic culture, are modern innovations, dating no earlier than the eighteenth century.

Key to our understanding of the Celtic measurement of time are the first-century AD bronze tablets found at Colingy in eastern France and thus called the Coligny Calendar. Employing Latin characters to express the native language, it was the most extensive extant document in Gaulish we had until the discoveries of the 1990s. The tablets detail sixty-two consecutive months, approximately equal to five solar years. Months are thirty or twenty-nine days and divided into halves. The lunar year was adapted to the solar year by the intercalation of an extra month of thirty days every third year. Months were ascribed character, as they were not in later Celtic calendars. They might be indicated MAT (good or auspicious) or ANM (an abbreviation for *anmat*, not good), implying that any calendar came with its build-in proscriptions.

Other information found at Coligny has much resonance for later centuries. The equivalent of New Year's Day, which falls in the autumn, is Samonios; and it marks the beginning of the new year because the dark precedes the light in the calculation of time. Although our reliance on scientifically measured solar time has caused us to put the beginning of the day at midnight, literally the middle of the night, the notion of dark preceding light is not strange to us, as Jewish religious practice measures time the same way. The Sabbath, Rosh Hashanah, Passover, etc., begin at sundown. Put in this context, the notion that the darkest part of the year, winter, begins the annual cycle in the northern hemisphere seems most logical, even if it has few counterparts elsewhere in human experience.

The Gaulish *Samonios* provides an unmistakable cognate for the classical Irish *Samain*, New Year's Day in pre-Christian Irish heroic literature. Such clear links between the continental and insular Celts are not always available. This endorsement of Irish antiquity's inheritance from earlier antecedents, added to the extensive texts and critical prestige of early Irish tradition, has meant that commentators prefer the classical Irish names for three of the calendar feasts. They are Samain (1 November), Imbolc (1 February) and Beltaine (1 May). The influence of Máire MacNeill (see below) favours Lughnasa for the fourth (1 August). The four days are also known by other names in other Celtic countries.

The Celts, like most other ancients, did not number each year. One year was, in a sense, much like another. Changes in technology came so slowly, even in the passage from the Bronze to the Iron Age, that one year *was* like another. We call such a vision of time circular, just as the stone calendar of the Aztecs in early Mexico was a large circle. The linear vision of time that seems so inevitable to us, where years are numbered and we remark on how styles and the ways we live change quickly, is derived from the Hebrew tradition, specifically the Book of Isaiah (eighth to sixth centuries BC) in the Old Testament or Hebrew Bible. Anticipating a Messiah, the Hebrews began numbering years in the second millennium BC, and projected the beginning of the calendar back to their understanding of the beginning of time, 3761 BC. Thus the Jewish calendar is always 3,761 years older than the Gregorian. The last turn of the century in the Jewish calendar was 5700, or 1939 in the Gregorian. The beginning of this millennium in the Gregorian calendar, 2000, was 5761 in the Jewish, and so on.

SAMAIN

Calendar stories based on the vegetation cycle abound in comparative mythology, the best known probably being that of the lovers Aphrodite (or Venus) and Adonis in classical mythology. When the lovers are together, nature blooms. Adonis, a hunter, seeks out a wild boar against Aphrodite's advice, and is severely wounded, descending to the underworld. Nature withers and dies. After six months Adonis makes his way to the land of the living, is reunited with Aphrodite, and nature flourishes anew. An antecedent of this story is found in the Babylonian myth of the lovers Ishtar and Tammuz, where, once again, the male figure 'dies' in the autumn and rises again in the spring. That fatal day when the hunters Tammuz and Adonis depart for the realm of the dead clearly corresponds to Samain of the Celts. As neither day was fixed in the solar calendar, however, they need not have been the identical day. Among the peoples of sunny Greece and Babylon, the day Adonis or Tammuz departs is the end of a cycle. The Celts, living in more northerly climes, saw it as a beginning.

Learned commentators' preference for the Irish form *Samain*

(Modern Irish *Samhain*), pronounced 'sow-ĭn', should not obscure the importance of the day in the calendars of all Celtic peoples. The Q-Celts use variations of the Irish form; in Scottish Gaelic it is *Samhuinn*, in Manx *Sauin*. The root of the word, *sam* [summer] and *fuin* [end] signals seasonal change rather than worship or ritual. The P-Celts celebrate the day but do not inherit the same word root. In Wales the day is Hollantide or Calan Gaeaf [first day of winter]; in Cornwall Allantide; and in Brittany Kala Goañv [beginning of November].

From the earliest records, Samain/Samonios is seen not simply as a day for the dead but when the dead might reach out to the living. Julius Caesar (first century BC) reports that the Gaulish Dis Pater was especially worshipped at this time. The Roman god Dis Pater [rich father] is an aspect of Pluto, ruler of the dead, but one 'rich' in the treasures of the underworld, especially the shades of all the living who have gone before. The native identity of his Gaulish counterpart is not known. More chillingly, other classical commentators depict deities venerated with human sacrifice. Sacrificial victims were drowned in vats to worship Teutates, the war god linked to Mars. Being burned alive in wooden vessels was the fate of victims sacrificed to propitiate Taranis, the 'master of war' sometimes linked to Jupiter. The spirits of the dead revisited their earthly homes on the evening of the holiday, and yet the time was thought favourable for examining the portents of the future and planning for future events.

After the Romans conquered the Gauls and partially integrated the subject population into the empire, aspects of the calendar feasts began to attach themselves to the Roman festivals. Samain/Samonios coloured the celebration of the harvest festival at the calend of the eleventh month (approximately 1 November), dedicated to Pomona, goddess of the fruits of trees, especially apples. The Hallowe'en festivities using apples, harvested just before this time, may date from this era.

Celebration of Pomona's day persisted well past the coming of Christianity. To lead the faithful away from such practices, Pope Boniface IV introduced All Saints' Day in the early seventh century, simultaneously consecrating the Pantheon in Rome as the church of the Blessed Virgin and All Martyrs. To separate further the Christian holy day from the pagan feast, the Church moved the date to 13 May. It is still observed among Eastern Orthodox churches in the spring, on the first Sunday after Pentecost, but in the West All Saints' Day moved back to 1 November, joined by All Souls' Day, 2 November, still a Roman Catholic observance. The root of the English word Hallowe'en, All Hallow E'en, testifies to the official supremacy of the Christian holiday and the survival in demotic form of the pagan calendar feast on the previous evening. In Scotland the pre-Christian and Christian were sometimes separated, with Samhuinn observed on 11 November.

Samain was the principal calendar feast of early Ireland. A festival, *feis*, was held at Tara every third year, to which each of the five provinces sent delegates. At Tlachtga, twelve miles west of Tara, the lighting of the winter fires was a key part of the Samain ceremonies commemorating Dagda's ritual intercourse with three divinities, the Mórrígan, Boand (goddess of the Boyne) and the unnamed daughter of Indech, a Fomorian king and warrior. No record survives that these were fertility celebrations, but in later Irish and Scottish Gaelic oral tradition, Samain was thought a favourable time for a woman to become pregnant.

The role of human sacrifice in early Irish Samain worship remains unclear. According to Christian scribes, the 'chief idol' of early Ireland, Crom Crúaich [bloody crescent] was venerated at Mag Slécht [plain of adoration or prostrations] in Co. Cavan, near the present village of Ballymagauran. The central idol was thought to be made of gold, surrounded by twelve others made of stone. The Killycluggin Stone from Cavan, now housed at the Cavan County Museum, Ballyjames-duff, does not match the received descriptions, but has nonetheless been associated with Crom Crúaich. The Stone, badly damaged in a move from the National Museum back to Cavan, dates from the third to the second centuries BC and is one of the few La Tène incised stones in Ireland in the Waldelgesheim style. The portrayal of cruel idols demanding human sacrifices may be an echo of the scriptural accounts of Tophet and Moloch (2 Kings: 23), as Eoin MacNeill suggested (1921). Whether Crom Crúaich as described actually existed cannot be proved, but it appears to be the model for the bogus god called Samhain (always with the Modern Irish spelling), invented in anti-Hallowe'en pamphlets. Sam[h]ain is, of course, a date or by extension a festivity, but the assertion that there was once such a god has made its way into at least one American encyclopedia.

Early Irish texts are always precise when pointing out that important action takes place at Samain. On this date the predatory Fomorians would exact their tribute of milk, grain and live children. The triple-headed monster Aillén Tréchenn would come from Co. Roscommon every Samain to wreak havoc on the entire island, especially Emain Macha and Tara, until he was eliminated by Amairgin, the first poet of Ireland. The fiery musician Aillén mac Midgna, known as 'the burner', came every Samain to Tara, where he would lull the inhabitants to sleep with dulcet melodies and then set fire to the place. The hero Fionn mac Cumhaill dispatched him on first meeting. Not all encounters were violent. Cúchulainn encountered a succession of otherworldly damsels at Samain, and the lovers Cáer and Angus Óg fly off in swan form on this day. It was, summarize Rees and Rees (1961), a time of confusion, the setting for voyages to the otherworld, sexual relations between mortals and others, and gender-blurring customs of cross-dressing.

Standing between the two halves of the Celtic year, Samain seemed suspended in time, when the borders between the natural and supernatural dissolved, and the spirits of the otherworld might move freely into the realm of mortals. It was also a time to relax after the most demanding farm work was done. Country lads would visit neighbours' houses, collecting pence and provisions for celebrations. It was a time for the building of bonfires, a custom that began very early in Irish and Scottish Gaelic tradition and continues into the twenty-first century. As people might perceive more of the realm of the dead at Samain, it was a time to look for portents of the future. James Joyce commemorates one of these practices in the story 'Clay' in *Dubliners* (1914).

Although they disappeared earlier, Welsh Hollantide celebrations were comparable, with post-harvest merrymaking, bonfire burning, divination games and ghostly visitations. The credulous reported encounters with *y ladi wen* [the white lady] and the *hwch ddu gota* [bob-tailed black sow]. On the night before Hollantide one could know if death would come in the next year by peeping through a church-door keyhole. Not all beliefs were grim. Young people sewing hemp at crossroads at night could make their future sweethearts appear.

IMBOLC, BELTAINE, LUGHNASA

In the pastoral and agrarian societies of ancient and medieval northern Europe, winter and spring comprised the quieter half of the year. War-making and cattle-raiding receded. The Irish historian Geoffrey Keating (c.1580–c.1645/50) reported that from Samain to Beltaine, the people of Ireland were required to house and feed the samurai-like *fianna*, who would offer their military service to different kings and princes in the other half of the year. In the dark months the greatest struggle was to make sure that provisions from summer and autumn lasted through the cold months without benefit of advanced food preservation technologies – not just something to eat but something approaching a balanced diet that would ensure health or at least the diminution of disease.

The return of fresh milk at this bleak time undoubtedly occasioned great joy. Ewes in Britain and Ireland begin lactation after lambing about February, midway between Samain and Beltaine. Cows' milk would have petered out by that time and not be available again until later in the spring. In any event, sheep's milk is richer in fat content than cows' milk and was greatly enjoyed in the early Irish diet. In the twelfth-century satire *Aislinge Meic Con Glinne* [Vision of Mac Con Glinne], a supreme delicacy is 'fair white porridge', made with sheep's milk. The ewes' lactation was a sign of lambing and the increase of the flocks. Sheep would lamb and therefore come into milk earlier than cattle at that time because of their ability to crop lower for grass and get along better than the cow on the sparse vegetation of late winter. Cows would safely be in calf by early March.

This experience appears to be behind the etymology given in the Glossary of Cormac mac Cuilennáin (d. 908) that the feast of Imbolc or Imbolg (early Modern Irish Óimelc) on 1 February marks the sheep's coming into milk. Despite his antiquity, modern commentators do not accept Cormac's judgements without exception. More recently it has been suggested that the root of the word *Imbolc* derives from the verb *folcaim* [I wash] and that February was originally a purification festival like the Roman Lupercalia. The assertion has not gained widespread acceptance. Inertia favours Cormac's explanation, despite learned scepticism.

Based on the link between Imbolc and lambing, Nerys Patterson (1992) has suggested that the day may have important connections with the seasons of human sexuality. Marriages in early Ireland tended to be concentrated between Twelfth Night (5 January) and Shrovetide (three days before the beginning of Lent, that is, from mid-January to early March). Newly married couples would live together until 1 May, when they separated, the men going with the cattle. Many first-born babies would then appear between mid-October and 1 February. New mothers' need for good nutrition came just as the sheep came into milk.

From the earliest times Imbolc was associated with Brigit, the fire goddess, and after Christianization with her successor, St Brigid of Kildare. The saint is often seen as a patroness of sheep, the pastoral economy and fertility in general. It is under her name that the day is now universally known in Celtic countries. The pre-Christian associations of the day have vanished from popular tradition. February 2, sometimes called Candlemas Day, is also sacred on the Christian calendar. It commemorates the feast of the Purification of the Virgin Mary, when Christ presented her in the Temple. The faithful may have their throats blessed on this day by having two crossed candles placed before them.

There are also teasing echoes of Imbolc in the secular American holiday Groundhog Day, 2 February, on which a large rodent (also called a woodchuck) seeks a subtle and ironic sign of the advent of spring. If it is a sunny day and he sees his shadow, winter will last another six weeks.

Whether in two, six or eight weeks, winter does lead to spring, and spring to summer. In pastoral societies, as those of so many of the early Celts were, the coming of warm weather meant the necessary dislocation of moving the herds to summer pasture, or transhumance. Before their departure, herdsmen would drive the cattle between two bonfires in hopes of protecting them from murrain and other ills. People would also make the passage between the two fires, hoping to invite good luck or forestall ill favour, and to cure barrenness. Cormac's Glossary testifies to the antiquity of this practice. Usually all fires would be extinguished so that they might be begun anew on Beltaine. In most of the Celtic lands the cattle drive took place on 1 May, but in Scotland, more northerly, darker and colder, it might be 15 May. The name in early Ireland for 1 May was Beltaine (also Beltane, Beltene, Beltine, etc.; Modern Irish Bealtaine). A three-syllable word, it is pronounced roughly 'bel-tin-ĕ'. Gaelic Scotland and the Isle of Man employ forms derived from the Old Irish, Bealltuinn and Boaldyn. An alternative name in early Ireland was Cétshamain, meaning roughly 'early spring'.

The etymology of the word Beltaine is tantalizingly uncertain. The second two syllables, *-taine*, appear to come from the word for fire, *teine*. Lore associated with the day specified the requirement for 'need fire', or fire begun afresh by rubbing two sticks, *teine éigen*. Fire was part of celebrations for the day in all the Celtic countries, on mountaintops in Scotland. In Cornwall the custom persisted until the late twentieth century. The first syllable *bel-* may mean 'shining, brilliant'. The same syllable has also invited speculation of a root in the name Belenus, the Gaulish god who may be an aspect of Apollo but who was usually worshipped under this name alone at temples from the Italian peninsula to the British Isles. The root of his name may be 'bright', like the Irish word. Nineteenth-century speculation linking Belenus with the Phoenician Baal is now rejected. Names for the day in the P-Celtic languages allude only to the time of year, not to fire or a lost god: Welsh Cyntefin, Dydd Calan Mai; Cornish Cala' Mē; Breton Kala Hañv, all of which mean either 'beginning of summer' or 'first of May'.

Apart from the fire-cleansing cattle drive, Beltaine also appears to have acquired aspects of the Roman spring festival Parilia or Palila, 21 April, a day for shepherds and herdsmen. In early Irish literature Beltaine is a good day to begin great projects. Both the Partholonians and the Milesians (see Chapter 7) invade Ireland on Beltaine, according to the pseudo-history *Lebor Gabála* [Book of Invasions]. The association with beginnings and departure may reflect the social experience of family members departing to the booleys or summer pastures.

A great body of oral tradition about Beltaine speaks of a continuing presence of fire, which could be put to different purposes. It might cook the Beltaine cakes or bannocks, which were very large, round and flat, usually made from oats or barley. They were large enough to be broken into several portions, one of which contained a black spot made of charcoal. The unlucky person who drew by lot the piece with the black spot could be subject to a mimed execution of being thrown into the fire or drawn and quartered.

It was also a time of anxiety. Food stocks from the winter would be running low. This is projected in oral tradition with stories of witches, animals or fairies who steal food from hungry families. Some of the anxiety was social. Nerys Patterson describes Beltaine as the day when peasants and landless cattle-owners were required to pay part of their tribute to overlords and decide whether to enter into new arrangements. May was also the end of the marriage season, and Beltaine was thought to be a singularly unlucky day for a wedding.

In later European history, Celtic May Day celebrations begin to merge with those of other countries, especially in the north. English peasants danced around beribboned maypoles until the Puritans, noting their unmistakable phallic symbolism, suppressed them in the mid-seventeenth century. May also being about the time many northern flowers first bloom, the day became a time to display garlands of blossoms. The pan-European May Day has roots in the Roman celebration of Floralia, 27 April–3 May, in honour of Flora, goddess of flowers, dating to at least the third century BC. A much studied phenomenon, this May Day began a month-long celebration of the oncoming of spring with the honorific 'election' of a May king and May queen noted as early as 1576. It was this version of May Day that was Christianized by the Roman Catholic Church when the entire month was dedicated to the Blessed Virgin Mary and a statue of her was crowned, or sometimes a young woman known to be of blameless character might be crowned as her surrogate. This practice, once common, has much diminished in recent years. Ceremonies more pertinent to Beltaine were of less concern to the Church, although it did suppress the burning of a ceremonial fire at the hill of Uisnech in Co. Westmeath, sometimes described as the centre of Ireland. Geoffrey Keating reports that the Uisnech fire was still current in the mid-seventeenth century.

When the Irish adapted European May Day to Beltaine, they did not allow many roles for women. Sir William Wilde noted in his *Irish Popular Superstitions* (1852) that there was no May queen in Irish spring parades, but that the leading female figure was played by a cross-dressing man. Folklorist Kevin Danaher (1972) retrieved a description of a Mummers' May Day parade in Wexford from 1897 in which the parts of the fool and his wife were both played by men. It may be, as Nerys Patterson has speculated, that cross-dressed men parading next to men dressed as men may indicate the hag-like female in the winter half of the year, her ritual potency now spent, while the male next to her is the summer half. Or the reason might have been male dominance and exclusion.

The all-male May Day parades appear to have led to the day's becoming an international holiday for labouring people. The link is found among Irish immigrants in the United States. After the Civil War, thousands of Irish-born workers joined the first American labour union, The Knights of Labor. Founded as a secret society in 1869, the Knights at first grew slowly, eventually claiming a peak membership of 700,000 in 1886. After some poorly directed strikes, its membership plummeted, losing ground to the rival American Federation of Labor. During its prime, the Irish-born members of the Knights paraded on what was in effect the first Labor Day, with men marching together on 1 May as they had in Ireland. Shortly afterwards the International Socialist Congress adopted 1 May as a day to honour the working man in 1889. Nearly four decades later the leaders of the Bolshevik revolution in Russia searched to find a holiday on which all of society might pay tribute to the contributions of labouring people. They chose the Irish-American May Day, now shorn of its religious and pastoral roots.

The last of the four calendar feasts, Lughnasa, may be the least perceptible in industrial, secular society, but we know more about its ancient roots than any of the other three. The Coligny Calendar found near Lyon, France, cites a 'great festal month' at Rivros, the counterpart of Irish Lughnasa or English August. We know today that Lyon was named for the Gaulish god Lugos/Lugus, whom the Romans called Gaulish Mercury, the ancient name of the city being Lug(o)dunum. At that city a festival was celebrated on the first of

Rivros (August) in honour of the emperor Augustus (d. AD 14). Lugos, as mentioned previously, is an anticipation of the Irish hero Lug Lámfhota, who gives his name to the Irish feast. According to early Irish tradition, Lug himself established the festival to honour his foster-mother Tailtiu at Brega, in modern Co. Meath. Tailtiu later became the name of one of Ireland's greatest fairs, held at nearby Teltown. Lug began the first festivities by leading horse races and martial arts contests. Soon, Lughnasa celebrations were held in many parts of Ireland as well as Gaelic Scotland, where the day is called Lunasduinn, and the Isle of Man, where it is Laa Luanistyn.

We prefer the unreformed Modern Irish spelling Lughnasa for the day because it was used in Máire MacNeill's landmark 700-page study *The Feast of Lughnasa* (1962), but to be consistent we should use the classical Irish *Lugnasad*, whose suffix *-nasad* may mean 'assembly, festive or commemorative gathering'. MacNeill's spelling also appears in the title of Brian Friel's admired drama *Dancing at Lughnasa* (1990), which draws thematically on festival traditions. The reformed Modern Irish spelling is Lúnasa, which is now more likely to denote the month of August than the nearly extinct festival. The August holiday has mattered much less in Wales and Cornwall, where the local names carry no echo of Lug's name, viz. Calan Awst [first of August] and Morvah, site of distinctive megaliths.

Lughnasa is a harvest festival of the first crops to ripen, wheat and barley. Once they became plentiful, it also marked the maturing of potatoes. Celebrants enjoyed climbing hills, both to pray and to gather bilberries that matured at this time. Six months after Imbolc, it was the time ewes' lactation ended the maternal phase of the flocks, and mating might begin again. Following nature's example, it was also a time of increased human sexual activity.

Surprisingly, Lughnasa has no mythological connection with the harvest in early Irish literature. Neither is it the date of many important events, only the invasion of Ireland by the Fir Bolg in the *Lebor Gabála*. The Fir Bolg would have a connection with the feast of Tailtiu, as it is named for one of their queens.

The date of Lughnasa was less securely fixed than those of the other calendar feasts. It might include many days, especially Sundays, from 15 July to 15 August. As the Christian Church often substituted the archangel Michael for Lug, the festival was transformed into St Michael's Day or Michaelmas and moved to 29 September. Meanwhile 1 August in Scotland and England became Lammas Day, from an Anglo-Saxon word *hlafmaesse* [loaf-mass], unrelated to Lughnasa despite the coincident initials. In a second move to Christianize the festival it was made a commemoration of St Patrick's victory over Crom Dubh [black crescent], renamed Domhnach Chrom Dubh and celebrated on the last Sunday in July or the first Sunday in August. In English these two days are known in Galway and Mayo as Garland Sunday, or its by-form Garlic Sunday.

MacNeill's study traces the transmutation and transmogrification of Lughnasa over the centuries, through open-air assemblies and pilgrimages at lakes, rivers and wells, and folk medicines, such as cures for insanity. Widespread practices through the insular Celtic countries as well as portions of England and France speak for the antiquity of the calendar feast as well as the importance it once had in the lives of most people. Perhaps there was no way for Lughnasa to survive in a society that has insulated us from the significance of natural processes, where people think of late summer as a time for escape from the routine of work and compulsory schooling. August has become a time for leisure activities, for holidays and vacations, not for shadowy commemorations of forgotten deities.

6

Otherworlds

THIS WORLD AND THE 'OTHER'

The 26-year-old William Butler Yeats framed the issue when he wrote of 'The Man Who Dreamed of Faeryland' (1891), set in Leitrim and Sligo in the rural northwest. The dreamy, spiritual Celts, it appeared, could perceive a world beyond the senses, an otherworld, imperceptible to their powerful, rational, practical neighbours, like the English. Not only does such a Celtic otherworld exist simultaneously with the empirical world of consciousness, but it is preferable to it, a gossamer ideal that contrasts with the grubby here and now.

The notion contributes to the burden of cliché. Play a word-association game with the 'Celt' and you can expect to hear such modifiers as 'intemperate', 'exuberant' and 'otherworldly'. None of these implies flattery when uttered by most non-Celts. The smile of condescension is implicit, as it was in the 1999 world press accounts of Co. Clare storyteller Eddie Lenihan's efforts to stop highway construction that would destroy a hawthorn bush where the fairies meet. Could the fairies find such a champion in contemporary Sussex or Kansas?

Cliché, of course, builds on caricature and exaggeration. The closer we get to the several otherworlds denoted in different Celtic texts, the less particular they appear. Earlier Europeans alluded to a realm beyond the senses, fairyland being one of many such conceptions. As a literary device fairyland becomes part of the action in Shakespeare's *A Midsummer Night's Dream* (1595) and Gilbert and Sullivan's *Iolanthe* (1882), appearing wholly English. Earlier European traditional literatures furnish examples of otherworlds that make striking parallels with those described in Ireland, Wales and Brittany. Still other examples from myth, legend and folklore abound in distant lands from Siberia to Hawaii.

Additionally, post-classical Celtic peoples, like other Europeans, long embraced the teachings of the Christian Church, which has defined visions of otherworldly realms of reward and punishment. The certitude of spending eternity in either heaven or hell tends to push aside older visions of a life beyond the physical, inherited from preliterate civilizations. Additionally, Christian vocabulary portrays an absolute dichotomy between *this world* and *the other world* that influences the connotations and nuances of our own English words in trying to speak about the subject.

Regardless of how much 'paganism' survives in Irish, Welsh and Breton traditions, the Christian faith of later scribes, ecclesiastical and secular, appears to have shaped the portrayal of worlds beyond the senses. The scribal vocabulary implies no shared belief, no single vision of a realm where the non-physical part of the self, the soul or psyche, might reside.

Of the thoughts of pre-Christian Celts there is little to tell. In an oft-cited text, the first-century Roman poet and historian Lucan remarks that according to druidical belief the souls of the departed survive not in Hades but in *orbe alio* (*Pharsalia*, I. 457). As Patrick Sims-Williams (1990) comments, *alius orbis* probably does not mean 'the otherworld' or even 'an otherworld', supernatural and divorced from 'this world', but simply 'another region'. The tiny Latin-writing learned elite of the Middle Ages used the phrase *alius orbis* to denote far-off lands separated from the known world by the impassable sea, lands such as Ceylon or the antipodes. The phrase would also be known to learned elites in the Celtic lands, but there is no evidence that they sought to find equivalents in their own languages.*

The retrieved ceremonial burials of the continental Celts imply the expectation of an afterlife but with fewer specifications than those left by the Egyptian pyramid builders. The extensive Iron-Age cemetery

---

* The Modern Irish phrase *saol eile* may denote 'another world' in Lucan's sense of a faraway place, such as China or Paraguay. In the poetry of Nuala Ní Dhomhnaill (b. 1952) and elsewhere in contemporary Irish usage *an saol eile* is a spiritual world that lies beyond empirical examination.

found at Hallstatt (seventh to sixth centuries BC) in Upper Austria includes many men buried with decorative swords and other weapons. These may only signal the wealth it took to assemble them or the prowess their bearers displayed in life. It is mere speculation to suggest that the departed warrior, weapon at the ready, expected to continue to do battle in the next life. On the other hand, the tall chieftain in the tumulus at Hochdorf (sixth century BC?), southwest Germany, was buried with golden plates and drinking vessels, in likely anticipation of a banquet worthy of his high station. The well-born woman buried at Reinheim (5th century BC) near Saarbrücken on the French–German border also has a fine eating and drinking service as well as a full display of her personal jewellery indicating her distinguished social rank: a neck ring, several golden arm rings, bracelets and finger rings. Her time in the afterlife would be stylish as well as comfortable.

VOYAGES TO THE BEYOND

Among the earliest narratives in Irish are those dealing with fabulous journeys, perhaps a projection of the intrepid travel undertaken by Irish monks in Dark-Age Europe, 600–1100 AD. These are categorized into two types by the first words in their titles. In *Echtrae*, a term meaning 'adventure', the distant regions visited are inhabited by men, even if they are shrouded by mist, beyond the sea or in the middle of the earth. *Imram* or *Immram*, meaning 'rowing about', denotes a sea voyage to one or more islands, often beyond the world inhabited by human beings. Put another way, while both the *Echtrae* and the *Imram* take the reader beyond the mundane, it is the latter that goes beyond the human to the otherworld. At the same time the current scholarly consensus holds that the *Imram* is a monastic genre and that later more vernacular versions of such fabulous voyages are probably secularizations. From the hands of the monks we try to piece together some of the oldest Irish portrayals of the otherworld.

The *Imram Brain*, dating from the early eighth century, is the oldest surviving example. Its title may be translated as 'The Voyage of Bran Son of Febal' or 'Bran's Journey to the Land of the Women'. The narrative is short, but the antiquity of its texts raises many questions of interpretation. Séamus MacMathúna's translation (1985) runs to twelve pages but is accompanied by 498 pages of commentary. The full text, assembled from eight manuscripts, consists of two long lyric poems filled with description and three brief prose passages of narrative. Bran, one of several Irish and Welsh personages of this name, is a king but a mortal one, distinguished only by his patronymic mac Febail.

While strolling about his fort one day, Bran hears music behind him, which follows and haunts him until he falls asleep from its sweetness. Awakening, he finds beside him a silver branch with blossoms he is unable to identify. When he takes the branch into the palace with him, a woman from 'The Land of Wonders' in strange attire appears and recites a poem to him. No one can explain where the woman has come from as all the entrances and ramparts are closed. The assembled kings both hear and see her.

Her poem begins with a description of the wondrous apple tree of *Emain*, whose twigs of white silver bear crystal leaves in blossom. This *Emain* appears to be identical with Emain Ablach, the realm of Manannán mac Lir, the sea god, and may be glossed as the 'Fortress of Apples' or the 'Land of Promise'. She describes the far-off island of Emain, held up by four pillars, just south of the plains of White Silver and Silver Cloud and near to the Silvery Land, the Gentle Land and the Plains of the Sea and of Sport.

In a quick transition, a host is seen rowing in a coracle or curragh, a small leather boat, across a clear sea to land with a large conspicuous stone, from which arise a hundred melodies. Here are many thousands of women clad in various colours, encircled by the clear sea. A very white rock on the edge of the sea receives its heat from the sun. On the nearby Plain of Sports people expect neither decay nor death.

The tone then shifts abruptly to Christian didacticism with a prophecy of the birth of Christ and a short description of the nature and extent of his kingdom. Bran, as the chosen from all the people of the world, is admonished not to be slothful and to cast off his drunkenness. He is about to begin his voyage to the Land of the Women.

After the silver branch springs from Bran's hand to that of the woman from the 'Land of Wonders', she departs and no one knows where she goes. Bran embarks with twenty-seven companions (a magical number: $3 \times 3 \times 3$), with each of his three foster-brothers in charge of one group. On their way the men encounter Manannán mac Lir driving his chariot over the sea. The sea god says he is destined after a long while to go to Ireland where he will father a son named Mongán upon an already married woman, a boy who will still be known as 'son of Fiachna' after the woman's husband. Parallel stories of Manannán's cuckolding of Fiachna and of Mongán's many adventures are told elsewhere in early Irish literature.

Bran's perceptions are not Manannán's. What Bran sees as a flowery plain is for Manannán the Plain of Sports or the Plain of Delights. Bran, it turns out, is really rowing over a beautiful fruitful wood. Manannán describes a gentle land where the inhabitants play a gentle game under a bush without any transgressions. They are ageless and do not expect decay, for the sin of Adam has not reached them.

The fall of Adam is then described, along with implications of gluttony and greed. Cautions are uttered against the sin of pride that leads to the destruction of the soul through deceit. This is followed by the prophecy of the coming of Christ and the introduction of a just law.

Manannán again predicts his procreation of Mongán and describes the son's life, death and ascension into Heaven. The prophecy that a divinely conceived child might achieve the realm of the gods is no doubt an echo of Christ's story in the Gospels, as more than one commentator has observed.

Leaving Manannán, Bran expects to reach Emain by sunset. He and his men row around the Island of Joy, whose people gape and jeer at them. Bran sends ashore one of his men, who immediately begins to act like the islanders and so is left behind. Arriving at the Land of Women [*Tír na mBan*], Bran does not dare to leave the coracle. The leader of the women calls out to Bran, 'Come here on the land, oh Bran son of Febal. Your coming is welcome.' When the woman throws a ball of thread to Bran, it clings to his palm but is sufficiently secure to allow the woman to pull the entire coracle into the harbour. They proceed to a large house where there is a couch for each of the men to share with a paired woman. Sumptuous food appears on dishes, more than the men can eat.

Bran's men lose all sense of time. What seems like one year is really many years. One of the shipmates, Nechtan mac Collbrain, acknowledges his homesickness for Ireland and asks Bran to return with him. Bran's unnamed lover cautions him against this, predicting that only sorrow will come of it. When it is clear that she will lose him, the lover counsels Bran to retrieve the man left on the Isle of Joy to complete his company. Further, she advises them to call out to friends when they reach Ireland but that no one should actually set foot on the land. The first point they see is Srúb Brain, usually identified with Stroove Point on the Inishowen Peninsula above Lough Foyle, Co. Donegal. Following the lover's instructions, Bran calls out to people on the shore and announces his name. No one knows him, but they say that such a person existed in their ancient stories. Nechtan's longing to return is so great he heeds no caution and leaps to the shore, immediately becoming a heap of ashes, as if he had been in the earth for hundreds of years. The shocking death causes Bran to sing this quatrain:

> Great was the folly for the son of Collbran
> To lift his hand against age;
> Without anyone who might cast a wave of holy water
> Over Nechtan, over the son of Collbran.

Bran then relates all his adventures in quatrains recorded in ogham, down to the time of this gathering. After bidding them farewell, he is not heard from again. (Summarized from Séamus MacMathúna's translation, 1985, 46–58, 286–90.)

For all its antiquity and exoticism, many elements in Bran's Voyage will be familiar to readers of traditional literature. One is the journey to the land of women, the very phrase MacMathúna uses as a subtitle for his translation. According to Stith Thompson's *Motif-Index of Folk-Literature* (1975), such an imagined journey bears the international number of F112. It can and does appear in traditional literatures anywhere. There is nothing exclusively Celtic or Irish about such a vision. Then again, it does appear in early Irish otherwordly voyages. Máel Dúin of the eighth- to tenth-century *Imram Curaig Maíle Dúin* [The Voyage of Máel Dúin's Boat] may return to Ireland a more pious Christian than he departed, but he too visits an Island of Women. Here the queen offers her seventeen daughters as bed-partners for the crew, providing uninterrupted pleasure and perpetual youth. After what the men perceive to be three months, they try to leave, but the queen throws yet another ball of thread, this one to prevent their escape. On a fourth attempt they succeed. Linked to the Land of Women motif are F111, journey to an earthly paradise, and F302.3.1, a man enticed to fairyland or the otherworld by a spirit or fairy.

Two other motifs, F373, the mortal abandons this world to live in the other, and F377, the mortal loses time in the otherworld, are also found worldwide, the latter perhaps best known in the story of Washington Irving's *faux* folk hero, Rip Van Winkle (1819). The Irish elaboration of the motif, Nechtan's immediate transformation into a pillar of ash at touching foot to the homeland, is repeated in dozens of later stories. After 300 years of lovemaking with the beauteous Niam of the Golden Hair in Tír na nÓg [the Land of Youth], incidentally producing three children, the Fenian hero Oisín returns to Ireland (see Chapter 11). Initially heeding the warning of his lover not to dismount, he nonetheless offers to help men in lifting a stone. His saddle girth breaks, and he falls to the ground. In an instant he is a withered old man. A comparable fate befalls the children of Lir in the early modern *Oidheadh Chlainne Lir* [The Tragic Story of the Children of Lir], who lose their human form rather than spending time in the otherworld. After being transformed into swans, they spend three exiles of 300 years each in the waters of central, northern and western Ireland (see Chapter 8). When a prophecy is fulfilled, they too re-inhabit human bodies, columns of dust that hold together long enough for them to be baptized into the Christian faith.

Testimonials of Christian faith initially appear intrusive in narratives such as *Imram Brain*, especially when the stories are reviewed in summary. There is no anticipation of the Gospels in the early passages or any foreshadowing of the traveller seeking salvation. Yet the presence of Christ's prophecies within the text changes the way the reader encounters Emain Ablach or the Land of Women. Such otherworlds, whatever their origin, are no longer absolutes but only by-ways on a traveller's journey, not unlike those encountered by the character called Christian in *Pilgrim's Progress* (1678), the Palace Beautiful or Vanity Fair. These do not look like the happy realms that the Hochdorf chieftain or the Reinheim matron were preparing to enter.

Then again, some readers wished those fantastic lands really existed. The desire to believe early Irish travellers' tales no doubt led to the popularity of the narrative whose manuscript circulated most widely in medieval Europe and was extensively translated and adapted in several languages. That text was *Navigatio Sancti Brendani Abbatis* [Voyage of the Abbot Saint Brendan], composed in the late ninth or early tenth century, the last notable Hiberno-Latin literary production. The historical St Brendan the Navigator founded two abbeys, Ardfert in Kerry and Clonfert in Galway, and died in 577 AD, at least 300 years before the composition of the *Navigatio*. While an interest in determining whether Saint Brendan actually sailed across the Atlantic has persisted down to contemporary times, scholars still dispute whether the *Navigatio* is a Christianization of a legend based on a nearly forgotten travel tale or a saint's story embracing secular episodes.

The impetus for the saint's two voyages is his hearing of the Land of Promise on the western ocean. Translated from *Tír Tairngire*, 'Land of Promise', this is one of the familiar Irish terms for the otherworld (see pp. 121–2). With fourteen companions in a leather coracle, St Brendan sets sail for the west and reaches what appears to be Iceland, where he stays five years. Iceland was indeed discovered by Irish monks before the Norse settled there, and a small archipelago is still named for those early seafarers, Vestmannaejar [Irishmen's islands]. Receiving acclaim on his return, St Brendan resolves to sail again, this time with an oaken boat and a crew of sixty. On his passage west he enters upon a sequence of fifteen adventurous landfalls and crossings: (i) an island with a large building sheltering travellers; (ii) an island of sheep bigger than cattle; (iii) an 'island' that turns out to be the back of the whale Jasconius [cf. Ir. *iasc*, fish], an episode paralleled in the voyages of Sinbad; (iv) the island of spirits taking bird form; (v) the island of St Ailbe, giving a detailed portrait of the lives of silent monks; (vi) the curdled sea, through which he passes without stopping; (vii) the island of Strong Men, populated by boys, young and old men, all of whom eat a purple fruit called *scaltae*; (viii) the island of the grape trees; (ix) a stream of clear water through which sailors can see to the bottom; (x) the great crystal column, possibly an iceberg; (xi) the island of Giant Smiths; (xii) a smoking and flaming mountain, perhaps a volcano; (xiii) a rocky mass, above which rises a man-shaped cloud, thought to be Judas, reprieved from damnation on Sundays; (xiv) the Island of Paul the Hermit; (xv) the Island Promised to the Saints.

Something in the *Navigatio* has always invited credulity in certain readers despite its prominent fabulous episodes. It was on Christopher Columbus's preparatory reading list. Despite its resemblance to such otherworldly voyages as *Imram Curaig Maíle Dúin*, not to mention the *Arabian Nights* (c.1450), the *Navigatio* has continued to inspire believers in its historicity. They seek to identify descriptions in the text with specific locations in Newfoundland, Florida and the Bahamas. Interest in St Brendan is allied to a wider popular fascination with purported pre-Columbian visits to North America, claims being made for different national groups, including the Irish, Scottish and Welsh. What appear to be ogham carvings have been found at many sites, from Nova Scotia to the Ohio River Valley. Genome studies of Native Americans indicate evidence of European DNA arriving on the continent well before 1000 AD. In the late twentieth century there were three transatlantic voyages in curraghs of the kind we know early ecclesiastical travellers used. Bill Verity led the first two in 1966 and 1970, and Tim Severin commanded the best known of the three in 1976–7, and followed it with his book *The Brendan Voyage* (New York, 1978) and a widely seen television documentary.

Still further accounts of otherworldly travel intersect with historical record. One appears in the eighth-century *Annals*, perhaps an indication of popular belief that did not find expression in narrative. The *Annals* are not history in the modern sense but rather records of facts and dates about such matters as dynastic marriages, the inaugurations and deaths of kings, the founding or destruction of monasteries.* Until the reforms of the twelfth and thirteenth centuries, their writing was a clerical franchise. Proinsias MacCana (2000) recounts the eighth-century depiction in the *Annals* of three ships sailing in the air. The entry for AD 743 reads, 'Ships with their crews were plainly seen in

---

* The reference '*Annals*' without prefix usually refers to what is called in English 'The Annals of the Four Masters', compiled by Micheál Ó Cléirigh and three others in the seventeenth century, translated by John O'Donovan in the seven-volume *Annals of the Kingdom of Ireland* (Dublin, 1849–51) and much reprinted.

the sky this year.' The episode would be retold with some variations in different kinds of literature over the next three centuries. In one of the stories, set during a royal assembly at Teltown, Co. Meath, an airborne sailor in a single boat spears what he thinks is a salmon. When he comes below to retrieve the fish, he is held by the people there until he protests that he is drowning.

THE SÍDH

This word has made a bumpy passage from Irish to English usage. Most readers encounter it first in the works of William Butler Yeats, as in the title of his poem 'The Hosting of the Sidhe' (1899). As the great poet knew little Irish, he seemed unaware that the final -e was appropriate only for the genitive or plural forms, and he neglected the diacritical slash over the letter í. The normative Irish spelling in the early twentieth century was sídh, pronounced 'shee'. When Modern Irish spelling was reformed about 1960, the word became sí, a form not yet widely used in English-language commentary. Classical Irish, preferred for most names in this volume, yields síd, which seems inappropriate here as most citations of the word are more modern. Aos (or áes) sídhe means 'people of the sídh'.

The first denotation of the word is the man-made mound or tumulus, of which there are hundreds in the Irish countryside. Called the 'fairy mound' in English, it is usually circular and often flat-topped, sometimes ringed with stones. Archaeologically speaking, the phenomena denoted by the term sídh are not mysterious and are known by a series of semi-technical terms. They may be commemorative, such as pre-Christian passage-tombs, low round barrows or burial mounds. Or they may be defensive, such as the fortified, circular earthen dwellings known as raths, pre-Norman defensive man-made mounds, or Anglo-Norman mottes (a yet more specific kind of mound).

Of beliefs associated with the sídh there is more to say. Farmers avoided having their cattle graze on the sídh and usually shunned paths leading to and from it. The notion that any small promontory, a hill or even more likely a tumulus, is linked to the supernatural or is 'haunted' is probably indigenous to Europe in general, and there is nothing uniquely Celtic about it. Implicit in the etymology of the word is the origin of its perception.

Summarizing scholarship on the word's roots, Patrick Sims-Williams (1990) argues that the derivation of *sídh* is *sed-* [sit] and that the Irish word originally meant 'seat, abode', later specialized as 'abode of divinities'. Pushed aside now are assertions that *sídh* can be traced to the Old Irish homophone *síd* [peace] or the Latin *sidus* [star], both of which would have implied something of the character of this abode of divinities.

In pre-Christian Ireland every district of importance might have its own *sídh* or hill that served as a route to the otherworld. T. F. O'Rahilly (1946) asserted that there was but one otherworld with many portals. More recent scholarship, led by Patrick Sims-Williams, finds the *sídh* to be a proliferation of independent kingdoms, much like the *tuatha* of mortal Ireland, but with friendlier relations with one another. Even the two neighbouring *sídh* between the breast-like hills known as the Paps of Ana in Co. Kerry had no subterranean communication. Each *sídh*, therefore, is local.

Early Irish scribes do not use any form of the word *sídh* as a substitution or calque for the Latin *orbe alio*. Indeed, there is no Irish calque or translation of *orbe alio* at all. Further, with the lack of a definite article, *sídh* appears to imply *an* otherworld rather than *the* otherworld. It is only our modern reading of the word, influenced by eight centuries of Christian learning, that leads us to impose the definite article *the* otherworld when it is not implied in early contexts.

Many stories survive of mortals, usually men, who enter the *sídh*. Curiously, the invitation to gain entry never seems to be the reward for virtuous or generous deeds or any kind of obeisance paid to residents. Often a perfectly ordinary male stumbles upon a rapturously beautiful maiden who beckons to him in ways he does not immediately understand. As in Bran's voyage to Emain Ablach, the mortal who enters the *sídh* loses track of time in the quotidian world he has left and is usually transformed for the worse when and if he returns.

Neither is the *sídh* the realm of the dead, the final resting place of the wicked or the virtuous. The Irish name for that place is Tech Duinn, the 'house' of Donn the ruler of the dead, sometimes known as Donn Tétscorach [abounding in furious horses (?)]. The location of this 'house' is not always specific, as it may lie beyond mortal geography. Often linked with Munster, it is sometimes identified with a rocky islet near Dursey Island at the extreme western end of the Beare Peninsula, west Co. Cork.

In earlier Irish literature the *sídh* is often seen as a palace or perhaps a very fine residence, much more *this*-worldly than otherworldly. Among the best known is Finnachad in Co. Armagh, the *sídh* of king Lir in *Oidheadh Chlainne Lir* [The Tragic Story of the Children of Lir] (see Chapter 7). Many of the most celebrated are understood to be otherworldly, even though *sídh* is not a part of their names: Brí Léith in Co. Longford, the residence of Midir, lover of Étaín; Clettig on the south bank of the River Boyne, residence of Elcmar, magician foster-father of Angus Óg; Femen in Co. Tipperary, home of Bodb Derg, the son of the Dagda; and Úamain in Connacht, childhood domicile of Cáer, lover of Angus Óg. Hundreds of others are known by the name of their most powerful resident, e.g. Sídh Nechtain, dominated by Nechtan.

The Modern Irish word *sídh* denoting 'fairy' in the broader sense, an extension of the more specific 'fairy mound', lends itself to dozens of compounds. These include *ceo sídhe* [fairy mist], *ceol sídhe* [fairy music], *sídh chóra*, *sídh ghaoithe* and *séideán sídhe* [fairy wind], *corpán sídhe* [changeling] and *suan sídhe* [fairy sleep]. Most fearful of these is *poc sídhe* [fairy stroke], in which the body is disabled or paralysed in ways inexplicable in the centuries before the development of modern medicine. A parallel belief among English speakers is the reason that 'stroke' is still the colloquial term for apoplexy or cerebral haemorrhage.

Knowledge of the *sídh* is not exclusively Irish and extends to nearby Celtic lands. Among the Manx the word *shee*, spelled like the anglicization of the Irish, denotes the fairy otherworld. In Scottish Gaelic it is *sìth*, which may be translated as preternatural or spiritual. *Sìthean* denotes a fairy hill, perhaps with a pointed top, but not a tumulus; *daoine sìth* [people of the *sìth*] is a name for the fairies. The Welsh phrase *caer siddi* (earlier *kaer sidi*) borrows the root of the Irish *sídh*, as Patrick Sims-Williams points out. The borrowing represents an uncommon instance of an Irish word used to express a Welsh idea. Caer Siddi is only one of a string of alternative names for the Welsh otherworld, Annwfn (see below), but in some texts it is depicted as a fortress in an overseas land.

MANY REALMS

Despite the widespread use in English of the Irish *sídh* under different spellings, there is no single word or phrase in either early Irish or early Welsh that translates 'the otherworld' as we understand that phrase in contemporary usage. Our contemporary vision is, once again, shaped in part by centuries of Christian teaching; 'the otherworld' is neither heaven nor hell. A concept much like 'the otherworld' certainly exists in early Irish and Welsh traditions, but it is denoted by a sequence of different terms, all with different connotations and shadings. These realms, both Irish and Welsh, appear in two locations. They may be under the ground, including under lakes and springs, or they may lie on an imperceptible island across the sea, usually the western sea, that is, the Atlantic Ocean, or under the sea.

The closest approximation to 'the otherworld' is the Welsh word *Annwfn* or *Annwn*, as seen from its linguistic roots. Patrick Sims-Williams (1990) endorses Eric P. Hamp's view (1977–8) that it derives from the intensive *an* and *dwfn* [deep]. The same root *dwfn* contributes to the Welsh word for 'abyss', *anoddyn*. The rival older theory put forth by Ifor Williams (1951) is more speculative. Williams argues from Gaulish cognates that *dwfn* should mean 'world' and that the first element *an-* is a negative rather than an intensive, which would make *Annwfn* a semantic cognate of the *alius orbis* cited by Lucan. *Annwfn* has no cognates in Irish but appears to resemble the Breton *anaon* [spirits of the dead; souls' society].

Unlike the *sídh*, Annwfn is a single realm that may be entered through many portals on earth and sea. This kingdom appears to be subdivided into separate sub-kingdoms dominated by a monarch who claims overlordship as the 'king of Annwfn'. In the first branch of the *Mabinogi* (see Chapter 13) Hafgan is seen as '*a* king of Annwfn' who challenges Arawn '*the* king of Annwfn'. Patrick Sims-Williams has noted that the Annwfn of *Mabinogi* seems contiguous with the earthly kingdom of Dyfed in south Wales and that the contention between

Hafgan and Arawn is a fair reflection of medieval Welsh politics. In some texts Annwfn is identified with the tiny island of Gwales (today Grassholm), off the southwest coast of Dyfed; Bendigeidfran's head rules over feasting here in the second branch of the *Mabinogi*. In the earlier *Culhwch and Olwen* Annwfn lies beyond Scotland.

Initially, Annwfn was seen as a place of joy and happiness, where life is enriched by enchanting music and a fountain flowing with an elixir sweeter than wine. Sickness and old age are unknown. Thus it may also be known as Caer Feddwid [W. court of intoxication or carousal]. The advance of Christianity, however, merged Annwfn with aspects of hell [W. *Uffern*], and its inhabitants came to be thought of as demons. The Arthur of Welsh tradition is nearly killed when he tries to retrieve a cauldron from Annwfn. Such dread gives rise to the feared *cŵn annwfn* [dogs of Annwfn], whose barks foretell death and who scavenge for the souls of the departed. In later folklore the dogs are led by Gwynn ap Nudd, king of the tylwyth teg, the 'fair folk' or fairies.

The passage of Annwfn from Elysian bliss to Stygian anguish finds no parallels in other Celtic traditions. In general, the variously named otherworlds, with two prominent exceptions, can be counted on to be places of abundant feasting and drinking, of sport and entertainment, of enchanting music, and of beautiful and submissive women. Even the two woeful domains, one Breton and the other Irish, do not present the entering spirit with the terrors Dante imagined would be visited upon sinning Christians.

Youdic, a name once uttered with fear in Brittany, is only the entrance to infernal regions. The full nature of what lies beyond was not spoken. In oral tradition Youdic was linked to a flat, dismal quagmire, Yeun or Yeun-Elez, in the Arrée mountains of Finistère *département*, northwestern Brittany. Those thought to be possessed by demons were cast into Youdic, and careless mortals who chanced to peer into it risked being seized and dragged down by unseen forces below. Fiends lying deep in the bog howled out at night, often taking the form of black dogs. At night also came the sounds of revelling among the lost souls. In Christian lore associated with Youdic, St Michael was named the protector who kept the innocent from falling in.

The Irish Dún Scáith [fort of shadow/fear], sometimes thought to be on the Isle of Man, may be entered and explored. It is a kind of Hades from which the deft and quick may steal a treasure. When the hero Cúchulainn and his champions land here, they have to overcome a series of challenges. Odious serpents swarm toward the men from a pit at the centre of the fortress. Next, hideous toads with sharp beaks attack; in their charging forth they turn into dragons. But the men vanquish them and thus procure an enchanted cauldron, gold, silver, an endless supply of meat and three magical crews to pull their ship back to Ireland. Escape is not simple, however. The evil spirits who protected Dún Scáith cause the Irish ship to capsize, sending the treasure to the bottom of the sea. Cúchulainn and his men swim back to Ireland where they live to tell the tale.

This Dún Scáith linked with the Isle of Man is easily confused with variations on the name, Dùn Sgàthaich, etc., which make play on Scáthach, the amazonian tutor of Cúchulainn thought to live on the Isle of Skye in the Hebrides. The Scottish Gaelic spelling Dùn Scàith may refer to a ruined fortress on the Sleat coast of Skye or to the whole of the island.

These specific locations for an otherworldly realm support John Carey's contention (1982) that the insular Celts did not adhere to a general notion of an unlocalized, 'overseas otherworld'. Islands that appear mythical or fabulous to us were sufficiently real to medieval cartographers to be assigned places on the map. As Carey sees it, the early Irish, especially, perceived otherworlds on actual islands. In early Europe, not just the Celtic-speaking lands, ship burials in seaworthy vessels were a common practice. Patrick Sims-Williams (1990) in commenting on Carey adds, there are 'multiple Irish Otherworlds, located in specific places, both underground and on islands'. *The* otherworld is a modern abstraction.

In the story of Saint Brendan's voyage, reviewed above, a lure for the quest was the hope of visiting Tír Tairngire [land of prophecy, promise]. It is presumed to be a land that can be reached by boat. Stories of Tír Tairngire depict a king and queen, Dáire (one of several to bear this name) and Rígru Rosclethan, who are called 'sinless' because they have intercourse only to produce their otherworldly son Ségda Sárlbraid. Half a dozen other stories tell of visitors to the land, some of whose behaviour is most earthly. The beautiful but wicked Bé

Chuma commits adultery here with Gaidiar, son of Manannán mac Lir, for which she is banished.

Another mysterious land made a lasting mark on the world's map. Hy Brasil is known today only in its Hiberno-English spelling, but it derives from an Irish original, perhaps *Í* [island] and *bres* [beauty, worth; great, might]. An earthly paradise lying at the same latitude as Ireland, Hy Brasil clearly builds on the much older European myth of the lost Atlantis. The Irish name may have been influenced by the boat-shaped fortress Barc Bresail built in Leinster and attributed to the shadowy king Bresal. Sometimes associated with the Aran Islands, Hy Brasil is one of many retreats attributed to the Tuatha Dé Danann after their defeat by the Milesians (see Chapter 7). Under different spellings the name appeared on a number of medieval maps in different parts of Europe and became the subject of cartographer Angelinus Dalorto's thesis *L'Isola Brazil* (Genoa, 1325). The Italian spelling, with a -z-, influenced the naming of the South American nation of Brazil, but maps continued to place the island of Brasil west of Ireland well into the seventeenth century. The notion of Hy Brasil as an island without labour, care or cynical laughter, where one might enjoy the conversation of such as Cúchulainn, persisted in oral tradition until the twentieth century. A fisherman claimed to William Butler Yeats, as cited in *The Celtic Twilight* (1893), that he had sailed out as far as Hy Brasil.

Other islands on the western horizon offer a paradise equal to that of Hy Brasil and are differentiated by names suggesting something of their inhabitants, their promise or their location. The beautiful, sexually inviting women of Tír na mBan [Land of Women] entertain many visiting heroes, beginning with Bran and Máel Dúin, as cited above. The Living of Tír na mBéo [Land of the Living] are some of the many otherworldly consolers of the defeated Tuatha Dé Danann; this is the same land where the hero Lug Lámfhota acquires his sword Frecraid. The resourceful Tuatha Dé Danann are also thought have sought refuge where no eyes could see them in Tír fo Thuinn [Land under Wave]. The fancifulness and generality of Tír fo Thuinn appear to suggest that storytellers gave it less credence than the other western Elysiums, but it is cited in a number of Fenian stories from oral tradition.

Tír na nÓg [Land of Youth], well known in English, conflates elements of many of the islands: usually in the west, a refuge for the Tuatha Dé Danann, a place of bountiful pleasure and sexual promise, where youth never expires. Oral tradition assigns Tír na nÓg to several locations, most popularly at the entrance of Lisconnor Bay, Co. Clare, south of the Cliffs of Moher. Or it may be inland, such as a cave on Knockadoon Island, Lough Gur, Co. Limerick, or in the north on Rathlin Island, off the Antrim coast. Niam[h] of the Golden Hair leads the Fenian hero Oisín to Tír na nÓg, where they sojourn for 300 years. The full nature of their doings there is never detailed. On his return to mortality, of course, Oisín, like others, finds himself ravaged by the time he does not perceive to have passed. The concept of Tír na nÓg may be traditional, but it was shaped by the literary imagination of Micheál Coimín's 1750 Irish-language poem *Laoi Oisín i dTír na nÓg* [The Lay of Oisín in the Land of Youth]. It is due not only to Coimín's well-wrought text that the name Tír na nÓg became so widely known but even more to the poem's dozen translations and adaptations, famously William Butler Yeats's 'The Wanderings of Oisin' (1889). Not a copyrighted name, Tír na nÓg may appear in contexts far from its roots. Any children's amusement park, like one in the resort town of Salthill, Co. Galway, may be called 'Tír na nÓg'. It is also the name of the mysterious white horse in Mike Newell's film *Into the West* (1993), written by Jim Sheridan.

The otherworld as distant island is less common in traditions outside Ireland. Stories of Roca Barraidh are still current on the Isle of Barra in the Outer Hebrides. On rare occasions privileged fishermen might see this enchanted island on the far horizon, which combines elements of Hy Brasil and Emain Ablach. The Scottish Gaelic *roc* denotes anything that tangles a fishing-hook or the tops of seaweed that appear above the water. Similarly, the Welsh Ynys Afallon [W. *afall*, apple] is a happy island of sensual pleasure, fertility, abundant feasting and perpetual youth on the western ocean. Ynys Afallon, along with Emain Ablach, which also contains an allusion to apples, have long been thought to contribute to the conception of Avalon in Arthurian tradition.

Lastly, not all islands are at sea. Expanses of flat land, plains, are like islands in that they offer the foot-traveller respite from rough ground. Perhaps that is why Mag Mell [pleasant plain] is sometimes portrayed at sea and sometimes on land. Bran passes it on his way to Emain Ablach in *Imram Brain*, where salmon romp like calves. At other times it is linked to the actual Mag Dá Cheó [plain of two mists], south of Medb's fortress of Cruachain in what is today Co. Roscommon, or it may lie in the southwest of Ireland. Not only is its location variable, but it may have as many as three rulers. Usually the monarch of Mag Mell is the forthright Labraid Luathlám ar Claideb [swift hand on sword] whose beautiful wife's name Lí Ban means 'paragon of women'. She is her husband's irresistible emissary to Cúchulainn in *Serglige Con Culainn* [The Sickbed of Cúchulainn] (see Chapter 10). Other attributed kings are Goll mac Doilb and Boadach.

Just as there is no single ruler of Mag Mell so there is no personality to lay claim to the title 'king of the otherworld'. Eochaid Iúil is the adversary of Labraid Luathlám of Mag Mell, but it is not clear where he reigns. Tethra of the demonic Fomorians has otherworldly resonances but he presides over no named realm. Neither does Eógan Inbir rule a happy kingdom, and he is diminished when his wife Bé Chuma cuckolds him with Gaidiar, the son of Manannán mac Lir. As his name appears more often in early texts than any of his rivals', Manannán, the otherworldly sea god, usually bests them. He appears in the four major cycles of early Irish literature and roams the Irish Sea, touching upon Scotland, the Isle of Man and Ireland at will.

PART TWO

Irish Myths

7

Irish Beginnings: the *Lebor Gabála Érenn*

PSEUDO-HISTORY

We do not know how the Celts envisioned the beginning of their world. No cosmogony, cosmology or creation myth in a Celtic language survives to our time. There is no Celtic document to explain the origin of the universe as one finds in Hesiod's *Theogony* among the Greeks or in the two *Eddas* from early Iceland. Classical commentators, including Julius Caesar (first century BC), testify that the Gauls had a cosmogony, but almost none of it can now be found. One line from the geographer Strabo (first century AD) speaks of the Gaulish belief in the indestructibility of the world. There is no trace of such beliefs in Irish, Welsh or Breton tradition, although John Shaw (1978) has found a story on the creation of the Milky Way Galaxy among the exiled Scottish Gaels in Nova Scotia (see Chapter 14). The most extensive origin story we have is Irish, and it does not address how the cosmos or humans came about but rather how different peoples, some of them fabulous, came to Ireland. This narrative, usually classed as a 'pseudo-history', is the *Lebor Gabála Érenn* (Modern Irish: *Leabhar Gabhála*), often translated as 'The Book of Invasions' or 'The Book of Conquests' or literally as 'The Book of the Taking of Ireland'.

For most readers the term 'pseudo-history' will be unfamiliar and sound unduly flippant or insulting. The compilers of the twelfth-century text of the *Lebor Gabála* thought they were writing a reliable record of human events but because of their credulous use of frequently fantastical sources they produced something very different. Several authors over different periods purported to synchronize myths, legends and genealogies from early Ireland with the framework of Biblical exegesis. Such stories as that of the Tower of Babel and Noah's Flood are taken literally, and Ptolemy's earth-centred vision of the cosmos orders the authors' globe. Alwyn and Brinley Rees in *Celtic Heritage* (1961) describe it as a 'laborious attempt to combine parts of native teaching with Hebrew mythology embellished with medieval legend'. Less charitably, Patrick K. Ford (1977) calls the *Lebor Gabála* a 'masterpiece of muddled medieval miscellany'.

The full five volumes of the *Lebor Gabála* appear to have grown over several centuries and were contributed to by many hands. Traces of identifiable but nameless poets appear from the ninth and tenth centuries, the final redaction coming after the eleventh century. Our oldest surviving version appears in the twelfth-century *Book of Leinster*. Compilers of the narrative do not demonstrate a profound knowledge of the Bible itself but rely instead on Biblical commentators and historians, especially Eusebius (third century AD), Orosius (sixth century), and Isidore of Seville (seventh century). The evidence of Latin learning has caused some modern commentators to suggest that there was once an original version in Latin from which the Irish text is derived, an assertion now largely dismissed.

Inevitably, the reader of the *Lebor Gabála* must wonder if there is some tiny grain of fact at the bottom of it all or whether the entire venture is built on moonbeams. The succession of different invasions of the island, culminating with the all-too-mortal Milesians, suggests a parallel with the Four Ages of Man outlined by the Greek Hesiod in *Works and Days* (*c.* seventh century BC). The narrative also provides a setting for the first cycle of Old Irish literature, which we now call 'The Mythological'. A key text of that cycle, *Cath Maige Tuired* [The (Second) Battle of Mag Tuired/Moytura], extends the action of the *Lebor Gabála* and is also discussed in this chapter, below. Yet the classification 'pseudo-history' reminds us that the *Lebor Gabála* was once thought a reliable record. Some of the most important historians before modern times struggled to coordinate the *Lebor Gabála* history to fit with information gathered elsewhere, including Geoffrey Keating (*c.*1580–*c.*1645/50), Micheál Ó Cléirigh (1575–*c.*1645) of the *Annals of the Four Masters*, and Roderick O'Flaherty (1629–1718). Even the conscientious post-Enlightenment figure Charles O'Conor (1710–91) thought the *Lebor Gabála* narrative could be accommodated with more trustworthy documents. In the later twentieth century John V. Kelleher of Harvard University devoted decades to solving the text's many riddles and also encouraged two generations of graduate students to work with shorter sections by using all the resources of modern technology, scrupulously edited manuscripts and more abundant data. Their efforts support the view that certain episodes in the *Lebor Gabála* contain distant echoes of events that can be demonstrated to have occurred. The same, of course, can be said of numerous medieval legends as well as later folktales.

To a degree, the *Lebor Gabála* resembles the earlier passages in the *Chronicles* compiled by Raphael Holinshed (1577), source for Shakespeare's *King Lear* and other dramas, or legend dressed up as history. A key difference is that whereas Holinshed contains the fanciful merging with the documentable record as it becomes available, in the *Lebor Gabála* early imaginative narrative is contorted to fit a framework inherited from biblical commentators. The text always comes with dates.

Human history begins with the biblical Flood, which commentators date at 2900 BC or in the supposed 'year of the world' 1104 Anno Mundi (abbreviated AM). Dates for all events in the *Lebor Gabála* vary a great deal, as medieval authorities could not agree on the date of Creation: the Anglo-Saxon historian known as the Venerable Bede (seventh century) argued for 3952 BC and the Septuagints, Greek-speaking Jewish scholars (third century BC), determined 5200 BC, while later authorities opted for 4004 BC. The ancestors of the Irish are known as the Scoti, a people presumed to have originated in Scythia (coextensive with modern Ukraine) who took their name from a daughter of the pharaoh of Egypt known as Scota or Scotia. In fact *Scoti* is a variant of *Scotti*, one of several names the historical Romans gave to peoples in ancient Ireland. Sixth-century historical migrations from Ulster to Argyll caused that name to be applied to what we now call Scotland. The *Lebor Gabála* portrays the Scoti as fellow exiles in Egypt with the Hebrews, whose leader Moses invites them to join the Exodus. This passage may be the source of the long-standing canard that the Irish are a lost tribe of Israel. While in Egypt the Scoti invent their own language. One Fénius Farsaid is described as being present at the separation of languages at Babel and leaving instructions to his grandson, Goídel Glas, to forge the Irish language out of the seventy-two tongues then in existence. The name makes play on the Old Irish word for the Irish language *Goídelc*.

The invasions or conquests of the title are found in the iteration of six successive waves of migration to Ireland, named for their leaders or dominant groups: (i) Cesair, (ii) Partholonians, (iii) Nemedians, (iv) Fir Bolg, (v) Tuatha Dé Danann, and (vi) Milesians, as well as the bellicose seafarers, the Fomorians, who are at war with most of the others. With linguistic inconsistency, the Partholonians, Nemedians, Fomorians and Milesians are cited by their English plural form, and the Fir Bolg and Tuatha Dé Danann by Irish forms. Of the seven groups only the last, the Milesians, are mortals, while the other six are either divine or removed to some degree from the human.

CESAIR, PARTHOLONIANS, NEMEDIANS, FIR BOLG

The first two invasions are more contrived and less grounded than the subsequent four. A woman comes from the Middle East for the first invasion in a story mixing pious credulity and teasings of sexual fantasy. Cesair (also Cessair, Ceasair, etc.) is the daughter of Bith, a son of Noah, and Birren, who escapes to Inis Fáil [Isle of Destiny, i.e. Ireland] just before the Flood. The disgrace of being denied entry to the Ark causes her to flee her homeland. In an alternative version, she is the daughter of Banba, one of the eponymous goddesses of Ireland. Forty days before the Flood, she arrives at Dún na mBarc on Bantry Bay in County Cork with fifty women and three men. Initially the women are supposed to be divided among the men in hopes that they will populate the island. Two of the men die, leaving the task to Fintan mac Bóchra, 'husband' of Cesair and a patron of poets, who feels inadequate to it and flees in the form of a salmon. Left alone, Cesair dies of a broken heart. The unnamed narrator of the story explains the origin of many obscure place names by tracing them to members of Cesair's retinue. Cold-eyed modern commentators have argued that the etymologies are invented and inserted in the narrative.

Ireland is empty for 312 years after the death of Cesair, and thus after the Flood, when the beneficent and industrious Partholonians, after seven years' wandering, land during Beltaine at Inber Scéne, which may be in Co. Kerry in southwest Ireland or Donegal Bay in the northwest. They settle first in the northwest near the falls of Assaroe but later clear four plains, introduce agriculture and are the first to divide Ireland into four parts. Nature welcomes them when seven lakes erupt of their own accord. Among their settlements is the plain of Mag nElta (anglicized Moynalty), coextensive with modern metropolitan Dublin.

These second invaders are named for their leader Partholón, another person with a Biblical pedigree. He is a descendant of Magog, who lived in the twenty-first year of the Patriarch Abraham. Additionally, he is a 'prince of Greece', who murders his own parents, costing himself one eye and bringing a lifelong propensity for bad luck. He is, despite this, 'chief of every craft'. Whether Partholón is Greek or Hebrew, his name is certainly not Irish, as the letter P was unknown in the earliest versions of the Irish language. The name is most likely borrowed from the Hebrew Apostle's name Bartholomew, which St Jerome and Isidore of Seville incorrectly glossed as 'son of him who stays the waters', i.e. a survivor of the Flood.

The Partholonians flourish for 520 years and rise to a population of 9,000, many of whom have developed characters, such as Partholón's three brothers, Eólas [knowledge], Fios [intelligence] and Fochmarc [inquiring]. Other specific names are attributed to the first teacher, first innkeeper and first physician. Others introduce gold, cattle-raising and jurisprudence. One Malaliach brews the first ale, later used in divination, ritual and sacrifice. Not all Partholonian innovations are so happy. Partholón's wife Dealgnaid seduces a servant in the first instance of adultery in Irish literature. In one version Partholón flies into a rage, but in another he is placated by his wife's verse protest that she should not have been left alone with great temptation.

Although the Partholonians do battle with the hated Fomorians, their victory does not extinguish the enemy. The Fomorians are sea pirates who use Irish offshore islands as bases for depredation. A hundred and twenty years after Partholón's death at Tallaght, near modern Dublin, all but one of his people die during a plague in one week in the month of May. According to a variant text, that one survivor is Tuan mac Cairill (sometimes mac Stairn), who lives on to the time of St Colum Cille (c.521–93/97) to tell the history of the invasions.

Thirty years after the extinction of the Partholonians, the Nemedians arrive, people who also improve the landscape. Like their predecessors, the Nemedians take their name from a leader with a biblical pedigree; Nemed is descended from Magog and a son of Japheth but still described as a 'Scythian'. It is from Scythia that the Nemedians depart in thirty-four ships, all but one of which is lost when the party greedily pursues a tower of gold seen at sea. The remaining ship wanders the world for a year before arriving in Ireland at a time and place not made specific.

Least remarkable and romanticized of the invaders, the Nemedians seem initially to be a shadow of the Partholonians. Four new lakes erupt during their occupation, and they advance civilization by clearing twelve plains and building two fortresses, one in Antrim, the other in Armagh. The latter is named for their queen Macha [Ir. *Ard Macha*: height of Macha], one of three important figures to bear that name. One of their druids, Mide, eponym for the kingdom of Mide, lights the first fire at Uisnech at the centre of Ireland; it blazes for seven years and lights every chief's hearth.

Their singular distinction is in doing heroic battle against the predatory Fomorians, whom they defeat three times. A fourth encounter, however, is catastrophic, forcing the Nemedians to pay a humiliating annual tribute at Samain. Seeking vengeance, the Nemedians storm the Fomorian tower of Tor Conaind on Tory Island off Donegal. The Nemedian hero Fergus Lethderg slays the Fomorian champion Conand, but most of the rest of the brave fighters are slaughtered, only thirty surviving to be scattered around the world. The offspring of those survivors become members of later invasions, the Fir Bolg and the Tuatha Dé Danann. One, Britán Máel, lives in Scotland until the arrival of the Picts, when he moves south, giving his name to Britain and the British.

Nemed's son Starn is the ancestor of the fourth wave of invaders, the Fir Bolg, who suffer oppression in a far-off land known as 'Greece', where their forced labour includes carrying dirt in leather bags from the valleys to the bare hills above. Under their leader, Semion, a grandson of Starn, they turn their bags into ships and effect an escape, arriving in Ireland at Inber Domnann (Malahide Bay, north of Dublin) on the August feast of Lughnasa, 230 years after Starn's departure. Their leader at that time is named Dela, whose five sons divide the island among themselves. As their predecessors had prepared Ireland for agriculture, they do not clear plains and no lakes are formed. Neither do they engage the vicious Fomorians. The Fir Bolg are, however, a military people. An early king Rinnal [cf. Ir. *rinn*: spear-point] is the first to employ weapons with iron heads.

The name *Fir Bolg* is usually glossed as 'men of Builg', a plural form in Irish. The words are also pronounced as they would be in Irish with a schwa inserted between the *l* and the *g*: 'feer BOL-eg'. The meaning of their name has been much disputed. The earlier folk etymology glossing the name as 'men of the bags' [Ir. *bolg*: bag], once dismissed, has recently gained new currency. Such bags would not be the ones cited in the narrative but ones that signal bellicosity through etymological routes. Within the *Lebor Gabála* they are thought to take their name from Bolg/Bolga, an ancestor deity. Another interpretation from the mid-twentieth century suggests that *Bolg* alludes to the Belgae, early historical invaders of Ireland speaking P-Celtic languages (ancient British, Welsh, Cornish, etc.).

Although the Fir Bolg prevail for a mere thirty-seven years, their era is distinguished by the rule of a great and generous king, Eochaid mac Eirc, who establishes justice and provides that all rain will fall as dew and that every year will yield a harvest. Eochaid also initiates a festival in honour of his wife Tailtiu; the actual festival of that name continued to be celebrated in Co. Meath until the late eighteenth century and was revived briefly in the twentieth.

The agricultural Fir Bolg meet their end at the hands of the invading Tuatha Dé Danann at the First Battle of Mag Tuired (distinguished from the better known Second Battle of Mag Tuired – see below). Subsequently, they scatter to distant parts of the Gaelic world, such as Rathlin Island off Co. Antrim in Northern Ireland, the Scottish coast and the far west of Ireland. The imposing archaeological site Dún Aonghusa on Inishmore in the Aran Islands is thought to be named for a Fir Bolg leader. Under heavy caricature, the Fir Bolg persist in Irish and Scottish Gaelic folklore as grotesque helots and cave fairies.

FOMORIANS

While not a part of the sequence of six invaders, the malevolent Fomorians exude a sulphurous presence over long stretches of narrative in the *Lebor Gabála*. They also figure prominently in the action of *Cath Maige Tuired* [The (Second) Battle of Mag Tuired], but portrayals are not coordinate across the two texts. Learned opinion today sees the Fomorians as euhemerized sea deities, pre-Christian divinities who came to be thought of as human, especially as demonic pirates. Earlier commentators invented lineages for them from the materials at hand. Their conception predates both the composition of the *Lebor Gabála* and the advent of Christianity. Linking them to the Bible, ecclesiastical scribes explained the Fomorians as the progeny of Ham, Noah's least favoured son. Later they were portrayed as giants or elves, or were seen with goat- or horseheads or other misshapen features. Historical experience contributed to their vilification as they took on the behaviour of sea-raiders from the north, first from the Scottish islands and more extensively from the Norse lands. Thus they are seen as wantonly cruel bullies, cutting off the noses of those who will not pay them tribute.

In their first appearance in the *Lebor Gabála* under their rapacious leader Cichol against the beneficent Partholonians, the Fomorians are seen as monstrous and fearsome, each having only one eye, one arm and one leg. To a modern, sceptical perception, the Fomorians may have seemed at some disadvantage because of missing parts, but their disfigurement must have thrown a fright into early readers and storytellers. Centuries later two figures from oral tradition, the Irish Fer Caille and the Scottish Gaelic Fachan, were described taking the same form. Later in the text the Fomorians are more anthropomorphic.

Unlike the six invaders of Ireland, the Fomorians never appear to be settlers but instead make raids from their distant, almost unassailable fortress on Tory Island, off the northwest coast of Co. Donegal. Their fortress is known as Tor Conaind, named for the chief Conand. They have an easy time against the gentle Partholonians, who are exterminated by a plague before the Fomorians can dominate them. The Nemedians, as recounted above, enjoy initial success against the Fomorians until they themselves are humiliated in a battle at Cnámros, Co. Laois (coextensive with the present village of Camross). As they are two generations apart, the Nemedians never face the Fir Bolg, which prompted some commentators to suggest they were doubles for one another, an unlikely assertion since rejected.

Individual warriors and champions of the Fomorians are surreally ugsome, as one might imagine, notably the leading military menace, Balor, often known as Balor of the Evil or Baleful Eye. Even his wife Caitlín or Céthlionn of the Crooked Tooth can send the timorous running. Balor does more than strike fear; he is lethal. He never opens the eye except on the battlefield, where four men are needed to lift the eyelid. Any army looking upon the eye is rendered powerless. The deadly capability of this eye comes from the child Balor's observation of his father's druids brewing potions and charms. Balor, however, need only extend his gaze to strike with dreadful effect. Earlier theories, now out of fashion, explained Balor as an anthropomorphic sun deity. In size and aggression, Balor is often seen as a counterpart of the Welsh juggernaut Ysbaddaden Bencawr, whose heavy eyelids require servants with forks to lift them.

TUATHA DÉ DANANN

Compilers of the *Lebor Gabála* are characteristically precise in dating the arrival of the Tuatha Dé Danann as thirty-seven years after the Fir Bolg, whom they displace, and 297 years before the Milesians, mortal equivalents of the Irish people. Other aspects of their arrival do not imply the earth-bound. Unlike the other invaders who arrive by ship, the Tuatha Dé Danann disembark from sombre clouds just before Beltaine, settling on an obscure mountain in the west, causing a three-day eclipse. An association with the west persists in their characterization. In an alternative text they do arrive by sailing over water, burning their ships on the shore, sending up a plume of dark smoke that causes an eclipse.

The name *Tuatha Dé Danann* is an Irish plural that translates roughly as 'people or tribe of the goddess D—'; earlier speculation asserted that the D— goddess was the familiar Danu, but linguistic analysis of early texts shows that the identity of D— is not so clear. It has no singular form. The Irish *tuatha*, commonly used in many contexts, does not translate explicitly into English, as it may mean 'people', 'nation', 'folk' or 'tribe'. As a phrase, *tuatha dé* predates the composition of the *Lebor Gabála*, describing the Israelites in translations of the Bible (cf. L. *Plebes Dei*) as well as the old gods. Danu, as mentioned in Chapter 4, is known only from the genitive form of her name and is tantalizingly close to, but not identical with, Ana/Anu, the earth goddess. The full origin of *Danann* (also spelled Danaan, Donann, etc.) is still disputed, as John Carey (1981) has shown. In English the group may be known as Tuatha Dé for short.

Although certain members of the Tuatha Dé Danann, such as the 'good god' Dagda and the great hero Lug Lámfhota [Ir. of the long arm], exist in Irish tradition before the composition of the *Lebor Gabála*, the compilers felt it necessary to invent a pre-invasion history for the group. Eleven generations removed from the Nemedians, the Tuatha Dé Danann were thought to have lived in 'Greece' but to have learned magic and druid lore in remote northern lands. They depart for Ireland from four magical cities: Fálias, Findias, Gorias and Murias. From these cities they take their principal treasures that appear again and again in later stories. From Fálias comes Fál or Lia Fáil, the stone of destiny, which cries out proclaiming the rightful king in coronation ceremonies. From Findias they take the sword of Nuadu, which allows no victim to escape. Gorias yields up Gáe Assail, the mighty spear of Lug Lámfhota, which guarantees victory. And from Murias they bring the cauldron of Dagda, which leaves satisfied all who take a draught from it.

Rounded, more humanized, even colourful personalities emerge from the host of the Tuatha Dé Danann. Although it would be an exaggeration to say they are counterparts of the Olympians of Greek mythology – there is no pantheon in *any* Celtic tradition – the more prominent personages from the Tuatha Dé do serve some of the functions of the Olympians. They reappear in dozens of later stories from all three of the major cycles, Mythological, Ulster and Fenian, often bringing superhuman powers to interfere with the lives of characters found there, not unlike the way Aphrodite and Poseidon shape some of the action in the *Iliad*.

Dagda, usually known with the definite article as the Dagda, is a warrior, artisan, magician and omniscient ruler. Among his possessions are the celebrated cauldron and two marvellous swine (one always cooking, the other still alive), and ever-laden fruit trees. His club is so great that it has to be dragged on wheels and leaves a track so deep that it marks the boundary between provinces. In size and potency it suggests parallels with the striker of the Gaulish god Sucellus or the hammer of the Norse god Thor. The Dagda is also known by other names in some stories: Eochaid Ollathair [father of all], Ruad Rofhessa [lord of great knowledge] and Deirgderc [red eye, i.e. the sun].

Boand is the goddess of the River Boyne, an anglicization of her name. While the lover of the Dagda, she conceives and gives birth to Angus Óg, the god of poetry. Some sources bowdlerize the episode and call Boand the 'wife' of the Dagda, but Nechtan is her usual husband. To hide her adultery, she asks Elcmar to be the foster-father of the child. Nuadu is her usual consort, but he is neither a foster-father nor a 'husband' in the Christian sense. Her residence is thought to be Brug na Bóinne [hostel of Boand], the Irish-language name for the great passage-grave of Newgrange, and, by extension, the forty tombs in the area. Competing stories explain her origin, both having her violate taboos, after which a well pours forth to drown her as she flees toward the sea, following a route that is now the River Boyne. Always feminine, she is attributed a lapdog, Dabilla.

Manannán mac Lir rules a mysterious land beyond the sea, as cited in the previous chapter, and is most associated with the powers of water. He is a giver of gifts with magical properties such as the concealing mist given to the Tuatha Dé Danann. Not always listed with the Tuatha Dé, his persona predates the composition of the *Lebor Gabála* and appears most widely in early Irish literature. The folk etymology that he gave his name to the Isle of Man is false, but the reverse may be true, that his name comes from an early name for the island. His patronymic, mac Lir, once thought to mean 'of the sea', remains puzzling. This Lir is not identical with Lir of Sídh Finnachad, the father of the swan children, a story composed at a later date.

Angus Óg, literally 'young Angus', is a god of youth and beauty as well as poetry. He may also be the god of love, if one can be said to exist. His name is spelled variously, Óengus, Áengus, Aonghas, etc., or he may be known as mac Óc or mac-ind-Óg, 'the son of youth' or 'young son'. Angus Óg drinks the ale of immortality and four swans circle over his head as he travels. He displaces his mother Boand at the residence of Brug na Bóinne or Newgrange. Although attributed many lovers, in his best known story he pines away for the inaccessible swan maiden Cáer. He protects himself with a cloak of invisibility but nonetheless defends many heroes, notably his foster-son, Diarmait Ua Duibne of the Fenian Cycle.

Nuadu Airgetlám [of the silver hand/arm] is a king who leads his people into Ireland but is later disqualified because of the 'blemish' of his severed hand, replaced with a silver prosthetic. His sword is one of the Tuatha Dé's treasures, a testimony to his prominence. Obliged to relinquish his throne temporarily, he was reappointed before the battle with the Fomorians, in which he fell to Balor. He appears to be the cognate of the early British god Nodons, who was worshipped at Lydney Park, an archaeological site on the west bank of the Severn; he also resembles the Welsh figure Nudd, who sometimes carries the epithet Llaw Erient [silver hand]. Nuadu is a consort of Boand.

Dian Cécht, the healing god, fashioned Nuadu's silver hand with moving fingers. In the battle with the Fomorians, Dian Cécht can restore every mortally wounded warrior except for the decapitated. For this he employs the *tipra sláine* [spring of life] to revive health and well-being. A cult of Dian Cécht predates the *Lebor Gabála*, and somewhat changed he also appears in later oral tradition; his porridge made of hazelnuts, dandelion, woodsorrel, chickweed and oatmeal can cure colds, sore throats and other ailments. His son Miach and daughter Airmid, of whom Dian Cécht is jealous, are also healing gods. The hero Lug Lámfhota is Dian Cécht's grandson but appears to be his contemporary in many narratives.

Ogma, the orator-warrior, is sometimes cited as one of the three principal champions of the Tuatha Dé Danann, along with the Dagda and Lug Lámfhota. A patron of eloquence and poetry, he is the fabled inventor of ogham, the earliest form of writing in Irish, a twenty-character alphabet made up of straight lines and notches carved on the edge of stone or wood. The word ogham (Old Irish *ogam*) is a philological cognate of his name. This Irish god bears a tantalizing resemblance to Ogmios, the Gaulish god of eloquence. Leading scholars such as Rudolf Thurneysen dispute any link between the two. Ogma memorably challenges Lug Lámfhota upon that hero's entrance into Tara (see below).

Donn, the god of the dead and ruler of the otherworld, is often portrayed as aloof and retiring, living in isolation from the other gods at Tech Duinn [Donn's house], a rocky islet at the extreme western end of the Beare Peninsula. He is, nonetheless, the first of the invaders to land in Ireland. Sometimes confused with the Dagda as an ancestor deity, Donn is often merged with another Donn, Donn mac Míled, from the Milesians, the next invaders. As the dead 'live' with him, he most resembles the Roman god Dis Pater, from whom he may derive through Gaulish intermediaries. In oral tradition he is thought to have caused shipwrecks, but in pious folklore his persona is adapted to portrayals of the devil.

Goibniu, the smith god, is one of three patrons of the crafts, along with Credne, a worker in bronze and gold, and Luchta the carpenter. He is seen most vividly in the battle with the Fomorians where he works tirelessly in forging both weapons and armour. His keen tips are always lethal. On occasion he joins the combat himself. Along with his martial skill, Goibniu is often seen as a god of healing. He is also the host of an otherworldly feast, *Fled Goibnenn*, where guests may drink all the ale they wish without getting drunk; instead, those attending are protected from decay and old age. His counterparts in Welsh tradition are Gofannon and Glwyddyn Saer.

Lug Lámfhota develops a vibrant dramatic personality when he enters into the battle with the Fomorians (see below). His principal epithet, 'Of the Long Arm', implies not the length of his limb but his power to hurl a weapon a great distance. One of the three great heroes of early Irish literature, along with Cúchulainn and Fionn mac Cumhaill (both possibly his doubles), he is cognate with Lugos/Lugus, the native name for the god Caesar called Gaulish Mercury. Caesar's description of Mercury as 'inventor of all the arts' translates Lug's second Irish epithet, Samildánach. The Gaulish god and the Irish hero

are both celebrated on 1 August. He also appears to be a counterpart
of the Welsh Lleu Llaw Gyffes.

Other important female figures among the Tuatha Dé Danann,
Brigit the fire-goddess and the triad of war-goddesses, Badb, Macha
and Mórrígan, are discussed in Chapter 4.

Once they have a secure foothold in Ireland, the Tuatha Dé Danann
prove to be masterful warriors. They drive the Fir Bolg before them to
the northwest of the island to a place called, in English, the Plain of
Pillars, or Mag Tuired. The Tuatha Dé demand to be made kings of
the Fir Bolg and are refused. King Nuadu is injured in battle and later
is fitted with his wonderful silver hand. He is replaced in kingship by
the handsome but contemptible Bres, the son of a Tuatha Dé woman
and the Fomorian king Elatha. The site of the Battle of Mag Tuired
may be Conga near what is now Cong, Co. Mayo. Rival claimants for
the site, all with tall megalithic stones, lie in Counties Galway and
Sligo. Wherever it is, the plain is unlikely to be identical with the Mag
Tuired, anglicized Moytirra, Moytura, etc., near Lough Arrow, Co.
Sligo, where the better known second battle takes place, pitting the
Tuatha Dé against the ever-despicable Fomorians. In the prelude to
this epic struggle, the Tuatha Dé set the tone of what will be their era
of fruitfulness by introducing pigs into Irish agriculture and having
three lakes erupt.

THE SECOND BATTLE OF MAG TUIRED AND LUG LÁMFHOTA

The *Lebor Gabála* does not address how the Tuatha Dé Danann drove
the Fomorians from Ireland. Instead, we read about that in a separate
narrative with a higher literary gloss, *Cath Maige Tuired* [The (Second)
Battle of Mag Tuired], whose language suggests composition in the
ninth or tenth century. Cross-references to the battle appear from the
twelfth century on, and most of the characters in it are introduced in
other narratives, not just the *Lebor Gabála*.

Three players dominate the action, the Fomorian Balor of the Evil
Eye and his two handsome grandsons, the greedy and cowardly
Bres (sometimes Eochaid Bres) and the stalwart and generous Lug

Lámfhota. Balor has been told he will be slain by a grandson, and, not surprisingly, the conception of both boys involves surreptitious lovemaking. Bres's mother Ériu (also Eithlinn), a woman of the Tuatha Dé, is visited by a splendid and mysterious stranger later revealed to be Elatha mac Delbaíth of the Fomorians. The young Bres grows at twice the rate of a common boy and is known for his beauty. Lug is also the fruit of a Tuatha Dé–Fomorian union. His mother, Eithne, is the daughter of Balor, who tries to keep her from consorting with any men. Cian, son of the Tuatha Dé healing god Dian Cécht, seduces her with the help of the druidess Birog. The union produces triplets, two of whom are killed at birth, leaving Lug to fulfil the prophecy that Balor fears. Fostered by Manannán mac Lir, Lug grows to be fair of face, charming and athletic.

When Nuadu is found disqualified for kingship because of his lost arm in the First Battle of Mag Tuired, the Tuatha Dé select Bres because his father Elatha ranks high among the nobles, even though he now lives with the rival Fomorians. Bres, though 'beautiful', is an odd choice for king, and he quickly proves unpopular. The odious Fomorians begin to hold sway over the Tuatha Dé, apparently an influence from Bres's parents' choice of residence. Under Bres's rule, the noble Dagda is reduced to building a fort for the new king and Ogma to fetching firewood. More galling, Bres lacks the most esteemed mark of a good king: generosity. Chiefs complain that 'their knives are not greased by him and however often they visit him their breath does not smell of ale'. Bres hosts no entertainment in the royal household. When the poet Cairpre comes to visit, Bres accommodates him in an outhouse. The poet's response is a satire that causes Bres to break out in red blotches. Fed up with his misdeeds, the Tuatha Dé ask Bres to abdicate in favour of the newly restored Nuadu. Weak-willed, Bres agrees, but soon begins to plot for his restoration.

The Fomorians require some suasion to take up Bres's cause. After he confesses to his father Elatha that his own arrogance and greed have brought about his downfall the older man offers little comfort. Not only should the prosperity of his people have been Bres's first concern, but Elatha sees dim prospects for his son's restoration. What has been lost through injustice should not be regained through injustice. Quite a different response comes from grandfather Balor, who

quickly associates Bres's grievance against the Tuatha Dé with Fomorian fortunes. The older man perceives that his tyranny could be broken
and his extortion ended. Rallying to Bres's side he assembles a fleet so
large that it forms an unbroken bridge from Balor's farthest island in
the Hebrides across to Ireland. Additionally, he gathers a mighty army
and starts to prepare for war.

Nuadu, unaware of Bres's conniving, is once again reigning justly
and happily over Ireland, restoring music to the court and prosperity
to the land. Tara resounds with the sound of feasting and spirited
entertainment. The worry that Balor and his raiders will one day return
lingers in the back of Nuadu's mind but does not darken his immediate
pleasure.

One day a princely young warrior, as handsome as Bres but of
nobler bearing, appears at Tara's gate with a retinue of other warriors.
When two doorkeepers, Gamel and Camel, ask his identity, he
responds that his name is Lug but he adds the obscure epithet 'Lonnan-
sclech'. After reciting his lineage and the names of his fosterers, Lug
asks that the king be told he has arrived and that he be allowed to join
the household.

'What skill do you have?' asks Camel. 'No one without an art enters Tara.'
'Question me,' Lug says, 'I am a carpenter.'
The doorkeeper answers, 'We do not need one. We have a carpenter
already, Luchta mac Luachada.'

And so the dialogue continues. Lug proclaims himself a smith, a
champion, a harpist, a warrior, a poet and historian, a sorcerer, a
physician, a cupbearer and a brazier. In each instance a doorkeeper
responds that the court already possesses an excellent practitioner and
cites a name. The itemization gives an inventory of the Tuatha Dé's
useful arts and, curiously, there is no implied hierarchy, with poetry
and war placed in the middle.

Lug's final challenge is, 'Ask the king whether he has one man who
possesses all these arts; if he has I will not be able to enter Tara.' Camel
the doorkeeper then announces that a warrior named Samildánach,
meaning 'master of all the arts', has come to help Nuadu's people. To
seal assurances of his excellence, Lug then defeats all the best court

competitors at a demanding board-game known as fidchell [Ir. wooden wisdom] and comparable to chess.

Recognizing that Lug does indeed possess the mastery he claims, Nuadu decides first to enlist the young man against Balor and his people. He cites the tyranny of their taxes, their piracy and their cruelty to captured sailors. Even though Balor is Lug's grandfather, the resplendent young warrior quickly agrees to ally himself with Nuadu. To further the cause, Nuadu decides to give Lug the authority to rule and steps down from the throne.

Lug rules uneventfully for thirteen days but then retreats with four other leaders, including Nuadu, to a quiet place to plan for the forth-coming battle. Three years pass. In one effort to gather intelligence, Lug dispatches Dagda to the Fomorian camp to spy and to delay the enemy until the Tuatha Dé are better prepared. Visiting their camp, Dagda asks for a truce. But they humiliate him by preying on his weakness for porridge and having him consume such an immense meal, with goats, sheep and swine for trimmings, that he is barely able to walk away. Dadga's efforts are not lost, however, as he encounters Domnu, the Fomorian goddess, who promises to use her magic against her own people.

The Fomorians advance to battle. As the Tuatha Dé assemble, Lug asks the many craftsmen to cite their magic powers. All comply – Goibniu, Dian Cécht, Luchta, Ogma and Credne the brazier, as does the witch-like Mórrígan so often associated with slaughter in battle. Joining also are Cairpre the satirist, assorted cupbearers, druids, witches, and Dagda himself, willing to give themselves to battle. Although Dagda flattens hordes of Fomorians, he is wounded by Caitlín, buck-toothed wife of Balor.

Once the fighting begins, the slaughter is great on both sides. The mêlée rolls over Mag Tuired like thunder and the ground becomes slippery with blood. The Tuatha Dé gain advantage when Dian Cécht restores fallen warriors with the aid of his three children. Lug aids his own armies when he assumes the characteristic pose of the sorcerer. Balor the formidable enemy can destroy an army with his baleful gaze. The four retainers are at the ready to lift the lethal lid. He has already made short work of Nuadu when he meets Lug on the battlefield.

Knowing that he cannot face his grandfather in hand-to-hand combat, Lug devises a way to assault him from afar. He thrusts a slingstone through Balor's eye that goes crashing through the back of his skull, killing twenty-seven Fomorians. Emboldened by Lug, the Tuatha Dé rout the Fomorians and drive them out of Ireland, never to return. The cowardly Bres, who has sworn to decapitate Lug before the combat was joined, is captured and pleads to save his life by promising abundant milk and harvests in every quarter. His promises are spurned but Bres is allowed to live on so that he may advise farmers on the time for ploughing, sowing and reaping.

Although the action of *Cath Maige Tuired* appears to be interpolated between the invasions charted by the *Lebor Gabála*, learned commentators agree that the text carries much deeper resonance in early Irish culture. At the very least it draws on more than conflicts between different early invaders. In his once influential study, *Early Irish History and Mythology* (1946), T. F. O'Rahilly argued that Lug's slaying of Balor is the centre of the narrative around which the rest has accrued. In his view Lug vs. Balor is a figurative treatment of the displacement of an older deity by a younger one in some undatable era from pre-Christian Ireland. He also felt that echoes of this conflict could be found in other early Irish stories. Of more lasting prestige have been the views of French theorist Georges Dumézil (1898–1986), especially as applied to early Ireland and Wales by Alwyn and Brinley Rees in *Celtic Heritage* (1961). Drawing on a comparative overview of Indo-European mythology, Dumézil and the Rees brothers see the Fomorians and the Tuatha Dé Danann representing different functions of stratified early society, a parallel of the conflict between the Vanir and the Aesir in the *Eddas* of Norse mythology.

MILESIANS

The Tuatha Dé Danann are a hard act to follow. As the final invaders, the Milesians sometimes feel diminished compared with their predecessors. Although just as mortal as the readers and hearers of the *Lebor Gabála*, the Milesians appear in two discontinuous narratives. The first, highly contrived and fanciful, imagines their origins in far-off

Scythia and in biblical lands. The second details the Milesian invasion of Ireland adorned with improbable and mysterious episodes while echoing the coming of historical Q-Celtic or Goidelic peoples to the island. Uniting these two streams is an imagined migration from north-western Spain to Ireland, providing the name of their eponymous founder, Míl Espáine [soldier of Spain].

Despite their origins in Scythia, the Milesians were thought to be descended from Japheth, Noah's third son, as were the earlier invaders, the Nemedians. The first Milesian leader was Fénius Farsaid, who was conveniently present at Babel during the biblical separation of languages. Fénius's son Niúl married a pharaoh's daughter named Scota; her name, from the Latin for 'Irishwoman', appears again in a later generation. Their son, Goídel Glas, fashioned the Irish language following his grandfather's instructions, taking the best of many languages. The Milesians were so chummy with their fellow captives, the Israelites, that Moses himself had saved the life of the infant Goídel with the mere touch of his rod. The child had been bitten by a snake, leaving him with a green mark that was the source of his epithet *glas* [green]. Moses pledged that Goídel and his descendants would live in a land free of serpents.

In the generations that follow, the Milesians suffer persecutions from the Egyptians and escape to seek their freedom. They return to Scythia but also spend seven years by the Caspian Sea, migrating eventually to Spain, which they conquer and settle. Míl Espáine, for whom his people are named, joins the narrative in Egypt and leads them through a circuitous itinerary to Spain, where he dies an unexplained death. Sources outside the *Lebor Gabála* posit a link with the ancient city of Miletus in Asia Minor as a possible explanation of the people's name.

The compilers of the *Lebor Gabála* share a fascination with Spain that crops up often in early Ireland. It arises in a wilful confusion between [H]Iberia and Hibernia. At the centre of the fascination is the assertion that a certain strain of the Irish population must be of Spanish origin. The notion survives in the still-heard folk genealogy that the 'black Irish', persons of distinctively dark hair but light skin, are descended from survivors of the Spanish Armada of 1588, a mathematical impossibility. Genome studies of the twenty-first century confirm that populations from the northern Iberian Peninsula do indeed share a genetic inheritance with portions of the Irish population, although such information was unobtainable before contemporary times. It is also possible that Ireland and the Iberian Peninsula share larger portions of pre-Indo-European Neolithic populations than are found in other European countries. Even though elements of Celtic culture survive among the Galicians of northwestern Spain as well as in part of Portugal, only flimsy evidence can be summoned to argue that large bodies of people sailed from the Iberian Peninsula to settle early Ireland. Galician literary tradition complements the Irish assertion. And Iron Age settlements in Galicia, called *castros*, were abandoned in about 600–500 BC, roughly the time the Celtic languages came to Ireland.

A more likely explanation is that both the Iberian Peninsula and Ireland are among the most westerly extensions of Europe and faced each other across a sea that invited early commerce. Agricola (first century AD) worried that Iberia and Hibernia might ally themselves against Roman rule in Britain. The Latin names *Iberia* and *Hibernia* make a slant rhyme. Additionally, Santiago de Compostela, capital of Galicia, was the focus of pious Christian pilgrimage from medieval times, visited by many but talked about by many more. Local tradition in Galway holds that Christopher Columbus stopped there on his voyage to America; this was commemorated in a bronze plaque in 1992.

Before he began his wanderings, Míl Espáine heard the prophecy of the druid Caicer that his people would live in Ireland, a country no Milesian had seen. After Míl's death, one sight of Ireland from afar crystallizes the resolve to go there. Breogan, a Milesian leader, builds a high, defensive tower at Brigantia (an old name for La Coruña, major seaport on the northwest corner of Galicia). Breogan's son Íth the magician climbs the tower in the cold winter twilight and sees the promised green island on the horizon. Íth then leads an advance party to Ireland, progressing to Ailech, a stone fortress in County Donegal, where he is killed by three kings of the Tuatha Dé Danann. Íth's nine brothers and the eight sons of Míl then vow revenge that will mean an occupation of the island.

A fleet of sixty-five vessels sails for Ireland just before Beltaine, but the crews suffer mishaps en route when two sailors, Erannán and Ír, are killed; the latter name becomes an eponym for Ireland (one of several). A fog closes round the approaching fleet so that the sailors lose their bearings and circle the island three times, frightened and helpless. The expedition at last lands at Inber Scéne in Co. Kerry (perhaps Kenmare). Amairgin the poet, a son of Míl, is the first to set foot on the island. After defeating a Tuatha Dé force at Sliab Mis (still known as Slieve Mish), the Milesians meet three goddesses, each of whom asks that Ireland be named for her: Banba, Ériu and Fódla. Each of the three is also named elsewhere in early Irish literature and assigned a complex pedigree as well as special powers. Only Ériu's wish is granted; Erin is her anglicized form, taken from the genitive. Names for the other two are cited as poetic synonyms for Ireland in the Irish language. At Tara the Milesians meet three kings, who may be, according to some texts, the husbands of the three queens: Mac Cuill, Mac Cécht and Mac Gréine. Speaking for all the Milesians, Amairgin asks that the Tuatha Dé either give over their country peacefully for the murder of Íth or fight to keep it. Unready for battle themselves, the Tuatha Dé ask the Milesians to strike a bargain. It is that the invaders will withdraw in their ships and stay nine waves from the shore with the promise that they will withdraw if the Tuatha Dé can muster the power to prevent them from landing again. Once at sea the Milesians are beset by a storm easily perceived as the nefarious magic of the Tuatha Dé. But Amairgin invokes the spirit of Ireland and brings a calm. The Milesians then swiftly cross the nine waves, and Amairgin goes ashore proclaiming that he is the wind on the sea and the god that puts fire in the brain. Colptha is the next to go ashore, and Inber Colptha at the mouth of the Boyne River is named for him.

Éremón, one of Míl Espáine's four sons, leads the Milesians in a sunwise turn (i.e. clockwise) around Ireland to bring good fortune to his enterprise. After a series of skirmishes, the Milesians crush the Tuatha Dé Danann in two battles. The better known is at Tailtiu [Teltown, Co. Meath], later the site of one of the most widely attended fairs in medieval Ireland. The second and lesser confrontation is at Druim Ligen in what is now Co. Donegal. Two leading sons of Míl, Éremón and Éber, divide Ireland between themselves, and they and a third brother, the poet Amairgin, continue to contend with one another. Their mother, Scota, Míl's widow, gives her name to the Irish people as Scoti and the island as Scotia. These were indeed some of the Latin terms for the Irish people and Ireland. Informed sources today tell us that Scoti (more often Scotti) and Scotia may have originated as a derogatory alternative for the usual Latin forms of Hibernian and Hibernia and may have meant something like raider or pirate. While Scotti first referred to the Gaels of Ireland, especially in the northeast, its denotation migrated across the Strait of Moyle to the Highlands of Scotland with the historical kingdom of Dál Riada from the sixth century on from Ulster to Argyll. Thus, Scotti first meant the Irish people and then came to mean the Scottish people when large numbers of Irish people conquered and united that land.

Milesian hegemony spread to all corners of the island, and for a century they ruled without challenge. Eventually there was a rebellion among the subject 'plebeian races', the Aitheachthuatha, made up in part of surviving elements of the Fir Bolg. They launched the usurper Cairbre Cinn-Chait upon his disastrous reign. Cairbre's son Morann, who could have maintained the ill-gotten dynasty, returned the Irish kingship to the Milesians.

Compilers of the *Lebor Gabála* strove to accommodate to the Ireland that existed before the arrival of the Anglo-Normans in 1170. One effort linked place-names with appropriate Milesian characters through creative pedigree-making or aetiologizing. The plain of Mag Ítha in Co. Donegal was thought to be named for Íth, the first Milesian to arrive in Ireland. The chieftain Breaga was linked to the medieval kingdom of Brega between the Liffey and Boyne rivers. The range of mountains known today as Slieve Bloom, earlier Sliab Bladma, were thought to have been named for Bladma, an otherwise insignificant figure. The Milesians do not appear in the Ulster Chronicles or in early Ulster and Connacht narratives. But the influence of the *Lebor Gabála* was so substantial that eventually many aristocratic families could claim a common ancestor in Míl Espáine.

Neither the *Lebor Gabála* nor *Cath Maige Tuired* addresses the question of what happened to the Tuatha Dé Danann. Although the most attractive of the invaders, they leave no narrative footprints. Other sources, some as early as the twelfth century, assert that they went underground. By agreement, the immortal Tuatha Dé leave the upper part of the earth to the mortal Gaelic people and their progeny, while they themselves descend beneath the surface to dwell in the ancient barrows and cairns so numerous in the landscape. The main route to their realm is the *sídh* (see Chapter 6), the distinctive circular-topped mounds still commonly found in Ireland. Under its different spellings, *sídh* becomes the nickname for their otherworld. This disposal of the Tuatha Dé was attractive to the Christian clergy because it explained the perennial association of ancient monuments and the spirit world while also demoting the Tuatha Dé to near-demon status.

Conflict between immortals and mortals causes the Tuatha Dé to deprive the living of their milk and edible grain, for which restitution is later made. Sometimes Dagda is described as not having been killed at Mag Tuired so that he may now rule under the earth. In other texts, his son Bodb Derg is the monarch. Although mortals might consider ancient ruins to be places of fear, especially during the dead of night, the subterranean Tuatha Dé are usually seen as living in an idyllic realm, some names of which were cited in the previous chapter. These include Mag Mell [Pleasant Plain], Emain Ablach [Fortress of Apples], a cognate of the Arthurian Avalon, and the best known, Tír na nÓg [the Land of Youth]. Like the classical Olympians, they may mirror human frailties in petty quarrels and intrigues, even though they enjoy beauty and agelessness. In time they become indistinguishable from the fairies, or *áes sídhe*, creatures widely known in European tradition. In oral tradition, the 'king of the fairies', Finnbheara, is depicted as having first been king of the Tuatha Dé Danann, but prominent figures from the *Lebor Gabála* are not reduced to this status.

A certain malevolence accruing to the underground deities may derive from Christian commentators linking the Tuatha Dé with the Fomorians. Or it may derive from their distinctive power of *féth fíada*, rendering them invisible, so that they may roam at will among mortals undetected. In long-standing folk belief, an old woman of the *sídh* can foresee misfortune in human households and will call out in the night as a warning. She is the *bean* [woman] *sídhe* [of the *sídh*], or banshee, whose lore is still widely known.

8

The Irish Mythological Cycle

SPINNING THE CYCLES

The notion that Old Irish narratives should fall into four cycles, Mythological, Ulster, Fenian and Kings, would have sounded strange to medieval storytellers and scribes. It was instead those great classifiers of data, nineteenth-century German academics, who sorted out these categories for us. They founded philology, the rigorous, systemized study of language. These were the same people who recovered the Old Irish language and compiled its first grammars and dictionaries. Their perception that the internal associations of characters, themes and places could link stories has persisted for more than a century and a half and is now standard. This is so even though the names for the cycles are sometimes troublesome; for example, how can we have a 'Mythological Cycle' when so much of early Irish literature may be subsumed in what is now often called Celtic Mythology? Additionally, the Ulster Cycle was once referred to as the Red Branch Cycle, the Fenian Cycle has been called the Finn or the Ossianic Cycle, and the Cycles of Kings, or the largest portion of them, are sometimes known as the Historical Cycle. Neither is the categorization tidy; some stories such as *Togail Bruidne Da Derga* [The Destruction of Da Derga's Hostel] might fit in more than one cycle while voyage tales such as *Imram Brain* [The Voyage of Bran] might not belong in any (see Chapter 6).

When strung together, the stories from a single cycle do not form a continuous, unbroken narrative or even a continuous timeline, although those dealing with Cúchulainn (Chapter 10) come closest. In some cases the episodes in one cycle appear to echo those of another, as the childhood deeds of Fionn (Chapter 11) are partially modelled on those of Cúchulainn. The love story of Diarmait and Gráinne (Chapter 11) makes several parallels with that of Deirdre and Noíse (Chapter 4), while coming to a dramatically different conclusion. Some characters, such as the legendary king Cormac mac Airt, may appear in more than one cycle. Lug Lámfhota, the principal hero of the Mythological Cycle, makes a significant appearance in the Ulster Cycle, and Manannán mac Lir the sea god may drive his chariot across whichever barriers he pleases.

The people who first memorized and later transcribed the early tales had other means of categorizing them. One was by using an identifying first word in the title. A story whose title begins with the word *Cath* . . . is about a battle. There were at least seventeen such classifications. A title beginning *Fís* . . . includes a vision, *Imram* . . . a voyage, *Tochmarc* . . . an elopement, and so on. While the national epic, *Táin Bó Cuailnge* [The Cattle Raid of Cooley] is often referred to in English as 'The *Táin*', there are several other stories of cattle raids beginning with the word *Táin*. We also have categories for which few examples have survived, such as a title beginning *Úath* . . . indicating stories whose incidents are set in caves.

Early storytellers were also burdened by meeting performance criteria modern readers pretty much ignore. In an oft-cited passage from the Book of Leinster [*Lebor Laignech*] (after 1150), poets are advised on the recitation of potentially 350 stories, of which 250 are 'prime' and the remaining 100 are 'secondary'. Prime stories deal with destructions, cattle-raids, courtships, battles, caves, voyages, violent deaths, feasts, sieges, adventures, elopements and slaughters. The same source actually cites only 200 prime stories and none of the secondary. The uncited stories may simply be missing or, in the case of the secondary, they may be segments of longer primary stories. Which story was performed may well have been determined by the occasion, such as departure on a voyage, the anticipation of a marriage or an appearance at a court of law. The storyteller's choice at such a moment would have nothing to do with our attribution of a cycle of stories on related characters.

Central to the action of the Mythological Cycle are the divinely derived Tuatha Dé Danann, especially the hero Lug Lámfhota, whose links to pre-Christian gods came to light early. The narrower definitions of 'mythology' current in the mid-nineteenth century laid more stake on narrative roots in religion, and through religion to explanations of the origin of the cosmos. No Celtic cosmology survives, as mentioned before, but the story of how the Tuatha Dé Danann and later the mortal Gaels had come to Ireland as told in the *Lebor Gabála* did present a narrative of social origins, at the least. Subsequent decades would uncover divine origins for other heroic figures outside this cycle, such as Cúchulainn, Fionn and the Mórrígan. Further, close examination of non-Western traditions, as well as revolutionary movements in psychology and philosophy, pushed out the limits of what could and could not be considered a 'myth'. In short, if we had done the sorting out of four different categories of stories today we would have given those in this cycle a different label.

Many of the stories in the Mythological Cycle appear to be taking place at an earlier time than the other three. Texts for the cycle appear in some of the oldest codices from the eleventh and twelfth centuries, while episodes within them find correlatives in the twelfth-century *Dindshenchas* or lore of places, implying they were widely known before the arrival of the Normans. This does not mean, however, that the creative energy for this cycle was all spent at an early date. The story from the cycle most popular with today's readers, *Oidheadh Chlainne Lir* [The Tragic Story of the Children of Lir], contains language suggesting it was composed well after great works from other cycles, such as *Táin Bó Cuailnge*; the manuscript dates from about 1500.

The narrative point of view in the Mythological Cycle is more accepting of wizardry and magical transformations. Étaín in *Tochmarc Étaíne* [The Wooing of Étaín] is turned into a butterfly; the Children of Lir become swans for 900 years, as do Angus Óg and his lover, but for a shorter period. These are distinct from the otherworldly intrusions found in all the cycles or the lure of the *sídh* so common in the Fenian.

The *Lebor Gabála Érenn*, discussed in the previous chapter, is not only the longest document of the Mythological Cycle, but is also a prelude and frame for most of the cycle's other stories. Most prominently *Cath Maige Tuired* [The (Second) Battle of Mag Tuired], the most profound and most commented-upon in the cycle, portrays action interpolated in the *Lebor Gabála*, which is why it was discussed in the previous chapter (pp. 140–44).

CHILDREN OF TUIREANN

In action peripheral to the clash between the Tuatha Dé Danann and the Fomorians at Mag Tuired, the three sons of Tuireann – Brian, Iuchair and Iucharba – come to their unhappy ends. *Oidheadh Chlainne Tuireann* [The Tragic Story of the Children of Tuireann] is a tale of animal shapeshifting, magic and revenge in which the three men run afoul of the mighty Lug Lámfhota.

The personage known as Tuireann plays little role in the story, once it is established that he has illustrious lineage (Dian Cécht the physician and possibly the goddess Brigit) and has fathered the three boys upon Ana. Brian and his brothers have reached maturity when the battle of Mag Tuired looms and they find themselves among the Tuatha Dé Danann gearing up for war. After two physicians speculate about healing the wounded king Nuadu, we meet Lug and his father Cian. While travelling north to the plain of Mag Muirtheimne, Cian becomes apprehensive about the approach of three armed men from a family gripped in an unexplained enmity with his own; they are Brian, Iuchair and Iucharba. Seeing himself outnumbered, Cian uses a golden wand to transform himself into a pig and begins rooting in the earth with a nearby herd. Brian knows that Cian is among the herd and thinks of him now as the druidical pig; even if they were to slaughter the herd, such a pig might escape and so Brian transforms his brothers into hounds who indeed separate their quarry from the rest. Once they have returned to human form, Iuchair and Iucharba ask to spare Cian, but Brian will hear none of it and instead demands that his brothers join him in stoning the druidical pig. Cian asks to be returned to his human form as well, and instantly tells the brothers he has tricked them. If they had killed him as a pig, there would be only a small fine to pay. Slain under his own form, his death will demand the far greater honour price or *éiric* demanded for a nobleman. He adds, 'My son Lug will know by the marks of your weapons who has slain me.' Brian then hurls a heavy stone at Cian's head and leads his brothers in pelting him until they reduce the champion to an insignificant, crushed mass. They struggle seven different times to bury the body as the earth rejects it on six occasions.

Lug Lámfhota, meanwhile, has led his armies to victory in battle, after which he asks the whereabouts of his father. When his men find the spot where Cian is buried, Lug travels there and learns from the earth itself the manner of the killing. He digs up the body and examines it, bringing waves of grief and anger upon himself. After chanting a mourning lay, he reburies the body, marks it with an ogham-inscribed monument, and holds funeral games. Lug then proceeds to Tara, where, after encountering Tuireann's three sons, he calls out to the assembly to name what penalty a man should ask of those who have murdered his father. Seeing the initial puzzlement, Lug announces that Cian is dead and that his murderers are present. The unnamed king of the assembly acknowledges that Lug could justly ask for the murderers' own death, but if he were the accused he would ask to pay the *éiric*. At this Brian stands up and confesses that he and his brothers dispatched Cian. Lug agrees to accept a fine instead of taking the brothers' lives.

The honour price requires the brothers to retrieve magical treasurers and to perform dangerous feats. The treasures to be brought back to Ireland are: (i) the three apples of the Garden of the Hesperides; (ii) the skin of the pig of King Tuis 'of Greece' that will cure all diseased and wounded people and will turn water into wine; (iii) the superb poisoned spear in the hands of Pisear, 'king of Persia', that will come to be known as Gáe Assail; (iv) two steeds belonging to Dobar 'king of Sicily'; (v) the magical seven pigs of Assal (sometimes Easal), king of the Golden Pillars, that, eaten at night, will reappear in the morning; (vi) the whelp or puppy Failinis of King Iruad (or Ioruaidh); (vii) the cooking-spit of the women of Inis Fionnchuire (or Findchuire), between Britain and Ireland; and, most enigmatically, (viii) three shouts on the hill of Miodhchaoin (or Midcháin) in Lochlainn, the realm of dangerous invaders. At first the three brothers are surprised by the apparent modesty of the penalty, fearing that each is a trick. After they swear their agreement before the king, Lug explains the necessity and exacting difficulty of each task. The apples from the Garden of the Hesperides, for example, will cure the diseases and wounds of anyone who eats them. Further, the person throwing such an apple will hit anything he wishes without losing the cast apple. Lug does not add, however, what the modern reader knows: that the apples originate in classical mythology and that retrieving them is also the eleventh of Heracles' twelve labours.

After departing from Ireland in silent dismay, Brian, Iuchair and Iucharba build on inexhaustible daring and intelligent resources to overcome the first seven of Lug's assigned tasks, but the eighth journey, to Lochlainn, almost breaks them. Miodhchaoin and his three sons, Áed, Conn and Corc, take the initiative in running their spears through the three sons of Tuireann. The men of Lochlainn are eventually killed, but Brian, Iuchair and Iucharba lie mortally wounded. Stricken though he is, Brian lifts his brothers' heads so that all three might make feeble calls, fulfilling Lug's *éiric*. Iuchair and Iucharba die soon after, and the weakened Brian returns their bodies to their father. Throwing himself on Lug's mercy, Tuireann begs for his son's life, which the hero can save with King Tuis' healing pigskin. But Lug refuses, still angry at the way his father has been cruelly slaughtered. The father then buries his sons in a single grave and dies himself soon after. Lug, however, values the treasures brought by the sons of Tuireann. He chooses to make Gáe Assail his favourite weapon and Failinis his lapdog.

Oidheadh Chlainne Tuireann is often classed as one of the 'Three Sorrows of Storytelling', along with the Deirdre story, Chapter 4, pp. 80–83, and *Oidheadh Chlainne Lir* [The Tragic Story of the Children of Lir], pp. 163–5 below.

MIDIR AND ÉTAÍN

Dating from perhaps the eighth or ninth centuries, *Tochmarc Étaíne* [The Wooing of Étaín] survives in mutilated, disconnected fragments, parts of which were found only in the 1930s. At the centre are the lovers Midir – described as a Tuatha Dé Danann lord of the *sídh* in the *Lebor Gabála* – and the immortal girl Étaín, a ravishing paragon of beauty. While elements of the story appear rooted in inexplicable mystery, it has the feel of a happy-ending fairy-tale for grown-ups, what Myles Dillon called 'a comedy in three acts'.

I

The story of how Midir and Étaín first meet lies under a narrative tangle of marital intrigue among the Tuatha Dé Danann. The Dagda tricks the magician Elcmar, lord of Brug na Bóinne (Newgrange and more than forty nearby tombs), so that he might sleep with his wife Boand, the river goddess. This produces Angus Óg, god of poetry in his maturity, who is given in fosterage to Midir at the *sídh* of Brí Léith (near Ardagh, Co. Longford). When the boy is grown, Midir goes to visit Angus Óg, now resident at Brug na Bóinne. While there, Midir claims to have suffered an injury for which he must be compensated with the fairest maiden in all Ireland, Étaín, daughter of Ailill (another of that name, not Medb's husband). Angus must first win her through the Heraclean task of clearing twelve plains, causing twelve rivers to flow, and delivering the equivalent of Étaín's weight in gold, which he does with Dagda's help.

When Midir returns home with lovely Étaín, his wife Fuamnach is understandably jealous. Taking a magical rod made from the rowan tree given to her by the druid Bresal Etarláim, Fuamnach strikes Étaín, turning her into a pool of water. As it evaporates, the water turns first into a worm and then into a butterfly (or in some translations, an exquisite, bejewelled dragonfly); its wonderful size and beauty fill the air with sweet music and fragrance. Even transformed, Étaín stays by Midir, and he knows it is she. Recognizing this, Fuamnach conjures up a wind to drive the butterfly out to the rocks and waves of the sea. After seven years of this misery, Étaín one day alights upon the breast of Angus Óg. For some time after, he carries Étaín-as-butterfly in a sunlit crystal cage. When Fuamnach learns of this, she drives Étaín in this form far to the north until she lands on a rooftop in Ulster. There she falls into a drinking cup of king Étar's wife, who immediately swallows the small creature. Nine months later Étaín is reborn as the daughter of king Étar. Although she has no sense of it, Étaín is now 1,012 years older than when she first began life as Ailill's daughter.

II

In the second story Étaín is now seen to be married to the mortal *ard rí* [high king] of Ireland, Eochaid Airem, whom she almost betrays accidentally through her own kindness. Her long-ago lover Midir makes a mysterious and unexpected appearance.

Another 1,000 years have passed, the Tuatha Dé Danann have retired to their fairy mounds, and the mortal Milesians or Gaels rule the land. After Eochaid Airem became high king, his subjects refused to pay him tribute because he had no queen. So Eochaid sent emissaries throughout the island in search of a suitable bride. When they found Étaín they were sure she was the right choice and notified Eochaid. When he came to claim her he found her washing her hair, surrounded by gold, silver and gems, beside a bright, bubbling spring at Brí Léith (Midir's residence, though he is not named). Enchanted by the sight of her bare white arms seen through a lush purple cloak, Eochaid immediately falls in love with Étaín. Everything about her seemed perfect: her long tapering fingers, slender ankles and even her delicate narrow feet. Her cheeks were like wild foxgloves, her skin white as newly fallen snow, making her lips seem even redder. Hers would be the standard of beauty against which others would be found wanting. Eochaid and Étaín are soon married.

The bride's almost otherworldly attractiveness becomes a burden for her. Eochaid's brother Ailill Anglonnach is so smitten with her that he becomes frenzied with desire, but he is shamed to speak of it and is thus without chance of a cure. Eochaid's chief physician, Fachtna, diagnoses Ailill's malady and knows that only Étaín's love can remedy it. When Eochaid departs on a royal circuit as part of his kingly duties, Étaín is left in charge of the afflicted Ailill, thought to be dying. The king's instructions are that Ailill's grave be dug, lamentations be made for him, and his cattle be slaughtered upon his death. As soon as they face each other, Ailill Anglonnach confesses the cause of his sickness to Étaín. Seeing his need, Étaín promises to help in the healing by giving herself to him but not in her husband's residence; rather the tryst should take place on a nearby hilltop. At the time of their appointed meeting, Ailill Anglonnach is overcome by a magical drowsiness, and an impostor in his likeness creeps into bed with Étaín. After three nights of lovemaking, Étaín senses that her bed partner is not Ailill, much as he might look like him. When she protests that she wished only to heal Ailill, her phantom lover reveals himself to be Midir of Brí Léith, her immortal husband from 1,000 years earlier. Midir explains that he paid a great bride-price for Étaín but that Fuamnach's jealousy had parted them. His filling of Ailill Anglonnach with deep longing for Étaín was but a ploy so that their meeting might be arranged. When he then begs Étaín to go away with him, she says she cannot without the consent of her current husband, Eochaid Airem. Upon her return to the king's stronghold there is great rejoicing that Étaín's honour has not been spoiled by sleeping with her husband's brother.

III

The third story follows immediately upon the second and portrays Midir's final attempts to have Étaín with him always.

Driven with unfulfilled desire for Étaín, Midir devises trickery to get around her husband Eochaid Airem. One lovely summer day Eochaid looks down from his ramparts at Tara to see a handsome warrior approaching, wearing purple and with long golden hair. Although Eochaid does not know the stranger, he extends hospitality to him. Saying that he knows the identity of his host, the stranger reveals himself to be Midir of Brí Léith and immediately challenges Eochaid to the chess-like game of fidchell, with golden pieces on a silver board. In gamblers' terms, Midir hustles the king, allowing him to win three successive matches, exacting rich prizes from the challenger. When Eochaid allows that the winner of the fourth match can name his own, Midir is, of course, victorious, and he asks to put his arms around Étaín and to kiss her on the mouth. Eochaid baulks at first but then agrees to Midir's request as long as it is in a month's time. Appearing handsomer than ever, Midir arrives on the appointed day only to find that Eochaid has surrounded Tara with armed men and secured the doors. Undeterred, Midir announces that Eochaid has given Étaín's very self to him, causing her to blush with shame. Sternly, the husband reminds Midir of the limits of their agreement and bids him to get on with the embrace and the kiss. Suddenly then, with his weapons tucked under his left arm and Étaín clasped in his right, Midir rises up through the smoke-hole in the ceiling and flies away. Guards stationed outside report seeing two swans, linked together by chains of gold about their necks, disappear in the distance.

Suitably enraged, Eochaid and his men upturn every *sídh* in Ireland, arriving at last at Midir's residence of Brí Léith in the very centre of the island. Hearing the demand that Étaín be returned, Midir responds by producing fifty women (in some accounts sixty) all resembling her so that no one can tell who is the true queen. Eochaid proclaims that his wife's skill and grace at pouring drinks will identify her, selects one of the multitude and returns to married life with her. He has chosen wrongly, however. Midir now tells Eochaid that the true Étaín was already pregnant from intercourse within marriage when she flew out of Tara with Midir. Worse, the simulation of Étaín Eochaid chose from the multitude was his own daughter; by sleeping with her Eochaid has unwittingly fathered a daughter upon his daughter. Horrified to be deceived, Eochaid Airem flattens Brí Léith, retrieves the true Étaín, his wife, and returns to Tara. Thus Midir loses his beloved Étaín for a second time.

Eochaid's incestuously begotten daughter is put out to die, but she is rescued by a herdsman and his wife. Reaching maturity, she exudes the stateliness of her royal forebears and is renowned for her fine embroidery. Another king of Tara, Eterscél, takes her for his queen. According to the *Tochmarc Étaíne*, Eterscél and the daughter of Eochaid's incest give birth to Conaire Mór, the young *ard rí* who meets a tragic and untimely death. This is but one of three versions of Conaire Mór's lineage, the best known of which comes in his own narrative, as follows.

CONAIRE MÓR AND
DA DERGA'S HOSTEL

The story of beneficent high king Conaire Mór, the innocent victim of
relentless fate, is a kind of sequel to the story of Midir and Étaín,
though compiled by a different hand and in a different style. It is found
in the eleventh-century text *Togail Bruidne Da Derga* [The Destruction
of Da Derga's Hostel], antecedents of which exist as early as the eighth
and ninth centuries. Although the action is set in what is now Leinster,
the story is often classed with the Ulster Cycle, in part because several
Ulster heroes appear in it, perhaps inserted by later redactors. Étaín,
lushly described, also appears, but now she is depicted as married to
Eochaid Feidlech, a brother of Eochaid Airem. Their stepdaughter
Mes Buachalla [cowherd's fosterling] marries Eterscél, but as she is
already pregnant, the true father of Conaire is a mysterious man who
appeared to her in bird form. At the moment of conception he declared,
'You will bear me a son, and that son may not kill birds, and Conaire
shall be his name.'

Such a command is called in Irish a *geis* (pl. *gessa*), an idiosyncratic
form of taboo found widely in early Irish literature. The unfortunate
person receiving the *geis* may have done nothing to merit such a
burden, and the person or forces applying it may appear wilful or
capricious. Yet the *geis* is not to be escaped. To violate it is to risk
death or catastrophe for one's entire family. And so it is with the
well-intentioned king Conaire Mór, whose just and prosperous rule is
threatened by the outcome of a host of *gessa*; all but one are prohib-
itions. (i) Birds must always be privileged in his kingdom. (ii) He may
not pass sunwise or righthandwise around Tara nor lefthandwise,
withershins, around Brega, the plain between the Boyne and Liffey
rivers. (iii) He may not hunt the *cláenmíla* [crooked beasts]. (iv) He
may not stay away from Tara on any ninth night. (v) He may not sleep
in a house from which the light of a fire is visible after sunset and into
which one can see from the outside. (vi) He shall not allow three red
men to go before him into a red man's house. (vii) He must not allow
plundering raiders to land during his reign. (viii) He may not allow a
lone man or woman to visit his residence after sunset. And finally (ix)

he may not try to settle a conflict between two of his subjects. In the run of *Togail Bruidne Da Derga*, however, Conaire Mór will unintentionally violate every one of these *gessa*.

Trouble begins when Conaire's three foster-brothers, Fer Gair, Fer Lí and Fer Rogain, all sons of the champion hunter-warrior Donn Désa, start to raid and plunder the countryside. Conaire banishes all of them from Ireland, as he does again with another band of brigands, the three Ruadchoin of the Cualu south of the Liffey, when they too begin to harass Conaire's subjects. At sea these unwanted exiles meet a band of despoilers or reavers led by the one-eyed Ingcél Cáech, a Briton, and together with the banished, outlaw sons of Queen Medb of Connacht – seven men all named Maine – they pillage first Britain and then Ireland. In Britain they slaughter a local king along with Ingcél's parents and brothers. Meanwhile, Conaire Mór is in Thomond in the south of Ireland, where he settles a dispute between two of his foster-brothers, two Corpres, an act of justice that is his first violation of the *gessa* that will lead to his own downfall. Accepting the hospitality of both foster-brothers, he stays five nights with each, breaking a second *geis*.

Ingcél Cáech and the other brigands land with 150 boats at Howth, northeast of what is now Dublin. Conaire, at the same time, is travelling south from Tara, in what is now Co. Meath, passing to the left of Tara and the right of Brega, and unwittingly hunting the forbidden *cláenmíla* of Cerna. His goal is the hostel of Da Derga, a friend on whom he has bestowed many gifts and who can be expected to welcome him. The hostel bestrides the small river Dodder to the south, which is perhaps Bohernabreena or Donnybrook in south Co. Dublin. En route Conaire meets a forbidding churl, Fer Caille, a dark man of the wood with one eye, one hand, and one foot who carries a black pig on his back. Approaching the hostel Conaire sees before him three horsemen dressed in red, and, recognizing another possible violation of a *geis*, asks his son to drive them off. The son fails, and the party enters the residence of Da Derga, which means 'red man'.

Fearful portents do not end at the doorway. A lone female seer of breath-stopping hideousness confronts Conaire. Each of her beetle-black shins is as long as a weaver's beam. A greyish woollen mantle does not cover her lower (i.e. pubic) hair, which reaches as far as her knee. Her lips are on one side of her head. They do not prevent her from speaking, as she puts her shoulder against the doorpost, casting an evil eye upon the king and the youths surrounding him. She is Cailb, and she prophesies that all the defenders will be destroyed except for what the birds can take away in their claws.

Eager for both revenge and booty, the invading reavers led by Ingcél Cáech and the three foster-brothers advance inland with 5,000 men. Da Derga's Hostel is in many ways a magical dwelling, described as having seven doorways (in some texts nine), but this does not mean it is invincible. Ingcél can spy upon the residence, describing the inhabitants to his fellow brigands. Fer Rogain, Conaire's foster-brother, identifies the defenders from the descriptions and predicts which among them will survive.

In three assaults on the hostel the attackers set it on fire, and three times the flames are extinguished. Many in the hostel are slaughtered, the first being Lomna the fool, as he had predicted for himself. The defenders, including Conaire, counterattack, slaying the thieving bandits left and right. Then the battle turns on a matter of water. Druids with the marauders cast an exhausting thirst upon Conaire, which he cannot slake as so much of the hostel's water has been thrown on the flames. The Dodder, flowing below, offers no help, and so the hero Mac Cécht searches Ireland for a drink for the king. (He is not identical with the Mac Cécht of the Tuatha Dé Danann; in some texts the Ulster hero Conall Cernach assists Conaire instead of Mac Cécht.) As he is returning with water from faraway Roscommon, two invaders are decapitating Conaire. Mac Cécht quickly dispatches both killers and pours the water he has brought into Conaire's headless neck. Astonishing all, the severed head then speaks: 'Excellent is Mac Cécht; good is Mac Cécht, who brings a drink to a king and does the work of a warrior.'

Despite the destruction of Da Derga's Hostel, Conaire's side suffers minimal losses, while of the brigands only five escape out of 5,000.

SWAN CHILDREN OF LIR

The story of Lir's four children magically transformed into swans could easily be mistaken for a fairy-tale until we note that father and children are all members of the Tuatha Dé Danann. The action is set during the period when the semi-divine Dé Danann are losing ground to the mortal and more prosaic Milesians. Despite this asserted link with events in the twelfth-century *Lebor Gabála*, the narrative appears to be of much later composition, the manuscript dating from about 1500. Events in *Oidheadh Chlainne Lir* [The Tragic Story of the Children of Lir] were not much celebrated in oral tradition but have more recently become among the best known from early tradition through the efforts of cultural revivalists and educators. Oisin Kelly's huge sculpture of the children changing back from swans into elderly humans is the focal point of the Garden of Remembrance, Parnell Square, Dublin. *Oidheadh Chlainne Lir* is one of the 'Three Sorrows of Storytelling', along with the Deirdre story (Chapter 4, pp. 80–83) and *Oidheadh Chlainne Tuireann* [The Tragic Story of the Children of Tuireann] (pp. 153–5 above).

When the Tuatha Dé Danann are defeated by the Milesians at the battle of Tailtiu, they seek out a new king so they will not be ruled by their conquerors. Two of the five candidates are Bodb Derg of Connacht and Lir of what is now Co. Armagh; he is not the Lir of Manannán's patronymic, mac Lir. Bodb Derg's selection disappoints Lir, who retreats to his *sídh* of Finnachad, where his unhappiness is compounded by the death of his wife. Magnanimously, Bodb offers the hands of his foster-daughters, and Lir chooses the eldest, usually named Áeb. In quick succession she bears two sets of twins, first the daughter, Finnguala, and son, Áed, and then two sons, Fiachra and Conn, after whose birth she dies. To compensate Lir for this loss, Bodb Derg offers the hand of a second daughter, Aífe, who cherishes her stepchildren, at least at first.

Proving childless in her own marriage, Aífe's attitude toward the four children takes a dark turn. Overcome with a debilitating jealousy, she takes to her bed, pretending sickness for a year. Brusquely pronouncing herself cured, she declares she will visit her father in Killaloe in what is now Co. Clare, taking the children with her. A wary Finnguala, who has seen evil portents in a dream, resists. On the way to the west, Aífe begins to rant against the children on patently false charges, claiming that they are depriving her of her husband's love. She orders her servants to butcher them on the spot – Lough Derraveragh [Ir. Dairbhreach: with an oak plantation] in what is now Co. Westmeath. When the retainers refuse, Aífe shoves the children into the water and produces a druidical wand (or sword) to metamorphose the children into swans. Finnguala, who like all the children has retained the power of speech, protests their blamelessness and asks Aífe how long their unjust punishment will last. The stepmother answers: 900 years in three sentences of increasing misery – 300 years here at Lough Derraveragh; 300 years in the North Channel, the narrowest passage between Ireland and the Mull of Kintyre in Scotland, sometimes called the Sea of Moyle; the last 300 years on the stormy west coast of Ireland between Erris and the small island of Inishglora, Co. Mayo. Aífe's spell upon the children, she explains, will end when a woman from the south, Deoch daughter of Fingen, king of Munster, unites with a man of the north, Lairgnéan, son of Colmán of Connacht. Now that Finnguala has asked the terms of the curse, any power of the Tuatha Dé Danann to lift it has been nullified. Aífe does allow, however, along with their power of speech, the children as swans to retain their senses and faculties, as well as an ability to sing, supremely among mortals. Leaving the children at Lough Derraveragh, Aífe proceeds to Bodb Derg's palace where her treachery is soon discovered and she is punished by being transformed into a demon (sometimes vulture) of the wind, condemned to wander through air until the end of time.

In the midst of their pain and sorrow, the child-swans can indeed sing and with eloquence, poetry and fine speech. People from all over Ireland flock to Lough Derraveragh to hear them. Bodb, Lir and other prominent figures attend. The original text includes many verse passages of their songs. At the end of each 300-year term, Finnguala reminds her three brothers to move on. During their second exile they encounter a party of horsemen, including two other sons of Bodb Derg, near an estuary of the River Bann. The men have been looking for the children and give them news of the Tuatha Dé Danann. Such

1. MAIDEN CASTLE

The hillfort in Dorset is the best preserved of more than 3,000 Iron Age settlements in Britain, but is somewhat misnamed. The man-made hill was never primarily a fort nor was it ever a castle. The 'maiden' derives from the early British *mai dun*: great hill.

2. TARA

County Meath's celebrated hill may never have been the court of early Irish epic or the palace of nineteenth-century romance, but it was long a centre of religious ceremony sacred to Medb, considered a goddess in pre-Christian time.

3. THE COLIGNY CALENDAR

These bronze first-century BC plates contain the oldest writing in any Celtic language. The sixteen columns represent a five-year cycle, complete with calendar festivals and days thought to bring good or ill fortune.

4. HALLSTATT EXCAVATIONS

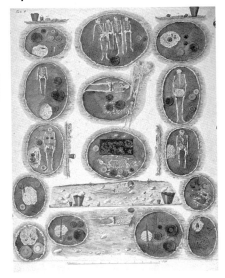

The discovery in 1846 of this early Iron Age cemetery in Upper Austria confirmed the existence of assuredly Celtic culture that predated the Romans. This is just one of a series of detailed illustrations that were made of the burials there. 'Hallstatt' now denotes the style of an epoch of Celtic art.

5. THE BOOK OF DURROW

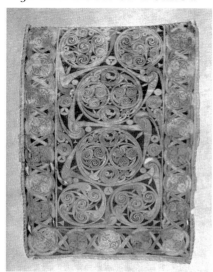

This illuminated manuscript of the Gospels was created *c.*660–680: more than a century and a quarter before the better-known *Book of Kells*. The book was found at Durrow, County Offaly, Ireland, and its distinctive artwork, especially the rondels, is a legacy from pre-Christian tradition.

6. THE BATTERSEA SHIELD

Red glass inlays on copper facing distinguish this shield found in the Thames at Battersea. The shield is of uncertain date (100 BC–AD 100?) and its outline identical to those from elsewhere in the Celtic world.

7. THE GUNDESTRUP CAULDRON

Although perhaps constructed in the Balkans (fourth to third centuries BC?) and found in Denmark, the silver vessel embraces the richest display of early Celtic iconography that we have. It stands 14 inches tall, lies 25.5 inches in diameter and holds 28.5 gallons.

8. GUNDESTRUP DETAIL: CERNUNNOS

An antlered divinity is widely known in pre-Roman Celtic Europe, but his name survives from only one inscription. He is seen here in the conventional half-lotus pose with two torcs, one around his neck and the other in his hand.

9. GUNDESTRUP DETAIL: HUMAN SACRIFICE OR REBIRTH

This may represent Teutates, one of the three principal divinities of Gaul, who, according to Roman commentary, accepted drowned human victims. But perhaps this scene depicts a dead man about to be regenerated through immersion.

10. GUNDESTRUP DETAIL: TARANIS

Wheel symbolism, conventionally associated with the sun, predates the Celts at Hallstatt by half a millennium, but continues in Celtic iconography. Taranis, the Gaulish god of thunder, often seen with wheel imagery, may be depicted in this panel.

11. THE GOD SUCELLUS

Cult partner of Nantosuelta, Sucellus, 'the good striker', was worshipped in Gaul and Britain. Opinion is divided about the hammer always seen in his hand: perhaps a weapon, cooper's tool, fencing instrument, wand or sceptre.

12. THE GODDESS EPONA

Epona, whose name means 'horse', was the focal point of one of the most widespread cults that ranged from what is now Britain to Serbia, through Rome to North Africa. She also appears in Apuleius' Latin proto-novel *Metamorphoses*, III, 27 (second century AD)

13. THE UFFINGTON HORSE

At 365 feet (112 metres), the horse was cut through turf to underlying chalk. The graceful design resembles horses found on pre-Roman British coins. Often thought to depict Epona, the horse was actually more likely to have been constructed before her cult came to Britain.

14. MINIATURE WAGON FROM MÉRIDA

This charming miniature from pre-Roman Spain foreshadows the boars of Irish and Welsh literature, such as Twrch Twryth hunted by Culwch or the unnamed boar pursued by Fionn and Diarmait. Mérida was later the Roman capital of Iberia.

15. SHEELA-NA-GIGS IN KILPECK

The meaning of these outwardly obscene figures is much contended: were they cautions against lust or patronesses of fertility? Their Hiberno-English name is of no help: it means 'Sheila of the breasts', but the figure's breasts are not prominent.

16. HEADS AT ENTREMONT

Evidence of the darker side of the early Celts survives at Entremont in Provence, where a shrine from the second century BC displays human heads plus models of heads. The heads of heroes were thought to possess talismanic powers.

fleeting gestures of good will are of little avail. Eventually the people of Ireland forget about Lir's offspring.

In their third exile the children's songs reach the ears of a new character introduced to the story. The young man is named Áebhric and appears to be a well-born cleric living in self-sustaining isolation near Erris [Ir. Irrus Domnann, Iorras Domhnann]. Like all the others, Áebhric is entranced by the children's singing, but he decides to write down their story so that we may read it now. Their 900-year exile complete, the children return to the *sídh* of Finnachad only to find it abandoned and desolate. Their only hope now is to wait at Inishglora [Ir. *Inis Gluaire*: island of Brightness] until Mo Cháemóc, a disciple of St Patrick, brings the Gospel of Christianity to the island. Hearing the evangelist's bell, the swan children begin to sing with it, making themselves known to him. To help the children forget their suffering, Mo Cháemóc brings them into his household and there links them together with a silver chain.

Meanwhile, without the children's knowing it, Aífe's prophecy is fulfilled. South and north are united with Deoch of Munster's marriage to Lairgnéan, and they now reign in Connacht. Once introduced to the reader, Deoch proves vain and grasping. She covets the singing swans for herself and demands that the king secure them for her. Bowing to her command, Lairgnéan tries to pull them away from Mo Cháemóc by yanking their silver chain, and in so doing unwittingly returns them to human form. That form is no longer childlike, of course. After 900 years of exile the four offspring of Lir are virtually pillars of dust. Mo Cháemóc baptizes them immediately, just in time to save their immortal souls.

ANGUS ÓG AND CÁER

The motif of swan transformation appears in yet another story from the Mythological Cycle, that of Angus Óg's impossible love for the beautiful Cáer. Angus's usual role is to aid imperilled lovers, as he does in the tale of Midir and Étaín (above). His own love for a woman he has never met presents his wit and inventiveness with its most ticklish challenge. The Old Irish version of the story (c. 1150) is titled

Aislinge Óenguso [The Vision of Angus], and the key elements of the narrative persisted in oral tradition until modern times under the title *Angus Óg agus Cáer* [Angus Óg and Cáer]. It is an Irish instance of the international tale type 400, the swan maiden.

A figure of youth (literal translation of Óg), beauty and poetry, Angus has the best claim to be the god of love among the Tuatha Dé Danann. Introduced in the *Lebor Gabála* (Chapter 7) he remained popular with storytellers in different cycles over the centuries. Stories of his conception and birth are extraordinarily complex and vary from text to text, as alluded to at the beginning of the account of Midir and Étaín (above). The most usual is that his father is the Dagda, 'the good god', who slept with Boand (the Boyne River) while she was still married to Nechtan. The Dagda had sent the cuckold Nechtan on a journey while the poor man was under a spell that took away his sense of time and hunger. When he returns in nine months he is deluded into thinking he had been away only a day. The parents of the newborn Angus ask Elcmar to be the child's foster-father as a means of hiding their infidelity. In rival versions, the Dagda is known by the name Eochaid Ollathair when he is seduced by the wife of Elcmar, one Eithne, probably an alternative name for Boand. In any case, Angus Óg displaces either Dagda or Elcmar to assume his usual residence, Brug na Bóinne [house, hostel of the Boyne]. The Irish phrase denotes the passage-graves at the bend of the Boyne River, Co. Meath: Dowth, Knowth and most famously Newgrange. People composing and recording early Irish narrative had no access to knowledge of the great antiquity (*c.*3200 BC) and functions of these monuments (e.g. the shaft of sunlight on the winter solstice), which is widespread today. At Brug na Bóinne, whichever monument was implied, trees are always in fruit, and a cooked pig is on the spit, always ready for eating. Angus Óg is given credit for bringing the first cows from India to Ireland, a feat attributed elsewhere to Manannán mac Lir. So blessed is Angus that four swans circle over his head when he travels, and while at home he drinks the ale of immortality. A protector of many male lovers, most prominently Diarmait Ua Duibne of the Fenian Cycle, Angus may intervene by interposing his cloak of invisibility; one wave of the cloak and the protected one cannot be seen by enemies.

Despite the efficacy of his help to other lovers, the torment of Angus's own love is hard to remedy. He is smitten by the beauty of a young girl he sees in a dream, a girl he has never met and cannot identify. The longing for her afflicts him with an ailment that demands he find her. He searches for her one full year. With the help of Bodb Derg, Angus learns that her name is Cáer, and that she is the daughter of Ethal Anbúail, the prince of a *sídh* in Connacht. Her nickname Ibormeith [yew berry] implies something of the nature of her character. The long-living evergreen yew is commonly a symbol of immortality in European tradition and is still often seen in Christian cemeteries. Wood from the tree is hard to burn and was the favoured material in druids' wands.

The girl's father Ethal reveals that Cáer is more powerful than Angus Óg. Further, if he were to win her, he would have to accomplish the conquest with assistance from the many Tuatha Dé Danann. Complicating matters even more, Ethal explains that his daughter is a shape-shifter, spending alternate years as a swan and in the form of the beautiful woman of Angus's dream.

She is in swan form when Angus finds her at a lake where she is surrounded by many other swans. Each of the other swan maidens is linked to another with a silver chain; only Cáer's chain is gold. Gifted with human speech, Cáer promises to join Angus if only he will let her return. Her transformation to and from swan form, as well as that of the other women, takes place at the festival of Samain. And, it appears, the only way for Angus to be with Cáer is when this metamorphosis is taking place. On the next Samain, then, Angus approaches Cáer's lake, embraces her, and then takes flight with her. He too has changed himself into a swan. The pair then fly three times around the lake, their enchanting song sending everyone who hears it into blissful sleep for three days and three nights. United at last, Angus Óg and Cáer take wing for his palace at Brug na Bóinne. While he lives at the bend of the Boyne, Angus Óg never ages, and his songs and poems remain as clear and fresh as the day he writes them.

9

The Ulster Cycle

Part I

STORIES ABOUT THE ULAID

So great has the literary prestige of the Ulster or Ultonian Cycle been, both in the Irish language and in English translation, that from a distance it sometimes appears to be the only cycle of early heroic stories. Contained within its mostly prose narratives are ferocious exploits of early Ireland's greatest mortal hero, Cúchulainn, and plangent tales of the celebrated tragic lover Deirdre, as well as the *Táin Bó Cuailnge*, the only epic in any Celtic language to stand comparison with *Beowulf* or even the *Iliad*. Some of the glow surrounding the phrase 'Ulster Cycle' derives from the attempts of nineteenth-century nationalists to recast the action in a chivalric mode. The impulse was to see the stories of the Ulster Cycle as equivalent to those of the Arthurian legends, exalted in Britain at that time as a kind of national myth. In the 1870s and 1880s writers such as Standish James O'Grady freely expanded upon fragments of early texts to fashion the kinds of figures, Cúchulainn especially, that would rally the aspirations of an oppressed people. Such sentiment favoured the alternative name 'Red Branch' for the Ulster Cycle and conceived of its leading male figures as knights. Seen with a colder eye, however, the narratives of the Ulster Cycle are much older than the high Middle Ages and their meaning is subject to wider interpretation than mere role modelling.

The wellspring of history at the root of the Ulster Saga concerns a powerful prehistoric people of the north of Ireland known as the Ulaid. With a traditional seat at the 18-acre Bronze Age hillfort of Emain Macha, now called Navan Fort, two miles west of the town of Armagh, the Ulaid dominated much of the northeastern quadrant of Ireland. At times their hegemony spread from the mouth of the Boyne River to as far west as Leitrim. The nine-county province of Ulster is named for them, 'Ulster' being a later coinage employing the Norse suffix -ster. The now archaic Ultonia, from the Latin for Ulster, also derives from the Ulaid. Six counties are still a part of the United Kingdom – Antrim, Down, Armagh, (London-) Derry, Tyrone and Fermanagh, while three are in the Republic of Ireland: Donegal, Cavan and Monaghan. All Irish counties were carved out and named by English occupiers in the seventeenth century and thus are not cited in early narratives, except as a means of interpreting archaic place names. Archaeological investigation at Emain Macha from the mid-twentieth century on has yielded extensive information about the wealth and power of the Ulaid, but it no more proves the historicity of the Ulster stories than excavation of the true Troy demonstrates that the *Iliad* is a historical document. Imagined Irish narratives, like Greek and also Welsh stories, exist with real-world references. Most of them, including most of the action of the *Táin Bó Cuailnge*, can be plotted on the map.

In most Ulster stories, Conchobar mac Nessa reigns at Emain Macha. He bears a matronymic rather than a patronymic, perhaps a nod to the intrigues of his mother Ness, who helped him to achieve the throne. Protagonist in several of his own stories, none of them recounted here, Conchobar is usually portrayed as a benign and just ruler, except for his unsavoury lust in the Deirdre story for a young woman whom he cannot have. As contemporary readers are likely to know the Deirdre story best, they often take a darker view of Conchobar than his portrayals elsewhere would warrant. One of his three residences is Cráebruad [Red Branch], containing a large roofbeam painted red, thus giving the alternative name for the Cycle, Red Branch. Given that his name may have three irreconcilable pronunciations, depending on the context, 'KON-ah-hoor', 'KONK-uh-var', and 'KRA-hoor', 'Conchobar' is often anglicized to the simpler 'Conor'.

Ulster struggles with mortal not supernatural enemies, the men and women of the five-county province of Connacht, west of the Shannon, comprising what today are Leitrim, Sligo, Mayo, Roscommon and Galway. Steeliest of these foes is Queen Medb, whose fortress at Cruachain lies near Tulsk, Co. Roscommon. Leading the Ulstermen against Connacht are three heroes. Cúchulainn, the most prominent, is the focus of the next chapter. The other two command much attention on their own.

Lusty Fergus mac Róich is a tutor and foster-father of Cúchulainn and had a prior claim to the throne at Emain Macha before Ness's machinations gave it to Conchobar. Tall as a giant, Fergus has something of the supernatural in him. He boasts the strength of 700 men and can consume at one sitting seven deer, seven pigs, seven cows and seven vats of liquor. His magical sword, Caladbolg, is as long as a rainbow. His sexual energy is implicit in his name. *Fergus* means man-strength or semen in Irish; his earliest patronymic *Roach* may derive from *ro-ech* [great horse]. He has huge genitalia, requiring seven women to satisfy him. The phallus-like upright stone at the hill of Tara, often known as Lia Fáil, was called *Bod Fhearghais* [Fergus's penis]* in the nineteenth century. In the *Táin Bó Cuailnge* Fergus goes into exile with the enemy Queen Medb but remains in touch with the Ulster champions. As cited in Chapter 4, Fergus encourages Deirdre and Noíse to return to Ireland, where they suffer Conchobar's treachery. Some commentators believe the Deirdre episodes may have become attached to the *Táin* as a means of explaining Fergus's sojourn with Medb. Six centuries after the action, his spirit is recalled from the afterlife to recount the story of the *Táin* to the poet Senchán Torpéist, to whom the writing of the epic is attributed.

Like Fergus, Conall Cernach embodies many supernatural elements. His names mean 'wolfish' and 'of the victories'. Conall too has a tremendous appetite, once consuming an entire boar, a beast so large it required sixty oxen to pull it. He has a distinguished lineage: Amairgin of the Milesians, the first poet in Ireland, lies with Findchóem, foster-mother of Cúchulainn, to become Conall's father. A guardian of boundaries, Conall appears to be an ancestor deity. He is a foster-brother and virtual twin of Cúchulainn, his partner in many adventures, whose death he will avenge. Like the classical Perseus and the Christian St George, he can be a dragon slayer. His aggression against the Connachtmen is relentless, but Medb asks Conall to kill her hus-

---

* Possibly named for local hero Fergus Caisfiaclach [crooked tooth], whose sobriquet was *Bód fo Bregaigh* [fire of Brega]; allusions to the two Ferguses may have become conflated in the 1830s when the Lia Fáil was erected.

band Ailill when he is caught in an act of infidelity. In Chapter 8 p. 162, Conall is an ally of Conaire Mór in *Togail Bruidne Da Derga* [The Destruction of Da Derga's Hostel], a story sometimes included with the Ulster Cycle.

Stories in the Ulster Cycle probably started in oral tradition and began to be transcribed as early as the seventh century. Surviving written texts are most numerous from the eleventh and twelfth centuries, and they continued to flourish in the oral traditions of Ireland, Gaelic Scotland and the Isle of Man through the eighteenth century, with some survivals in small communities as late as the twentieth century. Emain Macha, seat of the Ulaid, was founded sometime in the first millennium BC, and appears to be noted in Ptolemy's *Geography* (second century AD). It was destroyed or abandoned before the advent of Christian evangelization in the fifth century. Medieval ecclesiastical redactors of the stories contrived a pseudo-history in which Emain Macha was created in the seventh century BC and many Ulster events synchronize with episodes in the Bible. In such a reckoning the death of Conchobar mac Nessa occurs at the very moment of Christ's crucifixion on Calvary. This timetable is still found in popular memory.

As with the other four cycles, the Ulster stories do not form a continuous narrative whole, except as modern readers have imposed an order upon them. The narratives in the present chapter are disconnected, although the first dealing with the unique debility of the Ulstermen is usually seen as a *remscél* or foretale of the *Táin Bó Cuailnge* and bound with it. Another *remscél* of the *Táin* is *Longas mac nUislenn* [Exile of the Sons of Uisnech], which is recounted in Chapter 4 along with another Deirdre story, *Oided Mac nUisnig* [Death of the Sons of Uisnech]. Cúchulainn, principal hero of the cycle, does not appear in the first two stories in this chapter but provides dynamic presence in the second two. He dominates the action of the next chapter.

MACHA'S CURSE

The question of how the Ulstermen came to suffer debilitating pain at the time of their greatest difficulty, equal to that of a woman in the pangs of labour, is usually thought to precede the action of the *Táin*. Implications of Macha's fatal footrace, however, are implicit in many Ulster stories. The Irish title for this vignette is *Noínden Ulad*, an abbreviation of *Ces Noínden Ulad* or The Nine Days' Debility of the Ulstermen.

A rich landlord named Crunniuc mac Agnomain lives in a lonely place in the mountains of Ulster with his four sons. He is a widower without female companionship. While he is alone in the house a refined and elegant woman comes to him, and immediately settles in, taking on the domestic chores as if she were familiar with the house and used to the routines there. At evening she puts everything in order without being asked, all without speaking. Then she climbs into bed and lays her hand on his side, signalling that she wishes to be his wife. Together they prosper, Crunniuc much aided by his still unnamed wife's efforts. Good food and fine clothing abound. She delights in her husband's handsomeness, and soon she conceives their first child.

The announcement of a fair in Ulster attracts crowds of men and women, boys and girls. Crunniuc, dressed in his best finery, makes clear his desire to join the crowds. Darkly cautious, the wife warns her husband not to go. 'You will talk about us at the gathering, and that will bring us danger. Our happy union together will continue only if you do not speak of me at all.'

'I won't utter a word,' Crunniuc promises.

The brilliant festival turns out to be all that Crunniuc had wished for, with bright costumes and plenty of processions, games, combats, tournaments and races. At the ninth hour the chariot races begin, and the royal horses carry the day. Crowds praise the king (who is never named as Conchobar mac Nessa) and queen, repeating the poems of the bards. A retainer cries out, 'Never before have two such horses been seen to match these. They are the swiftest in all of Ireland!'

'My wife is faster,' boasts Crunniuc impetuously, forgetting his pledge.

'Seize that man,' thunders the king. 'And lock him up until his wife can be brought here to compete in the races.'

The king's messengers are quickly sent to Crunniuc's residence, where his wife greets them graciously, but asks why they have come. They explain that they have come so that she might release her husband because he has bragged that her speed is greater than that of the royal horses, news that fills her with dismay.

'He has spoken unwisely,' she murmurs. 'It was not fitting for him to say that. As you can see, I cannot come. I am about to deliver our child.'

'If you don't come,' the messengers remind her, 'he'll be a dead man.'

So she agrees to go with the king's messengers to the festival. Once there her advanced pregnancy draws unwanted attention, causing her to grumble, 'It is not becoming that I should be stared at because of my condition.' And then she cries out to them: 'A mother bore each one of you! Help me! At least wait until I have delivered my child!'

When the crowd is unresponsive, her tone changes. 'Because you have taken no pity on me, a long-lasting evil will come out of this and it will descend on all the Ulstermen.'

'What is your name?' asks the king.

'My name, and the name of my offspring will be attached to this place,' she answers. 'I am Macha, the daughter of Sainrith mac Imaith.'

In all of early Irish tradition there are three Machas, each a discrete personality, although each is a daughter of the same mother, Ernmass. One, a prophetess, is the wife of Nemed in the *Lebor Gabála*. The second, a warrior, also called Mong Ruadh [red-haired], is an Ulster queen who marries her rival, Cimbáeth, and dominates him. The Macha of this story is the daughter of a king whose name means 'Strange, son of ocean'.

The king's horses are brought forward, and the race begins. There is little suspense as Crunniuc's boast turns out to be well justified. Macha is ahead all around the track, and as she crosses the finish line she gives out a cry of pain. Her time has come. Having just won the race she falls to the ground and delivers not one but two children, a son and a daughter. As she gives birth, she cries out in her agony that all who hear her will suffer the same pangs for five days and four nights in their times of greatest difficulty. And this debility will be upon them for nine generations.

And so all who hear her are afflicted, made so weak with simulated labour pains they cannot lift a weapon. Some are exempted – Crunniuc, her still beloved husband, small boys, women and Cúchulainn because he is a son and avatar of the divine Lug Lámfhota.

According to the text, Macha's curse also explains the meaning of *Emain Macha*, as *emain* may mean 'twins'. The rival etymology, authorized by the seventeenth-century historian Geoffrey Keating, is that Macha wife of Cimbáeth marked out the area with her brooch, and *eo* [bodkin] + *muin* [neck] gives us *emain*.

CARVING UP MAC DA THÓ'S PIG

Two very old themes dominate the sometimes humorous ninth-century narrative of *Scéla mucce Meic Dathó* [The Story of Mac Da Thó's Pig]. The first is the incalculably ancient enmity between Ulster and Connacht. The second is the violent contest over the 'champion's portion' [Ir. *curadmír*], the favoured cut of pork given to the strongest man at a table. Posidonius (first century BC) described a similar competition among the ancient Gauls. This story is one of the very few in the Ulster Cycle where Cúchulainn does not make an appearance, even though thirty other heroes are cited.

Mac Da Thó [son of two mutes(?)] is a wealthy landowner in Leinster, who delights in his ownership of two animals. The greater of these is the mighty hound, Ailbe, who musters the ferocity of ten armies and can defend all of Mac Da Thó's properties by himself. Second is a huge, tame boar that has been reared for seven years and seven days on milk so that it may someday furnish a year-long feast when it is slaughtered. Interest in Ailbe, the fighting hound, prompts a bidding contest between two forces who despise each other, Ailill and Medb of Connacht on one hand, and Conchobar mac Nessa of Ulster on the other.

A host of innate nobility and generosity, Mac Da Thó receives visitors from the opposing forces at his well-appointed residence marked by the magical number seven: seven gates, seven doors, seven hearths and seven cauldrons always brimming with beef and pork. He explains his attraction to the number by explaining that guests receive hospitality as we have openings in our heads: two eyes, two nostrils, two ears and a mouth. And, further, he feels that to walk by a cauldron and not partake of the plenty would be an insult to the host.

Mac Da Thó's graciousness as a host is abruptly challenged when the two forces offer favours to him simultaneously to gain possession of the hound. Medb and Ailill will provide 160 prime dairy cows, and a prize chariot drawn by the two best horses in the western province, and these gifts will be repeated each year through the lives of his children and grandchildren. Not to be outdone, Conchobar responds with offers of jewellery, warm friendship and a secure alliance, and an offering of fresh cattle every year for ever. At the same time, Mac Da Thó senses a threat. If Medb and Ailill do not get what they want, they could easily assassinate Mac Da Thó and his wife, and if Conchobar is insulted by the host's response, he will surely attack as well.

Mac Da Thó finds the dilemma perplexing and thus scrambles for a solution. Although he has been cautioned (unwisely) never to share his secrets with a woman, he does speak of his difficulties with his wife, who hits upon a simple and deft solution: give the dog Ailbe to both parties and let them fight out the ownership between themselves.

To carry out this strategy Mac Da Thó acts with cool mendacious-ness in a humorous passage meant to invite the reader's admiration. As the two delegations arrive in different coloured finery, Mac Da Thó greets them separately and keeps them from seeing one another. When Ulster and Connacht confront each other in the hall, Mac Da Thó feigns surprise, followed by bland indifference to the electric tensions of the occasion. He asks the parties to sit on opposite sides of the hall in anticipation of the sumptuous feast he is about to present. The magnificent pig, now slaughtered, is ready for the table.

The question of who should carve Mac Da Thó's pig now becomes the centre of the action. Notorious for his mischief-making, the Ulster hero Briccriu, nicknamed Neimthenga [bitter-tongued], suggests that the magnificent mound of pork before them should be divided accord-ing to 'battle victories'. A long succession of warriors from both sides claims primacy, always with vain boasting followed by puncturing, abusive retorts. Conflict is momentarily resolved when Cet mac

Mágach, the Connacht hero, seizes the rhetorical moment by taunting and shaming the pride of Ulster's premier fighters. He claims the right to hang his weapons higher on the wall than anyone present and shouts that, unless anyone can best him, he will carve the pig. Sickened by Cet's reminders of their failures, the men of Ulster seem ready to submit.

At that moment the door crashes open, and in strides Conall Cernach, one of the three greatest Ulster warriors, who demands that Cet back away from the roast pig on the table. Never has he spent a day without slaying a Connachtman, he trumpets, never spent a night without plundering their property, and never slept without having a Connachtman's head beneath his knee. A bit shaken by Conall's thunder, Cet acknowledges that the Ulsterman may indeed be a better fighter but that his brother Anluan is greater still, and he if were present he would prove it. 'But he is,' Conall roars, throwing Anluan's severed head to Cet's chest with such force that blood gushes from his mouth. Flushed with his own bravado, Conall then proceeds to carve the pig, keeping the choicest portions for himself, and leaving only the forelegs to the humiliated westerners.

Enraged at this insult, the men of Connacht descend upon the men of Ulster, and soon bodies are heaped upon the floor and blood is flowing through the doorway. At just this moment of mayhem, Mac Da Thó decides to reintroduce Ailbe, the fighting hound at the centre of the current conflict between north and west. The host wants to see which side Ailbe will choose, and as the hound sees Conchobar's forces in the lead, he takes the side of Ulster. His rapacious teeth bared, Ailbe tears into the flesh of the Connacht fighters, giving Ailill and Medb such a fright that the royal couple take flight with their charioteer, Fer Loga.

In a startling reversal of expectations, the Connacht charioteer strikes a fatal blow against the hound as forceful as ten armies. Fer Loga uses a chariot pole to decapitate the majestic beast, letting the body fall to one side but keeping the head on his pole. At this point the storyteller adds that this episode lends itself to two place-names: *Mag nAilbe* [Ailbe's plain], in the valley of the River Barrow, where the action is taking place, and *Ibar Cinn Chon* [yew tree of the hound's head], a bogus etymology for 'Connacht' itself.

Seeking one last advantage for his province, Fer Loga lies in wait in the heather, ready to roll Ailbe's severed head into the roadway. His ambush succeeds as he springs into Conchobar's chariot and seizes the king by the throat. Realizing his disadvantage, Conchobar bargains for his freedom on Fer Loga's terms. Pausing, the charioteer thinks of a wish he would like fulfilled.

'I would like to see the women of Emain Macha and their young daughters sing choruses around me every evening for a year, with the words, "Fer Loga is my darling."'

Conchobar grants the request. He and Fer Loga proceed to Emain Macha where the maidens are obliged to follow the king's command. After a happy year, Fer Loga with a gift of two of Conchobar's horses returns to the west, fording the Shannon at Athlone.

BRICCRIU'S CONTENTIOUS FEAST

Trouble-making is ever Briccriu Neimthenga's pleasure. His insidious suggestions about how the pork might be carved at Mac Da Thó's dinner party are but a prelude to his grander shenanigans in the eighth-century story bearing his name, *Fled Bricrenn* [Briccriu's Feast]. His prey this time are three Ulster heroes, Conall Cernach, Lóegaire Búadach and Cúchulainn and, through them, their wives. His tactic, simple but effective, is an appeal to vanity: Which of you shall rank first? Who should take precedence? Who deserves to cut the champion's esteemed portion?

The story survives in four variant eleventh-century texts deriving from an eighth-century original, which in turn appears to have had antecedents of even earlier date. When coordinated, the entire narrative connects two barely related episodes: (a) Briccriu's inciting of competition for the champion's portion; and (b) the beheading contest or giant's challenge. Despite the modest caesura in the action *Fled Bricrenn* is often seen as one of the most finished stories as well as one of the longest, after the imposing *Táin Bó Cuailnge*.

As soon as they hear about the feast, the Ulstermen are reluctant to accept invitations to Briccriu's sumptuous new residence at Dún Rudraige [Dundrum, Co. Down], fashioned after the banqueting hall at Tara. The host's reputation for irascibility is enough to put them off. Knowing this, Briccriu forces acceptance by threatening to set all of Ulster into turmoil if they do not come: father and son will be set one against another, mother against daughter, even the two breasts of each woman will strike against each other until their milk is soured. Acknowledging the grief Briccriu could surely bring about, many give in and go, but only on the condition that the host himself should not enter the mansion. Untroubled by such ineffective limits on his deviousness, Briccriu sets about tickling the self-importance of the three heroes even before they arrive. He entices Lóegaire first, slathering him with flattery and then taunting him with questions such as why he does not receive the champion's portion, the choicest cut of succulent, milk-fed pork when he is at Emain Macha. Rising to Briccriu's bait, Lóegaire protests that he could have the champion's portion if he really wanted it.

Briccriu quickly plays the same tricks on Conall and Cúchulainn – unctuous flattery followed by prickly goads about unappreciated feats of valour and heroism. Cúchulainn is the angriest of the three, swearing that he will have the head of anyone who takes the champion's portion before him. At this Briccriu beams with satisfaction at his handiwork.

Once King Conchobar leads the Ulster party to Briccriu's residence, the host neglects his promise to stay away and attends to such household matters as the ordering of the musicians and the presentation of the banquet, from the wine to the much anticipated roast pig. Once he and his wife are sure that all is ready, they leave the dining hall with one last invitation to mayhem. Briccriu calls out that the magnificent champion's portion is to be set before the guests and that only the greatest champion deserves it. Retreating to a secure vantage point, the hosts wish to watch the forces they have set in motion without being scarred themselves. Cúchulainn's charioteer Láeg seizes the initiative by demanding that the champion's portion be delivered to his master. This provokes the expected clamour from the other two heroes' charioteers, and soon the retainers and their masters join in the raucous mêlée. Briccriu's hope that one hero will destroy another is dashed when a cooler head prevails. Sencha mac Ailella, Conchobar's chief judge and poet, steps forward with a disarmingly simple solution:

the champion's portion should be divided three ways, implying parity among the three contestants.

Thwarted in this, his first stratagem, Briccriu turns to the consorts of the three heroes, sure that he has readier prey this time. Observing that Fedelm Noíchrothach, wife of Lóegaire, is tipsy from too much wine, he praises her as the foremost woman of Ulster for her beauty, nobility and intelligence. Enjoying her rapt attention, he goads her to take precedence among the women by being the first to pass through the door of Briccriu's residence, an act that will confirm her rank. In quick order he uses the same simple ploys with Lendabair, wife of Conall Cernach, and Emer, wife of Cúchulainn. When the three noble women and their entourages meet three ridges away from the hall, each believes that Briccriu has spoken only to her and so projects a studied calm about making her way to the banquet. Measured, stately steps give way to a faster pace as they pass from the third to the second ridge. Briccriu's intrigue seems to be working as the parties draw closer to Dún Rudraige and each woman breaks into a run, hoisting her skirts and exposing her backside. Arriving at the door they compete in boasting contests over who has the more formidable husband, prompting Conall and Lóegaire to tear down the pillars so that Fedelm and Lendabair may enter. Cúchulainn takes more direct action, prising up an entire wall of the edifice, hefting it so high that stars in the sky are visible beneath the foundations. This allows Emer, unhurriedly, to step first into the house. Once she is in, Cúchulainn drops the wall, which crashes into the earth, sinking deeper than the length of a full-grown warrior. All this violence to the house's physical integrity undulates through the rest of the structure, sending Briccriu's balcony at a severe tilt, causing him and his wife to slide off and plop down farcically into a pile of slimy muck.

Fit to be tied, despite the absurdity of his condition, Briccriu demands that Dún Rudraige be restored to its earlier glory, screaming his rage before everyone present. The peacemaker Sencha mac Ailella then implores Cúchulainn to act, but the hero, exhausted from breaking in his horse, the Grey of Macha, cannot budge it. Suddenly, Cúchulainn seems transformed: his body is stretched like an extended bow, his face is distorted and his hair stands on end. This is an early instance of his empowering *ríastrad*, an untranslatable term known in English as his battle fury, battle frenzy or warp spasm. It usually comes upon him when he needs to draw on additional reserves of conviction and strength while threatened in combat; there are several instances in the next chapter. In this preview, *ríastrad* infuses Cúchulainn with all the muscle he needs to raise Briccriu's house in one thrust and restore it as it had been. With this Cúchulainn himself regains his normal appearance, and the entire company settles down to enjoy the rest of the feast.

Briccriu's challenge to the vanity of the Ulster heroes remains unsatisfied, of course, but he is not the immediate instigator of the third episode of the unfolding story. The Ulstermen themselves decide to take the question of who deserves the champion's portion to their usual enemies, Queen Medb of Connacht and her consort Ailill in their fortress of Cruachain. Everyone concerned with the question, headed by King Conchobar mac Nessa, packs up and begins to head west. So massive and extensive is the entourage that the rumble of humans and animals in motion extends all the way to the household of Medb herself, who remarks to her daughter Finnabair how odd it is to hear thunder on such a sunny day.

Taking a high vantage point in the fortress, Finnabair calls out detailed and particular descriptions of the approaching heroes for her mother to identify. Lóegaire has long braided yellow hair, brown at the root, blood red in the middle and golden yellow at the tip. Long braided hair also adorns Conall Cernach, whose bright, glistening face is half-red and half-white. Finnabair saves her highest praise for the third rider, whom she judges to be the most beautiful man in all of Ireland, even though he is sad and dark. It is Cúchulainn. His clothing brightens his appearance, a scarlet tunic fastened with a gold, ornamented brooch over his white breast.

In an instant Medb knows each of the warriors from her daughter's words but cautions that each of them could bring danger to the household. She orders that three vats of icy water be set aside to cool the battle fever of the three when they arrive.

Learning the reason for the Ulstermen's journey to Cruachain, Ailill is most uneasy, knowing that whatever he decides will make for him two implacable enemies. For a moment he is spared the invidious choice when three druidic cats are let loose among the Ulster threesome, scratching their food and baring claws. Lóegaire and Conall escape to the rafters while Cúchulainn remains calm, holding the demonic cats at bay all night. Seeing this, Ailill assumes his decision has been made and declares the champion's portion for Cúchulainn. But Lóegaire and Conall object vehemently, arguing that magic beasts cannot test a champion's strength, only other men.

Disgusted with her husband's indecision, which she calls cowardly, Medb proposes her own plan to separate the men, who she says are as different from one another as bronze is to silver, and silver is to gold.

She then speaks to the Ulster heroes one by one, telling each a variation of the same story. She allows Lóegaire and Conall to think they are her favourites, giving a bronze cup with a silver bird on the bottom to Lóegaire and a silver cup with a gold bird on the bottom to Conall, asking both not to divulge their little secret. Cúchulainn, playing the boardgame fidchell with Láeg, is harder to coax. She puts her arm around him and whispers in his ear that he is the greatest hero in Ulster and most deserving of the champion's portion. From under her garments she takes a splendid gold cup with a bejewelled bird at the base. As with the others, she asks him not to speak of this.

On their return to Emain Macha the three heroes are hosted at a banquet at which the champion's portion is carved but not served to anyone. Dubthach Dóeltenga [chafer-tongued], a man as rancorous as Briccriu, snarls that the expedition to Cruachain settled nothing and the champion's portion might as well be given to some hero other than the three current competitors. At that Lóegaire holds up his bronze cup to prove that he was Ailill's and Medb's choice, a secret until now. A startled Conall objects, brandishing his elegant silver cup, a sure sign that he had been favoured by the royalty of the west. Never one to be stampeded by the heat of the moment, Cúchulainn is slower to speak. Reaching into his cloak he produces his golden goblet, studded with jewels, and on the bottom the bird composed of precious gems. 'This is the best token of all,' he avows. 'With justice the champion's portion should be mine.' His presumption provokes Lóegaire and Conall to draw their swords and all three are about to flail one another when Sencha intervenes once more, reminding the trio that Medb had duped all of them, not each one individually. Thus, once again the question of who deserved the champion's portion is unresolved, and so the meat is cut up and distributed to the whole company.

Next, the three Ulster heroes seek the judgement of a wizard-warrior in the south, Cú Roí mac Dáiri of west Munster. He lives in a magical, impregnable fortress that revolves on its axis each night so that its entrance can never be found after sunset; it is identified with the Iron Age ruin of Cahirconree on the Dingle Peninsula, Co. Kerry. The host is away in far-off Scythia when the trio arrive; they are asked to keep watch at night until Cú Roí comes back. Lóegaire, the eldest, is keeping the first watch when a giant comes from the sea. Taking the Ulsterman up in one hand, the giant rolls him between his palms like a chess-piece turned on a lathe and then contemptuously throws him over the wall into the mud. Next night, Conall Cernach gets the same abusive handling. On the third night Cúchulainn fares better, overcoming attacks from nine warriors, a monstrous beast and finally the giant himself. When he enters the fortress the next morning, Cúchulainn sighs, to which the host's wife, Bláithíne, responds that his sigh should be for victory and triumph. After a short interval, Cú Roí enters, carrying the spoils of earlier conquests that Cúchulainn had left outside, and declares that he alone among the three Ulstermen is most deserving of the champion's portion. Cú Roí confirms his decision with a reward of gold and silver and promises, further, that Cúchulainn's wife Emer will enjoy precedence over all the women of the province.

When the troupe returns to Emain Macha that night, the matter is anything but settled. Lóegaire and Conall deny that Cú Roí has awarded the champion's portion to Cúchulainn as they did not witness what went on inside the fortress. Cúchulainn decides not to contend for his rightful prize as to do so would bring more sorrow than joy.

The final and crucial episode of the narrative is absent or illegible in the three recensions of *Fled Bricrenn* but survives in a separate manuscript found in Edinburgh. Determining the rightful claimant to the champion's portion is still the dominant theme, but in this last action Briccriu has completely disappeared, his role taken with lesser stature by the evil-tongued Dubthach.

One evening at Cráebruad, the Red Branch hall at Emain Macha, Conchobar and Fergus (who had preceded Conchobar on the throne) preside over a gathering that follows an exhausting tournament. Suddenly a huge, uncouth and churlish giant bursts into the hall, clearly looking for trouble. His yellow, ravenous eyes are as big as cauldrons and his fingers as thick as a man's wrist. He wears a tunic made of old hide covered by a dun-coloured mantle. The block he carries in his left hand would strain twenty yokes of oxen simply to budge. In his right hand he carries a huge axe whose handle would require six horses to carry and whose edge would cut hair aloft in the wind. He announces that he has been searching the world to find a man brave enough to keep a pact with him. With Conchobar and Fergus excepted because of their rank, the churlish giant asks that someone present agree to allow the giant to cut off his head with the axe. His part of the bargain will be to return the following night and place his own neck on the chopping-block to receive the same treatment. After some of Dubthach's gibes, the giant reverses the offer, submitting his neck to the chopping-block first.

As Lóegaire, Conall and Cúchulainn are absent, a lesser but strong warrior with an unfortunate name steps forward, Munremur mac Gerrcind [fat neck son of short head]. Doing what he is asked, Munremur raises the colossal axe and with one blow separates the giant's head from his shoulders. It rolls on the floor, leaving a trail of blood. Without wasting time, the giant reaches down to pick up the head, and with his axe over his shoulder strides from the room. On the following the night when the giant returns, head restored to his neck, Munremur is nowhere to be found.

On that second night, however, Lóegaire is present, prompting the giant to raise the question of the champion's portion. The giant calls out Lóegaire's name and asks that anyone contesting for the Ulster champion portion should be willing to carry out the beheading covenant. Lóegaire agrees, but his experience is the same as Munremur's. On the third night the giant challenges Conall, who, like the two before him, lops off the head easily but is elsewhere when it is his turn at the chopping-block.

On the fourth night, in Conall's absence, the giant rails against the court, Ulster in general and, finally, Cúchulainn in particular, who is present. Keeping his distance, the Ulster hero avers that he does not desire a covenant with the visitor, to which the giant snarls that he really fears death too much enter into the bargain. This gibe prompts Cúchulainn to leap toward the giant and swing the axe in a would-be lethal blow. For extra measure, Cúchulainn hurls the head to the top rafter and, when it falls to the floor, smashes it into smithereens. When this is done, the giant still rises, carrying with him what is left of the head.

Tension rises among the courtiers over how the dispute will be settled. On the fifth night the giant returns with his head restored, but Cúchulainn is keeping his half of the bargain. When Cúchulainn kneels and put his neck on the block, the giant teases him, telling him it is too short. Cúchulainn is willing to make his neck as long as a heron's but asks that he be killed quickly and not made sport of. The giant raises his axe on high, and he swings it so swiftly that the hissing is like wind through trees. But as metal meets skin, it appears that the giant has put the blunt side of the blade toward Cúchulainn's neck. The stroke is gentle, barely enough to mark the hero.

The giant then asks Cúchulainn to stand and declares that he has no equal for bravery, honesty and honour. He must take the champion's portion, and his wife Emer must take first place in the banqueting hall. At this the giant reveals that he is Cú Roí and swears that anyone who disputes with him puts his own life in danger.

The beheading bargain in *Fled Bricrenn* is much commented upon. It anticipates a better known sequence in the English romance *Sir Gawain and the Green Knight* (fourteenth century), written down many centuries later. As folk motif M221, it is found in more stories than these two.

THE INTOXICATION OF
THE ULSTERMEN

The reputation for sometimes raucous comedy that has attached itself to Irish literature over the past two centuries finds relatively little justification in the earliest narratives. Poets and storytellers might have ranked satire highly in their artistic repertory, but when applied it tended to be poisonous, with little to be laughed at. One of the very few stories that appears to be composed solely for humorous ends is the twelfth-century anti-clerical satire *Aislinge Meic Con Glinne* [Vision of Mac Con Glinne], with a mock exorcism of the 'demon of gluttony'.

Elsewhere comedy, when it appears, is often a surprise. The context may imply tones of stateliness, formality or heroic endeavour. In such stories we read of reversals of expectation or deflated pomposity, not in themselves laugh-out-loud funny. Even then, we must sometimes stand back from the text to perceive the author's intent.

The title of the twelfth-century story *Mesca Ulad* [Intoxication of the Ulstermen] signals a different tone from the rest of the cycle. Excessive boozing has been a staple comic theme since the time of Aristophanes (fourth century BC). In the two best-known translations of *Mesca Ulad* – the twenty-four pages of T. P. Cross and C. H. Slover (1936) or the thirty-one pages of Jeffrey Gantz (1981) – most of the narrative is anything but funny. Too much is given over to lengthy passages of static description and protracted runs of obscure personal and place-names, the kinds of things that would have been the stock-in-trade of medieval storytellers. Worse, the narrator does not follow a definite plot but instead ambles about the countryside, allowing for haphazard introduction of episodes unforeseen in earlier action. Inhibiting comedy further, the text is incomplete. The better-known fragment appearing in the twelfth-century Book of Leinster [*Lebor Laignech*] is more refined, with greater psychological depth. The shorter fragment in the earlier Book of the Dun Cow [*Lebor na hUidre*] appears to complete the narrative but with personal names in somewhat different forms and the key element of the iron house missing. Even with these impediments, the storyteller's desire to provoke smiles persists over the centuries and through translation.

The action begins with talk of the division of land. Just as Ireland had been divided first by the Tuatha Dé Danann and later by the Milesians, putting up borders that invited discord, so now Ulster is split into three parts. Conchobar mac Nessa commands the centre from Emain Macha while his fosterlings dominate the other two, Fintan son of Niall Noígiallach [of the Nine Hostages] in the north and Cúchulainn in the east. Other accounts put Fintan many centuries later and neglect to portray Cúchulainn in dispute with Conchobar, but *Mesca Ulad* imposes its own chronology and logic. With the feast of Samain approaching, Conchobar sends out trusted emissaries to invite the two younger men to a feast at the capital – Leborcham (Deirdre's nurse) to speak to Cúchulainn and wise old Sencha mac

Ailella to Fintan. Cúchulainn first blusters that he will not attend, but his wife Emer interrupts and says that he will. And so both foster-sons return to the hall of their protector.

Demands for safety and assurances from both sides are excessive. The hosts at Emain Macha ask that Cúchulainn give as hostages three prominent warriors: Conall Cernach, Conall Anglonnach and Lóegaire Búadach. In return, Cúchulainn asks that three young men from the household, all sons of prominent men including Conchobar, be held on his behalf. Meanwhile, Fintan is a harder bargainer. Whereas the hosts ask of him the guarantee of mid-level hero Celtchair mac Uithechair and two lesser figures, Fintan asks for the three sons of Uisnech, Ardan, Ainnle and Noíse, the lover of Deirdre.

At the centre of the negotiations is the request that Cúchulainn and Fintan give up their thirds of the province in a year's time so that Conchobar might rule the whole more peaceably. Praising their foster-father as a fountain of authority, they agree but caution that if the arrangement does not work out as planned Cúchulainn and Fintan will be returned their portions.

The guarantees for safety at Conchobar's banquet are worthless, however. Riot soon breaks out in the ranks despite all the efforts to prevent it. So ferocious is the squabbling between the different retinues that nine men are covered with wounds, nine with blood, and nine more writhe in death agonies, an equal amount for each side.

True to his usual role, Sencha shakes his branch of peacemaking and asks the reason for the quarrel. He reminds all that Conchobar will not be king for another year. Cúchulainn agrees to the household's wishes as long as no one from it tries to interfere with him during the intervening year. Sencha agrees. Then, for the next three days and nights, everyone present celebrates and drinks up all of Conchobar's bounty, before each returns to his own fortress.

Life in Ulster goes well for the following year. When the time comes for the three divisions of the province to be joined under Conchobar's leadership, both Cúchulainn and Fintan decide at exactly the same moment that they should hold their own feasts in honour of the occasion. Without any knowledge of what the other is doing, they somehow decide matters and take action at precisely the same instant. They prepare by assembling hundreds of vats of every kind of ale. Both swear an oath simultaneously that each will host Conchobar and the new regime on the same night. Both harness their horses and yoke their chariots at the same time. Then Cúchulainn takes an early lead by arriving first at Emain Macha and is making his case for hosting Conchobar as Fintan pulls up. The second man, true to his oath, will not yield to the first, and so violent a squabble breaks out between the two sides that Sencha does not dare to intervene in. Instead, Conchobar asks for help from his son Furbaide, who is also Cúchulainn's foster-son, hoping he can bring peace. The young man begins a loud chant of wailing lamentation, sobbing that just as the province is to become a wellspring of prosperity, all will be destroyed in one night. His tears have an immediate effect. Sencha proposes a compromise in which the entire entourage will spend the first half of the night with Fintan and the second half with Cúchulainn.

It is a compromise that overlooks geography. Things start well enough with the lavish entertainment during the first half of the evening at Fintan's northerly fortress of Dún Dá Benn in contemporary Co. Derry. Láeg, Cúchulainn's charioteer, reads the stars to determine when the middle of the night has come, but through the excruciatingly slow rules of protocol, he must delay this news. When it is heard, the party must scurry from Dún Dá Benn south and east over to Dún Delgan, coextensive with modern Dundalk, Co. Louth. The place names may sound a bit alike, but the distance between them is nearly ninety miles over rolling country. Cúchulainn instructs Láeg to begin their trek with leisurely indifference, but this pose does not last for long. Soon the previously dignified members of the court of Ulster take on a kind of Mack Sennett frenzy to drive forward. Mountains and great oaks seem to whiz by. The ensemble becomes the Keystone Kops in chariots. Forded streams and estuaries are left bone dry in their wake. Iron wheels level mountains and crags to the flattest of plains. When Conchobar observes that it does not look as though they are still in Ulster, wise Sencha answers that they are not. It appears that they are in the realm of their southern enemy Cú Roí in west Munster, 225 miles in the wrong direction, about as far from Dún Dá Benn as one could get without leaving the island. Then it starts to snow.

The narrative scene then shifts to the residence of Munster kings at Temuir Luachra; Cú Roí's rotating fortress in the previous story has been forgotten this time. Here he is playing host to the royal family of Connacht, also enemies of Ulster, Ailill and Medb, who has just given birth to a son. As a prelude to a possible future alliance between Munster and Connacht, Cú Roí has agreed to be foster-father to the infant.

Two druids in Cú Roí's household mount the fortress wall to begin a commentary on the approaching Ulstermen, about whom they are frequently mistaken. Cromm Deróil and Cromm Darail may be foster-sons of prime druid Cathbad but they often talk like a pair of vaudevillians. Cromm Deróil begins their dialogue with the words, 'Have you seen what I just saw? . . . What was that?' Cromm Darail answers, 'Only big oak trees.' 'Oh . . .', answers Cromm Deróil, 'Oak trees with chariots under them?' After a dozen such exchanges they both become dizzy and faint, Cromm Darail falling outside the wall, Cromm Deróil falling inside.

Reporting to the court inside the walls, Cromm Deróil and Cromm Darail recover themselves and comment further on the approaching Ulstermen, giving more detailed pictures than did Finnabair to Medb in *Fled Bricrenn* (see above) and also some deflating portraits. Cúchulainn comes off as a 'little black-browed man' but 'greatly resplendent'. Immortals of the Tuatha Dé Danann such as Angus Óg and the Dagda are also with them but visible only to the hosts at Temuir Luachra. Conchobar's fool, with a smooth, dark Ethiopian face, merits as much attention as the heroes do.

Medb asks if the unexpected arrival of the Ulstermen might possibly be in fulfilment of a forgotten prophecy. The blind seer Gabalglinde replies that it is and that the same prophecy foretold of the defensive use of an iron house with two wooden houses about it and a house of earth beneath. Sensing an advantage for themselves, the hosts at Temuir Luachra invite the Ulstermen in. Sencha accepts the welcome, acknowledging that they have not come to fight or do evil but rather because they have been on a drunken spree, and it would be dishonourable to leave the territory without spending so much as a night in it.

In accepting the invitation, one hundred Ulster champions clamour to be the first to enter the compound, but Sencha decides it should be Cúchulainn. When Cúchulainn returns with a company of minstrels and entertainers, the rest of the Ulstermen follow as though one.

Cúchulainn chooses the largest house, which turns out to be made of iron, as the prophecy foretold, and is flanked by two wooden ones. Servants provide ale and provisions for the guests, as well as a huge bonfire. At night the servants steal away and lock the door, fastening it with seven chains. The trapped men quickly understand what danger they are in, and Briccriu charges Cúchulainn with having brought them into the enemy's pen. 'I can perform a hero's feat,' Cúchulainn responds, 'that will get all the Ulstermen out.' He plunges his sword up to the hilt through the iron wall and through two houses of boards, and then announces to his comrades what he has found. 'This is the worst of all,' growls Briccriu.

At this point the fragment from the Book of Leinster ends, and we never learn the narrator's plans to complete the story. Action in the Book of the Dun Cow begins a few steps earlier with the Ulstermen disputing over who should lead them into Temuir Luachra. In this version many minor characters have slightly different names, and there is apparently no iron house. Instead, the men are locked into a wooden house, and Cúchulainn saves the day when he kicks down the door. He urges the men to hand-to-hand combat, and they eventually plunder the stronghold.

One defender, Crimthann Nia Náir, escapes and tries to wreak revenge on the Ulster hero through the wiles of the female satirist Richis, whose son was killed at Temuir Luachra. She strips naked in front of Cúchulainn, who turns his face downwards so that he might not see her private parts. Just as Crimthann is about to seize his opportunity against the Ulsterman, the charioteer Láeg throws a huge stone that breaks the back of the nude temptress. Recovering his strength, Cúchulainn charges forward to Crimthann and decapitates him with one blow, carrying away his head and other spoils.

Ailill of Connacht returns to his own country and lives in peace and unity with Ulster.

Conchobar's kingship does not suffer another threat as long as he lives.

Cú Roí and Cúchulainn remain adversaries in other stories. In one, Cú Roí, while allied with Ulster, gets the better of it by shaving the head of Cúchulainn and daubing his bare head with cow dung. Hair is also important in the resolution of their conflict. When Bláithíne,

Cú Roí's wife, becomes involved in an adulterous relationship with Cúchulainn, she agrees to tie her husband's hair to a bedpost. In one of his less admirable moments, Cúchulainn murders the discommoded cuckold.

10

The Ulster Cycle

Part II: Cúchulainn and the Táin

ROOTS OF HEROIC IDENTITY

Cúchulainn usually can be counted on to get the best of things, as his appearance in two stories from the last chapter shows. Of the three most dominant heroes of early Irish tradition, Lug Lámfhota, Cúchulainn and Fionn mac Cumhaill, he is usually ranked first. Like the other two, he appears to have roots in the earliest Celtic traditions, with links and analogues among the early continental Celts. Cúchulainn was favoured by learned storytellers for at least seven centuries, from the seventh through to the fourteenth. While his exploits greatly exaggerate human potential, several of the most important stories show him at his most human: growing to maturity, wooing a wife, and engaged in heartbreaking combat with a warrior who is his unacknowledged son. He is the most dynamic force in the *Táin Bó Cuailnge*, the national epic. Curiously, his adventures were barely extended in oral tradition, in contrast with those of Fionn mac Cumhaill, whose many portrayals are found in an immense body of later popular literature. For ordinary Irish people over the last 130 years, Cúchulainn's name has more often been relearned through books than inherited from everyday discourse. When, however, the Irish state looked for a heroic figure to commemorate the scene of the first bloodshed on behalf of national independence, the Easter Rising of 1916, in the lobby of the General Post Office on what is now O'Connell Street, they chose Oliver Sheppard's much-photographed statue of Cúchulainn.

At the time of the first translations of early Irish literature in the nineteenth century, commentators routinely compared Cúchulainn with classical heroes such as Heracles and Aeneas. More recent opinion holds that if Cúchulainn resembles early Mediterranean figures it is because early Christian redactors of his stories, themselves informed by Latin tradition, shaped him to look that way. Recent scholarship has also tended to downplay the 'Pagan survival' theories of early Irish narrative, but the deep appeal of his persona means that he could not have just been invented one day by an inspired scribe. Speculative links between Cúchulainn and the Gaulish god Esus appear to be insubstantial. More significant, perhaps, are his characteristic quickness and short, dark stature, features that Julius Caesar attributed to Gaulish Mercury. Inescapable are the implications of his birth name Sétanta. Although it has been glossed as 'god of routes and roads' and 'one who knows the way', the name bears at least a superficial resemblance to Setantii, the name of a people of northwest Britain described by Ptolemy (first century AD). His usual spear or javelin, the Gáe Bulga, evokes the name of the Belgae, the prominent early Celtic people described as the most ferocious of all by Caesar. There is probably also an echo of the Gaulish people the Manapii in the cognomen of Cúchulainn's father-in-law Forgall Manach.

The usual domain of Cúchulainn is Mag Muirtheimne, the plain adjacent to the Irish Sea in eastern County Louth, from Drogheda at the mouth of the River Boyne north to his fortress at Dún Delgan, next to the modern city of Dundalk. The same territory provides an entry route for invaders in the *Lebor Gabála*. It could well have served the same function for historical peoples such as the Manapii, Belgae or Setantii, who resided directly across the Irish Sea. Whatever the reason, early storytellers habitually link Cúchulainn with Mag Muirtheimne, whereas Lug Lámfhota is not ascribed a domain. Fionn mac Cumhaill might be thought to live at the Hill of Allen in County Kildare, but his adventures take him everywhere in Ireland as well as to hundreds of locations in Gaelic Scotland.

The translation of Cúchulainn's name, 'hound of Culann', usually strikes English readers as odd. Who is Culann and why should he have a hound at all? We are not used to such favourable associations for hounds or dogs. Depictions of the domesticated canine among the Celts offer some answers. The dog is portrayed on the Gundestrup Cauldron and is associated with the Gaulish goddess Sirona. Dog bones are commonly found in early holy wells, and a dog skull was uncovered by modern archaeologists at the base of the famous royal site, Emain Macha, in Ulster. A leader of pre-Claudian Britain (first century BC) was Cunobelinus, literally, 'the hound of Belinus'. More popularly, the cultivation of such noble breeds as the Irish wolfhound and the Irish terrier implies that many dogs in early Ireland were welcome in more esteemed places in a household than in barnyards and open fields.

Even so, the widely known story of how Cúchulainn acquired his name after killing Culann's dog (see next section) may have been a later invention to explain inherited practice. Dáithí Ó hÓgáin (1991) describes it as a 'secondary invention' and asserts that his original name meant 'warrior of Culann'. Ó hÓgáin's explanation for the identity of Culann lies in the archaic word *cul*, 'chariot'. In the story Culann is described as the kind of artisan/tradesman who would manufacture war chariots. A corrupted genitive or a compound of *cul* might have been the basis for the element *culann* so that 'Cúchulainn' would have originally been translated as 'chariot-warrior'.

The most plausible theory of Cúchulainn's origin, Ó hÓgáin says further, is that he symbolized a particular war-cult introduced into Ireland by a Celtic people who crossed over from Britain to the area of Muirtheimne.

YOUTH, EDUCATION, MARRIAGE

Like other heroes in world traditional literature, Heracles, Perseus or Siegfried, Cúchulainn is the product of an extraordinary, even miraculous conception. Actually, he has several such stories, all centring on the same mother, Deichtine, daughter of Cathbad the esteemed druid. Sometimes she is also seen as a sister or daughter of King Conchobar mac Nessa. In two stories Lug Lámfhota of the immortal Tuatha Dé Danann is Cúchulainn's ultimate father, even though the young hero has a host of mortal foster-fathers.

In the shortest version Deichtine is so distracted by grief for the death of a foster-son that she does not notice while drinking water that a tiny creature has passed into her mouth. That creature is Lug

Lámfhota. Or she may merely be dreaming that it is Lug. Dream or reality, Deichtine is impregnated by swallowing the small creature. People in the court, hearing that Deichtine is pregnant and not knowing of a father, assume she may have been compromised by a drunken Conchobar mac Nessa. Before she can deliver the child Cúchulainn, she is married to Sualtam mac Róich, but, given her condition, she is ashamed to enter his bed. No mere cipher, Sualtam becomes a foster-father of his wife's child and is later decapitated in defence of Ulster against the invasion of Ailill and Medb. Deichtine is ill as her confinement approaches and she suffers a miscarriage. Her virginity is restored, and she at last embraces her husband.

A separate version begins with Deichtine's disappearance, with fifty maidens, from the court of Conchobar mac Nessa. After three years a flock of birds settles on the field of Emain Macha and lays waste the crops. Conchobar and his retainers drive off the birds, which then lead the royal party to Brug na Bóinne, the residence of Angus Óg on the Boyne River. That night the men enter a splendid palace, where a noble young man is seen with what appear to be fifty maidens. The young women include Deichtine, and the noble youth is revealed to be Lug Lámfhota. Realizing this, Conchobar asks to see Deichtine, but she sends instead her newborn son Cúchulainn.

In a third alternative, less widely circulated, Conchobar, as either Deichtine's father or brother, commits incest with her to produce Cúchulainn.

There are also rival stories of the hero's fosterage, an important question in the unstable society of early Ireland where the sponsorship of a prominent fosterer could guarantee a lifetime of security and influence. Following the first of the conception stories, cited above, Sualtam mac Róich, Deichtine's husband, is seen as Cúchulainn's sole foster-father. More often leading members of the Ulster court vie for Deichtine's favour to be named fosterer, a possible contretemps she diplomatically resolves by agreeing to have seven in the role concurrently. They are: (i) Sencha mac Ailella the judge to give eloquence and poetry; (ii) Blái Briuga the hospitaller to provide for material comfort; (iii) Fergus mac Róich to take the young hero on his knee; (iv) Amairgin the poet to be his teacher; (v) Conall Cernach to be a foster-brother and virtual twin; (vi) Findchóem, Conall's mother, to be his wet nurse; and finally (vii) Conchobar to be his principal foster-father.

The boy Cúchulainn is still called Sétanta and must earn his heroic name, much as Heracles is first known as Alcides. How this happened along with other boyhood deeds is remembered by Fergus mac Róich, his tutor, in a lengthy early chapter of the *Táin Bó Cuailnge*. While still only five years old (or seven in many sources), Sétanta learns of a martial boys' corps at Emain Macha, headed by Follamain, Conchobar's son, and travels 25 miles by foot to reach it. To make the journey seem shorter, he plays games with weapons, such as throwing his javelin ahead of him, then racing forward to catch it. Upon his arrival Sétanta finds the boys, 150 strong, some practising fighting skills while others are playing hurling, a game like field hockey. He rushes headlong into the game, gets the ball, dodges around the surprised players and scores a goal. This does not go down well with the boys, and especially angers their leader Follamain. The rest of the boys throw their sticks, balls and finally their spears at Sétanta. Under this attack he experiences his first battle frenzy or warp spasm, baring his teeth, making his hair stand on end and putting a bright circle of light around his head. Thus transformed, Sétanta rushes the crowd, knocking fifty of the boys to the ground and chasing off others until Conchobar takes him by the arm. The king advises the impetuous boy that the corps is forbidden to play with the newcomer until he claims the protection of the group. Sétanta replies that he would have complied had he known. Conchobar then introduces the boy to the troop, and they all return to playing hurling. Quickly asserting himself, Sétanta begins knocking down the others one by one until Conchobar calls out to ask what he is doing. He answers that all the boys must come under his protection, which the terrified boys agree to do, even though Sétanta is younger than they are.

A little more than a year later, Sétanta is left behind playing hurling at Emain Macha while the rest of the royal household visits the residence of a wealthy smith named Culann in Cuailnge, next to the boy's home territory of Muirtheimne. Guests at the smith's lonely mansion know they can relax because they are protected against intruders by the host's huge, ferocious dog. In the midst of their merrymaking they hear a terrible sound. The late-arriving Sétanta, still only a boy, has slain the mighty dog by smashing it against a doorpost. An alternative version has Cúchulainn fling a ball into the dog's open mouth, mortally punishing the creature's innards. The guests at first cheer the boy's feats of strength, but Culann is clearly dismayed at the loss of his prized hound. Sensing this loss, Sétanta promises to raise another whelp to replace the guard dog, and will himself serve as the hound in the interim. Saluting his understanding and generosity, the crowd applauds and calls him the hound, *Cú*, of Culann, *Chulainn*, the name he retains thenceforward.

As we saw in the previous chapter with Finnabair's descriptions for her mother Medb, Cúchulainn is often portrayed as short, dark, beardless and filled with high spirits. Accounts vary from text to text, but his hair is usually thought to be of three colours, brown at the roots, blood red in the middle and blond at the crown. Some aspects of his person appear magical rather than what is usually thought handsome in a man. He has four dimples in each cheek, each dimple being of a different colour: yellow, green, crimson and blue. Seven pupils fill each eye. He clasps with seven fingers, and the seven toes on each foot allow him the grip of a hawk or griffin. As off-putting as some of these features may sound, Cúchulainn is conventionally described as handsome and highly attractive to women. Perhaps readers of early Irish literature did not always visualize the hero in his beguiling feats.

Difficult to visualize also is the singular transformation Cúchulainn undergoes before entering battle. The Irish term *ríastrad* is untranslatable, but the usual attempts are battle fury, contortion and warp spasm. When this overcomes him, he becomes a fearsome figure such as never has been seen before. His entire body quivers like a bullrush in a running stream. The muscles of his neck expand to the size of a baby's head, while his legs rotate on their axes, his calves, hams and heels shifting to the front and knees and feet to the back. One eye recedes to the interior of his skull, reduced to the size of a pin, while the other thrusts out. His mouth widens to meet his ears, and foam pours from his mouth like the fleece of a three-year-old wether. The thump of his heartbeat is as loud as a lion's roar as he rushes towards his prey. From his scalp a column of dark blood spurts forth, scattering in four directions, forming a gloomy mist. Lastly, a projection emerges from Cúchulainn's head, like a horn but the size of man's fist. It is the *lón láith* [light of the hero (?)], which signals he is about to begin combat.

As the paragon of Irish heroes, Cúchulainn's personal strengths are a continual theme among storytellers as well as among other characters in the narratives. Fergus mac Róich praises Cúchulainn while conducting his adulterous affair with Medb, Cúchulainn's soon-to-be adversary. No raven is more ravenous, no lion more ferocious. Obstacles and barriers do not exist for him. A characteristic expression of his energy is the distinctive salmon leap, which modern commentators compare to the jump of a soccer player. It may be both aggressive and defensive, enabling him to pounce on an enemy but also escape a predator. His ability to soar upward explains why nimbleness and brilliance are thought to be Cúchulainn's signal assets. The hero's vitality and attractiveness to women engender love-sickness in many an Ulsterwoman's breast. Warriors wish that Cúchulainn would take a wife so that their daughters would forget him. From the many he chooses Emer, daughter of the wily Forgall Manach. Even before he speaks to her Cúchulainn kills the three sons of Nechta Scéne as a demonstration of his lethal power, as the prevailing custom demanded he win Emer by force.

Upon their meeting, things begin well as Cúchulainn and Emer greet each other in riddles only they can understand. His stories of early exploits charm the maiden. Seeing the swell of her breasts above her gown, Cúchulainn coos that it would be a sweet place to rest. No one will rest here, she answers, until he accomplish three demanding tasks: (i) killing a hundred men at a range of fords in rivers, (ii) slaying three times nine men while leaving the middle man in each group still standing, and (iii) staying awake from February to May, and from May to November. Her father Forgall is less taken with the young swain, however. Going with friends to the court at Emain Macha disguised as Gaulish emissaries, he proposes that the only way for Ulster heroes, Cúchulainn in particular, to achieve greatness is to travel to distant Scotland to be schooled in the arts of war by the amazonian Scáthach. Not so secretly, Forgall wishes that Cúchulainn will perish on the journey or be slain by Scáthach herself. Even after heeding

Emer's warning of her father's intrigue, Cúchulainn departs for Scotland with Lóegaire, Conall and Conchobar.

The experience in Scotland turns out very differently from what Forgall wishes. In addition to receiving the required training, Cúchulainn enjoys successive romantic encounters with martial women. Upon arrival in Scotland, the four Ulstermen receive lessons in balance and endurance from Domnall Mildemail [the warlike], who still advises them to travel on to meet Scáthach. The tutor's hideous daughter Dornoll, meanwhile, becomes smitten with Cúchulainn, who does not return her affections. Hurt and angry, she vows revenge. In a short while she conjures up an enticing, roseate vision of Emain Macha, causing homesick Lóegaire, Conall and Conchobar to return to Ulster, leaving Cúchulainn alone in his quest for the right instruction. To reach Scáthach's fort, often identified with archaeological sites on the Isle of Skye in the Hebrides, the hero must cross the daunting 'Pupils' Bridge'. Designed to block the incapable, it is arched high in the middle and is low at each end. When he first steps on it, the bridge heaves low and throws Cúchulainn off, to the laughter of bystanders. Seized at that moment by his battle fury, Cúchulainn shifts to his salmon leap and flies to the middle of the bridge and then on, adroitly, to the far shore. He then treks on confidently to Scáthach's fort, hammering on the door with his spear, smashing through it in the process.

Recognizing that only a substantially trained fighter would have made it this far, Scáthach sends her daughter Uathach [spectre] to answer the door, and she immediately falls in love with Cúchulainn, like so many women before her. The Ulsterman also gets on well with the mother, who gives him a new spear, the Gáe Bulga, with which he is always later identified. Next she shows him how to cast it with his foot for maximum accuracy and deadly force. In time Cúchulainn comes to know the 'friendship of Scáthach's thighs', which may derive from a forgotten warrior initiation instead of being mere lovemaking. Scáthach grants Cúchulainn three favours: (i) to continue to instruct him most carefully; (ii) to give him her daughter Uathach, without exacting the bride price; and (iii) to predict his future career. In return Scáthach asks Cúchulainn's aid in fighting her enemies, an army of men and women led by the amazonian Aífe, whom even the formidable Scáthach fears. Despite her role in the narrative, Aífe may be a double for Scáthach; she is a different Aífe from the cruel stepmother of the Children of Lir. Cúchulainn charges into Aífe's army with heady success, slaying fighters left and right, and then comes into hand-to-hand combat with the warrior queen herself. She strikes the blade of his sword, leaving him with only the hilt, but he steadily gets the better of her, pinning her down and pointing the blade of another sword to her heart. Now he makes three demands of her: that she cease war upon Scáthach, stay with him that night, and bear him a son. She agrees.

The son she bears in nine months' time is named Connla (also Conlaoch, Conlai, etc.). Father and son spend no time together in Scotland, but they are destined to confront one another at a later date.

A fellow student of Cúchulainn in Scotland is Ferdiad [man of smoke], a bosom friend and sword brother. Ferdiad too is fated to find himself confronting Cúchulainn in the future.

On his return from Scotland to Emain Macha, Cúchulainn battles Emer's family and carries her off along with much gold and silver. In a struggle that lasts a year, he fulfils all the demands she had put upon him. Emer's father tries to escape the onslaught but tumbles from the fortifications to his death. Despite such violent courtship, Emer is usually portrayed as Cúchulainn's wife through the rest of the Ulster Cycle, and she is never said to leave him. In some stories Cúchulainn's wife is named as Eithne Ingubai, which may be but another name for Emer. Some of his dalliances have already been cited, such as the affair with Cú Roí's wife Bláithíne, and more are yet to come, as with Manannán mac Lir's wife Fand. He is also to be the love object of other women, such as the female warrior Cathach and the tragic swan maiden Derbforgaill.

The spear, Gáe Bulga, given him by Scáthach, is one of his major weapons along with his sword Caladbolg.* In later oral tradition he wields the Claidheamh Soluis [sword of light], which may also be known as Cruaidin Catutchenn. His charioteer is Láeg, and together they drive two horses, Saingliu or Dubh [Black] Sainglenn and Liath Macha [Grey of Macha]. Cúchulainn also has many associations with ravens and is once warned by two magical ravens.

---

* This sword was attributed to many heroes, more often Fergus mac Róich, and is often thought to be an antecedent of Arthur's Excalibur.

CONNLA'S RETURN

Cúchulainn is always seen as a boy or a very young man. Unlike Fionn mac Cumhaill or King Arthur, he never ages. Once again, as in the other cycles of Irish literature, there is no implicit timeline to show that one story comes before or after another. The same is true of Cúchulainn's portrayals in the previous chapter, competing for the champion's portion or racing across Ireland in the middle of the night. Imposing as the *Táin* is, storytellers saw no need to allude to it in Cúchulainn's other adventures, even in such foretales to the epic as this story. We can, however, understand that seven years have passed since Cúchulainn's sojourn in Scotland, learning the arts of war from Scáthach and fathering a child upon her rival Aífe. That son, Connla, has now reached the age of seven, and, like his father, he is ready to assert himself with arms.

Cúchulainn might have been an absent father, but he left instructions for the boy's upbringing. He was to be called Connla and sent to Scáthach for training as soon as he was able. He must step aside for no man, never refuse a challenge to single combat, and never tell his name to anyone except when overcome by another combatant. Further, Cúchulainn left a ring for the boy, asking that he should wear it when his hand was sufficiently big and then be sent to look for his father.

Seven years after the day of those fatherly commands, Cúchulainn and Conchobar mac Nessa are walking with other Ulster warriors on the beach at Tracht Esi (or Trácht Éisi, near Baile's Strand, Co. Louth) when they see a boy rowing on the sea in a bronze boat with gilded oars. The boy's power in using a sling to make birds do his will fills the men with awe. Cautiously, the Ulstermen send a lesser champion, hapless Condere, to prevent his landing or at least learn his name. The boy confidently defies him, refusing to give his name until he is bested in combat, which Condere does not wish to try. The more imposing Conall Cernach blusters, but with little effect. The mere noise of the boy's sling is enough to flatten Conall, after which the boy ties his arms with a shield strap.

This shifts the burden to Cúchulainn, standing angrily nearby, who is restrained by his wife Emer. She has already guessed the boy's identity. Challenged by the smirch on Ulster's honour, Cúchulainn ignores Emer and faces the intruder, sword in hand. His demand that the boy tell his name is enough to impel the youngster to draw his sword and rush forward. With one swing of the blade he shaves the hair off Cúchulainn's scalp, just missing the drawing of blood. Putting aside their weapons, Cúchulainn and the boy begin to wrestle. The grown man thrusts the boy down so hard that his feet penetrate into stone up to the ankles. They roll into the water, each hoping to drown the other. At last Cúchulainn casts his lethal spear, the Gáe Bulga, into the boy. It tears into the young flesh, barbs opening out, turning the surf red with blood.

With his last breath the boy cries out that Cúchulainn has used something that Scáthach did not teach him – and it has mortally wounded him.

The name of their common teacher is enough to reveal the boy's identity to Cúchulainn, confirmed by finding the ring the father had left with Aífe. The father then takes Connla's body in his arms and brings it before the assembled Ulstermen.

Known as *Aided Óenfhir Aífe* [The Tragic Death of Aífe's Only Son], the Cúchulainn–Connla story is an Irish instance of the international tale type N731.3, of which the best-known example is the Persian story of Sohrab and Rustum.

TÁIN BÓ CUAILNGE

For wealth of detail, richness of characterization and enumeration of episode, not to mention sheer length, the *Táin Bó Cuailnge* can stand comparison with the national epics of Europe. It is not, however, a highly finished work. To begin with it lacks a unifying narrative tone. Successive episodes do not advance continuing themes. Scant motivation appears for abrupt shifts in character. Some have derisively called it an 'epic-like saga' rather than an epic. What we have survives in two versions that differ in both character and specifics. Internal linguistic evidence suggests that narratives within the epic *Táin Bó Cuailnge* began to form as early as the seventh century, but the two versions that come down to us are of later date. The oldest recension, found in *Lebor na hUidre* [Book of the Dun Cow] (1106), exhibits lean prose and sharp humour but is somewhat disjointed. The text in *Lebor Buide Lecáin* [Yellow Book of Lecan] (completed *c.*1390) is clearly copied from the *Lebor na hUidre*. The second version, found in *Lebor Laignech* [Book of Leinster] (completed *c.*1150), can be more literary at best but is also given to florid alliteration and sentimentality. The *Lebor Laignech* version includes the *remscéla* or foretales, such as the Deirdre story, that are now usually cited as anticipations of the central narrative, even when Cúchulainn or Medb do not appear in them.

Táin Bó Cuailnge is often referred to as 'the *Táin*' for short, although that is a bit misleading. The words *Táin Bó* [cattle raid] follow a storyteller's device of categorizing in the first word of the title the kind of action that is about to be told. Several other early Irish stories have titles beginning *Táin* . . . , such as the *Táin Bó Flidais* [Cattle Raid of Flidias] or *Táin Bó Fraích* [Cattle Raid of Fraích]. David Greene suggested the title of the epic is inappropriate and may have been influenced by analogy with the others. The motive in the action is a quest for a single bull, not a herd of cattle. The English title, The Cattle Raid of Cooley, is not usually cited in learned commentary.

The first of the *remscéla* is a ninth-century anecdote giving the purported origin of the story. Fergus mac Róich returns from the dead and recites the entire text to the chief poet Senchán Torpéist. Internal evidence indicates that the *Táin* is the work of many hands, but the creation of Senchán Torpéist, whose name appears rarely elsewhere, suggests that the compilers wished for a native equivalent of Homer.

In other *remscéla* we learn of Macha's curse on the Ulstermen, of Conchobar's birth, his struggle to gain the kingship and his ill-fated love for Deirdre. Three stories of Cúchulainn, related earlier in this chapter, tell of his birth, his courtship of Emer and training by Scáthach, and the tragic combat with his son Connla. The final foretale is a story of magical transformation with comic undertones, explaining how the two great bulls, the Brown Bull and the White-horned Bull, came to be. Two swineherds, Friuch [boar's bristle] and Rucht [boar's grunt], are good friends, but their masters and everyone around them try to incite trouble between them. Friuch keeps pigs in the household of Bodb, king of the Munster *sídh*, while Rucht labours at the Connacht *sídh* of Ochall Ochne, bitter enemy of Bodb. Each plays a trick on the other as a test of power, which ends their friendship and sets them against one another. Dismissed for damage to the herds from their trickery, the pig-keepers spend two years transformed into birds of prey before returning to human form to tell of war-wailing and heaps of corpses. By now their enmity seethes through each change of form. Off again, they become, successively, two water creatures, warriors, stags, phantoms, dragons and finally maggots or water worms, each transformation bringing them different names. When a cow belonging to Dáire mac Fiachna in Ulster drinks water containing one of the worms, Medb's cow in Connacht swallows the other. Both cows beget bulls. Rucht is then Finnbennach, the White-horned Bull of Connacht, and Friuch is Dub [dark] or Donn Cuailnge, the Brown Bull of Ulster.

The body of the *Táin Bó Cuailnge* embraces fourteen episodes of varying length, of which the fourth is clearly interpolated. It tells of the boyhood deeds of Cúchulainn, as related earlier in this chapter. The other thirteen depict the collisions of Connacht and Ulster, Medb and Cúchulainn.

Action begins in disarming quiet, with 'pillow talk', a dispute between Medb and her husband Ailill mac Máta in their bedroom at Cruachain [Rathcrogan, Co. Roscommon]. Romance is not the issue; power, as measured by possessions, is. Medb's luxuries give her an initial edge, but Ailill seems to win the contest by laying claim to the great white-horned bull, Finnbennach. Possession of cattle was the standard of wealth in early Ireland, a herding society; in pre-Christian culture they had been worshipped. Sealing his superiority with a gibe, Ailill reminds his wife that the prized Finnbennach was born into her herds but left them because it did not wish to be ruled by a woman. All her possessions are thus diminished because she does not possess a bull to equal the great white-horned one of her husband. What should she do? Through her courtier (and lover) Fergus mac Róich, Medb learns how she can win advantage. The other of the two greatest bulls in all of Ireland is living now in the region of Cuailnge in Ulster, and she must have it. (Cuailnge is the Cooley Peninsula in northeastern County Louth in the Republic of Ireland, but then a part of Ulster.) She sends representatives to bargain with the owner, Dáire mac Fiachna, offering many treasures, including access to her 'friendly thighs' (a phrase that will reappear in the text). Dáire rebuffs her offer.

Enraged when the news is delivered, Medb resolves to take the bull by force and calls up the armies of Connacht and Leinster as well as Ulster exiles Cormac Connloinges, son of Conchobar mac Nessa, and Fergus mac Róich. Convincing Ailill that any insult to her is shared by the household, she gains him as an ally in the quest to assert her claim to superior wealth. Before the army decamps Medb consults two seers about what it is to face. One is the mysterious prophetess known only as Fedelm, who weaves a fringe with a gold staff as she rides on the shaft of a chariot. Asked what she sees Fedelm answers with the word 'Crimson'. When she is challenged by Medb and others, she repeats 'Crimson' and adds a description of the formidable deeds of Cúchulainn. The second seer, a druid, is more consoling; he tells Medb that she will return alive.

As the driving force of a huge army, Medb is attentive to the discipline and deportment of individual troops. Her judgement, however, sometimes appears impetuous. Noticing that the Leinster soldiers are more adept than the Connachtmen, she fears that they will outshine her own people, demoralizing them. Such allies could betray her. She thinks of sending them home or even of killing them. Dissuaded from such rashness, Medb agrees to distribute the crack Leinster fighters among her own soldiers, shoring up weaker regiments and reducing the threat that the allies will win more glory.

Fergus mac Róich, though an Ulsterman, takes command in the field. Why he has joined the enemies of his country is not always clear. He may be jealous of Conchobar mac Nessa, who is king in his place, or he may have exiled himself after the king's role in the murder of the sons of Uisnech, as told in the Deirdre story. He is uneasy about opposing his countrymen. Ulster is virtually defenceless as the warriors there still suffer under Macha's curse, binding them in the pain of a woman in labour. All, of course, except Sualtam and his son Cúchulainn.

In his first encounter with Medb's army, Cúchulainn merely leaves a posted, written warning. This happens at Iraird Cuillen [Crossakeel, Co. Meath], when the party is two-thirds of the way to Cuailnge. The hero cuts an oak sapling into the ring shape of a spancel, which could be used as a fetter for a cow or goat, a common item on the Irish landscape at that time. On this Cúchulainn writes a threatening message in ogham, 'Come no further, unless you have a man who can make a hoop like this one, with one hand, out of one piece.' At this time Cúchulainn sends his mortal father Sualtam to warn the rest of the Ulstermen.

Cúchulainn himself is far removed when the army reads his warning, as he is enjoying a tryst with a young woman – possibly Fedelm Noíchrothach, daughter of Conchobar, or possibly her bondswoman. This Fedelm is married to Ailill's elder brother Cairbre Nia Fer, whom Cúchulainn kills in a story outside the *Táin*. Cairbre's son Erc is destined to make Cúchulainn suffer vengeance for this particular killing, even though it is only one of thousands.

On the next night his message is more compelling. After cutting the fork of a tree with a single stroke, Cúchulainn thrusts two thirds of the trunk into the earth. Then he decorates the branches with the severed heads of four Connachtmen who strayed from the rest of the forces. In horror Fergus reminds his men that it would violate a *geis* to pass the tree without pulling it out. Medb asks him to do this, and it takes him seven tries to succeed. When asked who could have slaughtered the four and have the strength to drive the tree so far into the ground, Fergus replies that it could only be his foster-son Cúchulainn. He then gives a long account of Cúchulainn's boyhood deeds, as retold on pp. 194–7 above.

As the Connacht army advances further toward Cuailnge, it faces only one enemy fighter. Cúchulainn taunts and terrorizes, usually only one soldier at a time. Yet he can show disarming mercy. He assures one trembling Connacht charioteer that he has no quarrel with him and seeks his master instead. That master turns out to be Orlám, a son of Medb and Ailill. Cúchulainn instantly decapitates him, knowing that the head will be returned to the army command post. As the grieving parents examine it, Cúchulainn uses his long slingshot to crush the head of Fertedil, Orlám's charioteer, because he disobeys the exacting order to carry Orlám's head further, all the way to Medb's and Ailill's private camp. When the occasion presents itself, Cúchulainn also employs his sling to kill a bird perched on Medb's shoulder, and later casts a fatal stone at the pet marten on her warm neck. Three arrogant brothers try to avenge Orlám's death, but Cúchulainn makes short work of them.

Meanwhile in Cuailnge, Donn the Brown Bull begins to sniff the distant bloodletting. Hovering near him, croaking encouragement, is the many-shaped goddess of war Mórrígan, who is sometimes a woman, sometimes a beast, a bird or the wind. Now she is a raven on the bull's shoulder, capriciously reversing mood in decrying death and slaughter. Rampaging, Donn Cuailnge puts his head down and mows everything in front of him, ploughing a deep furrow in the earth, frightening everyone within earshot.

The Connachtmen's first encounter with Donn Cuailnge goes badly when the bull gores the herdsman who tries to capture him. With a retinue of fifty heifers, Donn tramples through Medb and Ailill's camp, killing fifty warriors before bounding into the countryside. Such mishaps do not keep Medb from pulling away from camp for amorous meetings with Fergus. A charioteer reports these indiscretions to Ailill, who accepts them but with rancour.

With the Ulstermen still debilitated by Macha's curse, Cúchulainn alone faces the western army. Each night he makes devastating raids, smashing heads with efficient use of his slingshot, leaving hundreds dead. Even with these losses, however, the army advances. Events put Fergus in a tight corner, as Medb and the Connachtmen expect him to strike a blow for their side. In a parley with Cúchulainn, Fergus negotiates an agreement committing both sides to single combat each day; the duration of the combat will be the only time the army advances. With Fergus at this meeting is Etarcomol, the headstrong foster-son of Medb and Ailill, who stares insolently at Cúchulainn. This is followed by insults and the boast that he will be the first westerner to face the Ulster champion the next day. Etarcomol persists in baiting Cúchulainn until the Ulster hero in exasperation slices the young man in two, from crown to navel. After rebuffing Fergus's claim that Cúchulainn has already violated the agreement, the Ulster hero has nothing left to do but drag Etarcomol's body back to Medb's camp.

In an unexpected turn of events Medb and her entourage head north, away from the path east to Cuailnge, setting their sights on Dún

Sobairche [Dunseverick, Co. Antrim]. This temporarily presents Cúchulainn with a dilemma as he wishes to track the queen but also wants to protect his own territory on the eastern coast. As he is doubling back he encounters Buide mac Báin and twenty-four followers who most unexpectedly are driving none other than Donn Cuailnge and twenty-four cows. Cúchulainn kills Buide easily, but in the fracas the great Brown Bull is driven off, causing the hero to suffer deep disappointment and dismay. Recovering, he resumes the slaughter of the enemy. One victim is Medb and Ailill's satirist Redg, who first asks for the Ulsterman's javelin. Cúchulainn responds by putting it through the satirist's head. Redg answers gamely in his death throes, 'Now, that is a stunning gift.' The remark inspires the early Irish name for the place of this combat, *Áth Tolam Sét* [Ford of the Overwhelming Gift]. Dozens of Cúchulainn's other combats are described as explaining names of places, some real and others probably imaginary, on the medieval map of Ireland. In the meantime Medb plunders Dún Sobairche to the north, a diversion from her principal mission.

Again and again, Cúchulainn is the superior in all encounters, even when Medb's side reneges on the agreement, sending as many as a hundred fighters, hoping to extend the length of the combat so that her army would have more time to advance. As this is happening Cúchulainn must also face another resourceful female opponent, the supernatural Mórrígan, goddess of war, who is adept at shape-shifting. Usually taking the form of a huge raven, she may also appear as an eel that coils around the hero's legs, a she-wolf and a red-eared (i.e. otherworldly) heifer. Once when he fights her off, wounding her in the process, she comes before him as a crone milking a cow with three teats, one for each of the wounds he has inflicted on her. So tired that he does not perceive her ruse, Cúchulainn asks for a drink. When he blesses the teats for nourishing him, he inadvertently heals the wounds he had inflicted on Mórrígan.

Another supernatural figure serves Cúchulainn's efforts to defend Ulster. It is the hero's divine father, Lug Lámfhota, who appears gloriously clad in brilliantly coloured clothes, carrying lethal weapons and invisible to everyone except his son. To give the young man respite, he stands guard for three days and nights, allowing time for restorative sleep. Lug also attends to his son's wounds, washing them and applying healing oils. On the fourth day Cúchulainn awakes to the fitness and strength of his first day in combat.

Cúchulainn receives mortal assistance from an unexpected source, the boy troop of Emain Macha, younger counterparts of the youthful corps that the hero had joined when he went to the capital. One hundred and fifty of them fight because they have been spared Macha's debilitating curse delivered only to grown men. Their initial foray yields costly success, as each boy takes down a single Connachtman before falling himself. But the greater numbers in Medb's army mean that the boy troop is eventually depleted, with only one boy escaping. When he makes a final dash at killing Ailill, he too is brought down, this time by the king's bodyguards.

News of the boy troop calamity sends Cúchulainn into an extreme *ríastrad*, with a red mist like a fog of vapourized blood rising from him. To avenge the boy soldiers who had honoured him, Cúchulainn lays into the Connacht army with greater vehemence than he had shown before. Mounting his chariot he drives around the perimeter of the massed armies, slaughtering the hapless westerners six deep in a standing. Soon 500 are gone, then dozens of petty kings, scores of animals, even women and children. The huge pile of corpses means that no one can keep count of the massacre. But Cúchulainn and his chariot sustain not a scratch.

Fergus, Medb and Ailill rethink the principle of single combat. After some false starts, one of which is Medb's deceitful attempt to send twenty-nine selected warriors on a fruitless attempt against Cúchulainn, the Connacht leadership is ready to comply. The question is to select the right champion for their side. Though his name has not been mentioned earlier in the *Táin*, only Ferdiad, best friend of Cúchulainn and former pupil of Scáthach, is judged worthy of the challenge.

Getting the combatants to square off takes some doing. Ferdiad is initially reluctant to face his boon companion. To push him, the Connacht forces threaten him with disgrace if he refuses but offer rich rewards if he consents, including the pledged troth of Medb's beautiful, fair-haired daughter Finnabair and access to Medb's lovemaking as well. Ferdiad responds that this will be a fight to the death, and if he must kill his old friend, he will return to camp and finish off Medb.

Yet Ferdiad has to be Connacht's man because he is the only one who could possibly match the Ulster hero. In his camp Cúchulainn admits he dreads the looming duel, not because he fears Ferdiad but rather because he loves him.

Ferdiad's duel with Cúchulainn, the climax of the *Táin* for many readers, is often cited as 'the combat at the ford', as if it were the only one. In a herding society like early Ireland's, a society without modern bridges, all paths must eventually cross shallow passages of rivers and streams. Armed men and the cattle they drive are at their most vulnerable at such crossings. Not surprisingly, then, many battles take place at the fords of rivers, not only in the *Táin* but also in other early Irish literature. So while there is no foreshadowing for the person of Ferdiad, his battle with Cúchulainn at Áth Fhirdiad [Ardee, Co. Louth] on the Dee River, 14 miles north of Drogheda, is the culmination of a long series.

The battle rages for four days and includes boasts and taunts as well as constant hand-to-hand combat. Pieces of flesh the size of a baby's head are hacked away, leaving wounds that gape so wide birds can fly through them. Each night Cúchulainn sends Ferdiad leeches and herbs to heal his wounds; the Ulsterman does not wish to have the advantage of better medical treatment. Ferdiad responds by sharing his food. For the first three days neither can gain an advantage while they fight with darts, slender spears, heavy spears and heavy swords. On the fourth day Cúchulainn calls for his Gáe Bulga, the mysterious and powerful weapon whose use he had learned from the amazonian Scáthach. It is a spear that enters the body at one point but opens to make thirty wounds within. Before he can act, Ferdiad plunges his sword into Cúchulainn's chest, and Cúchulainn casts his spear through Ferdiad's heart and halfway out of his back. But the *coup de grâce* is just now coming. With Láeg the charioteer helping him, Cúchulainn thrusts the Gáe Bulga against Ferdiad, killing him. Immediately Cúchulainn begins to lament the passing of his quasi-brother and friend, but he is prostrate from his own wounds.

The Ulstermen have little to celebrate in Ferdiad's death because their own hero lies so weakened. Into the breach steps another champion who achieves some Cúchulainn-like deeds. White-haired Cethern mac Fintain, known for his generosity and his bloody blade, flies into the camp of the western army, inflicting great damage. He, too, is severely wounded. Returned to the Ulster camp he makes a poor patient. Cethern kills the healers (fifteen or as many as fifty) who attempt to treat him because he does not like their unfavourable diagnoses. At the same time he tells stories of how he acquired his wounds, one of which has come from Medb herself. Cúchulainn gathers bone marrow and animal ribs to help restore him. Cethern returns to battle, felling many of the enemy before he himself is struck down.

Other single champions come forth from Ulster while Cúchulainn lies exhausted, but their futile efforts serve only to disturb Sualtam, the hero's mortal father. Frightened, he thinks that either the sky is falling or his son is continuing against unequal odds and so seeks him out on the battlefield. Unable to rise, Cúchulainn sends Sualtam back to Emain Macha to rouse the rest of the troops. Taking this call most seriously, Sualtam rushes to the palace shouting with all the fury he can muster: 'Men murdered! Women stolen! Cattle plundered!' Three times he calls out, but there is no answer. A *geis* forbids a commoner to speak before the king, and a king to speak before the druid. Cathbad asks about the meaning of Sualtam's cry, and learning that Sualtam has broken protocol by speaking before the king, refuses any help. Angered by the response, Sualtam shouts even louder, and in so doing loses his footing and trips on his scallop-edged but razor-sharp shield, instantly separating his head from his shoulders. The severed head is brought before Conchobar, where Sualtam still shouts the same warnings.

In death Sualtam achieves what he could not in life. Conchobar rouses the men of Ulster, and, at long last, the debilities of Macha's curse begin to fall away from the fighting men. The charioteer Láeg, speaking for Cúchulainn, joins in the call to arms. The narrative now recognizes that immense forces are hurtling toward each other. As the armed companies advance, the text includes more than 500 lines of description of colour and armaments, all in anticipation of the massed assembly at Gáirech and Irgairech, southwest of Mullingar in what is now Co. Westmeath. During the night before what must be the final encounter, Mórrígan incites both armies against each other. As the battle begins the Connacht forces under Fergus's command break through the lines. In Cúchulainn's absence, Conall Cernach rises to the fore and taunts Fergus for betraying his own kind for 'the sake of a whore's backside'. Undeterred, Fergus makes his way to Conchobar and almost succeeds in killing him but pulls back when he remembers the king is a fellow Ulsterman. Word of the assault on Conchobar reaches the still-recovering Cúchulainn, driving him from his bed and thrusting him into his battle frenzy. This is enough to drive Fergus from the field; as he had earlier promised, there would be no duel with Ulster's prime hero.

Ailill and Medb are now alone on the battlefield, and they have the Brown Bull with them. Suddenly, and to Ailill's displeasure, Medb announces that she has to relieve herself, and she withdraws. This is the time of her period, and the massive flow of her menstrual blood (urine, in an alternative reading) digs three great channels, each big enough to take a household. This is also just the moment Cúchulainn, restored from his bed of pain, comes upon her. He resists taking her when she is at a disadvantage. And when she pleads to be spared, he answers that it would be right to execute her, but he is not a killer of women. Thus he allows her to escape, taking the prized Donn Cuailnge with her. In anger Cúchulainn slices off the tops of three nearby hills. The human battle is over.

Surveying the carnage, Fergus observes: 'We followed the rump of a misguiding woman.' (The pun *tóin* [rump] and *táin* [cattle raid] disappears in translation.) And Fergus adds, 'It is the usual thing for a herd led by a mare to be strayed and destroyed.'

Once Donn Cuailnge is led to Cruachain, Ailill and Medb's residence, he gives out three mighty bellows, challenging Finnbennach the white-horned bull, which is grazing nearby. Finnbennach rises to the call, charging toward Cruachain, attracting a huge crowd. As Donn Cuailnge is tired from the trek across Ireland, Finnbennach gains an initial advantage. Briccriu Neimthenga, known for fairness as well as his bitter tongue, is called in as judge, but the raging beasts trample him under their hooves. In a reversal, Donn Cuailnge stamps his hoof on Finnbennach's horn, pinning him to the ground. Standing nearby, Fergus goads the Brown Bull, saying too many men have died to let the White-horned Bull throw away his honour so easily. Thus released, the two bulls continue the battle all over Ireland until, at dawn, Donn

Cuailnge emerges at Cruachain with Finnbennach's bloody remains dangling from his horns. With the battle decided, Donn Cuailnge starts out on a circuitous route home, scattering Finnbennach's body parts hither and yon. The loins are memorably dropped at the principal ford of the Shannon, Áth Luain [ford of the loins, modern Athlone]. When Donn Cuailnge reaches Ulster at last, he falls at Druim Tairb [ridge of the bull], victim of his own bursting heart.

Ailill and Medb make peace with Ulster and with Cúchulainn, but their beautiful daughter stays with the former enemy. The men of Ulster return to Emain Macha in triumph.

Medb meets an absurd death in an eleventh-century story retold on pp. 87–8. In it Furbaide Ferbend, son of her murdered sister, punctures her skull with a hardened piece of cheese on an island in Lough Ree, Co. Roscommon. Her prowess and resilience fail her at the end.

Cúchulainn, though destined to live only a short life, still faces many more adventures.

MORE TROUBLES WITH WOMEN

Having been trained in martial arts by Scáthach, Cúchulainn is a fit adversary for the bellicose Queen Medb. He is less prepared to resist women endowed with other wiles, the flatterers, the beguilers and the temptresses. His interactions with a series of women, where he often finds himself at a disadvantage, fill the curious tenth- and eleventh-century narrative *Serglige Con Culainn agus Óenét Emire*, known in English as 'The Wasting Sickness of Cúchulainn' or 'The Sickbed of Cúchulainn and the Only Jealousy of Emer'. As the title implies, there is a lack of coherence between two surviving portions, implying derivation from two earlier stories. Cúchulainn's wife is first known as Eithne Ingubai and secondly as Emer, a conflict resolved in this retelling.

At the always portentous Samain time, the men of Ulster assemble at Mag Muirtheimne, Cúchulainn's bailiwick, when a flock of birds descends upon a nearby lake. Learning that all the women desire the beautiful birds, one for each shoulder, Cúchulainn withdraws from an intense match of the board-game fidchell and goes hunting for them. He captures enough to supply each noblewoman with two, leaving none for his wife Emer, who thought herself deserving of the first pick of the lot. To repair relations with her Cúchulainn promises her two superior feathered creatures, ones linked with a golden chain who can sing a song of sleep-inducing sweetness. When he tries to hunt them down he only grazes them with his spear, after which Cúchulainn falls into a deep sleep while seated next to a pillarstone. In a dream more real than any he had known before, he envisions two beautiful women coming toward him, one in green and one in red. They begin to laugh, but their intentions are anything but coquettish. The one in green takes out a horsewhip and begins to flail Cúchulainn, and then she is joined by the woman in red. They beat him for such a long time that life seems drained from him. And then they leave without explanation.

Cúchulainn is carried to Emain Macha, where he does not answer any questions about how he finds himself in this state, nor does he speak a word for another year. He lies in his 'wasting sickness', prostrate for a full turning of the seasons.

On the next Samain a stranger of otherworldly mien appears at Cúchulainn's bedside, offering to cure him in a cryptic song. He is Angus the son of Áed Abrat (not related to Angus Óg). He invites Cúchulainn to come with him to Mag Cruchna (Co. Roscommon) where the hero can be healed and where Angus's lovely sister Fand is longing to be with him. On Conchobar's advice, Cúchulainn is carried back to the pillarstone where he had first fallen into his state, and there he meets an attractive woman. Clad in green, she is recognizably one of the two who whipped him in the dream. Identifying herself as Lí Ban [paragon of women], she promises that she means him no further harm and instead seeks his friendship and possibly an alliance. She brings the greeting of her husband, Labraid Luathlám ar Claideb [swift hand on sword] of the otherworldly Mag Mell. The husband promises him Lí Ban's extraordinary sister Fand [tear], now released from her husband Manannán mac Lir, the sea god. His demand is only one day of Cúchulainn's service against Labraid's three frightful enemies: Senach Siaborthe, Eochaid Iúil and Eochaid Inber. The offer interests Cúchulainn, especially in view of Fand's renowned beauty – but as he is still stricken with the wasting sickness, he sends his charioteer Láeg to look into the matter for him. The charioteer sails with Lí Ban in a bronze boat to an island where they are greeted by Fand and three fifties of women lying on three fifties of couches. Greeting Láeg also is Labraid who expresses his disappointment that Cúchulainn has not come. On his return Láeg speaks glowingly of his time in Mag Mell and the people he met there. On Cúchulainn's bidding, Láeg summons Emer to her husband, whereupon she tells him it is time to rise from his sickbed. Scolding him for being weakened by 'woman-love', she tells him it is time to throw off the wasting sickness. Her words have the desired effect. He rises to find that the debilitation has passed from him. With his strength restored, Cúchulainn returns to the pillarstone where he again encounters Lí Ban, who repeats her invitation to return to Mag Mell. Saying he does not wish to follow a woman's bidding, Cúchulainn refuses and again sends Láeg on his behalf, this time travelling by land. In Mag Mell Láeg is greeted by Labraid along with Fáilbe Finn, a regent. Fand is also there, and when she hears that Cúchulainn said he would not respond to a woman's call, she reminds Láeg to tell his master that the invitation came from her. On his return Láeg again recounts the wonders he has seen and tells Cúchulainn he would be a fool not to visit the island of Fand and Labraid for himself.

With Lí Ban and Láeg in tow, Cúchulainn harnesses his chariot and makes for Mag Mell, where he receives a warm welcome. Fand, seeing the Ulster hero for the first time, shows her pleasure at what she beholds. Cúchulainn has little time for ceremony and forges ahead, eager for combat. To Labraid's dismay, he announces he will take on all three enemies and their retinues. After reconnoitring during the night, partly with the help of ravens, Cúchulainn is seized by his *ríastrad* or battle fury at dawn. Then, single-handedly, he makes short work of Labraid's antagonists. A thrown spear impales Eochaid Iúil as he bathes in a river. Wielding his sword with lightning speed, Cúchulainn flattens thirty-three soldiers to the left and right before crushing the skull of Senach Siaborthe with a terrible blow. Heartened by the Ulsterman's swift success, Labraid's army surges forward to drive the invading forces away, and Labraid himself asks that the killing cease. To withdraw from his battle fury, Cúchulainn is cooled in three vats of water, the first of which his body heat causes to boil over.

All of Mag Mell rejoices, and both Lí Ban and Fand honour Cúchulainn with poetry. Fand's offering is more warmly accepted. Soon she and Cúchulainn are off by themselves and they make love continually for the next month. As he makes ready to depart, Cúchulainn agrees to tryst with her by the yew tree at Ibor Cind Trácha, near the modern town of Newry, Co. Down. News of this reaches Emer's ears, and she is quickly consumed by her own fury. She leads fifty women with whetted knives to the appointed spot at the appointed time. What follows, however, reverses expectations. Emer delivers an oration denouncing men's lust for what they do not have and their rejection of the familiar, which causes Cúchulainn to pledge his intention to live with his wife for ever. Seeing such exquisite love, Fand asks to be abandoned. Touched by the lover's unselfishness, Emer then asks to be left behind. Each woman would deliver Cúchulainn's love to the other. This ticklish impasse is resolved by the unanticipated arrival of Manannán mac Lir, Fand's husband, who spirits her away with him. Cúchulainn, anguished at this turn of events, wanders the mountains of Munster, unwilling to eat or drink until the druids give him a vial of forgetfulness. The same drink also washes away all of Emer's jealousy. In a magical conclusion, Manannán mac Lir shakes his cloak of forgetfulness between Cúchulainn and Fand so that they may never meet again.

DEATH OF CÚCHULAINN

Stories of how Cúchulainn dies began to circulate as early as the tenth century, well before the *Táin Bó Cuailnge* reached its final form. In all accounts he is no more than twenty-seven years old, the magic number built on Celtic triplism: $3 \times 3 \times 3$. Always invincible in combat, Cúchulainn is brought down by a combination of the physical and the metaphysical: the deceptions of wizardry, the violations of *gessa*, and the implacable vengeance of wronged heroes. The vision of the champion forcing himself to stand tall in his final moments has appealed deeply to later generations of readers. It is the unmistakable inspiration for Oliver Sheppard's famous statue in Dublin and has been the starting point for numerous modern illustrators.

In his battles with Medb, Cúchulainn had killed a warrior named Cailitin, who was also a wizard and possibly of Fomorian origin. After this Cailitin's wife gave birth to sextuplets, three boys and three girls, all of them hideous and misshapen. As their father had been her ally, Medb takes the venomous little creatures under her protection and sends them all to Scotland to study sorcery. On their return she incites them against her long-time adversary, Cúchulainn. She begins with an invasion of Cuailnge, to the southeast of Emain Macha, certain of drawing Conchobar mac Nessa into the fray. Hearing that treachery is planned against Ulster's prime hero, Conchobar orders Cúchulainn to come to Emain Macha, while still sharing the company of Emer, his druids and the women of Ulster. The loathsome children of Cailitin come to the plain before the fortress and fling up showers of dead oak leaves and withered stalks of thistles. They raise an ear-splitting clamour that sounds like a vast army. Thinking Emain Macha undefended, Cúchulainn starts to rush out to meet the invaders when Cathbad, the wise druid, tells him it is all a hallucination, designed to lure him to his death. Wait three days, he adds, and it will all be gone. One of the witches transforms herself into a crow and flies over Cúchulainn's head, taunting him with reports of the destruction of Dún Delgan and of his followers.

Within the fortress, Cúchulainn is comforted by his Emer as well as by other women. One of them is Niam, usually seen as the wife of Conall Cernach, who in this context has become Cúchulainn's mistress with Emer's apparent compliance. (She is not the Niam who is the lover of Oisín.) On Emer's advice, Niam tries to take Cúchulainn to the Glen of the Deaf [Silent Valley in the Mourne Mountains], where the bewitching sounds of the supposed attack cannot penetrate. After first refusing, Cúchulainn agrees to leave for a safe place. Meanwhile, the children of Cailitin scour the landscape, filling valleys and glens with their howling and screaming. A daughter of Cailitin magically takes the form of one of Niam's attendants, and in this guise leads Niam away from the safety of the assembled company. This allows another daughter to assume Niam's lovely form in which she tells Cúchulainn to leave Emain Macha to save Ulster from Medb's armies. Surprised but still deluded, he agrees. As he readies himself to depart a gold brooch falls and punctures his foot, a decidedly bad omen.

Departing with Láeg he is subject to more hallucination from clan Cailitin, that Emer's headless body has been thrown from the ramparts of Dún Delgan and then the entire fortress burned and levelled. Immediately, Cúchulainn and Láeg return to Emain Macha, where they find Emer safe and whole. She reminds him that he has been victim of continuing wizardry, and pleads with him to stay with her. Still hearing the call to save Ulster, and sensing that his end may be near, Cúchulainn's answers Emer's imploring by telling her that he has never shirked a fight and that fame outlives life. With this he and Láeg depart for the south.

After passing the house of his nursemaid, where he stops for some refreshment, Cúchulainn comes upon three crones, all blind in the left eye. They are cooking something on a rowan-tree spit over a fire; it is the carcass of a dog. As the crones also have poisons and spells, Cúchulainn is wary, much more because the eating of dog meat is a violation of a *geis*, incumbent upon him because of his name, '*hound of Culann*'. But he cannot simply withdraw because he would violate another *geis* if he visited any cooking hearth and did not accept food offered to him. His chariot speeds by, implying he does not wish to stop, when one of the crones calls out to him to stop and be sociable. He refuses, but she entreats him further by saying her small meal is only a roasting hound. Then she adds the taunt that it is unseemly to see the great ones of the world who cannot stand the company of the humble and the poor. With this he relents and draws near to her fire, where she gives him a dog shoulder-blade with her left hand. He eats some of the meat, holding it in his left hand. Uneasy, he then tries to put the meat aside, hiding it under his left thigh. Forces beyond Cúchulainn's person are not deceived, and immediately he feels a seizure. The strength in his left arm and thigh begins to diminish. Cúchulainn and Láeg quickly leave the crones' fire and push on to Muirtheimne.

Racing to the plain near his fortress of Dún Delgan, Cúchulainn and Láeg bound through enemy forces, scattering them like hailstones in a storm or leaves in a gale. Greater challenges lie ahead in the persons of the clan Cailitin, Erc son of Cairbre Nia Fer, still smouldering with anger from Cúchulainn's murder of his father (p. 205, above), and Lugaid son of the murdered Cú Roí. The clan Cailitin supply their allies with three spears, throwing the first one themselves. After missing Cúchulainn, their intended target, the spear impales Láeg, spilling his intestines on the cushions of the chariot. Erc hurls the second spear, which again misses Cúchulainn, finding its mark instead in the flesh of the Grey of Macha. Lugaid, the third adversary, has a lethal thrust. His spear pierces Cúchulainn's armour and tears the flesh away from the entrails. This panics the remaining horse, Saingliu, who gallops off with half the chariot's yoke, leaving Cúchulainn to die alone with the rest of the vehicle.

Enemies, watching from a cautious distance, know the champion is nearing his end but dare not approach him as they can still see the hero's light flickering around his head. Holding the huge wound together, Cúchulainn drags himself to a nearby lake for a soothing drink and a chance to wash himself. Seeing a pillarstone nearby, he struggles toward it, putting his back against it for support. Taking his belt, he ties himself to the stone so that he might die standing up, as he had once pledged. Lugaid and Erc banter between themselves over who should have the courage to act. Cúchulainn's faithful horse, the Grey of Macha, though bleeding from his wounds, returns to make a last pass with teeth and hooves against the timid attackers. The agony continues for three days while the ravens of battle, Badb and Mórrígan, hover about the champion's head until the hero's light at last flickers out. Cúchulainn then lets out a great sigh, splitting the stone at his back. A raven lights on his slumped shoulder and settles there. The Grey of Macha fetches Conall, brings him to Cúchulainn's body and lays his head on the dead hero's breast.

Emboldened by the sight of the raven where it would otherwise never perch, Erc and Lugaid approach Cúchulainn, lifeless but still standing. As Lugaid pulls back Cúchulainn's hair, hoping for a clean swipe at the neck, the Ulsterman's sword falls, severing Lugaid's hand at the wrist. In revenge Lugaid and his men remove both the right hand and the head of Cúchulainn, which they bear in triumph to Tara. The hero's body, still tied to the pillarstone, remains in the field. Tradition associates Cúchulainn's death with the stone called Clocharfarmore [stone of the big man] still standing about four miles south of Dundalk.

Later Conall Cernach avenges his friend's death by killing Lugaid.

11

The Fenian Cycle

FÉNI, FIANNA, FENIANS

Stories from the third cycle of Irish heroic literature are often set far from the seats of royal power and usually depict men in battle. Sometimes the men are in conflict with rapacious mortal invaders, at other times with different bellicose factions of their own warrior caste, or perhaps with alluring supernatural figures. At the centre of the action, not always portrayed favourably, is the poet–warrior–seer Fionn mac Cumhaill, along with his armed companions, the Fianna Éireann. Many of the later stories of the cycle are set within a narrative frame that asserts that Oisín, Fionn's son, and Caílte mac Rónáin, Fionn's cohort or nephew, have survived to a later date and are recalling wondrous deeds from earlier days. The third is also the most voluminous of all the cycles, with more stories recorded in manuscript tradition than from the other three, as well as much celebration in oral tradition. It is the only cycle still alive in the mouths of traditional Irish and Scottish Gaelic storytellers at the beginning of the twenty-first century. Some stories, old and new, are filled with rollicking adventures told with a *Boys' Own Paper* depiction of hard-won victories. Stories told within the Oisín and Caílte narrative framework, especially when the listener is a Christian figure such as St Patrick, are tinged with a sense of loss and regret for a stout-hearted, generous heroism that cannot be regained.

Today 'Fenian' is the usual name for the cycle, but this has not always been so, and many commentators are uncomfortable with it. In much of the nineteenth century, 'Ossianic' was the preferred name, under the influence of the Scottish charlatan James Macpherson's invention of 'Ossian' for 'Oisín'. Macpherson's *Poems of Ossian* had borrowed heavily from oral traditions of this cycle, and the use of 'Ossianic' seemed to imply that here one might find the untainted originals. Oisín is indeed the narrator of many of the stories of the cycle. From the nineteenth century through to the present some observers have preferred 'Finn Cycle', employing an Old Irish form for Fionn mac Cumhaill, the foremost presence. One still sees that phrase in print, but it is not the most common.

The word 'Fenian' is a neologism coined in 1804 by yet another charlatan, Colonel Charles Vallancey, outwardly appearing to be an anglicization of the Irish 'fianna'. Contained within it, however, is an apparent word-play on the Old Irish *Féni*, another name for the early invaders of Ireland, the Goidels, the people who brought the Irish language to the island. They are often thought 'true Gaels'. In early Irish law the Féni are the old, aboriginal or purest population, free land-tillers, never to be confused with servants or slaves. To someone who knows no Irish the words *Féni* and fianna might appear similar, but from their roots they have no linguistic connection. 'Fenian' none-theless entered popular usage in the nineteenth century and acquired political associations that do nothing to illuminate Old Irish literature. The Irish Republican Brotherhood, the revolutionary body founded in 1858, adapted 'Fenian' as an alternative name, and so it was cited in story and song, as in 'The Bold Fenian Men'. Fenian activity peaked in 1866–7, with an armed invasion of Canada by US members, most of them veterans of the Union Army in the Civil War, and open rebellion in British-occupied Ireland. More recently 'Fenian' has been the popular designation for Republican, anti-British advocacy, especi-ally in the six counties of Ulster still a part of the United Kingdom.

If 'Fenian' is seen as the equivalent of fianna, there is a certain appropriateness in naming the cycle after the band of men instead of their leader. Fionn, after all, does not appear in every story, whereas the fighting men do. Furthermore, the fianna (sing. fian) are rooted in history, while Fionn, despite sustained and passionate belief in his historicity, was never a mortal being. The capitalized Fianna Éireann are the creatures of the third cycle of Irish heroic literature, but the lower-case fianna were an everyday part of medieval Irish life. The Brehon Laws tell us that they were bands of non-subject, landless men, who were not foreigners. They stood apart from the rest of society and were responsible for defending Ireland against external enemies, both natural and supernatural. Their first allegiance was to the *ard rí* [high king]. In exchange for lodging and board, they might serve a regional king who did not maintain an army of his own. We read of their resistance to the Norsemen in the eighth and ninth centuries, but there is no mention of them when the Normans arrived after 1170. How early they might have existed is a question that invites speculation. The Irish fianna may have an antecedent among the ancient Gauls known as the *gaesatae* [spear-men?]. The Greek historian Polybius (second century BC) describes them in the Upper Rhône Valley, armed men who were not a part of the Celtic settlements they defended. In the past 200 years or so of Celtic studies, commentators have differed over what status the fianna held in Irish life. Initially they were seen as Irish counterparts of the chivalrous Knights of the Round Table, and later as samurai. Such a vision encouraged the leading political party of independent Ireland to call itself Fianna Fáil, or the 'soldiers of destiny'. Others have seen them as parasitic marauders, living off the fruits of common labour that they disdained.

Membership in a fianna was exclusive but not hereditary. An applicant had to distinguish himself intellectually as well as physically. He must become a prime poet and master twelve books of poesy. Among the ordeals he had to endure was standing waist-deep in a hole armed only with a shield and a hazel stick while nine warriors threw their spears at him from a distance of nine furrows; to suffer even one wound was to fail. He would be rejected if his weapons quivered in his hands, if his braided hair was disturbed by hanging branches, or if his foot cracked a dead branch as he strode through the forest. He should have the ability to make a running leap over a bough equal to the height of his brow or to pass easily under one as low as his knee. One of the most difficult tests required him to pull a thorn from his foot while running, without slowing down.

Although the names of Fionn, his son Oisín and his grandson Oscar are among the most widely known from early Irish tradition, their relative celebrity owes little to the influence of individual Fenian texts. The bulk of narratives is much larger than in the other three cycles, a testimony to their appeal to popular audiences over many centuries.

But readers whose tastes have been formed on prestige Western literature are likely to find Fenian heroics wanting. Sean O'Faoláin called
Fenian stories the 'sow's ear of Celtic literature'. Contrast the Ulster
Cycle's *Táin Bó Cuailnge* with the Fenian near-epic *Cath Fionntrágha*
[The Battle of Ventry], which probably dates from the twelfth century
but survives in a fifteenth-century recension. Ventry is an actual place,
four miles west of the modern town of Dingle, Co. Kerry. In it Fionn
and his men ferociously resist Dáire Donn, 'the king of the world',
probably a stand-in for the Holy Roman Emperor. Clash of arms
might be the climax to a suspenseful narrative, but page after page of
uninterrupted sword-play and derring-do make for tedious reading.
Such a narrative evidently brought a different effect when recited
to audiences with few other entertainments. Folklorists speak of the
'endless battle' motif, formula Z12, tale type 2300. Many of the
English-language adaptations of Fenian stories have been in juvenile
fiction, heavily edited and bowdlerized. The most often adapted narratives, the love stories of Diarmait and Gráinne or Oisín and Niam, are
not typical of the cycle. When William Butler Yeats embodied the
spirit of old Ireland in his depiction of the 1916 insurrectionists, he
chose Cúchulainn not Fionn mac Cumhaill.

Some of the most admired passages from the Fenian Cycle are not
narrative but rather nature poetry, such as those in the fifteenth-century
Duanaire Finn [The Poem Book of Fionn], which cannot be known
adequately in translation. The twentieth-century poet and fiction
writer James Stephens evoked the earlier tradition in a widely quoted
passage in his *Irish Fairy Tales* (1920). In it Fionn quizzes his men as
to which sound provides the finest music to be heard. Their answers
are all worthy: the calling of a cuckoo from a high tree, the ring of a
spear on a shield, the belling of a stag across water, the baying of a
tuneful pack of hounds heard in the distance, the song of a lark, the
laugh of a gleeful girl or the whisper of a beloved. The master then
answers his own question. 'The music of what happens,' says great
Fionn, 'that is the finest music in the world.'

FIONN ASCENDANT

Fionn's stories are known in all parts of Ireland, Gaelic Scotland, the Isle of Man and Gaelic-speaking Nova Scotia. His usual fortress or 'palace' is the Hill of Allen [OIr. *Almu*; ModIr. *Almhain*] in County Kildare, a claim not supported by archaeological research. Appearances in so many texts over centuries in different lands mean that Fionn has such a shifting persona he can sometimes appear to be an entirely different personage. Not surprisingly, there are more than twenty spellings of his usual name, including the anglicized Finn Mac-Cool. Many commentators prefer the classical Irish spellings Finn and Find, consistent with most others in this volume. The spelling 'Fionn mac Cumhaill' cited here is Modern Irish, in part because he is portrayed in more Modern Irish stories than other heroes, but also to distinguish him from the more than two dozen other early Irish figures named Finn or Find. And as with Cúchulainn, this is a name he acquires as he matures.

Chronicles assigned Fionn the death date of AD 283, and Geoffrey Keating (*c.*1580–*c.*1645/50) sanctioned his historicity. He is thought to have lived during the reigns of the legendary kings Cormac mac Airt and his son Cairbre Lifechair. The lack of evidence for there ever having been such a person as Fionn did little to restrain the confidence of oral storytellers in his having once walked the byways of Ireland. In the early 1970s an Irish countryman soberly advised folklorist E. Estyn Evans that Fionn was not a giant, as some held, but actually stood at only five foot six.

Linguistically, Fionn's antecedents are incalculably ancient. The gloss of his name as 'fair' or 'light-haired one' links him to a continental Celtic divinity Vindonnus – cf. Gaulish *vindos* [white] – whose name is cited in a dozen place-names from the Roman occupation, notably Vindabona along the Danube on the site of the modern Vienna. This is not to suggest that Fionn is directly descended from Vindonnus, but rather that the name of the continental deity is refracted in scores of names of figures from early Ireland and Wales, including the Welsh Gwynn ap Nudd, whose name is the equivalent of Fionn's although the two are not exact counterparts.

A more immediate anticipation of the heroic figure is Find, the early Irish personification of wisdom suggested by the geographer Ptolemy (second century AD). According to Dáithí Ó hÓgáin (1988), this Find was venerated by Leinstermen in the Boyne valley who were driven from their homeland by the depredations of the Uí Néill dynasty from Ulster. Certain families among them, such as the Uí Fháilghe, then projected Fionn the poet-warrior-seer who lives in the countryside, prepared to defend his people while not ruling them. His continuing enmity is with the Uí Néill, the most powerful political force in pre-Norman Ireland. Fully formed as a persona as early as the sixth century, Fionn had been accommodated in Leinster genealogies by the seventh.

While his pedigree might have been fabricated, the names within it remain fixed, even when personalities behind them are almost vaporous. His father is always Cumhall, cited in the ubiquitous patronymic, mac Cumhaill, of the Clan Baíscne. Cumhall is killed by the rival Clan Morna, led by Goll mac Morna, even before Fionn is born. The young Fionn will enter upon a world in which bloody rivalry between the two clans is a given; his challenge will be to reunite them under his leadership. Fionn's mother is Muirenn Muncháem [of the white neck] through whom the hero claims his most important ancestor, Nuadu Airgetlám [of the silver hand], king of the Tuatha Dé Danann; or perhaps it was only Nuadu Necht, a Leinster manifestation of Nuadu Airgetlám. When his widowed mother is unable to raise Fionn, she has him nursed by her sister Bodhmall, a druidess. Another family member, Fiacclach mac Conchinn, also fosters the boy, endowing him with a spear that never misses its mark.

From birth the hero is known as Demne Máel, a name implying short hair and associations with druids, craftsmen and poets. Like Cúchulainn, born Sétanta, or Heracles, born Alcides, he must win the name by which he will be known. His growth to young manhood is outlined in a short text *Macgnímartha Find* [The Youthful Exploits of Fionn], unmistakably modelled on the boyhood career of Cúchulainn as told in early sections of the *Táin Bó Cuailnge*. Setting out to seek his fortune, Demne comes to a group of boys on the plain of the Liffey and engages them in a series of athletic contests, including the early stick–ball game of hurling or hurley. No matter what the sport, young

Demne is victorious, even when all of the others are against him. The jealous chieftain of the nearby fortress urges the boys to be rid of the upstart by drowning him in a nearby lake, but Demne drowns nine of them. A spectator calls out, 'Who is the fair boy?' [ModIr. *Cé hé an giolla fionn?*]. And thus he becomes Fionn the son of Cumhall.

Young Fionn may excel at what all men must do, being a superior runner and jumper in a milieu that lacks cavalry, but he also gains from exploits denied to ordinary mortals. Among the most famous stories attached to him is how he acquired 'knowledge' – not erudition or learning, but what we would call occult or esoteric knowledge. While still a youth he becomes the pupil of the druid or seer Finnéces, who has been waiting seven years to find the Salmon of Knowledge at Linn Féic [Fiac's Pool], along the Boyne River. A later tradition places this episode at the falls of Assaroe on the Erne in Co. Donegal. The druid's name means 'Finn the seer', which might imply a link to old Find, the early personification of wisdom or a doubling with Fionn himself. Finnéces' patience is rewarded when he at last catches the salmon, which he roasts on a spit over an open fire. Wanting the salmon's power for himself, he asks the boy to leave it alone. But when Fionn touches it and burns his thumb, he thrusts the injured digit into his mouth. He has not eaten the fish, but merely tasting the salmon's flesh is enough to deny Finnéces wishes. When the druid asks the boy his name he still answers 'Demne'. Finnéces responds, 'Your name is Fionn, for it was prophesied that a fair-haired man would eat the Salmon of Knowledge, and you are that fair-haired Fionn. Eternal knowledge is yours now, not mine.' An alternative, less well-known story of the eighth century has Fionn gain superhuman knowledge when he catches his thumb in the door of an otherworldly dwelling on Sliab na mBan [Slievenamon], Co. Tipperary. The thumb motif is constant, however. Through a thousand stories Fionn can always summon up his special powers of knowledge by bringing his thumb to his mouth.

The Modern Irish name for Fionn's esoteric knowledge is *fios*, which in other contexts may also denote second sight. Above this he is attributed powers of divination known by specific if cryptic names that were earlier seen as the province of the druids. *Díchetal do chennaib* [OIr. extempore incantation (?)] is a kind of spell or incantation composed on the spot, often using the fingertips. It may have been a kind of clairvoyance or psychometry in which Fionn conveys his message in quatrain or verse. Druids and certain poets also possess this power, which St Patrick did not condemn because it did not involve pagan rites. Such rites are called for in *imbas forosnai* [poetic knowledge that illuminates], in which the practitioner chews a piece of red flesh from pig, dog or cat. He then sleeps for three days and nights, after having placed the flesh on a flagstone, chanting invocations to unnamed gods. He must also chant over his two palms, asking that his sleep be not disturbed. After the three-day sleep Fionn judges if *imbas forosnai* has come to him. This is a power shared by the highest rank of poet, the *ollam*. Lastly is the enigmatic *teinm laida* [OIr. breaking open of the pith], another chewing of the thumb with powers greater than *fios*, perhaps a combination of some of the others. St Patrick banned this as 'giving offerings to demons'.

Like Cúchulainn, Fionn is trained by an amazonian tutor, Búanann, but he also studies with a male, Cethern mac Fintain. His unnamed spear that never misses its mark is not his only weapon; he also wields the famous sword Mac an Lúin. When charging into battle Fionn and his men intimidate their enemies by shouting the war cry of Dord Fían. When hunting, his favourite quarries are wild boar and deer. His favourite animal is the dog, and the two most associated with him, Bran and Sceolang, are his transformed cousins. He is described as slaying a serpent in nearly every body of water in Ireland, the Isle of Man and Gaelic Scotland.

Despite Fionn's customary association with the countryside, and the hundreds of allusions to him in surviving, often remote place-names, the first great feat usually attributed to him is a defence of the seat of the *ard rí* [high king] at Tara. Aillén mac Midgna, usually known as 'the burner', had been a fairy musician of the Tuatha Dé Danann, who lived at Sídh Finnachad in the north (also home to Lir, father of the swan children) or nearby Sliab Fúait [Slieve Fuad]. Each Samain Aillén would come to Tara, playing on his *timpán*, a kind of drum or tambourine. The sweetness of Aillén's music concealed his darker motives. Once the men of Tara were lulled to sleep, even those suffering from wounds, Aillén would spew forth flaming rock from his mouth and burn the residence to the ground. Unresisting, the powers at Tara allowed this to continue for twenty-three years. Each year they would dutifully rebuild the palace, and when Samain came they submitted to Aillén's next visit. Sensing their despair, Fionn offers to rid them of Aillén if all those present at Tara – nobles, poets and druids – will guarantee his heritage, meaning the restoration of Clan Baíscne with Fionn at its head. They agree. The hero first makes himself immune to Aillén's musical charms by inhaling the poison of his own spear, whose point is so venomous as to forbid sleep. This immunization against the allure of music evokes Odysseus' resistance to the songs of the sirens in Book XII of the *Odyssey*. Aillén's magic has the expected effect on the rest of the party, which falls into a deep sleep. When Aillén's mouth opens to send out a great, engulfing flame, Fionn is prepared, thrusting forward his crimson, fringed cloak. The garment drives the fire downward, where it scorches a massive crater deep in the earth. Seeing his power thwarted, Aillén flees to his underground lair in the north with Fionn in hot pursuit. Before Aillén can reach safety, Fionn impales him with his spear. Quickly cutting off Aillén's head, Fionn returns with it to Tara, where he fixes it on a pole for everyone to see the next dawn. Overjoyed at his deliverance, the king of Tara proclaims that Fionn son of Cumhall shall be the new chief or *rigfhéinnid* of the fianna. Goll mac Morna, slayer of Cumhall, agrees, striking his palm against Fionn's, making himself the ally of the son of his old enemy. In subsequent tales Goll may be a cohort or a rival. Goll is also linked to Connacht, home of many of Fionn's mortal rivals.

Fionn is a defender, never an invader. With fair hair, broad shoulders and a broad brow, he enjoys the good looks of a romantic hero, early or modern. His enemies may be from other parts of the Gaelic world, often Connacht, or Scandinavia, that is, Lochlainn. Sometimes his enemies are exotic, like 'The King of Greece' or 'The King of the World'. Some with names implying darkness, Arca Dubh [Black Arky], Borba [harsh, arrogant], or Dealra Dubh [dark sheen], seem to pop up only so Fionn can knock them down. While highly mobile, Fionn is always portrayed on foot, never in a chariot like Cúchulainn. He is not assigned a favourite horse. John V. Kelleher once remarked that allusions to Fionn and the Fenians in local place-names are as common as 'lover's leap' and 'devils' washtub' are in North America. Often the attribution implies giant strength such as the 'Parallel Roads' that line Glen Roy in Inverness-shire, which are actually markers from ancient glacial lakes. Fionn is thought to have cut mountain passes with his sword, but also lends his name to lesser landscape features such as caves and 'fingerstones' (bare, vertical rocks).

In still another class of stories Fionn tangles with the supernatural. Among the most common of these are many of the *bruidhean* [hostel, banqueting hall] type, in which Fionn and his men are lured into an attractive residence and find all exits closed once they are inside. Anne Ross (1967) has suggested that the fear associated with the *bruidhean* derives from the burning of human sacrifices in wickerwork images in pre-Christian times. The motif is not unique to the Fenian Cycle and a close parallel can be found in *Togail Bruidne Da Derga* [the Destruction of Da Derga's Hostel], part of either the Ulster or Mythological Cycle. Often, but not always, the seducer is a beautiful but treacherous woman. In the widely known (both Ireland and Scotland) *Bruidhean Chaorthainn* [Hostel of the Quicken Trees] the villain is Midac, a young man of Lochlainn who had been raised with the Fianna at the Hill of Allen. He invites his former benefactors to his residence along the Shannon River only in hopes of betraying them to the King of the World. Yet other stories are clearly allegorical, as in the fifteenth-century text where Fionn and his men encounter an old man, a ram, and a beautiful young woman. The ram who butts the men's food from their table and will not be restrained is the world. The woman who tells Fionn he has had her already, as she rejects him, is youth. And the old man who makes quick work of the ram is old age, which eventually subdues all.

Among Fionn's many powers is the ease he has with most women. Unlike Cúchulainn with Emer, he lacks a constant mate. Encounters with more than fifty named women produce innumerable progeny. One of the many named Áine swears she will sleep with no man except Fionn. The imposition of Christian ideas of monogamy classifies some of these women as 'wives' and others as 'lovers', a distinction not made by the original storytellers. The best remembered of these today, though not necessarily the most important, is Sadb the deer-maiden, also known as Saba or Blaí. Her story comes in two versions. In the first she has been enchanted into deer form by Fer Doirich the druid.

After the hounds Bran and Sceolang chase her into the Hill of Allen, Fionn gives the deer shelter and is delighted when it turns into a beautiful young woman. They become lovers, and she gives birth to the child Oisín, whose name is the diminutive of deer, *os*. When Fionn returns to hunting, Sadb is again enchanted by Fer Doirich, and so abandons her infant son. Seven years later Fionn finds him naked under a rowan tree near the storied mountain of Ben Bulben in Sligo. In the second version the lover, sometimes named Blaí, is usually a beautiful young woman married to Fionn who is transformed into a deer by a malicious but unnamed magician while her husband is away. Once again the mother abandons the child, only to have the father find him some years later. Oisín becomes an important member of the fianna though not necessarily as an heir of Fionn or as a leader of men. Within the older, Irish-language manuscript tradition the favoured offspring is Oisín's son Oscar, Fionn's grandson, the 'Galahad of the Cycle'. In certain later narratives, to be considered in this chapter, Oisín becomes the lover and poet who inspired James Macpherson's chicanery.

THE HERO AND THE ANTI-HERO

Standish James O'Grady put it most simply: 'Heroes expand into giants, dwindle into goblins, or fling aside the heroic form and gambol as buffoons . . .' (1878). He should have made the qualification that the arc from acclaim to pratfall is followed by popular heroes such as Heracles, rather than by epic heroes such as Achilles. Heracles was the subject of an immense body of popular literature, not all of which survives, that inverted his most admirable virtues. By the time of Aristophanes' *The Frogs* (405 BC) he had been reduced to a figure of slapstick motivated by gluttony and lust. Achilles, whose character is fixed in the *Iliad*, suffers no such transmogrification, and neither does Cúchulainn, whose character is kept in place by the *Táin Bó Cuailnge*. The popular Fionn, the Fionn of oral tradition, is a highly protean character, much cruder than the Fionn of manuscript tradition, as Gerard Murphy points out in the introduction to volume III of *Duanaire Finn* (1953), one of the most searching and profound analyses of the cycle. To a certain extent, the very ubiquity of a heroic character is enough to invite his deflation. Raphael Patai (1972) has observed a parallel phenomenon in modern popular literature in which industrialization can reproduce characterizations with a speed and thoroughness unanticipated before the printing press. In such media the hero-buffoon, Buster Keaton or Dagwood Bumstead, is a commonplace.

Portrayals of the comic and anti-heroic are more common in later oral literature, and more common in English-language and Hiberno-English stories than in Irish, Scottish Gaelic or Manx stories. David Krause in *The Profane Book of Irish Comedy* (1982) traces the roots of the comic Fionn to an eighth-century manuscript whose English title is 'The Quarrel Between Finn and Oisín', in which the son speaks antagonistically to his father. Whereas we are used to Oisín singing his father's praises in dialogue with the authoritarian St Patrick, Krause asserts that this older Oisín was a rebellious Oedipus set on humiliating his father, Laius. As the centuries passed and Christianity became more a part of the narrative, Oisín transferred his aggressions to the new religious authority imported from abroad and began to puff up the reputation of his departed father.

A taste for coarse humour is more evident in the Fenian Cycle than any of the other three. In later folktales the once-heroic Fionn has his vanity deflated with such demeaning challenges as being asked to whistle with a mouth full of oatmeal. Only the Fenian Cycle has produced anything like the 128 surviving Céadach tales from both Ireland and Gaelic Scotland, with still more from Nova Scotia. The mischievous and querulous Céadach is an interloper to the Fenian milieu. Often disguised in skins, he seeks to elbow into the fianna for reasons that are never clear. Often an unwanted 'helper', he may be called Céadach or may bear any of many names, or he may have a nickname like 'the hard gilly/servant' or the 'churl'. Fionn is rarely the butt of his contrivances, but leading members of the fianna are. Once he persuades them all to climb on the back of a tired old horse, which then collapses under the weight. After urging them all to mount another horse, he watches as the horse rushes off to take the warriors under the sea.

The best-known story of Fionn as a buffoon-hero is not recorded before the nineteenth century, and then only in English without a known Irish-language antecedent. William Carleton (1794–1869), an Ulster-born Catholic turned Protestant novelist, gave his fifteen-page version the title 'The Legend of Knockmany' in an 1845 collection of stories. Knockmany is a hill in Carleton's native county of Tyrone, a site with no special Fenian associations. Carleton's story probably first appeared in a serial now lost. The early folklorist Patrick Kennedy published a variant in his *Legendary Fictions of the Irish Celts* (1866). But after William Butler Yeats republished the Carleton text in the influential *Fairy and Folk Tales of the Irish Peasantry* (1888), its prominence was assured. More than twenty plagiarisms and un-credited adaptations have made this the portrait of Fionn that many in the English-speaking world outside Ireland, especially children, are most likely to know.

In 'The Legend of Knockmany' Fionn the giant, here in the Hiberno-English form 'Fin M'Coul', is at work on the Giant's Causeway in County Antrim when he hears that another giant, named 'Cucullin' [*sic*], is headed his way, spoiling for a match of strength. In manuscript tradition, of course, Fionn and Cúchulainn never meet, their cycles being discrete. Popular literature is not troubled by such distinctions, and, as we shall see, this may be a case of mistaken identity. Fin returns home to his wife Oonagh at Knockmany, quaking in fear that he is going to be 'skivered like a rabbit' by his enemy. Oonagh is more confident, knowing that the rival giant's power resides in the middle finger of his right hand, and so sets about to outwit him. She has Fin dress as a baby and hide in an unnamed son's cradle, while she prepares to bake bread in which she has inserted granite stones. Giving false hospitality to Cucullin, who is annoyed at not finding Fin home, Oonagh offers Cucullin the granite bread. After trying twice to eat the bread, losing teeth in each attempt, Cucullin refuses to take another bite. At this point Oonagh offers another loaf, minus the granite insert, to Fin whom she blandly describes as her baby. Fin, of course, has no difficulty in eating at all, which leaves Cucullin amazed and apprehensive about confronting the father of such a child. Cucullin now wishes to leave Knockmany, but not before feeling the teeth of such an astonishing infant. Readying for the climax, Oonagh invites Cucullin to place his magic finger well into Fin's mouth. Fin immediately bites the finger off, jumps out of the cradle and makes short work of the visiting giant – now debilitated.

The implications of castration with the severed finger are likely to leap out at the contemporary reader, but they should not obscure the humiliations heaped upon Fionn: cowering in fear from an invader, dressed in infant's clothes and protected by his resourceful wife.

Carleton certainly did not invent this story, nor was he the first to attach it to the Fenian Cycle. The central motif of deception to over-come an enemy is at least as old as the anonymous *Maistre Pierre Pathelin* (*c.*1464), one of the original French stage farces, which can still raise a laugh when performed today. Eleven years before Carleton's publication, novelist Frederick Marryat put a variant of the story into the mouth of an Irish character named O'Brien in his *Peter Simple* (1834). Here Fionn is called Fingal, after Macpherson, and he, not his wife, thinks of the granite-loaf strategy. The rival giant is described as Scottish. If the story is of foreign origin, this is hardly the first time a narrative from abroad has been interleaved into an Irish corpus. The origins of the story of the conflict between Cúchulainn and his son Connla are in early Indo-European tradition and are found as far afield as Persian literature.

A year before *Peter Simple* yet another version, entitled 'The Legend of Fin-Mac-Cool', appeared in the pages of the *Dublin Penny Journal* (1833) with intriguing variants. The anonymous author, cited only as 'Q', follows the same scenario we find in Carleton, with the location switched from Knockmany to Ballynascorney in County Dublin. The Scottish giant is here named 'Usheen' for Fionn's own son, Oisín. As the identity of the invading giant is flexible, one is tempted to think that Q simply plucked an available name, one that the Macpherson controversy had made prominent. Then again, 'Usheen' is a phonetic rendering of what *Oisín* sounds like to English ears, a spelling that derives from hearing spoken Irish. Q's tone never responds to the thunderous Oedipal implications of father Fionn quailing in terror at the advance of his grown son striding toward him. But here in the nineteenth-century penny press is an unmistakable reprise of the eighth-century 'Quarrel Between Finn and Oisín'.

The lack of an antecedent for 'Knockmany' in Irish or Scottish Gaelic does not mean the story has not entered Celtic oral tradition.

Variants, with significant changes from Carleton's model, are recorded in the Hebrides in the 1860s and in Ulster in 1913. Whether they predate the printed sources or follow from them is difficult to know.

The more significant issue is that the Knockmany story, whatever its origin, should have attached itself to Fionn mac Cumhaill instead of to another hero. Part of the reason must be that he was the most available because Fenian tradition was very much alive in oral tradition in the late eighteenth and early nineteenth centuries, whereas the other cycles had receded from the popular mind until the revival of Old Irish from the mid-nineteenth century and after. Whoever asserted this connection – not Carleton, Marryat or Q – saw within Fionn's persona a wiliness and resilience that would triumph over humiliation as well as over redoubtable adversaries. The capacity to fall and rise again is what attracted James Joyce in linking his *Finnegans Wake* (1939) to Fenian lore. The myth of Fionn does not serve the same function in the *Wake* that Odysseus does in *Ulysses* because Joyce had much wider ambitions in portraying language, man's fate and the fortunate fall. His famously challenging narrative is larded with Fenian allusions, one of which is present in the pun of the title, 'Finn again wake', a call to Fionn to begin his career again, from preening hero to gambolling buffoon.

Early sources disagree about accounts of Fionn's death or even whether or not he was mortal. In one of the better known, Fionn and the fianna have worn out their welcome at the court of Cairbre Lifechair, Cormac mac Airt's son and successor. As different factions squabble among themselves, the king himself provokes a climactic battle by killing Fionn's servant Ferdia. It takes fully five men to murder Fionn at what is now Garristown, County Dublin. In another source an assassin named Aichlech mac Dubdrenn slays Fionn at the Ford of the Brea on the Boyne River, not far from where the hero first tasted knowledge. A variant version has Goll mac Morna dispatch Fionn at the same site. Yet other stories cite locations in Cork, Kerry, and the Scottish shire of Perth. Fionn may be reincarnated as Mongán in the Cycles of the Kings, or he may be a part of the Sleeping Army (folk motif E502), at rest in a remote cave, like King Arthur, Charlemagne or Barbarossa, biding his time until his people call for him again. Many

sites are also named as his burial mound, including Druim Derg in
Co. Meath.

FIONN, DIARMAIT AND GRÁINNE

Far darker than Fionn the farcical hero is Fionn the jealous cuckold in
Tóraigheacht Dhiarmada agus Ghráinne, the greatest, most resonant
prose narrative of the Fenian Cycle, usually known in English as 'The
Pursuit of Diarmait and Gráinne'. Fionn's portrayal in this story
resembles what happens to the otherwise admired Ulster king Conchobar mac Nessa in the nearly parallel Deirdre story. In both stories we
have an ageing powerful man who cannot have what he wants, a
reluctant, beautiful young woman, the woman's preferred lover, and
flight. Among the great differences are that the Diarmait and Gráinne
story is more than six times as long, chock full of digressions and
colourful supporting characters, and comes to quite a different conclusion. Both the Fenian and the Ulster stories anticipate the love
triangle between Tristan, Iseult and King Mark of Cornwall, a stand-in
for Arthur. Needless to say, the Arthurian story is the most widely
known of these in Western culture, but the two Irish narratives have
long been recognized as the older. James Carney (1955) has argued
that the roots of the two Irish stories are older still, having been
adapted from the late Roman love triangle between Mars, god of war,
Venus, god of love, and Adonis, Venus's consort. References imply
that this Fenian story was known by the tenth century although it did
not take the form we now recognize until well after 1200. A named
author, Dáibhí Ó Duibhgeannáin, composed a full manuscript version
in 1651. This did not stop the Diarmait and Gráinne story from being
immensely popular in oral tradition. Until well into the twentieth
century a common appellation for the megalithic dolmens or portal
tombs that dot the Irish countryside was 'beds of Diarmait and
Gráinne'.

While grieving for a wife named Maignis, Fionn complains that a
man alone cannot sleep well and so goes in search of a new mate. His
retainers tell him of the lovely Gráinne, daughter of King Cormac mac
Airt, who is reported willing, if he can only prove a worthy son-in-law.

Fionn succeeds, but at the betrothal feast Gráinne is disappointed to see that her prospective husband is older than her father. Her eye travels to other members of the party, first Oisín, who rebuffs her, and then to dark, curly-haired Diarmait Ua Duibne, with whom she is soon smitten. In versions of the story in oral tradition Gráinne cannot resist Diarmait's mysterious *ball seirce* [love spot], which he usually keeps modestly covered with a cap. Listeners familiar with Fenian stories would know two of Diarmait's aspects without their being explained in this text. One is that he is Fionn's favourite among the Fianna, and the other that he must constantly be on the lookout for a wild boar, the transformed spirit of a murdered half-brother. Taking the initiative, Gráinne slips a sleeping potion to all present except Diarmait, whom she entices to run away with her. When he delays out of loyalty to Fionn, she threatens him with a *geis* of destruction, and so, somewhat shrug-shouldered, he follows her. The lovers flee to a forest across the Shannon River, where Diarmait builds a dwelling with seven doors. Fionn and the Fianna are upon the couple in no time, but the men restrain their leader's hunger for vengeance. Oisín sends two warnings to the lovers, but Diarmait ignores both. Instead he plants three kisses on Gráinne's compliant mouth in full view of the enraged Fionn. At this the lovers, aided by Diarmait's patron Angus Óg, the god of poetry, envelop themselves in a cloak of invisibility and make a magical escape in one bold leap over the heads of Fionn and the Fianna.

The route of the fugitive lovers takes them to all corners of the Gaelic world, in Ireland and Scotland. The fever of the chase does not quickly light Diarmait's passions, however, which may be restrained by a reserve of respect for Fionn. This disappoints Gráinne. When they are crossing a stream, some water splashes her leg, prompting her taunt that it is more daring than he. Not long afterwards their love is consummated, and soon Gráinne is with child. The pregnancy causes Gráinne to crave the red berries of the rowan tree retrieved from Tír Tairngire [the land of promise] – now found in the forest of Dubros in Co. Sligo – and guarded by a one-eyed surly troll named Searbhán. This ugly ogre, skilled in magical arts, is a formidable guard of the berries, but Diarmait learns how to turn his own weapon, an iron club, against him. Both mother- and father-to-be feast on the berries, finding those on the highest branch to be the most delicious.

While Diarmait is aloft, Fionn and the pursuing fianna come to rest under the very same rowan tree. The men try to relax by playing the chess-like board-game of fidchell. Looking down, undetected, Diarmait sees that his ally Oisín is getting the worst of the match with Fionn. The skilful lover then aims berries toward specific points on the board, indicating the best next move, and so determines the outcome of three successive matches. Recognizing how the games have been won, Fionn demands that Diarmait show himself. In complying, though, Diarmait gives Gráinne three more kisses before Angus Óg can spirit her off to his residence at Brug na Bóinne in the Boyne valley. Diarmait once more escapes by leaping over the heads of his pursuers.

The lovers retreat to safety at Céis Chorrain [Keshcorran], Co. Sligo, where they rear four or five children and live peacefully. Diarmait easily turns back further attempts to capture them. In some versions Fionn contents himself with another of Cormac's daughters, but in most he still longs for his betrothed. Eventually, Angus Óg negotiates a peace between the chieftain and the pursued, and so the fugitive lovers can come to rest, almost like a settled domestic couple. One night Diarmait's sleep is troubled by the cry of a hound on the scent, a beckoning to return to the chase. Ignoring Gráinne's warning of the implicit danger, he leaves his bed to join the hunt with his former comrades. Fionn has organized a boar hunt near Ben Bulben in Sligo. In some versions Fionn warns Diarmait of his *geis* never to hunt pig; in others he is silent. The old chieftain certainly knows the danger to Diarmait, which would deliver a widowed Gráinne to her betrothed, but the young man is also a warrior who had been nearly a surrogate son. Diarmait knows what he is entering upon but happily rejoins his brothers-in-arms. But the hunt does not go well: Diarmait's arms are useless. The boar charges Diarmait as all expect and gores him mortally. This leads to Fionn's most odious scene in the story. Standing over the wounded Diarmait, Fionn gloats that all the women of Ireland should see him now that his beauty has been so sullied. Nearly breathless, Diarmait nonetheless reminds his old captain that he has the power to heal this grievous wound by carrying water in his magical hands. Fionn's grandson Oscar seconds this plea for help, with which Fionn reluctantly complies. Finding water nearby, he cups his hands to carry a quantity back to the stricken Diarmait, but when he arrives it has all drained away. This half-hearted attempt to save the rival is repeated twice more until, at last, Diarmait succumbs.

The remainder of the story is told in many ways. Sometimes Gráinne exhorts her sons to wreak vengeance upon Fionn. In others she wears widow's weeds, mourning Diarmait until her own death. In still others – the versions that remain popular with English-language adapters of the story – she is reconciled with Fionn. Stories from oral tradition portray Gráinne harshly as a lewd woman, unworthy of Diarmait's chastity. In the Fenian ballads surviving in the seventeenth-century collection *Duanaire Finn*, Gráinne puts aside her disgust with Fionn's age and his vile treatment of Diarmait, and embraces him in marriage.

COLLOQUY OF THE OLD MEN

Fionn's death date of 283 AD is a fiction, of course, but a useful one. While Fenian lore was a part of a living literary tradition, both written and oral, stories about him at different stages of his life, or as a splendid hero, a clown or an oaf, might be told side by side. By barely spoken convention, all the stories about him are happening in the third century, before the advent of Christianity and literacy. The date for St Patrick's arrival, 432 AD, may be a pious contrivance, but the organized preaching of the Gospels can be demonstrated to have begun in Ireland in the fifth century. The actual date for the beginning of Fenian storytelling is impossible to name, but the early years of the cycle unmistakably coexisted with the rise of what we now call Celtic Christianity, forms of monastic discipline not regulated by the Bishop of Rome. At some time in the twelfth or thirteenth centuries, a time of great literary flowering all over Europe, an unnamed churchman set himself toward a reconciliation between the old heroic tradition and the new learning, as well as between Fionn the warrior-hunter and Fionn the poet. The result is *Acallam na Senórach* [colloquy/dialogue of the elders/ ancients]. Inspired by the innovating tendencies of his century, the author drew heavily upon volumes of the traditional lore, especially the codified lore of places known as the *Dindshenchas*, as well as history, lyric poetry, ballad and learned poetry and Christian commentary.

The interface of Christian practice and pre-Christian or 'pagan' heroic lore is not the only aspect that makes the *Acallam* unusual. Although composed by a single personality, the narrative was copied extensively in different manuscripts, with additions and emendations, all the way down to the nineteenth century. In Modern Irish it is known as *Agallamh na Seanórach*. None of these manuscripts is ever complete, as they nearly always lack an end and often lack a beginning. Seemingly set in the twelfth-century present, *Acallam* gives us a 700-year-old St Patrick, very much an 'ancient' himself, who contends with 900-year-old warriors of a lost ethos. As for the Fenian protagonists, Caílte mac Rónáin, the runner and steward, and Oisín, they represent what Joseph Nagy (1997) calls a 'fortuitous glitch in time', disseminating a once lost, now recovered, lore. He adds, 'Caílte and his companions transcend time and sequence, paralleling the innumerable anachronistic references which they and the text make . . .' Among the most important of these is knowing the location of Mellifont Abbey (founded 1142), a vanguard in twelfth-century reforms. Surprising also is the author's favouring of Caílte as the Fenian spokesman while Oisín, nominally a leading companion, sometimes disappears from the scene. Later oral tradition, of course, much prefers Oisín.

The narrative begins with a pseudo-historical paragraph describing the several catastrophic battles that nearly annihilated the fianna and left them scattered into groups and bands all over Ireland. Only two leading warriors survive, Caílte and Oisín, along with the female chief and custodian, Cáma, who had watched over Fionn from childhood until the day he died. The comrades-in-arms repair to Cáma's residence for three days and three nights before they begin their journey, each accompanied by nine retainers. It takes them to Druim Derg, possibly Fionn's burial mound, and the plain between the Boyne and Liffey rivers, where they encounter St Patrick, who is chanting the divine office and praising the Creator. The clerics with Patrick are initially horrified at the size of the old Fenian fighters and their hounds, but the saint calms matters by bringing out his aspergill to shake holy water on the giants, driving away the devils that had been hovering about.

Conversation begins graciously between pagan and Christian. Over 200 anecdotes of the past are shared. Caílte, it is remembered, had led Patrick to the spring suitable for baptizing the peoples of nearby north

Dublin and Meath. At all times Caílte is unwavering in allegiance to Fionn. When Patrick asks if the lord he served was a good man, the old Fenian answers in verse:

> Were but the brown leaf,
> Which the wood sheds from it gold,
> Were but the white billows silver,
> Fionn would have given it all away.

Despite Patrick's anxieties about the distraction from prayer that listening to stories requires, he cautiously smiles and repeats the phrase, 'May victory and blessing attend you.' His guardian angels soothe his fear when they appear to tell him that the ancient warriors can tell no more than a third of their stories because of their forgetfulness and lack of memory. To delight noblemen of later times who might listen, what is remembered should be written on poets' staves and in learned men's words.

Patrick and Caílte begin their peregrinations around Ireland, first to the south and then to the west. Oisín takes a different route, going north to find his mother. As they pass, Caílte narrates the lore of place, linking myth and legend with specific sites. The old warrior's ability to cite the older place-name than the one now in use may reflect the contemporary unease that the Normans were displacing earlier strata of civilization. They complete this circuit at Tara, then the court of the *ard rí* Diarmait mac Cerbaill, leader of the Uí Néill, and reputedly the last pagan monarch of Ireland. Oisín has arrived separately before them. Together they attend the Feast of Tara, currently in progress, where the Fenian comrades relate the brave deeds of earlier times.

Time after time, the pagan–saint dialogue serves as a frame to introduce stories of the Fianna. Both prose and verse passages have an almost Arthurian flavour, especially with repeated mention of the generosity of Fionn. A discernible anti-clerical humour often portrays Saint Patrick as a bigot, predicting the doom of hell for the Fenians. On the whole, the temper of the *Acallam* is cheerful, despite Caílte's decrepitude, loneliness and laments for the vanished heroic past.

OISÍN AND NIAM

The tale of Oisín's sojourn in a pleasure-filled otherworld seems barely connected to the rest of the cycle, although always one of the most popular of Fenian narratives, a staple of Irish and Scottish Gaelic storytellers until the nineteenth century. In the earliest manuscript version, the tale is structured to look like a double of the *Acallam na Senórach*. An aged Oisín is in a dialogue with St Patrick, explaining how he has reached this state of infirmity. But Oisín the lover cannot be seen as an extrapolation of the persona he projects in most Fenian stories in general or the *Acallam* in particular. Some of the story's popularity and free-standing independence can be explained in noting that it is a blend of two international tale types, 470 and 766, and embraces fully five folk motifs, of which D1338.7 is the extended stay in the land of youth. Along with these persistent appeals to the popular imagination, Oisín's tale benefits by having been smoothed into a more polished format during the eighteenth century. Micheál Coimín [Michael Comyn] (1688–1760) was a member of the Protestant ascendancy with a deep regard for Irish-language tradition, unusual in his caste. His *Laoi Oisín i dTír na nÓg* [Lay of Oisín in the Land of Youth] (*c*.1750) is written in Modern Irish, where the fairy lover's name is spelled Niamh, employing the archaic, accentual metre known as *amhrán*. Coimín's *Laoi* was not translated into English for a hundred years but inspired several elegant adaptations, such as W. B. Yeats's first long poem, 'The Wanderings of Oisin' (1889).

One day a feeble, blind old man is taken to St Patrick, weakened in body but strong in spirit. He scorns the doctrines of the newcomers and sings the praises of the code of honour and way of life of the fianna. His claim to be Oisín son of Fionn mac Cumhaill looks doubtful to Patrick as more than a span of a full human life has elapsed since the old leader's death. To convince the saint of his veracity, Oisín relates the following tale.

After the defeat of the fianna at what is now Garristown in north Co. Dublin, Fionn, Oisín and a few others retreat to Lough Lein [Killarney] in Co. Kerry, a favourite haunt. They have much to lament. Most poignant is the slaughter of Fionn's favourite grandson, Oscar,

Oisín's son. Fionn weeps. The beauty of the countryside suggests a means of raising the men's spirits: they will take their hounds on a hunt. They soon espy a young, hornless doe bounding through the forest with the dogs in barking pursuit. Hot on the trail, the men come upon an arresting vision. Instead of a deer it is a beautiful young woman galloping toward them on a nimble white horse. Her startling loveliness suggests something above the human: her gold crown and shining golden hair hanging in loops over her shoulders. Her luxurious cloak, brightened with gold-embroidered stars, hangs down over the silk trappings of her horse. More alluring still is her face: her eyes as clear and blue as a May sky, her glowing white skin and her mouth as sweet as honeyed wine. A silver wreath adorns the horse's head, and gold glints from the saddle and even from its hoofs. Who had ever seen a finer horse? She identifies herself as Niam Chinn Óir [of the golden hair], daughter of the king of Tír na nÓg. Fionn asks if she has left a husband and why she has come. She has refused many suitors, she explains, because she desires only Oisín, son of Fionn, renowned for his handsomeness and sweet nature.

Silent until this point, Oisín is initially thunderstruck but then clearly pleased. He agrees to marry her, the most beautiful woman he has ever seen. She wants not only marriage but for him to come away with her to Tír na nÓg, where he will never grow ill or old, and where he can never die. There he will be crowned and enjoy every imaginable pleasure, food and wine in abundance, fine silks, powerful weapons and jewellery. Tall trees bend low with fruit. Hundreds of gorgeous maidens will sing his praises, and a hundred brave warriors will follow his every command. He will still be able to hunt, accompanied by a hundred keen hunting dogs. And he will have Niam for his wife.

Tír na nÓg lies to the west. On his journey there with Niam, Oisín encounters an ugly giant carrying a load of deerskins. They struggle for three days and three nights, but, powerful and threatening as the giant is, Oisín overcomes him. Such victory ensures a triumphant welcome for Oisín in Tír na nÓg, with the award of Niam as his consort. In embrace Niam is all the lover her appearance had implied. Their union produces three children, a daughter and two sons, one of them named for the slain Oscar.

All the wealth, comfort and pleasure does not, however, prevent

Oisín from feeling a small measure of homesickness. He longs to see Fionn and his companions again. Niam's father grants his wish to visit his home, but Niam is perturbed by her husband's longing. She tells him she will refuse him nothing but fears he may never return to her. He reassures her by reminding her that the white horse knows the way back, and he's really only going to look around. Consenting, she gives him a sterner warning. He should never dismount from his horse when he is back in mortal Ireland. If his foot so much as touches the ground there, he will never be able to return to Tír na nÓg. Lastly, sobbing, she tells him he will never be able to see Fionn again, only a crowd of sour-faced monks and holy men. As he mounts his horse, she kisses him and tells him he will never come back to her or the land of youth.

What Oisín does not quite comprehend is that while he feels he has been in Tír na nÓg only long enough to start a family, it has been 300 years in the lives of earthbound mortals. His white horse takes him to Ireland swiftly, and he arrives in high spirits. They begin to dissipate when he interviews the people he finds there. They all know stories of Fionn mac Cumhaill, more than they could begin to tell. Not only have they never seen Fionn or any Fenians up close, but they perceive Oisín to be a giant, a curiosity. He proceeds to the Hill of Allen in Leinster and finds it a bare hill, overgrown with nettles, chickweed and ragwort. The heartbreaking but unmistakable news can no longer be denied: Fionn is dead, and there is no trace of his companions to be found anywhere.

Moving on to Glenasmole in County Dublin, favourite hunting ground of the fianna, he answers the shouts of some sturdy men nearby who are trying to lift a heavy stone into a wagon. The name of the glen means 'Valley of the Ember', and it lies at the headwaters of the Dodder River, a modest body of water cited in many early Irish stories. As he stoops to help them, the girth around the horse's belly snaps and Oisín falls to the ground. As Niam had predicted, he is immediately transformed into a very old man, looking all of his 300 years. The crowd of mortals watch in horror because on horseback Oisín had towered over them. Now he lies at their feet, helpless and hopeless, a spent, blind old man.

12

The Cycles of the Kings

KINGS, HISTORY AND LEGEND

Once we spoke of only three cycles. When commentators began the disciplined study of early Irish literature after the middle of the nineteenth century, they perceived the three cycles we have already considered, the Mythological, the Ulster and the Fenian. Perhaps because the concept of a cycle – of interrelated if not continuous narratives – was imposed from modern times, many stories could not be categorized within the three rubrics. These include place-name stories, voyages and adventures to the otherworlds (such as the Voyage of Bran), saints' legends, and many stories pertaining to persons and realms of great kings. Over the decades it appeared that some of these stories, especially popular ones such as *Buile Suibhne* [The Frenzy of Suibne/Sweeney], might constitute a fourth cycle. Inconveniently, there is no single king at the centre of the stories, like Ulster's Conchobar mac Nessa, but rather successive kings in unrelated stories. This led Myles Dillon to coin the phrase 'The Cycles of the Kings' (1946), the plural implying that this fourth narrative body is made up of several sub-units. Habit and the impulse for uniformity often reduce the plural to a singular, 'The Cycle of the Kings'. As some of the fabled kings have at least a tenuous claim to historicity, the stories may also be known as 'The Historical Cycle'. Tom Peete Cross and Clark Harris Slover in their often-cited *Ancient Irish Tales* (1936) compromised with 'Tales of the Traditional Kings', a sensible alternative that never gained currency.

As we considered in Chapter 3, early Ireland is richly endowed with kings, the great majority of whom are only names, ciphers, in chronicles and genealogies. Some of the most storied bear evocative sobriquets and are the attributed ancestors of numerous families. Such a figure is Conn Cétchathach [of the Hundred Battles], who may have lived in the second century AD, and who is commemorated in the name of the western province, Connacht. He is the first to hear the Lia Fáil [Stone of Prophecy] speak, telling him not only how many of his line will follow him in the kingship at Tara, but also of the coming of St Patrick.

Among Conn's heirs is his admired grandson Cormac mac Airt, thought to have reigned for forty years in the third century. He is such a bountiful king that all the rivers of Ireland abound with salmon, cows produce more milk than vessels can hold, and calves are born after only three months' gestation. He is, again, the reigning monarch during most of the adventures of Fionn mac Cumhaill and the fianna. The magical story told about him, *Echtrae Cormaic*, recounted below (pp. 255–7), has prompted many commentators to suggest he could not possibly be historical. T. F. O'Rahilly (1946) argued that he was only an idealization of the first Gaelic-speaking king of Tara. This was not the position of early, powerful families, several of which claimed descent from him.

Coming over a century later is Niall Noígiallach [of the Nine Hostages], a warrior-king closely linked with the unmistakably historical Uí Néill dynasty that dominated Ireland for six centuries. He is their reputed ancestor, for their name translates as 'grandchildren/spiritual descendants of Niall'. The attribution of 'Nine Hostages' to Niall testifies to his military prowess and capacity for dominating his neighbours. There are two stories about the identity of the hostages. The older version, more likely but less widely known, is that they were all taken from the Airgialla, a once powerful people who had settled in a region near Lough Foyle in what is now Northern Ireland. The later version, probably invented, is that Conn captured one hostage from each of Ireland's five provinces as well as from the Scots, Saxons, Britons and Gauls.

Much later and certainly historical is Brian Bórama or Boru, the victor over the Norsemen at the Battle of Clontarf (*c.*1014). From his birthplace at Killaloe in Co. Clare and his usual residence or 'palace' at nearby Kincora on the Shannon River, Brian became the ruler first of a small kingdom named Dál Cais or Dál gCais, anglicized to the

Dalcassians. He ruthlessly extended his power over nearby neighbours in Limerick and Cashel, eventually becoming the dominant force in all of southern Ireland. He also achieved his ultimate goal of having himself crowned *ard rí* at Tara in 997, seventeen years before he perished during his defeat of the Norsemen at Clontarf, in what is today a suburb of Dublin. So many heroic stories have accrued to the career of Brian Bórama that they can be seen to constitute a small cycle of their own. Alan Bruford (1969) has dubbed it 'The Dalcassian Cycle', no examples of which are included here.

The presumed rooting in history changes the tone of many of the stories in this chapter. Much depends on the distinctions between myth and legend, and from that the expectations of the listener/reader. The English word 'legend' derives from the Old French *legende* and denotes a 'traditional tale popularly regarded as historical', or 'an inauthentic story popularly regarded as true' (*Shorter OED*, 1993). The concept is not defined in classical culture, although the story of Theseus and the Minotaur might share some features. The term might first be applied to saints' stories, as in the thirteenth-century *Golden Legend*, fabulous tales collected by Archbishop Jacobus de Voragine. By extension we call the stories of Charlemagne and King Arthur 'legends', even when they share motifs with the narratives of Greek and Roman mythology. Perhaps Conn, Cormac, Niall and Brian can be put in the same box with Charlemagne and Arthur.

For all we know, the early audience of the *Táin* might have thought that Cúchulainn, Conchobar and Medb were historical figures. Certainly, the credulous listeners to oral traditions about Fionn mac Cumhaill as late as the twentieth century felt they were partaking of the heroic exploits of an actual defender of the Irish people, even when the stories portrayed enchantments and magical transformations. Whatever the certitude of the listeners, it could only be enhanced when stories depicted sovereign rulers commemorated in genealogies, local place names, and the names of powerful families. Experience outside the narrative implied that the elements in it came from life.

The commonplace observation of the stories in the Cycles of the Kings is that they are less magical than in the Mythological, less heroic than in the Ulster, and less romantic than in the Fenian. That should not imply, however, that they are grim or pedestrian. Enchanted flights from the everyday are still present. Missing instead are characters like Lug Lámfhota, Balor, Mórrígan, Medb, Fionn or the Fomorians whose roots are in the pre-Christian divine. In this chapter we are more likely to see transparent borrowings or parallels with non-Irish traditions. Suibne has clear counterparts in Scotland's Lailoken, a madman of the forest, and Britain's Merlin, who was a woodland madman in a story separate from his becoming Arthur's magician. The story of how Rónán killed his son borrows more than a little from the classical myth of Hippolytus and Phaedra, the lying seductress. Within these cycles we also encounter the most familiar solitary spirit from Irish tradition, the leprechaun.

MAD SUIBNE

Suibne or Suibhne, the antecedent of Sweeney, was a common enough name in early Ireland, but there is no indication that Suibne, the cursed king who went mad, ever existed. He does not appear in the genealogies of the people he is supposed to have ruled. The setting of his three-part story is linked to the Battle of Mag Rath (or Moira) of AD 637, the culmination of a momentous dynastic struggle in what is today Co. Down. Citations for Suibne *Geilt* [Mad Sweeney] appear in a ninth-century law tract, but his main story, *Buile Suibhne* [The Frenzy of Suibne], did not take its present form until the twelfth century, surviving in three manuscripts written five centuries later. Redactors of his narrative are careful to present the Church most favourably, especially as a repository of native learning. The two stories preceding *Buile Suibhne* are *Fled Dúin na nGéd* [The Feast of Dún na nGéd], which deals with events leading up to the battle, and *Cath Maige Rátha* [The Battle of Mag Rath], a description of the carnage there.

Action begins in the petty kingdom of Dál nAraide, which straddled the border of counties Antrim and Down in what is now eastern Northern Ireland. King Suibne, son of Colmán, seeks to expel the evangelizing St Rónán from his realm, but his wife Eórann tries to temper her husband. Enraged by the sound of Rónán's proselytizing bell, Suibne dashes out of the front door of his castle while Eórann tries to stop him by grabbing his coat. This leaves the pagan king stark naked but still carrying weapons, like the ancient Gaulish warriors described by Posidonius. In a fit of fury, Suibne hurls Rónán's psalter into a lake and is about to give the saint a pasting when his kingly responsibility calls him to the Battle of Mag Rath. Piously the saint gives thanks to God for being spared, but he also curses King Suibne, asking that he be made to wander through the world naked, just as he had come naked into Rónán's presence.

The king's second encounter with the saint has a more lasting effect. After an otter magically restores Rónán's psalter, so that it appears it was never dropped in water, the saint approaches the Mag Rath battlefield, hoping to bring peace. He is not successful. As he blesses the armies, his sprinkling of holy water irks Suibne so severely that he thrusts a spear through an attendant, killing him. He hurls another at the saint himself, only to see it break against Rónán's bell, its shaft flying into the air. Thus the saint curses the king a second time, declaring that he should fly through the air like the shaft of his spear and that he may perish of a cast spear. Initially unconcerned, Suibne rejoins the battle and finds himself increasingly disoriented amid the clamour of bloodletting. Seized with trembling like a wild bird, he flees the battlefield. As he races madly, his feet barely touch the ground and he alights in a yew tree. Meanwhile, at the battle, his opponents are victorious after Suibne's withdrawal. After a kinsman fails to restore the king to his senses, Suibne flees to a remoter corner of Ireland, perching on a tree in Tír Chonaill [Donegal].

Always tormented, Suibne wanders the land, described in passages filled with arrays of poetic place-names, often wishing that he had been killed in battle. His lamentations come in long verse narratives, or lays. While not a member of the privileged, powerful caste of poets, *filid* (sing. *fili*), Suibne is a king who speaks poetry. He describes himself as a madman, and as he is naked, shivering in the trees, he looks like one. Eventually he finds respite in the valley of the lunatics, Glen Bolcáin. This appears to have been an actual place and is identified with the modern Glenbuck near Rasharkin, Co. Antrim. A Fenian text places the valley on the Dingle Peninsula in Co. Kerry, which may have been another such retreat.

At some of his stops Suibne gives cryptic advice. Reaching the lyrically named church of Snám Dá Én [Swim Two Birds] on the

Shannon, near the monastery of Clonmacnoise, the mad king observes the clerics reciting their Friday canonical prayers, the nones. Nearby, women are beating flax, and one of them is giving birth to a child. Unsettled by what he sees Suibne announces that it is unseemly for women to violate the Lord's fast-day, which is how he views what the rest of humanity sees as the miracle of childbirth. Then he compares the beating of the flax with the bloody beating his folk had taken at Mag Rath. Hearing the vesper bell, he complains, 'Sweeter indeed were it to me to hear the voices of the cuckoos on the banks of the Bann from every side than the cacophony of this bell, which I hear tonight.' His lay that follows repeats this theme, praises the beauty of nature and ends with a plea to Christ not to sever Suibne from His sweetness.

Throughout this torment, Suibne's one faithful friend is Loingsechán, perhaps a foster-brother or a half-brother sharing the same mother. On three occasions Loingsechán rescues Suibne and keeps him informed about his family. In his unsettled mental state Suibne sometimes does not wish to be approached so on one occasion Loingsechán has to take on the guise of a mill-hag. She had won the king's confidence by giving him food.

Led by Loingsechán, Suibne speaks of his desire to be with his wife Eórann, who has gone to live with a friend of the king, Guaire. At first he reproaches his wife for this, but when she says that she would rather live with him, even in misery, he takes pity on her and recommends that she stay with her new lover.

When a crowd gathers, Suibne flees again to the wilderness, coming to rest in a tree. On Loingsechán's second visit the subject turns to Suibne's kingdom. The sad news is that the king's father, mother and brother have died. So too his only daughter, a needle to the heart. When he learns that his son also has died, Suibne is so overcome by grief that he falls from his tree. At this Loingsechán grabs Suibne, ties him up and tells him that his family is actually alive after all. The news shocks the king back to sanity, at which Loingsechán takes him back to Dál nAraide and helps re-install him as king.

Sanity and lucidity do not last long. When Suibne is alone in his palace, he is approached by the once-helpful mill-hag, whom Loingsechán impersonated. She reminds him of his period of madness and persuades him to jump, as he had often done in his former state. Maliciously, she competes with him, and they both jump into the wilderness where Suibne falls back into his lunacy. The mill-hag and her contest reappear in Irish oral tradition and probably originate there. Arriving at the northern cliff-edge fortress of Dún Sobairche [Dunseverick, Co. Antrim], Suibne clears the battlements in a single bound. Trying to equal his feat, the mill-hag falls from a cliff and is killed. Following this, Suibne migrates to Britain and keeps company with a madman, who had been cursed by his people for sending soldiers into battle dressed in satin. This man eventually drowns himself in a waterfall, but his presence underscores the links with the Welsh-Arthurian figure Merlin, called Myrddin *(G)wyllt* in his madness, perhaps an anticipation of Suibne Geilt. Returning to Ireland once again, Suibne is afraid to enter his own house for fear of capture. His wife Eórann complains that she is now ashamed of his madness and as he does not choose to live with her, she wishes he would depart for ever. Crestfallen, Suibne departs, bewailing the fickleness of women.

More torments beset Suibne's flight around Ireland before he can find deliverance. A severely wet and cold night brings another interval of lucidity in which he seeks to return to Dál nAraide. But when this news is miraculously transmitted to St Rónán, he prays that the mad king not be allowed to persecute the Church again. Following this, a horde of fiendish phantoms vexes and harries Suibne, sending him deliriously in every direction. At last, finding forgiveness for his many misdeeds, Suibne comes to the monastery of St Moling, Tech Moling, which is now St Mullins, Co. Carlow. Moling, or Mo Ling, is an historical figure (d. 697), whom Giraldus Cambrensis (eleventh century) called 'one of the Four Prophets of Ireland'. This saint takes pity on the wandering madman and allows him to return to the monastery each evening for a meal. More importantly, Moling also writes down his adventures. Reception from the saint's household takes a different tone. The monastery cook delivers sustenance by poking a hole in a cowdung with her foot and then filling it with milk for Suibne to lap. Even this demeaning favour is too much for the cook's husband, who runs Suibne through with his spear. Fainting in weakness from the wound, Suibne confesses his sins to St Moling and is given the last rites. Taking the forgiving saint's hand, Suibne is led to the door of the church where he collapses and dies, freed from his double curse.

Although the names are changed, Suibne is unmistakably the model for Goll in William Butler Yeats's early poem, 'The Madness of King Goll' (1887).

HOW KING RÓNÁN KILLED HIS SON

This story and the one preceding it have many elements in common, although composed at different times by different people. We have yet another figure named Rónán, a king this time, unrelated to the saint, and some of the action takes place at Dún Sobairche in Co. Antrim. The central narrative is tied to putative historical figures whose names appear in the Chronicles. It is unlikely that the main players in the narrative, Rónán and Eochaid, knew each other in life. King Rónán mac Aeda of Leinster died in 610 or 624. His father-in-law, presumably an older man, Eochaid or Echaid Iarlaithe, is recorded as having died more than forty years later, in 665. The story citing both kings was probably invented a century or two later by a genealogist drawing on classical sources. A surviving text, perhaps of the tenth century, is found in the *Book of Leinster* (after 1150). More than in other stories of this cycle, the metaphysical element is absent. There are no gods, taboos or enchantments. Tension arises from everyday human elements such as love, jealousy, hate and violence. The usual Irish title is *Fingal Rónáin* [How Rónán Killed his Son], but it is sometimes known as *Aided Maíl Fhothartaig Maic Rónáin* [The Death of Máel Fhothartaig Son of Rónán].

Rónán, king of Leinster, is the father of Máel Fhothartaig, the handsomest and most admired young man in the province. Men gather around him whenever he appears. As he matures, he increasingly becomes the darling of young girls in the court, whose favours he returns. His father Rónán, meanwhile, is a sad widower, his wife, a certain Eithne of Munster, Máel Fhothartaig's mother, having died sometime previously. His thoughtful son recommends he seek a wife, perhaps a settled woman. Rónán chooses instead an attractive young woman, the daughter of Eochaid of Dún Sobairche in the north. The bride is never named, but she is certainly not what the son had in mind for his father. He describes her as 'skittish'. Once she arrives at Rónán's residence, however, she has a much more positive view of her stepson the he does of her. Indeed, she is immediately smitten with him and sends her beautiful maidservant, under threat of execution if she fails, to solicit him to come to the new queen's bed. To strengthen the case, the maidservant sleeps with Máel Fhothartaig herself, but also reveals the new stepmother's desires for him. Taking heed, the young hero departs with fifty retainers for Scotland, where he soon acquires an admirable reputation as a warrior and hunter. His two hounds, Doilín and Daithlenn, are swifter than those of the host Scottish king. When his fellow Leinstermen insist that he return home, he comes via Dún Sobairche where King Eochaid tells him that his daughter should have been sleeping with him, Máel Fhothartaig himself, instead of that old churl Rónán. The young man is displeased to hear this, but continues his travels to Leinster anyway.

On his arrival the unfortunate maidservant is again sent, under pain of death, to cajole the young man to come to the queen's bed. In despair Máel Fhothartaig asks advice of his foster-brother Congal, who responds that he has a solution but for a price. He rejects an offer of the horse, bridle and clothes and says he will take nothing but the two prize hunting dogs. The ruse is simple. Máel Fhothartaig must leave early in the morning to herd cattle before Congal goes to the queen and tells her that the young man is hoping to tryst with her later that day at an appointed spot marked with white stones. After displaying her eagerness all morning, the queen sets off for the white stones and twice she runs instead into Congal, who reviles her with abusive language, like 'Harlot!' and 'Wicked woman!' The third time he escalates his attack with a horsewhip. Beaten but unbowed, she snarls back at him, 'I shall bring blood into your mouth.'

That night back at Rónán's residence, the king is praising his son, who has not yet returned from the herding mission on which Congal had sent him. The dishevelled queen grumbles that the king is always puffing up his son. Rónán responds by extending his admiration and adds that the son does it all for the comfort of his father and his father's new wife. In a surly voice she answers that the son does not get the comfort in return that he desires. 'Three times Congal brought him to me,' she charges, 'and it was hard for me to escape from him.'

Rónán angrily denounces her, 'A curse on your lips, you evil woman.' But she responds that she can prove her charges. Soon Máel Fhothartaig enters and begins to dry his legs by the fire, presenting the queen with her moment to act. He recites half a quatrain about cold weather, which she is able to complete with words about how cold it is for a man to be without his lover.

'It is true, then!' exclaims Rónán, signalling to one of his men, Áedán. The retainer immediately casts his spear toward the son, its shaft transfixing Máel Fhothartaig to his chair. A second catches the foster-brother Congal, and a third rips out the bowels of the jester Mac Glass. In his death throes, the son tells his father that he has been taken in by a miserable lie. Further, he relates how the young queen had been pestering him, how Congal led her away three times, and that he would no more sin with her than with his own mother. He swears by the tryst with death, to which he goes, that he is innocent.

The words have their desired effect. After Máel Fhothartaig dies, Rónán mourns for three days, singing an eloquent, restrained lamentation that describes his wife as a guilty, lustful woman. In seeking vengeance, Congal's brother Donn journeys to Dún Sobairche where he lures the queen's father, Eochaid, from his palace, the better to slaughter him, his wife and his son. Donn carries the heads back to Leinster where he flings them on to the queen's breast. At this she rises and throws herself on her own knife.

The story ends with the introduction of Máel Fhothartaig's previously unmentioned sons, whose mother's name is neither given nor implied. They come to Rónán's door and announce that a fight is to be held outside at which an old champion cannot stand. With that, blood comes to Rónán's mouth, and he dies at once.

Whoever constructed the story of *Fingal Rónáin* very likely borrowed from the widely known Greek tale of the virtuous charioteer Hippolytus and the lustful, vicious Phaedra, found in Euripides' *Hippolytus* (428 BC) and elsewhere. Often misogynist early churchmen were fond of stories of erring women, and might also have drawn from the

Biblical Joseph's unwanted encounter with Potiphar's wife (Genesis, 39: 12). The theme of mistaken sexual rivalry between son and father carries the folk motif number of K2111. See also tale type 870C.

CORMAC'S GOLDEN CUP

The following story revisits a fairy-tale world of mysterious strangers, trios of wishes asked and granted, and spoken words that have the power of defying the laws of nature. The storyteller attributes these fabulous events to the pre-Patrician king most famous in early Irish tradition, Cormac mac Airt, who, the *Annals* assert, reigned, with interruptions, from AD 227 to 266. Another of his titles, Cormac Ua Cuinn, links him with his almost equally famous grandfather, Conn Cétchathach [of the Hundred Battles]. The frequent citing of his name in early genealogies testifies to the depth of credence given his presumed historicity as well as the desire of ambitious families to be associated with him. His exploits related here, *Echtrae Cormaic* [Cormac's adventures], splice together several early narratives with proffered moralizing and implied social criticism. Several commentators have noted that Cormac's visit to Tír Tairngire [The Land of Promise] anticipates Perceval's visit to Grail Castle. The motif of the testing cup of truth can also be found as far afield as early India.

At dawn on a May morning, Cormac mac Airt is walking the ramparts of Tara when he espies an extraordinarily dressed stranger approaching. Grey-haired, the visitor wears cloth-of-gold attire with bright colours, the sort that would only befit a warrior or prince of high station. He carries a silver branch with three golden apples on his shoulder. When Cormac learns that the golden apples if shaken will produce a marvellous music that will bring sleep to even the most troubled, such as women in childbed, he asks to have it. The strange warrior gives his assent, asking only that Cormac promises the fulfilment of three wishes, to which the latter readily agrees.

A year and a day pass, and the stranger returns. He asks to have the king's daughter Ailbe. The request raises three loud cries from the women of Tara, but Cormac shakes the silver branch at them, banishing grief and casting them into sleep. And so his daughter Ailbe is delivered. In a month the stranger returns and asks for Cormac's son Cairbre Lifechair. Again, despite courtly displeasure, Cormac agrees.

On a third visit the stranger asks for Cormac's own wife, Eithne Tháebfhota, daughter of Dúnlang, king of Leinster. Before Cormac can act, the stranger takes the woman with him. This is a loss that Cormac cannot endure. He pursues the stranger's party with its captive until a great mist envelops them all in the middle of a plain. At this point the narrative takes a sharp turn, suggesting the remainder of Cormac's adventures are from another source.

All alone on the plain, Cormac comes upon a huge fortress with a wall of bronze around it. Within the walls lies a house of white silver, half-thatched with the wings of white birds. In all respects, what Cormac beholds is exceedingly strange. A fairy host of horsemen is thatching the rest of the roof with more white feathers, even though a gust of wind will carry off all they have completed. A stoked fire immediately consumes all the timber thrown into it, even a thick-boled oak. Moving on, he comes to yet another bronze-walled fortress, one containing four palaces. He enters and finds beams of bronze, wattling of silver and more thatch of white feathers. His hosts are drinking water from the five streams flowing from a shining fountain. Adjacent to the water are nine hazelnut trees that drop their nuts into the fountain, where they are eaten by five salmon. The euphonious sound of water falling in the streams is more melodious than any music that men sing.

Once inside, Cormac is hospitably welcomed by a handsome warrior and a beautiful blonde woman in a golden headdress. Once a pig is put on a spit, the guest and his hosts enter upon a unique storytelling contest. A truth must be told for each of the pig's quarters or it cannot be cooked at all. Three others at the banquet are not named but identified: a kitchener, the warrior and the woman. They relate what sound like tall tales that strain credulity, but they please the host with their truthfulness. Then it is Cormac's turn. He tells the story we know has just happened, how first his son, then his daughter, and finally his wife were taken by a mysterious stranger. When this story is also judged true, the pig is now properly cooked. Cormac's only complaint is his lack of company; he usually dines with fifty. At this the warrior-host begins a mellifluous lullaby that puts Cormac to sleep. Upon waking he finds fifty warriors as well as his lost family – daughter, son and wife.

The ale and food are portioned out, and a cup of gold is placed in the handsome warrior's hand. As Cormac is admiring its strange workmanship, the host explains the cup's unique qualities. If three falsehoods are spoken under it, the cup will split into three parts, which he proceeds to demonstrate with three successive lies. To weld the cup back together he follows with three testimonies about Cormac and his family. He declares that Eithne has lain with no man since she left Tara, nor has Ailbe, and that Cormac has lain with no woman. These words fuse the cup together, making it whole again. At this the host reveals that he is Manannán mac Lir, the god of the sea. It was he who appeared at the walls of Tara with the silver branch. Manannán explains the wonders Cormac had beheld, that, for example, the shining fountain is the fountain of knowledge, and the five salmon represent the five senses.

On the next morning Cormac arises to find himself on the green of Tara, and with him are his wife Eithne, son Cairbre and daughter Ailbe. With him also are the silver branch with the golden apples and golden cup of truth.

FERGUS, MONSTERS AND LITTLE PEOPLE

Although Fergus mac Léti is a mythical king of Ulster, his story is usually classed with this cycle through a kind of filing accident. The earliest version of his narrative, the seventh- or eighth-century *Echtra Fergusa maic Léite* [Adventure of Fergus mac Léti], survived in legal texts because it was cited in the study of the proper disposal of disputed property. As in other early Irish stories, place-names refer to real places, even though the dispute suggested in the story could hardly have taken place. That is the only rooting in history to be found here. This Fergus, a swimmer, is very likely only a double of the hero Fergus mac Róich, so prominent in Ulster stories.

Instead of inhabiting the realms of great kings, *Echtra Fergusa maic*

Léite includes fantastical elements that would later prove enchanting to storytellers in oral tradition, such as sea monsters and the first appearance of the leprechaun in Irish literature. The inherent popularity of such motifs may help explain why a later burlesque, Rabelaisian version of the story appeared in the thirteenth century.

At the beginning of the story, Fergus mac Léti is a powerful king in Ulster, the north of Ireland, who has under his sworn protection the nobleman Eochaid Bélbuide [yellow mouth]. When, during a war, a group of men from the midlands sent by Conn Cétchathach [of the Hundred Battles] come and kill Eochaid, King Fergus finds it an outrageous offence; indeed, it is known in Irish law as a *díguin* (slaying of a person under a king's protection) and Fergus demands compensation. When he comes south to insist on compliance, Conn and his followers are unable to stand up to him. They cede to him a tract of land, which may be Mag Muirtheimne (coincidentally Cúchulainn's country) or farther south, near the mouth of the Delvin River. Also in the package is the mother of one of the assassins, a noblewoman named Dorn, whom Fergus makes a household slave. Satisfied, Fergus makes peace and returns to the north.

Next day at an unnamed spot on the shore, Fergus and his charioteer stop for a rest, and in the heat of the day fall asleep. Otherworldly visitors come to them in their slumber. Water-sprites swarm out of the sea and lift Fergus, still sound asleep, out of his chariot. They separate him from his esteemed sword Caladhcholg (a counterpart of Fergus mac Róich's Caladbolg). Next they carry him into the water, and when one of his feet dips below the surface, he wakes instantly and seizes three of the tiny creatures. He demands that they grant him three wishes, namely the power of swimming under water in (a) seas, (b) pools and (c) lakes.

The word for sprites with small bodies is *lúchoirp* or *lúchorpáin*, which through metathesis, the switching of the consonants *c* and *p*, and anglicization becomes the familiar term leprechaun. These eighth-century creatures, water-sprites, bear only the slightest resemblance to the solitary fairies found in T. Crofton Croker's *Fairy Legends and Traditions of the South of Ireland* (1825), followed by nearly two centuries of commercial and popular distortion and caricature. In spite of the figure's instant recognizability, the leprechaun is neither the most striking instance of fairyhood within Irish tradition nor is it that tradition's most representative character. In Irish tales the leprechaun is neither cute nor charming, qualities ascribed to him by Albion's patronizing attitudes toward Hibernia.

The little men grant Fergus's three-part wish, firstly by something like earplugs made from magical herbs and secondly by a waterproof tunic wound round his head that anticipates a modern diving helmet. These gifts come with an important proviso. Fergus will not be allowed his new power at Loch Rudraige [Dundrum Bay, Co. Down] in his own country.

Recklessly, Fergus ignores this prohibition. He does indeed attempt to swim under water at Loch Rudraige, where he comes face to face with the fearsome monster known as the *muirdris*. The beast alternately inflates and deflates itself like a bellows. Just the look of it is poisonous, and Fergus finds himself suffering a horrifying disfigurement. His mouth is wrenched backward from his face and pushed round to find a new berth on the back of the king's head. Lacking a mirror, Fergus cannot sense what he has suffered, but his charioteer's horror at seeing him sends an unmistakable signal.

Fergus flees to the land and falls asleep there. His charioteer travels on to Emain Macha to meet with wise men of Ulster and tell them what disaster has befallen the king. Under the custom and laws of the time, no person having a serious physical blemish could serve as king, and any reigning king suffering the freakish disfigurement visited upon Fergus would have to abdicate. As testimony to their faith in this king, the wise men agree to enter into a conspiracy to conceal what has happened. Even Fergus himself will not know the full extent of his misfortune. His residence will be cleared of all strangers when he returns, as well as anyone else who would betray the secret. At Emain Macha his head will always be washed while he is lying on his back so that he cannot see his own reflection in the water. Only servants trusted not to tell either Fergus or anyone else will be allowed to serve him. As difficult and unlikely as this scheme is to execute, it succeeds for seven years.

One servant had been forgotten, the highborn and resentful Dorn, held as a slave because of her son's actions. When she is commanded to wash Fergus's head one day, the king is exasperated with the slowness of her ministrations and strikes her with his whip. After enduring constant humiliation for years, Dorn loses her composure and begins to taunt Fergus about his grotesque appearance. As well as being insulted, Fergus now must acknowledge what happened to him in the loch. At this he takes out his sword and cuts the queen/slave in two.

Fergus's next move is clear. He must drive straight to Loch Rudraige to find and to overcome the monster. Its terror has disfigured him and he must now triumph over the object of his fear. He plunges into the lake and battles under water with the *muirdris* for a day and a night. Ulstermen gather along the shore to watch as the loch seethes like a cauldron while huge waves crash upon the beach. At last the king emerges from the water and climbs to a high sandbank separating the inner from the outer bay, declaring his victory and brandishing the head of the monster. This sweet moment of triumph vanishes as Fergus falls back dead in the water, having conquered his fear at the cost of his life.

The burlesque thirteenth-century version of *Echtra Fergusa maic Léite* embroiders details to lengthen the narrative and also greatly expands the roles of the water-sprites or leprechauns. They are much smaller here, able to stand in the palm of the hand of a normal-sized man. New also are the names for the sprites, Iubdán the king, Bebo his queen, and Eisirt their court poet. Eisirt has psychic powers, like the leprechauns of later tradition. He knows when Fergus is having an affair with his steward's wife and that Fergus's own wife is having another with her stepson. King Fergus once again does battle with the monster of Loch Rudraige, now called *sínach*. Fergus's mouth is turned to the back of his head, but his wife is the one who reveals the secret. Before the revelation, they have a petty dispute over a bathroom trifle. Fergus uses his sword rather than his bare hands to kill the monster in the second encounter.

It has long been suggested that an English translation of the thirteenth-century version of *Echtra Fergusa maic Léite* was read to Jonathan Swift and thus influenced the creation of the Lilliputians in Book I of *Gulliver's Travels* (1726). Vivian Mercier's *The Irish Comic Tradition* (1962) argues convincingly that this is so.

The transfer of land to Fergus for the violation of *díguin*, which prompted early lawyers to preserve the eighth-century manuscript, plays no role in the resolution of the action.

PART THREE

Welsh and Oral Myths

13

British Roots and Welsh Traditions

NATIVE FOREIGNERS

In their early literature, the Welsh people describe themselves as living on *Ynys Prydain*, the Isle of Britain. It was not simply that the Cambrian Peninsula containing the principality of Wales was a part of the island of Britain. Instead, the early Welsh correctly perceived that they were the cultural and linguistic descendants of the ancient Britons who were conquered and colonized by the Romans. Their literary purview extended in pre-modern times to regions of Great Britain that we today do not think of as 'Wales'. The lengthy early poem *Y Gododdin*, attributed to Aneirin of the sixth and seventh centuries, begins near what is today Edinburgh and continues into northern Yorkshire. Large areas of the Lowlands of Scotland, especially in the southwest, remained Welsh-speaking for many centuries into the Middle Ages. The later, almost wistful name for these lost provinces is 'the Old North'.

The word 'Wales' derives from the Old English *wealh, wealas* (pl.) meaning 'foreigner' or 'not a Saxon'. The Angles, Saxons and Jutes, who arrived in Great Britain from the middle of the fifth century, brutalized the native population and showed scant interest in learning the British language. Pushed to the western periphery of the island, the ancient British language survived in Wales, Cornwall and, after some delay, Brittany. Wales came to be thought of as a separate entity before the time the eighth-century King Offa of Mercia ordered construction of the long earthwork, Offa's Dyke, separating native Celtic speakers from the Germanic Angles and Saxons. Earthwork remains still lie a bit east of the modern border of Wales. Eventually the Welsh came to refer to themselves as *Cymry* and their principality as *Cymru*, from the earlier *com-brogos*, compatriots.

The Welsh are culturally but not ethnically distinct from the rest of Britain. Genome studies beginning in the mid-1990s confirm what anthropologists had long thought. Genes of the ancient Britons survive in many inhabitants of Britain, whether they think of themselves as Welsh, English or Scottish. There was no fifth-century ethnic cleansing. Many of the Britons, for whatever reason, learned English and blended in with the invaders. Neither should the centuries-old link between ancient British or Brythonic and Modern Welsh coax us into emphasizing a widespread survival of pagan religion and worldview in Welsh tradition. Such a view was highly seductive in the early decades of nineteenth-century Celtic scholarship but has been severely discredited since. The Welsh Dôn certainly appears to share the same roots as the Irish Danu, but they are hardly identical. The children of Dôn who appear in the *Mabinogi*, Gwydion, Gilfaethwy, Gofannon, etc., do not have Irish counterparts. Similarly, Modron, the mother of the abducted child Mabon in the eleventh-century *Culhwch and Olwen*, derives from the ancient goddess Matrona, eponym of the Marne River in Gaul, just as Mabon derives from Maponos [divine youth], a god of Roman-occupied Britain and Gaul linked to Apollo. The fascinating presence of these very old names in medieval stories may intrigue the reader, but it does not mean that the literary products of Christianized Wales are actually pagan. A modern analogy can be seen in the many culturally archaic artefacts of Christmas. Mistletoe (of druidic origin), the yule log and the decorated conifer known as the Christmas tree are, to the learned observer, unmistakably of extra-Christian origin. To most people decorating a Christmas tree, its exotic origin is merely incidental, not a sign that the household with the tree has returned to ancient worship.

Writing in the Welsh language began after the advent of writing in Irish and survives in smaller bulk. Although the literary tradition extends from about the middle of the sixth century to the present, most pre-Norman work (i.e. before 1094), with two or three exceptions, survives in twelfth- to fifteenth-century manuscripts. The Latin *Historia Brittonum* (*c*.800) alludes to Welsh poets who sang in the sixth century, works attributed to two of whom, Taliesin and Aneirin, survive. Fanciful lore associated with such poets, recounted in the next section, testifies to their early renown but undercuts their claim to historicity.

The early Welsh and Britons, as mentioned before, never perceived that they formed a community with the Irish, Manx or Scottish Gaels. The unity of the Celts was not defined until the beginning of the eighteenth century. The Welsh and the Irish were certainly aware of one another and each made frequent raids on the other, often returning with captive slaves. They also settled on each other's territories and integrated themselves into the native social fabric. It would be a mistake, nonetheless, to overplay linguistic and narrative parallels. They do not conclusively demonstrate that there was a long-lost common origin for the literatures of Wales and Ireland, as there is for the two languages. The issue is elusive and contentious, with learned opinion divided between accepting and rejecting the single-origin theory. A fuller discussion would require more space and specialized terminology than would be appropriate here, but a few examples can define the problem. The name of the Irish hero Fionn mac Cumhaill finds a cognate in the name of the Welsh figure Gwynn ap Nudd; *gwyn* also means fair or white, and Fionn is of the family of Nuadu. But within their traditions Fionn and Gwynn are far from identical, having differing statures and contrasting careers. Gwynn is first ruler of the otherworld and dwindles down until he is merely king of the fairies. A similar discontinuity can be seen with Manawydan fab Llŷr, the title character and protagonist of the Third Branch of the *Mabinogi* (see pp. 277–80, below), and Manannán mac Lir. Despite his skill with magic and certain crafts, Manawydan lacks the divine capabilities of the Irish sea god. In still other instances the points of comparison are internal rather than linguistic. The wild man of the woods, Myrddin Wyllt, goes mad at the sight of a battle and gains the gift of prophecy. Narratives about him invite comparison with the Irish Suibne Geilt as well as with the Scottish figure Lailoken. But all three, Myrddin, Suibne and Lailoken, are examples of the Wild Man of the Woods theme found elsewhere in early European tradition, and Myrddin contributes to the persona of the celebrated Arthurian magician Merlin.

As in Ireland, Welsh heroic prose narrative draws on much earlier oral tradition, whose existence is easily inferred. Early readers evidently recognized resonant characters at their first introduction. The vividness and succulence of innocent Rhiannon or guilty Blodeuedd are Welsh gifts to Western literature. The earliest surviving Welsh narrative, *Culhwch and Olwen* (*c.*1100), may be late compared to Irish examples but it still predates most of the development of prose narrative elsewhere in Europe. *Culhwch* also contains an early portrait of King Arthur with a roll-call of his companions and appears before such often-cited Arthurian texts as Geoffrey of Monmouth's *Historia Regnum Britanniae* (*c.*1135), Wace's *Roman de Brut* (1155) or Chrétien de Troyes' *Lancelot* (*c.*1178).

Eleven anonymous tales redacted in Norman times are found in *The White Book of Rhyderch* (*c.*1325) and *The Red Book of Hergest* (*c.*1382–1410). During the nineteenth century Lady Charlotte Guest recovered and translated them in three volumes (1838–49), along with the story of Taliesin of later provenance, to make an even dozen. She called the collection *Mabinogion*, an anglicization of *mabynnogyon*. The title was once thought to mean 'tales of youth', comparable to the French *enfances*. More recent scholarship suggests it may be translated as the 'stories of the divine Maponos/Mabon'. The term appears only once in early texts and has long been recognized as a scribal error or ghost-word, a presumed plural for *Mabinogi*. Lady Guest's term has wide currency and was endorsed by the esteemed translation by Gwyn Jones and Thomas Jones (1910–72), but the more authentic term *Mabinogi* used in Patrick K. Ford's translation (1977) is preferred here. While the eleven medieval tales are still often bound together, the term *Mabinogi* should only apply to the four interconnected stories: *Pwyll, Prince of Dyfed*; *Branwen, Daughter of Llŷr*; *Manawydan, Son of Llŷr*; and *Math, Son of Mathonwy*. Together these are known in Welsh as *Pedair Cainc y Mabinogi* or the Four Branches of the Mabinogi and are summarized on pp. 271–83, below. 'Branch' is preferred to 'chapter' or 'book' because it does not imply a linear continuum.

TALIESIN

Taliesin is one of the three best-known names from early Wales, along with Dylan and Rhiannon, even among people who pay little attention to anything Welsh. An examination of what little is known about the life of Taliesin [W. radiant brow], or even of the resplendent stories that later attached themselves to him, does not explain why his name should be so familiar. The reason is that diverse forces have popularized him both in the United Kingdom and in North America. The Anglo-Welsh fantasy fiction writer Charles Williams (1886–1945) greatly expanded Taliesin's characterization, based on Welsh originals, in a series of popular novels. From there Taliesin entered the food-chain of fantasy fiction, making his way eventually to role-playing games such as Dungeons and Dragons. Travelling in more elevated artistic circles, the Welsh-American architect Frank Lloyd Wright (1869–1959) made Taliesin a personal culture hero and built two estates named for him, one in Wisconsin and the second in Arizona. The second compound, Taliesin West, has since become a teaching centre accepting only select, highly qualified students. The effect has been to give the name 'Taliesin' connotations of innovation and excellence.

The historical Taliesin, if he existed at all, may have been a native of the central Welsh mini-kingdom of Powys who spent much of his adult life in the Old North praising the merits of several patron princes. He is, with Aneirin, one of the two surviving *cynfeirdd* [oldest poets]. Nearly 800 years after his lifetime, scribes assembled sixty poems linked to him in the *Book of Taliesin*. Of these, twelve have been ascribed to a sixth-century author by the modern scholar Sir Ifor Williams. Despite their antiquity, the dozen do not include the kinds of works that generations of Welsh schoolchildren might have been obliged to memorize, shaping their sense of idiom and style. Six are eulogies to Taliesin's prince, Urien Rheged, and to the prince's son, Owain ap Urien, figures of verifiable historicity. Two of the eulogies include intercessions with the patron after a period of estrangement. Of the remaining six poems, two are graphic descriptions of battles fought by Urien and Owain with the Angles and Picts, and yet others are praise poems for more remote Welsh rulers.

Taliesin includes Christian elements in the poems, beginning and ending with prayers for the soul, for example, but his exaltation of the warrior-leader feels pagan. His ideal ruler, Urien Rheged, protects his people by his personal bravery and his ferocity in battle, yet he is generous and magnanimous in peace. He is not unlike Fionn mac Cumhaill. In all the poems Taliesin is an upholder of the received social order and a conscientious craftsman.

Such a sober figure fired the Welsh imagination. He is assigned a minor role in *Branwen*, the second branch of the *Mabinogi*. Later, poems were attributed to him that he could not possibly have written, depicting encounters with predatory, supernatural beasts, the *cûn annwfn* [dogs of the otherworld] and with Annwfn, the otherworld itself. A comparable impulse led to Taliesin's role in the magical origin of poetic inspiration, the *Hanes Taliesin* [Story of Taliesin], sometimes known as *Ystoria Taliesin* [History of Taliesin], with some episodes found in parallel fragments. Elements in the tale may date from as early as the ninth or tenth centuries, but the surviving narrative was compiled in early modern times by Llywelyn Siôn (1540–c.1615).

During the reign of the historical Maelgwn Gwynedd (sixth century) in north Wales, Ceridwen, a shape-shifting goddess, lives at the bottom of Bala Lake with her husband Tegid Foel [*teg*, beautiful; *foel*, bald]. He is alluded to in what is still the Welsh name for the lake, Llyn Tegid. All day she brews in a magic cauldron named Amen, whose contents she intends for her own ugly son Morfran [sea crow] so that he might be gifted. With a lack of kindness the text also refers to Morfran as *Afagddu* [utter darkness], an unworthy beneficiary of his mother's attentions. Her intentions are thwarted when her servant Gwion Bach [little Gwion] snatches three drops from the cauldron on his thumb and forefingers and immediately jams them into his mouth, giving himself the gift of poetry. Blazing with fury, Ceridwen sets after Gwion Bach and each of them undergoes a series of metamorphoses of prey and hunter. Gwion Bach becomes a hare, and Ceridwen a greyhound. He a salmon, and she an otter; lastly, he a grain of wheat and she a hen who swallows him. In the particular magic of Celtic myth, this grain impregnates Ceridwen. The entity that had been Gwion Bach is reborn from her womb as an infant of such stunning loveliness that she cannot bring herself to butcher him and so casts him adrift on the sea. The baby drifts to the weir, near Aberystwyth, of the mythical ruler Gwyddno Garanhir, whose feckless son Elphin finds him on Calan Mai [May Day]. When the young man opens the blanket he exclaims, '*Dyma dâl iesin!*' [what a beautiful forehead]. To which the child, only three days old, replies, '*Taliesin bid*' [let it be Taliesin]. Gwyddno takes him as a foster-son.

As the boy grows older, he forms a bond with the bumbling Elphin, often advancing the fortunes of his foster-father. In a telling episode, Taliesin accompanies Elphin to the court of Maelgwn Gwynedd at Deganwy (near the mouth of the Conwy River, north Wales), where he employs magic and his superior poetic powers to overcome the household poets. As he is the adult, Elphin gains more from this contest than the poet does. Puffed up in vanity, Elphin boasts to Maelgwn's court that his (unnamed) wife is the fairest in the land, his horses the swiftest, and his bard (Taliesin) the wisest. For this hubris Maelgwn imprisons Elphin and sends the royal son Rhun [grand, awful], an irresistible seducer, to test Elphin's wife's virtue. In each instance, Taliesin proves a resourceful aide to his foster-father. He substitutes a female servant in disguise for Elphin's wife, and the helpless girl succumbs to Rhun's predatory charm. Later, when Rhun cuts a finger from the unfortunate servant to prove his conquest, Elphin is able to prove that his wife, with all fingers intact, is innocent. Taliesin next frees Elphin from Maelgwn's chains by singing a magnificent song on his own origin from the time of Lucifer's fall. Lastly, Elphin's horses defeat Maelgwn's, and, following Taliesin's instructions, a jockey drops his cap, revealing a cauldron of gold that repays the foster-father's generosity in rescuing the infant poet from the weir.

CULHWCH AND OLWEN

Although included by Lady Charlotte Guest in her *Mabinogion*, the tale of Culhwch and Olwen has quite a different character from the Four Branches. It is both older and often cruder, but relieved by passages of rare beauty. There are long runs of obscure names and built-in oral recitation devices, such as repeated questions and answers, designed to allow a performer to have some fun but that are a bit tiresome on the printed page. They are not repeated here. The story also feels more like a folktale, with a cruel stepmother, a wicked witch and a central plot-line classed by folklorists as 'The Giant's Daughter' (motifs G530.2; E765.4.1.1; H335). At the same time several figures, including Culhwch himself and Mabon, appear to derive from divine origins, according to some commentators. Perhaps most conspicuously, the narrative also includes an early portrayal of King Arthur, quite different from the way he will appear in later romances in other languages.

Cilydd, son of Celyddon Wledig [W. *gwledig*, ruler, prince], seeks to marry a woman as well-born as himself. His choice falls on the lovely Goleuddydd, daughter of Anlwdd Wledig. Unsettled by her almost immediate pregnancy, Goleuddydd leaves the household to wander through wild country, giving birth to her noble son in a pig-run. A swineherd names the child *Culhwch* [pig-run]. Although an unlikely appellation given his station and his mother's violent antipathy to pigs, Culhwch, the reader can expect, will have future interaction with porcine creatures, including boars. Goleuddydd dies shortly after, and to replace her Cilydd murders the king of Doged and carries home his widow. Understandably unhappy, the stepmother curses Culhwch, prophesying that he will not lie next to a woman until he has accomplished a seemingly impossible task. It is to win the rapturously beautiful Olwen, daughter of the crafty and cruel giant Ysbaddaden Bencawr. Cilydd reassures his son that he can make easy work of the task only by seeking help from King Arthur, a cousin. A few of the right words will aid him: on meeting the king he should only ask to have his hair trimmed. Meanwhile, the stepmother's curse has had an unanticipated effect on the young man. Without having seen Olwen, he falls deeply in love with her, and so sets out for Arthur's court.

Like a young god or hero, Culhwch fares forth in splendour, with a glowing aura about his face, fully armed with two silver spears and a sword that can bring blood from the air. His reception at court is less than cordial as the porter Glewlwyd Galfaelfawr refuses him entry. The moment is reminiscent of the arrival of Lug Lámfhota at Nuadu's court in *Cath Maige Tuired* [The (Second) Battle of Mag Tuired]. Culhwch's persistence pays off as the king demands that the young man be admitted. Following his father's instruction, Culhwch asks that his hair be trimmed, evidently a rite of passage from youth to manhood. He also recites a lengthy roll-call of Arthurian heroes, including the children of Dôn. So charming is Culhwch that Arthur agrees to help him in winning Olwen. Members of Arthur's court join them – Cei, Bedwyr, Cynddylig Cyfarwydd the guide, Gwrhyr Gwastad Ieithoedd the interpreter, and Menw the illusionist. These figures do not have the character of Arthur's men as we know them in English. Cei, to cite but one, does not yet show the surliness of Sir Kay, his later counterpart.

Culhwch and Arthur hear ominous reports on their long journey. The herdsman Custennin, brother-in-law of Culhwch's mother, reports that no one leaves Ysbaddaden's castle alive. Undeterred, the party advances to the nearby castle where Culhwch meets Olwen, whose name means 'flower track' because four trefoils or white clovers spring up wherever she steps. She seems pleased to accept Culhwch's pledge of love but reminds him that she cannot join him without her father's consent, which he is unlikely to give: his life will end when she takes a husband. She urges him to try anyway, saying that if he can meet the giant's demands, Culhwch will have her.

Ysbaddaden is not receptive to guests. When Culhwch and Arthur approach, he casts three poisoned stone spears at the party, each one of which is turned back to the thrower. The wounds cause the giant to hear the young man's entreaty. Before the dialogue can begin, he asks servants to use large wooden forks to lift his heavy eyelids, a characteristic he shares with the Irish divinity Balor. Ysbaddaden agrees to give his daughter's hand to Culhwch if he can accomplish forty seemingly impossible tasks. The recitation of the tasks is accompanied by a verbal exchange in which Culhwch repeats the boast over and over, 'It is easy for me to accomplish that, though you may not think so.' Some of the tasks are frivolous, such as finding honey nine times sweeter than that of the first swarm out of the hive. Others show the possible influence of the twelve labours of Heracles in classical mythology. Culhwch's first group requires eight primary agricultural labours, such as ploughing waste land so that food might be grown, and five secondary labours to complete the ploughing. In each instance Culhwch makes light work of the challenge and quickly accomplishes thirteen of the original plus three not previously mentioned. Often he is aided by the folkloric magic of enchanted animals and birds.

Three of the tasks loom larger than the others. One is to secure the blood of the pitch-black witch, daughter of the bright-white witch from the Valley of Grief in Hell's back country. The blood is needed to stretch out Ysbaddaden's hairs, which must be shaved before the taking of Olwen. This is accomplished, as Culhwch promises.

A second is to enlist the help of Mabon the Hunter, who is locked up in Gloucester Castle and of whom nothing has been heard since he was snatched from his mother Modron when he was but three days old. Though not much time in the narrative is spent on him, Mabon interests commentators because of his divine antecedents in Maponos of ancient Britain and Gaul. Further, he is cited as one of the Three Exalted Prisoners of the Isle of Britain, in the Welsh *Triads* (*Trioedd Ynys Prydain*), that medieval treasure-trove of Welsh lore. Once he is released from his enchanted imprisonment, Mabon is the oldest of all living beings, quite a paradox for someone whose name means 'youth'. His aid is still valuable to Culhwch's quest.

More formidable is the challenge of securing the shears, razor and comb from between the ears of Twrch Trwyth, son of Taredd Wledig. The huge destructive boar was once a king who, with his followers, had been transformed as punishment for his evil ways. Arthur and Culhwch begin the chase, which extends through south Wales, Cornwall and Ireland. With Mabon's help, the party catches up with the boar and retrieves the necessary implements before driving him into the sea.

Returning with their booty, Culhwch and Arthur face Ysbaddaden. One of their party, Caw of Britain, shaves the giant's beard, and his flesh and skin down to the bone, and his two ears. Thus subdued, Ysbaddaden agrees that Culhwch has won his daughter but gives credit to Arthur for this turn of events. He also admits it is time to end his life. Another member of the party, Goreu, strikes off his head and places it atop a courtyard post.

Culhwch takes possession of the giant's fort and his kingdom. That night he sleeps with Olwen. As long as he lives, she is his only wife.

PWYLL, PRINCE OF DYFED;
MABINOGI, BRANCH I

Proinsias MacCana has written that the *Mabinogi* 'is not a mythological document in any primary sense; it is a literary construct which makes use of mythological, and other, materials' (1992). Its author is not, he adds, a mythographer conscientiously recording the traditions of the gods for their own sake, but instead a gifted writer shaping the shattered remains of a mythology to his own literary ends. We do not know that author's name, but he lived in Dyfed in southwestern Wales and worked between 1050 and 1120 during the transition to Norman occupation. Action in the *Mabinogi* takes place in the real world, with frequent citations of actual place-names, as in Irish stories. Triads within the narrative testify to an origin in oral tradition. Many hands and many heads contributed materials, but only one personality shaped the text we read. He was probably a cleric; he always praises patience and chastity, and he certainly knows the law.

Later than the author is the redactor, the person who put the stories in the form under which they were copied in manuscript. The redactor, in contrast to the author, was a stylist rather than a storyteller. His sophisticated diction and rhetoric display a knowledge of Latin and blend the colloquial judiciously with the learned. Adjectives are used sparingly, and there is little figurative language.

Although the title 'Four Branches' was imposed in modern times, there seems little doubt today that the four tales belong together. They may be juxtaposed so that a reader might compare them. J. K. Bollard (1975) argues for their essential unity by stressing the three themes that unite all four stories, namely friendships, marriages, and feuds. He sees, further, a continual interplay between the three that functions as a unifying element in the stories, an interplay that also comments on social attitudes and relationships. The four stories embrace many repetitions and cross-references, and no incident in the *Mabinogi* is superfluous or isolated.

The story of Pwyll is told in two barely connected portions. In the first the prince encounters Arawn, ruler of Annwfn, and agrees to exchange forms with him for a year. In the second Pwyll meets the dazzlingly beautiful Rhiannon, who becomes his wife. She suffers from a false accusation, but they produce a son, Pryderi. Dyfed was earlier the name of a region in southwestern Wales. The modern Dyfed, reconstituted in 1974, embraces a much larger area.

While hunting one day near Glyn Cuch [glen scowl], Pwyll, Prince of Dyfed, becomes separated from his companions. He is startled by a pack of hounds, not his own, running down a stag. They have a certain ominousness about them because they bear the colours of the otherworld: snow-white fur with red ears. Pwyll is about to drive them away when the dogs' master appears and chides the prince for his discourtesy. The stranger identifies himself as Arawn, a king of Annwfn. Medieval readers would identify Annwfn as the otherworld, but the two men discourse as if it were just another mortal kingdom. Arawn tells of being harried by a rival king, Hafgan [summer white], and proposes Pwyll redeem his bad manners by taking on Hafgan in single combat in a year's time; to work out this plan, Pwyll and Arawn should exchange both shapes and kingdoms for a year. The bargain will be concluded when Pwyll in the shape of Arawn lays Hafgan low with a single blow – because a second would allow the villain to revive.

Without a moment's consideration of what a year's imposture would entail, Pwyll agrees to the adventure. As Arawn he is a wise and good ruler of Annwfn, but he has overlooked his obligations to the king's beautiful wife. At bedtime, Pwyll as Arawn sets his face to the wall and says nothing, never so much as touching the wife, much to her surprise and disappointment. The impostor king is nonetheless courteous to the wife on all public occasions. When the appointed time comes, Pwyll as Arawn meets Hafgan in combat at a river ford. In a single gallant blow Pwyll sunders Hafgan's shield and knocks him the length of an arm and a shield over his horse's hind end. In deathly bravado, Hafgan asks for another blow as a *coup de grâce*, but Pwyll remembers the dangers of delivering a second stroke. Arawn's court and retainers rejoice that the kingdom is again united. His promise kept, Pwyll returns to Glyn Cuch, where he greets Arawn. The two rulers thank each other for their stewardship and return to their own kingdoms in their own shapes. That night when Pwyll returns to his own marriage bed, he is pleased to learn from his wife (not named) that Arawn chastely kept his part of the bargain. Arawn also maintained Pwyll's reputation as a just ruler in his absence. In payment for his service the mortal king is given a new title: Pwyll Penn Annwfn [ruler of Annwfn].

The second portion of Pwyll's story seems barely connected to the first. The king is seated on the magical mound of Arberth, where one might be expected to see wonders. The mound's lore is fulfilled when Pwyll beholds a woman approaching dressed in brilliant gold brocade and mounted on a majestic, pale white horse. No one knows her name, but the king's men pursue her, and on a fourth attempt determine that she is Rhiannon. This is the most theatrical entrance in the Four Branches and partially explains why the name 'Rhiannon' has such resonance outside Welsh literature; she is also a figure with ancient roots (see pp. 79–80). Rhiannon identifies herself as the daughter of Hyfaidd Hen, who has arbitrarily betrothed her to another man, while she loves only Pwyll, whom she has been seeking. Pwyll allows that, yes, he loves her as well and asks that they be married at a feast to follow in a year and a day. She agrees. In a year's time Pwyll brings one hundred men with him to the expected feast at Rhiannon's father's palace. The festive mood changes abruptly when a tall, auburn-haired stranger, his regal bearing enhanced with satin garments, enters and asks a favour of Pwyll. To Rhiannon's dismay, Pwyll grants it, in a moment of reckless high spirits. Shortly, alas, the stranger is revealed to be Gwawl son of Clud, the father's choice as suitor, who wants his promised bride now. Honest Pwyll feels bound to his promise of granting a favour, but Rhiannon refuses to marry Gwawl before another year has passed. Portentously, Rhiannon gives Pwyll an enchanted bag, advising him to make good use of it when the time comes.

After a year a second great wedding feast is held with Gwawl in the honoured place as prospective groom. During the merrymaking, an old beggar clad in rags and rough shoes enters, asking charity from the party: just a bag of extra food to take with him. Gwawl graciously agrees, but something begins to go wrong. No matter how much food servants place in the bag, they cannot fill it. The bag cannot be filled, the beggar offers, until someone endowed with wealth and land gets into the bag and stamps it down. Rhiannon asks Gwawl to see if this is true. The would-be groom has only to put his two feet into the bag for the ruse to be revealed. The beggar, Pwyll in disguise, pulls the bag over Gwawl's head and ties it. The Prince of Dyfed then blows his horn and invites the other merrymakers to join him in a game of 'badger-in-the-bag', striking and kicking the bag stuffed with the hapless Gwawl about the hall. Only when the captive Gwawl agrees not to seek revenge is he released. Pwyll and Rhiannon are then happily married.

Trouble of a different kind befalls the couple. After a period of barrenness, Rhiannon gives birth to a son who inexplicably disappears the very next morning. Household servants, fearing they will be charged, contrive to make it appear that Rhiannon has murdered her own son. Although stunned at this charge, Pwyll will not put his wife away. He agrees, instead, that she should suffer a unique punishment, that of sitting each day at the castle gate's horse block. There she should tell her tale to every passing stranger while offering to carry each one on her back. Some commentators feel this episode implies Rhiannon's antecedent in the ancient horse-goddess Epona.

Relief from Rhiannon's torment comes from across Wales in the little kingdom of Gwent Is Coed, where a lord named Teyrnon Twrf Lient raises horses. On each Calan Mai [May Day], his prize mare always foals, but no one knows what becomes of the offspring. One year Teyrnon investigates by waiting in the horse barn through the night of the birth. A huge clawed arm comes through the window. Moving quickly, Teyrnon hacks off the arm at the elbow and then dashes outside to see what lies behind it. In darkness, he can see nothing. On his return to the barn he finds an infant boy wrapped in the finest satin. As Teyrnon and his wife are childless, they raise the boy as their own, calling him Gwri of the Golden Hair. As the boy matures rapidly Teyrnon and his wife recognize that he bears a striking resemblance to Pwyll, Prince of Dyfed. They take the boy to Pwyll's castle, where there is understandable rejoicing and Rhiannon is released from her humiliating punishment. The rightful parents now claim their son and name him Pryderi [care (?)].

BRANWEN, DAUGHTER OF LLÔR; *MABINOGI*, BRANCH II

Unlike Branch I, the title character Branwen [white or sacred raven] here is more of a supporting player than a lead. The focus instead is on her family, the Children of Llŷr, offspring of the Welsh sea-god. It is led by the giant Bendigeidfran (or Bran [crow/raven?] the Blessed), in the company of his stalwart brother Manawydan and their beautiful sister Branwen. In their house also are two half-brothers born of the same mother, the rancorous Efnisien [unpeaceful] and the mild Nisien [peaceful]. The action switches to Ireland when Branwen marries the Irish king Matholwch, where war breaks out after Efnisien insults the in-laws. Branwen dies, and Bendigeidfran is killed, but his severed head remains to protect the Isle of Britain.

Action begins in the ancient coastal seat of Harlech, where Bendigeidfran the new king of the Isle of the Mighty (Britain) reigns with his court and family. One day the new king sees thirteen ships with embroidered satin pennants coming from Ireland with a fair wind. On them is the Irish King Matholwch, seeking to make an alliance. Bendigeidfran and brother Manawydan agree to marry Branwen of the snowy breast to the Irish King Matholwch, which she appears to accept. At first this seems like a boon to both parties. A huge celebration is held in a tent because Bendigeidfran cannot fit into a conventional building. Then things begin to turn sour. Half-brother Efnisien rages that he was not consulted about the nuptials and takes his vengeance by mutilating Matholwch's horses; he cuts their lips, ears and tails so that they are both disfigured and useless. The Irish guests are shocked. Covering for the household, Bendigeidfran explains that the misdeed was only a whim of his malevolent half-brother and offers to make up the loss, horse for horse. Sweetening his contrition, Bendigeidfran offers three gifts: silver, gold and, most importantly, a cauldron of regeneration that overnight will restore slain warriors to life. In giving the gift, Bendigeidfran explains that the cauldron originated in Ireland. One Llassar Llaes Gyfnewid with his wife Cymidei Cymeinfoll retrieved it while escaping from a fiery house there. They turned over the cauldron of regeneration to Bendigeidfran, who offers it now for the merging of the families. This is sufficient for Matholwch, who has heard the story of the cauldron. He returns to Ireland with wedding gifts, his entourage and his bride.

The first year as queen of Ireland goes well for Branwen. She receives love and acclaim, which increases when she produces a son named Gwern [alder]. In the second year suppressed resentment begins to surface. Matholwch's brothers keep remembering Efnisien's old insult and ask that Branwen be made to suffer for it. She is removed from queenship and sent to the kitchen where the cook bullies her and kitchen boys box her ears. For three years Branwen suffers while the Irish cease all commerce that would return word of her humiliation to her family. Resourcefully, she trains a starling that carries the news to the court at Harlech, whereupon Bendigeidfran immediately prepares a great army to invade Ireland. Welsh armed men board ships for the crossing, but Bendigeidfran is so huge he must wade the Irish Sea. Matholwch's defenders are stupefied by the Welsh king's immense size, but Branwen knows that her brother has come to rescue her.

The Irish scurry west. When in their flight they destroy the last bridge over the Shannon River, Bendigeidfran must make of himself a human bridge, allowing his men to cross on his back. Seeing their cause weakened and wishing to ingratiate themselves with the invaders, the Irish make an entreaty. To compensate for their mistreatment of Branwen, Matholwch offers to build a house big enough to hold Bendigeidfran. Stealthily, though, they use pegs to hold a hundred bags filled with armed men inside the house. Efnisien's malevolence is then put to rare good use. He asks what is in the bags, and being told they are filled with flour, squeezes each until he has cruelly murdered every warrior. Trapped by their own ruse, the Irish are left with nothing to say.

Despite the discomfort of this moment, both sides share in a night of feasting. In a gesture of conciliation, the Irish confer their sovereignty on Gwern, the son of Branwen and Matholwch. The boy wins the affection of both Irish and Welsh, all except scowling Efnisien, who jealously plunges Gwern into the fire. This unleashes latent tensions on both sides, with widespread fighting and slaughter. Having the cauldron of regeneration, the Irish could seize the advantage by bringing their dead back to fight. In a climactic act of contrition, Efnisien hides himself among the Irish corpses, waiting to be thrown into the cauldron. Once he is cast inside, his body stretches out and breaks the cauldron in four ways – bursting his own heart at the same time.

All the Irish men are slaughtered, and only five of their women are spared. The Welsh suffer as well, but seven of their number survive, including Pryderi, Manawydan and Bendigeidfran. The giant king is later mortally wounded by a poisoned spear in the heel. His death request is most unusual. He implores the Welshmen to cut off his head and take it to Gwyn Fryn [white mound] near London but facing France. On their route the men hear the sweet music of the three small birds of Rhiannon. Branwen's return brings deeper sadness. She can still see Ireland when she sets foot in Wales, and, turning, cries out, 'Dear Son of God – alas that I was born! These good islands have been destroyed because of me.' Sighing deeply, she dies of a shattered heart.

The five surviving Irish women, we learn, are pregnant, and each bears a son. In maturity, each young man mates with a different woman, producing the tribes that become the five provinces of Ireland.

MANAWYDAN, SON OF LLŶR; *MABINOGI*, BRANCH III

The title character of the third branch, Manawydan, continues his role as brother and heir of Bendigeidfran in the second branch. Joining him are characters from the first branch, Rhiannon and her son Pryderi, who is now ascribed a wife, Cigfa. Most of the action is set in south-western Wales with successive forays into England. While there is much magic in this branch, there are also depictions of the lives of tradesmen.

On their return from the foray to Ireland to rescue Branwen, Manawydan and Pryderi settle in Dyfed, where Pryderi is lord of seven *cantrefs* (100 townships each). Seeing that Manawydan lacks a companion, Pryderi promises the hand of his still beautiful mother, Rhiannon. Both parties are highly receptive to this match and sleep together as soon as they can. Pryderi chooses Cigfa, daughter of Gwyn Gogoyw, for himself. The two couples get on together prosperously and happily until an inexplicable mist comes upon them quite suddenly. This occurs while the four are feasting at Arberth, the very same spot where Pwyll first encountered the splendid Rhiannon. The mist is equally mysterious but far less benign. It devastates the country, turning what had been some of the most verdant land on earth into a desolate waste. At first they are able to get by with what they can hunt, but Manawydan speaks of his unhappiness and urges them all to migrate to Lloegyr [England]. There they might support themselves in lucrative trades, starting with saddlemaking just across the border in Hereford. Within a short time the quartet is a raging success, turning out products of premium quality. Soon, none of the other saddlers have any business, and they rail against the Welsh intruders, threatening violence. Pryderi wants to stay and fight, but Manawydan cautiously advises retreat. And so the same pattern follows with the manufacture of shields and shoes: success, resentment, Pryderi arguing resistance, Manawydan counselling retreat. Weary of it all, the group returns to Dyfed and attempts again to live by hunting.

Hunting in the wild brings unexpected challenges. A ferocious but gleaming white boar charges them one day, drawing all the hunting dogs in his train. Worse, the boar heads for a fort and disappears, taking the dogs with him. Always impetuous, Pryderi also enters the fort, but against Manawydan's advice. Hearing of this Rhiannon is cross with her husband for allowing her son to rush into what appears to be an enchanted snare. Rhiannon then goes in search of Pryderi. Inside the fort she finds him clinging to a bowl but unable to speak. When she too touches the bowl, she is also struck dumb and immobile. A thunderclap sounds and, poof, the fort disappears. This sets Cigfa to sobbing for her lost husband. Manawydan, always a comforting counsellor, offers to be a helpful companion to her. Cigfa then finds herself travelling with a man not her husband and not a blood relative, in effect her husband's stepfather. Like Pwyll in the first branch, however, he is an honourable respecter of a woman's marriage vows.

When Manawydan and Cigfa return to England, they are a celibate couple. Once again they enter the trade of shoemaking and follow the same cycle as on their first enterprise. Acclaim for their craftsmanship leads to commercial success, followed by the jealousy of English shoemakers, recriminations, and, eventually, return to Dyfed. After a period of fishing and hunting without dogs, they till the soil in three crofts sown with wheat. This brings a new trouble. The first croft is devastated before Manawydan can bring in a single harvest. On the following night the same fate befalls the second croft. Before he loses the third croft, Manawydan keeps watch on the third night. The culprits are revealed to be an enormous host of mice ravaging the field. Manawydan suddenly grabs one of the tiny creatures and thunders that he will hang this one. Cigfa upbraids him for such trifling behaviour beneath his dignity, but Manawydan answers that he will execute them all if he can catch them. To solemnize the execution, Manawydan takes the mouse to the mound at Arberth the next day. Before the execution begins, three strangers, the first seen in seven years, arrive at the mound. Each one argues that it is unseemly to put to death such an insignificant creature as a mouse. Stepping forward, the first traveller, a shabbily dressed scholar, offers a ransom of one pound. Raising the ante, the second traveller, a priest, puts up three pounds. The grandest of the three, a bishop, offers a ransom of seven pounds. He quickly raises this to twenty-four pounds as well as his own horses and seven loads of baggage and seven horses to pull the loads. All this if only the mouse can be spared. Manawydan refuses to yield, which prompts the bishop to ask what else he could possibly want. The answer is immediate: 'The release of Rhiannon and Pryderi and the removal of the magic enchantment from the seven *cantrefs* of Dyfed.'

Astoundingly, the bishop agrees to Manawydan's demands. He will pay any price because the mouse is really his pregnant wife, magically transformed. The 'bishop' is actually Llwyd, son of Cil Coed, a friend of Gwawl, whom Pwyll, Pryderi's father, had humiliated with the game of 'badger-in-the-bag' in the first branch. Llwyd and his family have been harassing Dyfed because of the remembered hurt of that episode. The devastation of the crops, the enchantment of Dyfed and the entrapment of Rhiannon and Pryderi are all means of revenge. Contrite now, Llwyd promises never to trouble Dyfed again. Manawydan releases the mouse, who is immediately restored to her natural form as the fairest young woman anyone has ever seen. In return the herds, dwellings and habitations of Dyfed are now again as good as ever. Rhiannon and Pryderi are released from their servitude, and the two couples live together in happiness.

MATH, SON OF MATHONWY; *MABINOGI*, BRANCH IV

Action in the fourth branch shifts to the north, to Gwynedd, the medieval kingdom often at odds with Dyfed of the south. Featured here are Math, son of Mathonwy, and his niece and nephews, the children of Dôn. More complex and longer than the previous three, the fourth branch combines mythological, magical and human elements. Despite abrupt transitions, this branch is frequently the most appealing to modern readers. Novelistic episodes of intrigue and betrayal are peopled with arresting characters such as the unscrupulous enchanter Gwydion, the adulterous Blodeuedd and the heroic Lleu Llaw Gyffes.

Math reigns in Gwynedd while Pryderi has come to power in Dyfed with portions of allied nearby kingdoms. Vital to Math's stability on his throne is his participation in a seemingly bizarre custom. Unless he is away for war, he must, when seated, keep his feet in the lap of a chosen virgin, Goewin, who is renowned for her beauty. Why this should be so is never hinted at in the text, but modern commentators have many suggestions. M. J. Green (1993) asserts that Math may represent the survival of a sacral kingship in which the life-force of the land is concentrated in the undissipated and undiluted sexuality of the virgin. Or there may be a parallel with the concept of the ritual marriage between the king and a female incarnation of sovereignty, a personified force of the territory, in order that the land may be prosperous and fertile. The king has no romantic attachment to the footholder. Other members of the court, including Math's nephews Gilfaethwy and Gwydion, do have their eyes on her. Because he has supernatural powers, Gwydion perceives that Gilfaethwy is smitten with Goewin and so devises a complicated plan to allow his brother to be with his heart's desire. His scheme turns on a taste for pork. Pigs are new to Wales at this time, and their meat is proclaimed sweeter than beef. Gwydion promises to scout out some of the precious comestible by taking ten companions and going in disguise as a bard to Dyfed, where Pryderi is raising a herd. Although the delegation charms Pryderi, the Dyfed king is looking for comparable exchange before he will hand over such prized beasts. The enchanter Gwydion at last turns to magic; he ensorcells Pryderi with twelve phantom steeds and twelve phantom hounds and then leaves immediately with the pigs. Next morning when Pryderi realizes he has been defrauded, the two petty kingdoms are at war. Math's subsequent departure for the battlefield means that he must leave foot-holder Goewin behind, which allows Gilfaethwy his moment with her. As virtuous as she is lovely, Goewin refuses. He then forces his affection upon her dishonourably. Elsewhere the war ends quickly when Gwydion slays Pryderi in single combat.

The outrage committed on Goewin yields consequences. When she confesses to Math that she is no longer a virgin, the king marries her to spare her further shame. His anger is directed toward his nephews instead. He has them transformed successively into a pair of deer, pigs and wolves. Simultaneously their sexes are changed so that one must be female while the other is male. As stag and hind in their first year they produce the fawn Hyddwn, the second as boar and sow gives Hychdwn Hir [tall piglet], and their third as wolf and bitch, Bleiddwn [wolf cub]. Their three-year punishment ended, the brothers return to human form, cleansed and anointed, to rejoin the court.

So well restored to good graces is Gwydion that he may again advise the court, even on such delicate matters as finding a new virgin foot-holder. He nominates his own sister, Arianrhod, the daughter of Dôn. Math says he will accept her after she has passed an infallible test of virginity. A magician's rod is placed on the floor, and she must step across it. Arianrhod agrees but fails spectacularly. As her foot crosses over the rod, a golden-haired infant drops from her womb and gives out a loud cry. In humiliation Arianrhod bolts for the door, dropping another little thing on the way, which Gwydion seizes. The sturdy, golden-haired infant dropped in the test is named Dylan [ocean, wave], and immediately leaves for the sea. In maturity he will be described as dark and will bear the epithet *Eil Ton* [son of wave] and can swim as well as any fish. The cryptic 'thing' dropped by Arianrhod as she flees turns out to be another child. Gwydion, the unacknowledged father of both infants, nurtures this second boy away from prying eyes, until one day he decides to present him to his mother. Arianrhod is furious to see the boy, a reminder of her foiled deception. After scolding Gwydion for bringing him, she rages that she does not want the boy to have a name until she herself decides what would be appropriate. In an attempt to have the mother view the child with more equanimity, Gwydion has him work as a shoemaker, and in that guise he throws a stone with accuracy and skill. Suitably impressed, Arianrhod admiringly calls the stone-thrower Lleu Llaw Gyffes [light/fair one of the sure/steady hand]. Returned to anger when she realizes Lleu's true identity, she swears that he cannot have weapons until she gives them to him. But she soon has to swallow this threat when her palace appears threatened and she acknowledges that she does indeed have to give Lleu weapons. In a third fit of anger, Arianrhod proclaims that young Lleu cannot have a bride of any race on this earth. Gwydion and Math respond by constructing a wife of fragrant materials: oak, broom and meadowsweet. Her name Blodeuedd [flower face] is appropriately descriptive. She and Lleu are instantly taken with one another and make love on the first night.

The young couple's wedded bliss is short-lived. They settle in the far *cantref* of Dinoding, where Math and Gwydion help them establish a household. Lleu then returns to Math's court, leaving Blodeuedd by herself. One day a hunter named Gronw Pebyr stops nearby, and as soon as he and Blodeuedd lay eyes on each other they instantly fall in love. As she did with Lleu, Blodeuedd sleeps with her paramour as soon as she can. Alert to the dangers of their love affair, the adulterers agree that they must murder Lleu before he uncovers their deception. She knows that her husband is nearly invulnerable. Pretending an interest in his safety and welfare, she asks Lleu how he might be killed. Although most weapons are useless against him, Lleu recklessly allows that he can be killed only by a spear made over a year's duration. Further, the spear must be hurled at him as he is bathing in a special kind of tub and only when one of his feet is touching a billy goat. Complicated as they are, Blodeuedd and her lover meet every one of the demands. Just as Gronw Pebyr is about to run the hero through, Lleu Llaw Gyffes lets out a horrible scream and takes flight in the shape of an eagle. Soon he is out of sight. Gronw Pebyr then shows himself to be more than a mere adulterer by adding Lleu's castle and lands to his own property.

News of the adultery and attempted murder weighs heavily on Math and Gwydion. After exhausting effort they track down Lleu in eagle shape. His magic now more benign, Gwydion puts his wand to the eagle and returns Lleu to his familiar human form. The hero is unexpectedly emaciated and weak. Finding the strumpet Blodeuedd as well, Gwydion is harsher. To shame her he turns her into an owl and condemns her never to show her face in light again. Aware of his guilt, Gronw Pebyr offers compensation for the thwarted murder. Lleu thinks it would be appropriate for him to return whatever blow was delivered to him. For his protection, Gronw Pebyr is allowed to hide behind a rock. It is not enough. Lleu's thrust of the spear is so ferocious that it sunders the rock and pierces the adulterer's back, ending his tawdry life. Lleu Llaw Gyffes retakes his possessions and rules them successfully. Later he becomes lord of all Gwynedd.

Thus end the four branches of the *Mabinogi*.

14

Survivals in the Oral Traditions of
Celtic Lands

LEARNED TEXT AND HUMBLE SPEECH

Great medieval narratives such as the *Táin Bó Cuailnge* and the *Mabinogi* command much of our attention in this volume. Their substantial bulk, artistic complexity and depth sustain extensive critical scrutiny. For all that we have discovered about them, most of their secrets remain to be unravelled. And they exist in written documents.

If we think of post-classical Celtic mythology as consisting primarily of Irish and Welsh materials, it is because only in Ireland and Wales was there an early written literary tradition in the indigenous languages. In both Ireland and Wales there is also a huge body of oral literature, much of it collected from illiterate storytellers in the nineteenth and early twentieth centuries. In some of the stories characters from earlier written tradition, such as Fionn mac Cumhaill or Deirdre, appear again often strangely transmogrified. In oral tradition Fionn the hero of written narratives can be seen as a giant or as a clumsy buffoon. While mnemonic oral formulae among storytellers may allow for set passages to stay intact over many generations, it is also true that the more often and more widely a story is repeated the more often variations will occur in characterization and plot detail.

So it is in Gaelic Scotland and Gaelic Nova Scotia, the Isle of Man, Cornwall and Brittany, places with Celtic language traditions that produced no manuscripts from small learned castes in medieval times. Apart from Scottish Gaelic poetry published in the early sixteenth century, narrative lore in these five areas comes from nineteenth- and twentieth-century collectors who travelled among the illiterate peasantry. We can never be sure what status a story held within the society where it was collected. Was it mere entertainment or was it thought to contain an esteemed truth of the tribe? Nineteenth-century publication occurred before collection from oral sources had attained professional academic standards. We cannot always guess the collector's limitations or biases. Given these limitations, the information received from collectors is often difficult to reconcile with what documents tell us. The Brahan Seer, a gifted practitioner of 'second sight', is one of the most widely known and cited figures in Scottish Gaelic oral tradition. But the two life records that support his existence are eighty-six years apart and could not possibly describe the same person. In oral tradition variations over time and place may produce tales of contradictory themes. In the Breton 'Legend of the City of Ys', the usual narrative point of view is somewhat misogynist, in that the villain is Dahut, the dissolute princess. In other versions her otherwise saintly father Gradlon may take this role, making a story of radically different import.

A certain fluidity of character and theme is hardly the only distinction of oral tradition. Prompted by the rise of television and mass communications after the middle of the twentieth century, many scholars have re-examined the transforming impact of literacy on the mind of Europe. Their attention has ranged from writing itself to the introduction of the printing press at the beginning of the Renaissance and the rise of mass literacy after the Industrial Revolution. In the view of Walter J. Ong, in *Orality and Literacy* (1982), writing changes the *way* we think as much as it changes *what* we think. His findings are as much diachronic as synchronic and can apply to medieval literacy as well as to modern, even when that literacy is drawn from a long-ago orality.

There is a sociological dimension as well to the difference between medieval written stories and those collected from the unlettered. The ecclesiastics who produced the manuscripts in Ireland and Wales were but a tiny fraction of the population in which they lived. Their housing might have been intolerable by modern standards – unheated stone cells – but they usually came from the most privileged families. Along with reading their own languages, they also knew Latin and perhaps Greek, giving them access to worlds far beyond their own. The illiterates interviewed by nineteenth-century collectors could have been anyone who happened by. Such people subsisted on the impoverished fringes of Europe, the 'Celtic Fringe', while a few hundred miles away other minds were unravelling the mysteries of science or amassing unprecedented fortunes. Tied to archaic economies and inhibitive and repressive social structures, these were 'folk' rather than citizens.

Collections from the oral traditions of the illiterate among the Celtic fringe came fairly late in the century. The impulse to rescue stories of the peasantry had begun at least a generation earlier on the continent with scholars such as the Brothers Grimm – Jakob (1785–1863) and Wilhelm (1786–1859). With the amassing of stories from dozens of languages came a new understanding of the stories' nature. Earlier narratives collected from illiterate peasantry were thought to be 'popular antiquities': 'popular' because they were known among common people, and 'antiquities' because they were presumed to have been derived from ancient originals, perhaps in Greece and Rome. In the 1850s English collectors coined the term 'folktale' to imply that the phenomenon should be considered on its own, not as some degraded form of a learned original, whether we call it 'mythology' or not. Because they are not written down their age and origin are incalculable. Just as speech precedes writing, however, many could well be older than comparable stories recorded by learned elites.

SCOTLAND

Scotland comprises five traditional ethnic groups, only one of which has given its name to the nation. These are the Gaels or *Scotti*, who began migrating from Ireland about the fifth century. *Scotti* was one of several names for Irish people, especially in the northeast of that island. Before they arrived, the land in the north of Great Britain was known as Caledonia or Alba. In 844 the Gaelic leader Cináed mac Alpín [Kenneth MacAlpin] united with the neighbouring Picts (an indigenous, essentially Celtic-speaking people) to form Scotland. Eventually Scottish Gaelic hegemony extended over the Angles (i.e. English) in the southeast and the Britons (or Welsh) in the south and southwest kingdom of Rheged, as well as the many Norse enclaves. For several centuries Scottish Gaelic spread over the entire kingdom.

Derived from Old Irish, it underwent so many changes in vocabulary and pronunciation as to become a separate language. Eventually it was replaced as the medium for law and commerce by the Scottish language, a linguistic cousin of English, often known as Scots, Broad Scots or Lallans. 'Lallans' means, literally, 'Low Lands', and denotes the more heavily populated, industrially advanced and prosperous areas of the country in the centre and south, including Edinburgh and Glasgow. Gaelic, no longer the national language, retreated behind the Grampian Line, a range of mountains that separate the Highlands and Hebridean Islands of Scotland from the rest of the country, where it continues to be spoken and written in the twenty-first century.

Spectacularly beautiful but mostly unarable land, the Highlands have been so obscured by more than two centuries of romance set among their misty crags that few readers perceive how impoverished they have been and how cut off from the mainstream of European culture. There were almost no roads in the Highlands until the eighteenth century and thus few wheeled vehicles. Individuals did not own land, which was held by powerful clan chiefs, much like medieval lords. In 1745–6, many Highlanders supported a disastrous rebellion to restore the Stuart pretender, Prince Charles Edward or 'Bonnie Prince Charlie', to the thrones of Scotland and England. The misguided effort ended in the last battle fought in Great Britain, at Culloden Moor, in April 1746, a catastrophe for Highland culture. In the subsequent repression of the rebels, traditional dress was forbidden and the Gaelic language vehemently discouraged. In time the clan chiefs, most of whom now resided in distant cities, decided that flocks of sheep would be more profitable on their lands than humans were, and so began the Clearances. These led to the destruction of tenants' cottages and the driving off of the inhabitants, often at gunpoint. They were put on ships and settled in distant lands, such as Canada and Australia. In their famous walking tour of the Highlands in the 1770s, Samuel Johnson and James Boswell described an exotic, semi-savage population living in debilitating poverty. On entering villages they were greeted by barefoot, begging children, their faces blackened by living in smoky stone cottages without chimneys. Today the Highland population still residing on traditional lands is a tiny fraction of the whole of Scotland, about 270,000 people in a nation of nearly 6 million.

Although Scottish Gaelic literary tradition has been Christian since the establishment of the monastery of Iona in the Inner Hebrides by St Colum Cille (d. 597), it did not produce great ecclesiastically fostered medieval collections of written narratives as Ireland and Wales did. Scottish Gaelic marginal notes appear in the Latin texts of the Gospels in *The Book of Deer* (1131–53) but more substantial writing in the language did not appear until early modern times with *The Book of the Dean of Lismore* (1512–26). Seventeenth- and eighteenth-century bards, patronized by clan chiefs, left substantial written records of their carefully wrought poetry. But the great body of narrative lore was passed down through oral tradition of the illiterate peasantry and not recorded until the nineteenth century. Among the great collections are John Francis Campbell's *Popular Tales of the West Highlands*, 4 vols. (1861), and Archibald Campbell's *Waifs and Strays in Celtic Tradition*, 4 vols. (1889–91). In these and other volumes we find familiar Irish characters such as Cúchulainn, Deirdre, Fergus, Angus Óg and especially Fionn mac Cumhaill. When James Macpherson uncovered Fionn and Oisín in Scottish Gaelic ballads sometime before 1760 and fashioned Fingal and Ossian from them, he clearly did not perceive their Irish provenance. Scottish Gaelic texts often replicate narratives found in Irish, sometimes transforming earlier stories but also embroidering new episodes onto old patterns. Further, different themes command priority in Scotland, especially an interest in second sight.

From the Scottish Gaelic *dà shealladh* [two sights], second sight or clairvoyance is a widespread phenomenon in traditional belief. A person with the power is known as a *taibhsear*, best translated as 'seer'. Among the Irish the Fenian hero Diorruing is credited with such ability. A generic model would have the *taibhsear* behold a phantom funeral cortège passing along a road, escorting the body of a man still in robust health with no thought of death, only to have the person die shortly after this vision. What is seen in second sight need not be dour or gloomy, but in Scotland that is usually the case. A person endowed with *dà shealladh* does not cause unpleasant events to take place or receive any joy in having them come to pass.

The most celebrated Scottish Gaelic possessor of second sight is known, fittingly, as 'Sombre Kenneth'. Despite the intense belief in his historicity and dozens of websites proclaiming his prophecies into the Internet age, there is only skimpy evidence that there ever was such a person. He is usually known in English by the late coinage 'Brahan Seer', after Brahan Castle, about fifteen miles northwest of the city of Inverness. If he lived he would have been known in Gaelic as Coinneach Odhar Fiosaiche, 'Sombre Kenneth of the Prophecies'. Some sources boldly give his name as Kenneth MacKenzie because he is thought to have been part of Clan MacKenzie, but as a Gaelic speaker he is unlikely ever to have been addressed under this English form. Anglicized phonetic renderings like 'Kenneth Oaur' or 'Owir' are more probable.

A substantial body of oral traditions in Scottish Gaelic about the person and prophecies of the Brahan Seer began to gather in the late seventeenth and early eighteenth centuries. This lore has been widely known from the Outer Hebrides in the west, across the Isle of Skye and the former shire of Inverness to eastern Ross-shire, especially the peninsula in the Moray Firth known as the Black Isle. At the centre of this lore is the episode of the Earl of Seaforth's sojourn in Paris in 1663, in which Coinneach, still at home, reveals the absent nobleman's adultery. No record of the Brahan Seer and his prophecies appears in print until Thomas Pennant's *A Tour in Scotland* (1769), a century later. Now that the Seer has become a recognized phenomenon, modern scholars have scoured documents for references to him, and what they find is inconvenient to his legend. One 'Kennoch Owir' was prosecuted for witchcraft, on 23 January 1577, on the Isle of Lewis in the Outer Hebrides, eighty-six years before the Seaforth revelations.

Elizabeth Sutherland (1985) has concluded that while there may have been a man known as Coinneach Odhar, in oral tradition this has become a collective name for a number of *taibhsears*, and that the named persona has drawn a whole prophetic tradition to it. A representative pronouncement that defines that personal vision is the often repeated, 'The Highland people will become so effeminate as to flee their native country before an army of sheep.' The depopulation of the Highlands was, of course, the central tragedy of Gaelic history. And while the calamity of Culloden could eventually be romanticized, the departure of whole families from a once warlike people, not always through the forced Clearances, evoked only bitterness and shame.

Frequent citation of the Brahan Seer within Gaelic oral tradition colours the tone of all adjacent stories. He is also said to have foreseen, in more surreal language, the building of the Caledonian Canal linking Loch Ness and the sea. We have no assurance, however, that any such prophecies were ever uttered. The words of the Brahan Seer began to appear in newspapers in the late 1850s and were not collected in book form until 1877. Even if we could prove that a vision predated the described event, there is no way of knowing if Coinneach Odhar was the originator of it.

Persistent as interest in the Brahan Seer has been, his persona is hardly a unique phenomenon. Some of his gloomier utterances have been traced to Norse antecedents, perhaps derived from the large number of Scandinavians who settled in Gaelic Scotland. Some part of the lore surrounding him is probably derived from that of the thirteenth-century Scottish poet called Thomas the Rhymer, who is credited with living with the Queen of the Fairies and predicting the death of Alexander III, the Battle of Bannockburn and the union of Scotland and England. In his retention of a band of true believers into the twenty-first century the Brahan Seer also invites comparison with the French astrologer usually known as Nostradamus (1503–66). The prophecies of both include highly gnomic language requiring some interpretation in order to be applied to any event. Yet some of the Brahan Seer's visions are quite specific, especially those dealing with the family of the Earl of Seaforth, including birth deformities of children, family tragedies and the eventual extinction of the line. All of these came to pass. Further 'proof' of the Brahan Seer's veracity appears from time to time in the press. He is thought to have said, 'When the ninth bridge cross the Ness, there will be fire, flood and calamity.' That ninth bridge was built in 1987. Within two years there was a disastrous fire: the Piper Alpha oil rig exploded in the North Sea, killing 167 workers. This was followed by flood when the 127-year-old rail bridge across the Ness was washed away. And lastly calamity: Pan Am flight 123 crashed on Lockerbie, Scotland, killing 279 and burning portions of the town. In the next decade we see fulfilment of a more benign vision: 'When men in horseless carriages go under the sea to France, then Scotia shall rise anew from all oppression.' The tunnel under the English Channel opened in spring,

1994. And the Scottish Parliament, closed for nearly 300 years, reopened in July, 1999.

NOVA SCOTIA

The furthest flung, newest and least studied canton of the Celtic world lies in the Canadian Maritime province of Nova Scotia. Large numbers of impoverished, landless Gaelic-speaking Highlanders were settled there from the late eighteenth century through to the middle of the nineteenth. They came from the former shires of Inverness, Argyll and Ross, both the mainland and the Hebridean Islands. Some were victims of the Clearances. Whereas Irish, Welsh and Scottish Gaelic were once spoken, written and published elsewhere in North America, only in Nova Scotia did a widespread oral tradition flourish, one that has persisted until the twenty-first century. The 1900 census recorded 100,000 speakers, most of them born in the province. This *Gàidhealtachd* [Gaelic-speaking region] encompassed most of Cape Breton Island and the mainland counties south of the Cumberland Strait.

Given the relative poverty of Gaelic-speakers in the hinterlands of a remote province, traditions there were little heeded by the majority culture. Official disdain helped suppress the language until the late twentieth century when most native speakers had died off. Conventional observation held that Cape Bretoners, or 'Capers', had scant literature meriting much attention. Recent study corrects this misapprehension. Margaret MacDonell's *The Emigrant Experience: Songs of Highland Emigrants in North America* (1982) shows how a highly sophisticated, disciplined Gaelic literary culture extended uninterrupted from Scotland to Nova Scotia and smaller settlements in Ontario and North Carolina. Despite the emphasis on adapting to a new environment, the texts MacDonell examines include continuing references to Scottish experience and place-names, such as Strathglass, Gairloch and Islay. Their isolation and linguistic separateness foster a striking cultural conservatism in Nova Scotian Highland settlers.

The ambience of the Scottish homeland is more evident among the tales of unlettered Gaelic speakers, with references to kings and castles never seen in the New World. Adventures of Irish heroes such as Cúchulainn, Fionn mac Cumhaill, Oscar and Diarmait (also known in Gaelic Scotland) are extended in a land of herring fisheries and maple trees. Some of the traditions that migrated to Nova Scotia, however, are not recorded in Scotland. Their existence supports the documentable pattern that archaic survivals are found at the periphery of a given cultural area. Most of the Highlanders in Nova Scotia emigrated before folklore and folktales were thought worth recording.

Recording of Gaelic lore in Nova Scotia did not begin until the twentieth century, and the storyteller with the most extensive repertory, Joe Neil MacNeil (1908–97), was not interviewed until the 1970s. The Harvard-trained scholar John Shaw transcribed, edited and translated his stories in *Tales Until Dawn* (1987) when MacNeil was in advanced years. A fragment not included in the collection gives what is possibly the only item of cosmology from the Celtic world. In it the origin of the Milky Way galaxy is depicted as emerging from two trees separated by a loch, as if to complete an arch between them. The narrator places this episode within the well-known Ulster story of Deirdre, here spelled 'Deirdire'. Her lover here is named Nois [Noíse], one of the 'Children of Uisneach' [Uisnech]. In this variant the sons of Uisneach are killed in a great, unnamed battle, after which Deirdire falls into the grave with the men. The bodies of the two lovers are exhumed and reburied on either side of the burial mound. Soon a tree grows from each grave and rises until the two join. This arouses a great deal of vengeful malice in an unnamed king, who orders that the trees be cut down. Soon another pair of trees grows and joins until the king has them cut down as well. This sequence of events recurs repeatedly until the king decides to have the bodies placed on either side of a loch, a distance too great for the trees to span. Between the trees a cluster of stars gathers in a light trail, *Sgrìob Chlann Uisnich* [track of the Children of Uisneach]. Shaw reports having also heard this phrase elsewhere in Gaelic Nova Scotia.

Elements in the three-word Gaelic phrase invite speculative interpretation. Uisnech, along with its associations in the patrimony of Noíse and his brothers, is also a prominent hill in Co. Westmeath, an omphalos of pre-Christian Ireland. The druid Mide lit the first fire in Ireland there.

THE ISLE OF MAN

A widely known folktale has it that Fionn mac Cumhaill once tore a huge sod of earth from the province of Ulster, thus creating Lough Neagh, and hurled it into the Irish Sea where the sod became the Isle of Man. Thirty-two miles off the coast of Ireland, the Isle of Man has closer cultural ties to Leinster than to nearby Ulster. Further, the island tends to be rocky, not sandy like the shores of Lough Neagh. Metaphorically, however, the story has something useful to impart. The Isle of Man is not the discrete cultural entity that its quasi-independence would imply. It is a 220-square-mile Crown Dependency of the United Kingdom with its own parliament, the Tynwald, and its own banking laws. Until 1974, when the last native speaker died, it had its own language called Manx or Manks. Ancient monuments, such as neolithic chambered tombs and Bronze Age cairns and ring-forts, correlate with Irish design. The earliest people of the Isle of Man came from both Britain and Ireland; later there was extensive Norse settlement. For a while in the Middle Ages, the Norse rulers of Man extended their power into the Hebrides in the west of Gaelic Scotland. The Manx language unmistakably derives from Old Irish but has more in common with Scottish Gaelic than with Modern Irish. Its real distinction lies in its being written in English phonetics. The Irish hero Fionn mac Cumhaill, for example, becomes Finn McCooil on Man, while his son Oisín is Oshin. In the Manx language, the Isle of Man is known as *Mannin* or *Ellan Vannin*.

Known to the ancient geographer Ptolemy (second century AD) as Manavia, and to the Romans as Mona, the Isle of Man has a peripheral presence in many early Irish narratives. The sea god Manannán mac Lir takes his name from the Isle of Man, rather than the other way round, as was once thought. Manannán's realm, Emain Ablach, which has no specific place on the map, is sometimes confused with Man. The otherworldly realm of Dún Scáith and the shaggy-haired warriors known as the Fir Fálgae are speciously associated with the Isle of Man. Absent from the Isle, however, was a native tradition of learning, ecclesiastical or secular, to record Man's traditions in medieval times. Manx was not a written language until the translation of *The Book of Common Prayer* (*c.*1625). After some isolated references in the eighteenth century, disciplined collection of Manx lore did not begin until after the middle of the nineteenth century with William Harrison's *Mona Miscellany* (1869), Edward Callow's *The Phynodderree* (1882) and Arthur Moore's *Folk-Lore of the Isle of Man* (1891).

The most distinctive figure in Manx oral tradition, and virtually the only one with any currency in the wider English-speaking world, is the solitary fairy known as the fenodyree or phynodderree. The name, never capitalized, may be spelled in nine or ten different ways, testimony to the figure's persistence in the popular mind and his reappearance before different collectors over time. He is an individual rather than a class, and is often portrayed naked but covered with body hair. In most of European lore, the solitary fairy, as opposed to the trooping fairy, is usually ominous and malignant. Not so this Manx figure. The fenodyree, like the Scottish brownie, can be helpful by performing tasks requiring formidable strength and endurance, such as carrying a huge block of marble a long distance or harvesting an entire field of crops. Admired for this second generous task, he may be known by the complimentary epithet *yn foldyr gastey* [the nimble mower]. At some earlier point he bore the name *uddereek*, suggestive of handsomeness, but he was transformed into his familiar but ugly persona for courting a mortal girl from Glen Alden. The fenodyree's hairy legs suggest to some commentators a parallel with the satyr of classical tradition, but he lacks the requisite sexual aggression. Sometimes the fenodyree is ascribed a wife, with whom he often quarrels. Sometimes he is capable of mischief. When one imprudent man invokes the fenodyree to cure his little red cow he is disappointed with the results. Indeed, the fenodyree can summon powers to heal the little animal, but he also carries it off in the end.

CORNWALL

Occupying a long narrow peninsula in southwestern Britain, Cornwall suffers from being thought of as a tourist destination. W. S. Gilbert and Sir Arthur Sullivan set their *Pirates of Penzance* (1879) in the Cornish resort town to imply what a familiar and domesticated place it had become. The extinction of the Cornish language in the eighteenth century has diminished a sense of separateness from the rest of England. The modern county, coextensive with the former duchy of Cornwall, is known in the Cornish language as *Kernow*. Still known from many documents, as well as from contemporary attempts to 'revive' it, Cornish is a Brythonic cousin of Welsh and Breton. As with Scottish Gaelic and Manx, Cornish lacked a learned tradition in medieval times, although the area had been evangelized by Irish monks beginning in the sixth century. Many Arthurian legends are set in Cornwall, notably the story of Tristan, Iseult and King Mark, and some of them take Cornish form. The best known word from the language is 'Jennifer', the Cornish form of 'Guinevere' or the Welsh 'Gwenhwyfar' [white, smooth], once a characteristic woman's name there. The Gospels began to be translated in the tenth century, and the Cornish mystery plays of the fifteenth century are much admired as supreme examples of late medieval drama. Despite some odd snatches in Edward Lhuyd's *Archaeologia Britannica* (1707), collections of Cornish oral tradition did not appear until a century after the death of the language when stories were known only in English form. These collections were by Robert Hunt, *Popular Romances of the West of England* (1865) and William Bottrell, *Traditions and Hearthside Stories of West Cornwall* (1870).

The most resilient figure from Cornish oral tradition to have made its way into English discourse is the pixie, an adaptation of the earlier piskie. The more historical spelling 'piskie' has been so displaced by the more familiar 'pixie' that it is no longer recognizable to most readers, but somewhat different phenomena are denoted by the different forms. In the collections of Hunt and Bottrell, the piskie (also pigsie) is a wizened-looking, weird old man who threshes grain. He may mislead folks through a 'piskie-ride' on horseback. The term 'pixie' was known in English at least sixty years before Hunt and Bottrell and derives from traditions in Somerset and Devon as well as Cornwall, perhaps carried to neighbouring counties by Cornish migrants. These pixies, even when they rise to mortal size, have definable characteristics: they are red-headed, with pointed ears, turned-up noses and short faces. They are usually seen naked, are known to squint, and like to steal horses at night. Like other figures in English oral tradition, Puck or Robin Goodfellow, they are fond of giving wrong directions or misleading travellers. This association gives us the still useful English word 'pixilated', adapted from 'pixie-led'.

While most Cornish stories are episodic or extended anecdotes, the one known as 'The Giants of Morvah' may once have stretched to epic length. Nineteenth-century storytellers report that its many complex details and turns of plot required three nights to recite, but only a précis has been recorded. Morvah of the title is one of Cornwall's most significant archaeological sites on the windswept northern slopes of the Land's End promontory, four miles northeast of the town of St Just, in the far west of the county. Standing stones at Morvah include the granite *Men-an-Tol* [holed stone], a spectacular annular or doughnut-shaped megalith once thought to have curative properties. It is an area where Cornish language and folk customs survived until the latest date. Morvah was also the scene of an annual fair on the first Sunday in August, a counterpart to Lughnasa celebrations in Ireland. 'The Giants of Morvah' was recited at the fair. Teasingly, the story contains elements suggesting a possible link to the Irish hero Lug Lámfhota, whose worship lies at the root of Lughnasa.

There are four giants in the story, Tom the protagonist, Jack his visitor and later friend, and two who are unnamed. One summer's night when Tom is driving his wagon home, he finds his way blocked by a huge stone and so takes a short-cut across what he thinks is common land. It is not. The resident giant challenges him for trespassing and uproots an elm tree with which to beat Tom. Without losing his composure, Tom overturns his wagon, removing the axle and wheel to use as weapons against the giant. The ground shakes with their blows, but just as exhaustion is about to overtake Tom, he triumphs. He hears people dancing around festive fires but knows he must bury the giant and take possession of his castle and land. A woman named Joan whom Tom had known bathes his wounds, and together they take possession of the castle, which brims with jewels and golden treasure. They live together happily for many years and produce several children of which the oldest is a beautiful daughter named Genevra (variant of Jennifer, Guinevere, etc.). Like the giant before him, Tom tries to keep the curious away from his treasures.

The serenity of Tom and his happy family does not last. One morning another giant smashes through the front gate with a hammer in his hand. It is Jack the tinkard, with a toolbag on his back. Tin had long been mined in Cornwall, and a handler of tin, a tinker or 'tinkard', does not carry the questionable status that calling bears in Ireland. Impatient that Tom's desire for safety has blocked the road to St Ives, Jack challenges him to combat in wrestling or by slinging stones. Tom responds with a thrust of his axle wheel, but Jack wields his staff so quickly it looks like a spinning wheel. Soon Tom's weapon is flying over a fence. Rather than gloat at his prowess, Jack offers his friendship and demonstrates that he has many talents, like Lug in his epithet *Samildánach* [many-skilled]. Jack makes a bow from an elm sapling and quickly slays ten animals for Tom and Joan's larder.

Shown the treasures in Tom's castle, Jack is less impressed with the gold and jewels but more taken with the bits and pieces that he could use in his own work. He uses them to fashion a pearl necklace that he places on Genevra's head when he takes his place beside her at table. To honour Genevra further, Jack does battle with a second unnamed giant at Morvah. He takes the stone cover off an old mineshaft and his adversary falls down it. Jack thus becomes the possessor of the Morvah giant's treasures. He weds Genevra during a huge feast on the first Sunday in August. In each successive year the anniversary is celebrated, with Jack teaching friends and relations skills they did not know existed. In time the commemoration grows to such an extent that it seems more like a fair, Morvah Fair, than a wedding anniversary.

BRITTANY

The name 'Brittany' (cf. Fr. *Bretagne*) enjoys a strange euphony in our ears. This is true despite – perhaps because – the region is so little known in the English-speaking world. The ancient name for the peninsula jutting out from northern France was Armorica, a term still occasionally seen in print. The current name, which means literally 'Little Britain', commemorates a migration of Brythonic-speaking peoples from the island of Great Britain in the fifth and sixth centuries. Modern Bretons see themselves as descended from the ancient Britons, although their gene pool gains from many other peoples, including the ancient Gauls pushed westward by the advancing Franks. Why the Britons should have left Britain has been subject to much interpretation. An earlier view that they were driven out by predatory Saxon invaders now seems less likely. More prosaic reasons like famine and economic hardship are more probable. In Welsh tradition the emigrants from Britain were led by St Cynan Meiriadog (or Meriodoc), who was rewarded with tracts of land for his service to the Roman emperor known to the Britons as Macsen Wledig. First composed of a series of culturally related petty kingdoms, Brittany was an independent duchy through the Middle Ages until 1532. It remained a mostly Breton-speaking province of France until Napoleonic times, when it was divided into five (later four) *départements*. Despite the efforts of sometimes violent nationalist groups, the four *départements* remain integrated into the rest of the nation, but important cultural distinctions remain. New houses, for example, must by law be constructed in Breton style, with black slate roofs and cream stucco walls. Urban industrial workers retain deep enthusiasm for traditional Breton dress and folk dances. And though records are inconclusive, several hundred thousand people still speak the Breton language. The name for Brittany in the Breton language is *Breizh*.

The Welsh ecclesiastical traveller Giraldus Cambrensis (*c.*1146–1223) tells us that spoken Breton was more closely related to the Cornish of his day than to the Welsh. Modern linguistic analysis confirms his observation. In recent centuries Breton has made many borrowings from Welsh, but contemporary spoken Breton and Welsh are not mutually comprehensible. Neither early Welsh literary development nor written Cornish, like the miracle plays, seems to have had much influence on Breton writers. The Anglo-Norman Marie de France (fl. *c.*1160–90) introduced a purported Breton narrative form, the *lai* or *lay*, to mainstream European literature. Many of her *lais*, in addition, employ Breton themes. Several Arthurian stories have Breton settings, such as the forest of Brocéliande, where Merlin was imprisoned, and Arthurian figures are reshaped in Breton form, for example Perceval as Peronnik. Giraldus also speaks of many 'tale-telling Bretons and their singers', but no Breton literature of any kind is known before 1450.

Written Breton literature did not commence for almost another 400 years when Théodore Hersart de La Villemarqué (1815–96) produced

Barzaz Breiz [Breton Bards] in 1839. As an admirer of James Macpherson's spurious *Poems of Ossian*, as well as of the Welsh charlatan Iolo Morganwg (1747–1826), La Villemarqué looks like a pseudo-medievalist to the modern sceptical eye. Although his poems and stories lacked the antiquity of the originals of his contemporary Lady Charlotte Guest's translations in *The Mabinogion* (1838–49), and he was a bowdlerizer, La Villemarqué was a better linguist than Macpherson and more faithful to sources in oral tradition. His texts are still used today in university courses in Breton literature.

Relatively few Breton narratives have any currency outside Brittany, but the best-known of them has also been widely known within Breton tradition, surviving in three versions. Its usual Breton title is *Kêr Is* [City of Is], known in English as 'The Legend of the City of Ys'. One of a half-dozen flood legends in Celtic languages, the story explains how a once sinful city came to be submerged beneath the Bay of Douarnenez in southwest Brittany. Turning on the central theme of pagan excess in conflict with Christian restraint, its three permutations always include at least three characters. The first is Gradlon (or Gralon) Meur [the great], a pious and saintly king who protects his city by building a dike. His name is still much associated with the city of Quimper (Bret. Kemper), where his statue sits between the two towers of the cathedral. Second is his beautiful, wilful and lascivious daughter Dahut (also Dahud, Ahé, Ahés), who brings grief to the kingdom. And third is the abbé Guénolé, an historical figure credited with founding the first monastery in Brittany at Landévennec in the fifth century.

In his youth, King Gradlon had practised the old faith. When he took a wife, it was thought in his kingdom that she was not of this world. After the birth of her daughter, Dahut, the wife returns to the sea whence she came. While hunting one day with his men, Gradlon happens upon a pious hermit in the woods, Corentin (or Korentin), who appears to have no food to feed his guests. The hermit then performs a miracle that deeply impresses the king. He takes a minnow from a well and cuts it in half with his knife. The half he keeps becomes the basis of a bounteous feast, with fish, meat and fruit in abundance. The half of the fish returned to the water grows whole again so that Corentin can repeat the miracle on another occasion. Thunderstruck at what he has seen, Gradlon declares himself for the new faith,

Christianity, and sees to it that Corentin is installed as bishop in Quimper. Churches, chapels and cloisters begin to appear, and under Corentin's urging Gradlon passes new laws curbing fleshly excesses and promoting temperance, virtue and restraint instead.

Dahut is displeased with this turn of events, finding the new Quimper joyless. Her father calls her tone blasphemous. Changing the subject, she complains that she lives too far from the ocean. She begs her father to build her a city by the sea and says she will then be content. And so Gradlon spares no expense to meet her wishes, constructing the new city of Ys with spacious public squares and tall white towers. Bishop Corentin notes that Ys lacks churches and, to Dahut's chagrin, Gradlon adds them. The king's daughter recommends other additions. Seeing that Ys has been built on low ground, she asks that her father construct a protective dike, with sluices that can be opened to fill the city's needs. He complies.

In the oldest and simplest version of the story, Dahut secretly entertains her lover, and the two of them, driven to frenzy by wine, steal Gradlon's key to open the sluice gates, flooding the city.

The more familiar second version has much more to say about Ys as a commercial centre given to luxury and debauchery. To ensure her dominance over the churches Gradlon has built, Dahut consults the pagan sisterhood of the isle of Sein, women who still worship the old gods. They conjure up the korrigans, small but lustful creatures who seek carnal relations with innocent Christians and are also magnificent builders. They fashion a new castle for Dahut, both elegant and imposing, that towers over Gradlon's church. Before long the church is nearly abandoned, with weeds pushing up between the stones at its door. Learning of this, as well as of Dahut's fostering of public practice of the seven capital sins, abbé Guénolé is filled with loathing and disgust. Taking the tone of the Old Testament prophet Jeremiah, Guénolé foretells the ruin of the City of Ys.

A small boy named Kristof sets in motion some of the forces working against Ys. After casting stones in the water with a crooked stick, the boy catches a magical fish who offers riches in exchange for his liberty. With her usual haughtiness, Dahut mocks this exchange, and so the fish responds with a magical spell upon her, making her pregnant with a son who can claim no father. About a year later, Dahut's father

Gradlon puts his daughter, Kristof and the baby boy in a cask and sets them out to sea, where yet another city with palaces appears. Ys remains in danger, however, because Kristof has magically removed a protective oak.

Although Gradlon is nominally king of Ys, his paternal indulgence to Dahut means that she sets the tone for the city, especially the moral tone. With the help of the korrigans, she contrives that Ys may become a lure for unwary sailors, capsizing their ships nearby so that they may be looted by the immoral city's depraved denizens. Each night she takes a new lover whose face is covered in a black silken mask. When she tires of his attentions, she ties a fatal knot in the mask's strings, leading to the painful death of the rejected gigolo. This pattern continues until she receives a suitor unlike any of the others. Dressed all in red he refuses to wear her black mask and meets her bare-faced. Charming her with his impudence, he tells her that he will make her his bride in his palace of fire with columns of smoke, if only she gives him what he wants: the key to the sluices in the dike. She responds that this is impossible for the key is tied around her father's shoulder. Then, with much stealth, she retrieves the key and gives it to the stranger, but when she reaches up to touch his cheek he is no longer there.

As soon as the key enters its slot, the sea begins to rush into the city. Guénolé raises the alarm in Gradlon's palace and urges the king to flee on his steed Morvarc'h [horse of the sea] before they are all inundated. Still the doting father, Gradlon pulls up his worthless daughter behind him as he sets off at a gallop. The water is seething and foaming at Morvarc'h's fetlocks, ready to submerge them both, when a voice from behind calls out to him, 'Throw the demon you carry into the sea if you do not wish to perish.' At that moment Dahut falls from Morvarc'h, and the water recedes, allowing Gradlon to escape and to reach Quimper safely. Ys is now submerged, but Dahut lingers on as a siren-like mermaid, calling out to sailors about to be shipwrecked.

Roles are substantially changed in a third version, known only in ballad tradition. This time Gradlon leads the people in extravagance and debauchery, and freely gives the key to Dahut, who misuses it. Once again she survives as a mermaid who haunts the waters at Douarnenez.

The popularity of the story in Breton oral tradition invites a wide array of variants. The City of Ys may also be located on the Étang de Laval on the desolate shores of the Bay of Trépassés [the dead]. A later narrative appendix describing an underwater church whose bell was still ringing but which would emerge on a clear morning inspired Claude Debussy's piano prelude *La Cathédrale engloutie* [the sunken cathedral] (1910). That same popularity has made the corruption of Ys proverbial, as in the Breton slurring pun on the name of the French capital, *par Is*, from the Breton *par* [like], that is, Paris = 'like Ys'.

GALICIA AND ASTURIAS

Chapter 7 reminds us that the historical links between early Ireland and Spain as depicted in the *Lebor Gabála*, once dismissed as pure fantasy, have been substantiated by recent scientific study. Research into national DNA patterns shows that the two countries are indeed closely connected. Upon a closer look, however, the tie is more than genetic. Barry Cunliffe in *The Ancient Celts* (1997) traces archaeological links between Spain and Ireland going back as far as the fourth millennium BC. Language once supplied another bridge, now vanished. Celtic speakers flourished in the Iberian Peninsula for several centuries before their culture was overcome by the Romans. The most significant numbers were in the northwest corner, the former province of Gallaecia, where Latin displaced the native language after the third century AD. That region is coextensive with the modern provinces of Galicia in the far northwest and Asturias its neighbour to the east. The pre-eminent twentieth-century specialist in Galician folklore, Vicente Risco (1884–1963), reckoned that Galician culture was basically Latin, but with a Celtic soul.

Evidence from early Iberian tradition supports the vision of Spain found in the *Lebor Gabála*. An early tower did indeed stand in the harbour of La Coruña, which could have served as the model for the one which Breogan builds and Íth climbs to see Ireland on the horizon. Lost now, it was replaced in the second century AD by the oldest working Roman lighthouse, known as the Tower of Hercules. Hundreds of abandoned *castros*, small defended Celtic-era towns consisting of round stone houses dating from as early as 1000 BC, can be found throughout the area. 'Céltigo' turns up frequently as a name for a village or rural district. Monte Pindo, a pink granite mountain on the Atlantic coast near Fisterra in Galicia, is also known as *Olimpo Celta*, 'the Celtic Olympus'.

Galicia's claim for a place at the Celtic table seems not yet to have entered a wider consciousness, but the case continues to be made. Traditional music groups from Galicia such as Milladoiro find a warm welcome at Pan-Celtic festivals. The distinguished Galician literary figure Leandro Carré Alvarellos (1888–1976) has argued that the legends of his home province reflect a Celtic culture and psychology, and the Irish academic Elizabeth Frances Keating has devoted a book, *Afinidades Culturais entre Galicia e Irlanda* (1990) to these cultural affinities.

The links are not to be found with lengthy narratives, such as the *Táin Bó Cuailnge* or the *Mabinogi*. Instead, better examples are seen in older oral tradition, especially when malign figures fit well with the Church's efforts to demonize Celtic inheritance. Such a personage is the *lavandeira nocturna*, a male devil in female disguise who tries to seduce young women. A counterpart in the north is the 'washer at the ford', who is found in all six traditions under a variety of names, *bean nighe* in Gaelic Scotland and *tunnerez noz* in Brittany. The washer is also an aspect of the Irish war goddesses Badb and Mórrígan. She is a death omen, sometimes gorgeous and weeping, sometimes hideous and grimacing, who washes bloody garments at the ford of a river and turns to tell the beholder that they are his or hers.

A close parallel with Ireland and other Celtic countries is the phantom funeral. In Irish folk belief, people who have been 'taken' by the fairies are not dead but can sometimes be seen in fairy processions, the *sluagh sídhe* or *slua sí* [fairy host] or the *sluagh/slua na marbh* [host of the dead] from which they might be rescued. A fairy funeral can foretell the death of a person known to the viewer. The *Santa Compaña* [Holy Company] in Galicia and the *huestia* [host] and *gente buena* [good people] in Asturias, complete with coffin, priest and mourners bearing candles, are likewise ghostly funeral processions presaging death.

The *xana* is a Galician and Asturian otherworld woman responsible for changelings. Typically, a mother is working outdoors with her infant nearby, but when she returns home in the evening she notices that the child is different. The *xana* (var. *inxana*), who lives in a cave, has taken the human mother's toddler and replaced it with her own. One remedy, collected in 1985 near Llanes on the Asturian coast, is for the mother to bring the *xana*'s child to the mouth of the cave and shout, 'Inxana Mora, take your child and give me mine.'

Irish fairies are associated with mounds or ringforts or earthen circles sometimes called 'daneforts' for their supposed connection with Danish Vikings. In Galicia and Asturias the otherworld denizens of ancient monuments, especially the *castros*, are called *mouros* (cf. standard Spanish *moros*). The word is believed to be a corruption of the regional word for 'dead person', *morto* (Spanish *muerto*), and not related to the Moorish conquest. The *mouros* are nearly always associated with hidden treasure, usually gold, which makes them close cousins of the Irish leprechaun.

The Irish fairy known as the *púca* often takes the form of a ferocious-looking but ultimately harmless large black dog with fiery red eyes; a Scottish Gaelic variant, the *cù sìth*, is dark green rather than black. The *urco* of Galicia is also a fierce-looking large black dog, with the addition of long ears and horns and a piercing howl but without the red eyes. It always presages misfortune.

Other examples bring together verbal formulae more specific than motifs and tale types that might be found in many European countries. In one of the better-known Irish tales, the fairies reward a good hunchback when he adds 'and Wednesday' to their monotonous song that goes 'Monday, Tuesday, Monday, Tuesday'. A bad hunchback tries to emulate him by abruptly breaking into the fairies' revels with 'and Thursday and Friday', and is then saddled with the first hunchback's hump.

The Galician parallel, collected in Verín in the early twentieth century, shows the characteristic demonizing of fairy lore. A woman disguises herself as a witch by painting wrinkles on her face and wearing smoked glasses, mounting a broom and flying to Seville to join a witches' Sabbath. She finds them dancing in a circle and singing, 'Monday, Tuesday, Wednesday, three; / Thursday, Friday, Saturday, six.' The intruder adds, 'and Sunday, seven', and all the witches vanish in a puff of smoke.

Select Bibliography

Agallamh na Seanórach, ed. and trans. Nessa Ní Shéaghdha (3 vols.). Dublin: Oifig an tSolathair, 1942–5.

Aigner, August, *Hallstatt*. Munich, 1911; rpt Munich: Reinhardt, 1971.

Aislinge Meic Con Glinne, ed. Kenneth H. Jackson. Dublin: Dublin Institute for Advanced Studies, 1990.

[*Aislinge Óenguso*] *The Dream of Óengus. An Old Irish Text . . .* , ed. Francis Shaw SJ. Dublin: Brown & Nolan, 1934, 1977.

Allason-Jones, Lindsay, *Women in Roman Britain*. London: British Museum Press, 1989.

Anderson, Marjorie O., *Kings and Kingship in Early Scotland*. Edinburgh: Scottish Academic Press, 1980.

Annals of the Kingdom of Ireland, ed. and trans. John O'Donovan (7 vols.). Dublin: Hodges & Smith, 1849–51; rpt New York: AMS, 1966.

Anonymous ['Q'], 'A Legend of Fin-Mac-Cool', *Dublin Penny Journal*, 1 (41) (6 April 1833): 327–8.

Anwyl, Edward, *Celtic Religion in Pre-Christian Times*. London: Constable, 1906.

Audacht Morainn, ed. Fergus Kelly. Dublin: Dublin Institute for Advanced Studies, 1976.

Bhreathnach, Edel and Newman, Conor, *Tara*. Dublin: The Stationery Office, 1995.

Binchy, D. A., *Celtic and Anglo-Saxon Kingship*. Oxford: Clarendon Press, 1970.

Bitel, Lisa, *Land of Woman: Tales of Sex and Gender from Early Ireland*. Ithaca: Cornell University Press, 1996.

Bollard, John K., 'The structure of the Four Branches of the Mabinogi', *Transactions of the Honourable Society of Cymmrodorion*, 1975: 250–76.

Book of Leinster [*Lebor Laignech*], ed. R. I. Best, Osborn Bergin, M. A. O'Brien and A. O'Sullivan (6 vols.). Dublin: Dublin Institute for Advanced Studies, 1954–83.

Bottrell, William, *Traditions and Hearthside Stories of West Cornwall*. Penzance: W. Cornish, 1870; rpt Newcastle upon Tyne: Frank Graham, 1970.

Brasseur, Marcel. *Les Celtes*. Vol. 1: *Les Dieux oubliés des Celtes*. Vol. 2: *Les Rois oubliés des Celtes*. Rennes: Terre de Brume, 1996–7.

Bromwich, Rachel (ed. and trans.), *Trioedd Ynys Prydain: The Welsh Triads*. Cardiff: University of Wales Press, 1961; 2nd edn, 1978.

Bruford, Alan, *Gaelic Folk-Tales and Mediaeval Romances*. Dublin: Folklore of Ireland Society, 1969.

[*Bruidhean Chaorthainn*] 'The Fairy Palace of the Quicken Trees', in *Old Celtic Romances*, trans. P. W. Joyce. Dublin: 1961 (1879), pp. 123–53.

Buile Suibhne (The Frenzy of Suibhne), Being the Adventures of Subhne [sic] Geilt, A Middle Irish Romance, ed. James G. O'Keeffe. Irish Texts Society, vol. 12. London: David Nutt, 1913; rpt Dublin: Stationery Office, 1931; Dublin Institute for Advanced Studies, 1952, 1975.

Byrne, Francis J., *Irish Kings and High Kings*, 2nd edn. Dublin: Four Courts, 2001.

Callow, Edward, *The Phynodderree, and Other Legends of the Isle of Man*. London: J. Dean, 1882.

Cambrensis, Giraldus, *The History and Topography of Ireland*, trans. John J. O'Meara. London: Penguin, 1984.

Campbell, Archibald (compiler), *Waifs and Strays in Celtic Tradition* (4 vols.). London: David Nutt, 1889–91.

Campbell, John Francis (compiler), *Popular Tales of the West Highlands, Orally Collected* (4 vols). Paisley: Gardner, 1861; rpt London: Gardner, 1890–93.

Carey, John, 'The Name "Tuatha Dé Danann"', *Éigse*, 18 (1981): 291–4.

Carey, John, 'The Location of the Otherworld in Irish Tradition', *Éigse*, 19 (1982): 36–43.

Carleton, William, 'The Legend of Knockmany', in *Tales and Sketches, Illustrating the Character, Usages, Traditions, Sports and Pastimes of the Irish Peasantry*. Dublin: J. Duffy, 1845, pp. 97–112.

Carney, James, *Studies in Irish Literature and History*. Dublin: Dublin Institute for Advanced Studies, 1955.

Carr, Gillian and Stoddard, Simon (eds), *Antiquity Papers 2: Celts from Antiquity*. Cambridge: Antiquity Publications, 2002.

Carré Alvarallos, Leandro, *Las Leyendas Tradicianales Gallegas*, 7th edn. Madrid: Espasa Calpe, 2002.

Cath Finntrágha, ed. Cecile O'Rahilly. Dublin: Dublin Institute for Advanced Studies, 1962.

Cath Maige Tuired: The Second Battle of Mag Tuired, ed. Elizabeth A. Gray. Irish Texts Society, vol. 52, Dublin: Irish Texts Society, 1982.

Celts, The. A five-part Opus Television production for S4C International/ Rhyngwladol [Cardiff], 2000. Commentaries by Proinsias MacCana, Anne Ross, Miranda Aldhouse-Green, Barry Cunliffe, et al.

Chapman, Malcolm, *The Celts: The Construction of a Myth*. London: Macmillan; New York, St Martin's, 1992.

Charles-Edwards, T. M., *Early Irish and Welsh Kinship*. Oxford: Clarendon Press, 1991.

Charles-Edwards, T. M., *Early Christian Ireland*. Cambridge: Cambridge University Press, 2000.

Cogitosus, 'Life of Saint Brigit', ed. Seán Connolly and Jean-Michael Picard, *Journal of the Royal Society of Antiquaries of Ireland*, 117 (1987): 5–27.

Coimín, Micheál [Michael Comyn], *Laoi Oisín i dTír na nÓg, The Lay of Oisín in the Land of Youth*, trans. Dáithí Coinín. Dublin: Chamney, 1880.

Condren, Mary, *The Serpent and the Goddess: Women, Religion and Power in Celtic Ireland*. San Francisco: Harper & Row, 1989.

Cremin, Aedeen, *The Celts*. New York: Rizzoli, 1998.

Críth Gablach, ed. D. A. Binchy. Mediaeval and Modern Irish Series, XI, Dublin: Dublin Institute for Advanced Studies, 1941, 1979; trans. Eoin MacNeill, 'Ancient Irish Laws: the Law of Status of Franchise', *Proceedings of the Royal Irish Academy*, C, 36 (1923): 265–316.

Croker, Thomas Crofton, *Fairy Legends and Traditions of the South of Ireland*. London: John Murray, 1825; 2nd edn, 1838.

Cross, Tom Peete and Slover, Clark Harris, *Ancient Irish Tales*. New York: Henry Holt, 1936; rpt New York: Barnes & Noble, 1969.

Cunliffe, Barry, *The Ancient Celts*. Oxford and New York: Oxford University Press, 1997.

Cunliffe, Barry, *Facing the Ocean: The Atlantic and Its Peoples*. Oxford: Oxford University Press, 2001.

Danaher, Kevin, *The Year in Ireland*. Cork: Mercier Press, 1972.

Davies, John, *The Celts: Based on the S4C Television Series*. London: Cassell, 2000.

Davies, Sioned, *The Four Branches of the Mabinogi*. Llandysul: Gomer Press, 1993; *Pedeir Keinc y Mabinogi*. Caernarvon: Gwasg Pantycelyn, 1989.

Dillon, Myles, *The Cycles of the Kings*. Oxford: Oxford University Press, 1946.

Dillon, Myles, *Early Irish Literature*. Chicago: University of Chicago Press, 1948.

Dillon, Myles and Chadwick, Nora, *Celtic Realms*. London: Weidenfeld & Nicolson; New York: New American Library, 1967; rpt London: Cardinal, 1972.

Doan, James E., *Women and Goddesses in Early Celtic History, Myth and Legend*. Working Papers in Irish Studies, 87(4/5). Boston: Northeastern University, 1987.

Duanaire Finn: The Book of the Lays of Finn, 3 vols. Irish Texts Society, vols. 7, 28, 43. Vol. I, ed. Eoin MacNeill, London: David Nutt, 1908. Vol. II, ed. Gerard Murphy, London: Simpkin & Marshall, 1933. Vol. III, ed. Gerard Murphy, Dublin: Educational Company of Ireland, 1953.

Dumézil, Georges, 'Le Trio des Macha', *Revue de l'Histoire des Religions*, 146 (1954): 5–17.

[*Echtra Fergusa maic Léite*, eighth century] 'The Saga of Fergus mac Léti', ed. D. A. Binchy, *Ériu*, 16 (1952): 33–48.

[*Echtra Fergusa maic Léite*, thirteenth century] 'The Death of Fergus mac Leide', in Standish H. O'Grady (ed.), *Silva Gadelica*, II. London: Williams & Norgate, 1892, pp. 269–85.

[*Echtrae Cormaic*] '*Echtra Cormaic maic Airt*, The Adventure of Cormac mac Airt', trans. Vernam Hull, *PMLA*, 64 (1949): 871–83.

Ellis, Peter Berresford, *The Mammoth Book of Celtic Myths and Legends*. London: Constable and Robinson, 1992, 2002.

Espérandrieu, Émile, *Recueil général des bas-reliefs de la Gaule romaine* (16 vols.), completed by Raymond Lantier. Paris: Presses Universitaires de France, 1907–66.

Fee, Christopher R. and Leeming, David, *Gods, Heroes and Kings: The Battle for Mythic Britain*. Oxford and New York: Oxford University Press, 2001.

Fingal Rónáin and Other Stories, ed. David H. Greene. Mediaeval and Modern Irish Studies, no. 16, Dublin: Dublin Institute for Advanced Studies, 1955.

'*Fled Bricrenn*, a Critical Edition of . . . ,' ed. Kaarina Hollo. Unpublished dissertation, Harvard University, Cambridge, MA, 1992.

[*Fled Bricrenn*] *Fled Bricrend* [*sic*]: *The Feast of Bricriu*, ed. George Henderson. Irish Texts Society, vol. 2, London: David Nutt, 1899; rpt 1993.

Ford, Patrick K., 'Introduction' to Patrick K. Ford (ed. and trans.), *The Mabinogi and other Medieval Welsh Tales*, University of California Press, 1977.

Freitag, Barbara, *Sheela-na-gig: Unraveling an Enigma*. London, New York: Routledge, 2004.

Gantz, Jeffrey, *Early Irish Myths and Sagas*. Harmondsworth: Penguin Books, 1981.

Gimbutas, Marija, *The Goddesses and Gods of Old Europe, 6500–3500 BC: Myth and Cult Images*, rev. edn. Berkeley and Los Angeles: University of California Press, 1982 (first published 1974).

Green, Miranda Jane, *Celtic Myths*. London: British Museum Press, 1993.

Green, Miranda, *Celtic Goddesses: Warriors, Virgins and Mothers*. London: British Museum Press, 1995.

Green, Miranda J. (ed.), *The Celtic World*. London and New York: Routledge, 1995.

Guyot, Charles, *The Legend of the City of Ys*, trans. Deirdre Cavanagh. Amherst: University of Massachusetts Press, 1979.

Hamp, Eric P., 'Intensives in British and Gaulish', *Studia Celtica*, 12–13 (1977–8): 1–13.

Hanes Taliesin. See *Mabinogi, The*, ed. and trans. Patrick K. Ford.

Harrison, William, *A Mona Miscellany: A Selection of Proverbs, Sayings, Ballads, Customs, Superstitions, and Legends Peculiar to the Isle of Man*. Douglas, 1869.

Henken, Elissa R., *The Welsh Saints: A Study in Patterned Lives*. Cambridge: D. S. Brewer, 1991.

Hull, Eleanor, *The Cuchullin Saga in Irish Literature*. London: David Nutt, 1898; rpt New York: AMS Press, 1972.

Hunt, Robert, *Popular Romances of the West of England; or, The Drolls, Traditions, and Superstitions of Old Cornwall*. London: John Camden Hotten, 1865; 3rd edn, 1881, rpt New York: Benjamin Blom, 1968.

Immram Brain: Bran's Journey to the Land of the Women, ed. and trans. Séamus MacMathúna. Tübingen: Niemeyer, 1985.

[*Imran Curaig Maíle Dúin*] *The Voyage of the Máel Dúin: A Study*, ed. and trans. H. P. A. Oskamp. Groningen: Wolters-Noordhoff, 1970.

Judge, Roy, *Jack-in-the-Green: A May Day Custom*. Ipswich: D. S. Brewer, 1979; rpt London: FLS Books, 2000.

Keating, Elizabeth Frances, *Afinidades Culturais entre Galicia e Irlanda*. Vigo, Spain: Editorial Galaxa, 1990.

Keating, Geoffrey [Séathrún Céitinn], *The History of Ireland. Foras Feasa ar Éirinn*, 4 vols. Irish Texts Society, vols. 4, 8, 9, 15. Vol. I, ed. David Comyn, London: David Nutt, 1902. Vols. II, III, IV, ed. Patrick S. Dinneen, London: David Nutt, 1908–14. Rpt, ed. Breandán Ó Buachalla, London: Irish Texts Society, 1987.

Kelly, Fergus, *A Guide to Early Irish Law*. Dublin: Dublin Institute for Advanced Studies, 1988.

Koch, John T. and Carey, John, *The Celtic Heroic Age: Literary Sources for Ancient Celtic Europe and Early Ireland and Wales*. Malden, MA:

Celtic Studies Publications, 1994, 1995; Andover, MA, Oakville, CT and Aberystwyth, Wales: Celtic Studies Publications, 2000, 2003.

Krause, David, *The Profane Book of Irish Comedy*. Ithaca, NY: Cornell University Press, 1982.

La Villemarqué, Théodore Hersart de, *Barzaz Breiz: chantes populaires de la Bretagne*. Paris: Charpentier, 1839. Translated by Tom Taylor as *Ballads and Songs of Brittany*, London and Cambridge: Macmillan, 1865, 1907, 1978; rpt Norwood, PA: Norwood Editions, 1976; also Henry Carrington, *Breton Ballads*, Edinburgh: privately printed, 1886.

Lebor Gabála Érenn: The Book of the Taking of Ireland, ed. R. A. S. Macalister, 4 vols. Irish Texts Society, vols. 34, 35, 41, 44. Dublin: The Educational Company of Ireland, 1938–56. Rpt, ed. John Carey. London: Irish Texts Society, 1993.

Le Roux, Françoise and Guyonvarc'h, Christian-J., *La Souveraineté guerrière de l'Irlande: Mórrígan, Bodb, Macha*. Rennes: Ogam-Celticum, 1983.

Löffler, Christa Maria, *The Voyage to the Otherworld Island in Early Irish Literature*. Salzburg Studies in English Literature 103, Salzburg: Institut für Anglistik und Americanistik, Universität Salzburg, 1983.

Longes mac nUislenn, ed. Vernam Hull. New York: Modern Language Association; Oxford: Oxford University Press, 1949.

Lucan [M. Annaeus Lucanus], *The Civil War: Translated as Lucan's Pharsalia*, trans. Nicholas Rowe. London: Everyman, 1998.

Mabinogi, The, and Other Medieval Welsh Tales, ed. and trans. Patrick K. Ford. Berkeley and Los Angeles: University of California Press, 1977. Includes *Hanes Taliesin* (pp. 159–81).

MacCana, Proinsias, *Celtic Mythology*. London: Hamlyn, 1970.

MacCana, Proinsias, *The Mabinogi*. Cardiff: University of Wales Press, 1992.

MacCana, Proinsias. See *Celts, The*, Opus Television S4C, 2000.

McCone, Kim, *Pagan Past and Christian Present in Early Irish Literature*. Maynooth: An Sagart, 1990.

MacDonell, Margaret, *The Emigrant Experience: Songs of Highland Emigrants in North America*. Toronto: University of Toronto Press, 1982.

[*Macgnímartha Find*] 'Boyish Exploits of Finn', trans. Kuno Meyer, *Ériu*, 1 (1904): 180–90.

Mackenzie, Alexander, *The Prophecies of the Brahan Seer, Coinneach Odhar Fiosaiche*. Inverness, 1877; rpt London: Constable, 1977.

MacKillop, James, *Fionn mac Cumhaill: Celtic Myth in English Literature*. Syracuse: Syracuse University Press, 1986, 2001.

MacKillop, James, *Dictionary of Celtic Mythology*. Oxford: Oxford University Press, 1998.

McMahon, Joanne and Roberts, Jack, *The Divine Hag of the Christian Celts: An Illustrated Guide to the Sheela-na-Gigs of Britain and Ireland*. Cork: Mercier Press, 2001.

MacManus, Diarmuid, *The Middle Kingdom: The Faerie World of Ireland*. London: Parrish, 1959; rpt Gerrards Cross: Colin Smythe, 1973.

MacNeil, Joe Neil, *Tales Until Dawn: The World of a Cape Breton Story-Teller*, ed. and trans. John Shaw. Kingston and Montreal: McGill–Queen's University Press, 1987.

MacNeill, Eoin, *Celtic Ireland*. Dublin: Martin Lester; London: Leonard Parsons, 1921.

MacNeill, Máire, *The Feast of Lughnasa*. Oxford: Oxford University Press, 1962; rpt Dublin: Comhairle Bhéaloideas Éireann, 1982.

Macpherson, James, *The Poems of Ossian, Son of Fingal*. London: W. Stachan and T. Becket, 1765; rpt Edinburgh: Patrick Geddes, 1896.

Maier, Bernhard, *Lexikon der keltischen Religion und Kultur*. Stuttgart: Alfred Kröner, 1994. *Dictionary of Celtic Religion and Culture*, trans. Cyril Edwards. Woodbridge: Boydell Press, 1997.

Marryat, Frederick, *Peter Simple*. London: R. Bentley, 1834.

Marsh, Richard, *The Legends and Lands of Ireland*. New York: Sterling; Sayvon, Israel: Penn Publishing, 2004.

Massey, Eithne, *Legendary Ireland: A Journey through Celtic Places and Myths*. Dublin: O'Brien Press; Madison: University of Wisconsin Press, 2004.

Megaw, J. V. S., *The Art of the European Iron Age*. New York: Harper & Row, 1970.

Megaw, Ruth and Megaw, J. V. S., *Celtic Art*. London: Thames & Hudson, 1989.

Mercier, Vivian, *The Irish Comic Tradition*. Oxford: Clarendon Press, 1962.

Mesca Ulad, ed. J. Carmichael Watson. Dublin: Dublin Institute for Advanced Studies, 1941, 1983.

Moore, Arthur W., *Folk-Lore of the Isle of Man*. Douglas, Isle of Man: Brown; London: David Nutt, 1891.

Murphy, Gerard. See *Duanaire Finn*.

Murphy, Gerard (ed.), *Early Irish Lyrics: Eighth to Twelfth Century*. Oxford: Clarendon Press, 1956.

Nagy, Joseph Falaky, *The Wisdom of the Outlaw: The Boyhood Deeds of Finn in Gaelic Narrative Tradition*. Berkeley: University of California Press, 1985.

Nagy, Joseph Falaky, *Conversing with Angels and Ancients: Literary Myths of Medieval Ireland*. Ithaca: Cornell University Press; Dublin: Four Courts, 1997.

Navigatio Sancti Brendani Abbatis: The Voyage of Saint Brendan, Journey to the Promised Land, trans. John J. O'Meara. Portlaoise: Dolmen Press, 1985.

New Catholic Encyclopedia, 2nd edn. Detroit: Thomson/Gale; Washington: Catholic University of America, 2003.

Ó Cróinín, Dáibhí, *Early Medieval Ireland: 400–1200*. London and New York: Longman, 1995.

Ó Crualaoich, Gearóid, *The Book of the Cailleach: Stories of the Wise-Woman Healer*. Cork: Cork University Press, 2003.

O'Faoláin, Seán, 'Ossian – the Sow's Ear of Celtic Literature', *Modern Scot* [Edinburgh], 6 (1935): 44–51.

O'Grady, Standish James, *History of Ireland: The Heroic Period*. Dublin: Ponsonby, 1878.

Ó hÓgáin, Dáithí, *Fionn mac Cumhaill: Images of the Gaelic Hero*. Dublin: Gill & Macmillan, 1988.

Ó hÓgáin, Dáithí, *Myth, Legend, and Romance: An Encyclopedia of Irish Folk Tradition*. London: Ryan; New York: Prentice-Hall, 1991.

Ó hÓgáin, Dáithí, *The Sacred Isle: Belief and Religion in Pre-Christian Ireland*. Woodbridge: Boydell Press; Doughcloyne: Collins Press, 1999.

Ó hÓgáin, Dáithí, *The Celts: A History*. London: Collins, 2004.

[*Oided Mac nUisnig*] 'The Death of the Sons of Uisnech', trans. Whitley Stokes. *Irische Texte*, ser. 2, 2. Leipzig: S. Hirzel, 1887, pp. 109–84.

[*Oidheadh Chlainne Lir*] *Oidhe Chloinne Lir: The Fate of the Children of Lir*, ed. and trans. Richard J. O'Duffy. Dublin: Gill, 1883, 1905, etc.

[*Oidheadh Chlainne Tuireann*] 'The Fate of the Children of Tuirenn', ed. and trans. Eugene O'Curry, *The Atlantis* [London], 4 (1863): 157–240.

O'Leary, Philip, 'The Honour of Women in Early Irish Literature', *Ériu*, 38 (1987): 27–44.

Olmstead, Garrett S., *The Gods of the Celts and the Indo-Europeans*. Innsbruck: Verlag des Instituts für Sprachwissenschaft der Universität Innsbruck; Budapest: Alaptvány, 1994.

Ong, Walter J. SJ, *Orality and Literacy: The Technologizing of the Word*. New York: Methuen, 1982.

O'Rahilly, Thomas Francis, *Early Irish History and Mythology*. Dublin: Dublin Institute for Advanced Studies, 1946.

Patai, Raphael, *Myth and Modern Man*. Englewood Cliffs, NJ: Prentice-Hall, 1972.

Patterson, Nerys T., *Cattle-Lords and Clansmen: Kingship and Rank in Early Ireland*. New York: Garland Press, 1992.

Posidonius, 'The Celtic Ethnology of Posidonius', ed. J. J. Tierney, *Proceedings of the Royal Irish Academy*, vol. 60, sec. C, no. 5 (1960); rpt Dublin: Royal Irish Academy, 1985.

'Quarrel Between Finn and Oisín, The', *Fianaigecht, Being a Collection of Hitherto Inedited Irish Poems and Tales, etc.*, ed. and trans. Kuno Meyer. Royal Irish Academy, Todd Lecture Series, vol. XVI, Dublin: Hodges, Figgis, 1910, pp. 22–7.

Rees, Alwyn and Rees, Brinley, *Celtic Heritage*. London: Thames & Hudson, 1961.

Ross, Anne, *Pagan Celtic Britain: Studies in Iconography and Tradition*. London: Routledge; New York: Columbia University Press, 1967.

Scéla mucce Meic Dathó, ed. Rudolf Thurneysen. Dublin: Stationery Office, 1935; rpt Dublin: Dublin Institute for Advanced Studies, 1975.

Serglige con Culainn, ed. Myles Dillon. Mediaeval and Modern Irish Series, vol. XIV, Dublin: Dublin Institute for Advanced Studies, 1953.

Shaw, John, 'A Gaelic Tale of the Milky Way', recited by Joe Neil MacNeil, *Cape Breton's Magazine*, 19 (June, 1978): 31.

Sims-Williams, Patrick, 'Some Celtic Otherworldly Terms', *Celtic Language, Celtic Literature: A Festschrift for Eric P. Hamp*, ed. A. T. E. Matonis and Daniel F. Melia. Van Nuys, CA: Ford & Baillie, 1990, pp. 57–81.

Stephens, James, *Irish Fairy Tales*. London and New York: Macmillan, 1920; rpt New York: Abaris, 1978.

Strabo, *Geography*, trans. Horace L. Jones. Cambridge, MA: Harvard University Press, 1969.

Sutherland, Elizabeth, *Ravens and Black Rain: The Story of Highland Second Sight, Including a New Collection of Prophecies of the Brahan Seer*. London: Constable, 1985.

[*Táin Bó Cuailnge*] *Táin, The: Translated from the Irish Epic Táin Bó Cuailnge*, Thomas Kinsella. Dublin: Dolmen Press; London: Oxford University Press, 1969.

Thompson, Stith, *Motif-Index of Folk-Literature: A Classification of Narrative Elements in Folktales, Ballads, Myths, Fables, Medieval Romances, Exempla, Jest-Books and Local Legends*, rev. edn. (6 vols). Bloomington: Indiana University Press, 1975, 1989.

Thurneysen, Rudolf, *Die irishe Helden- und Königsage bis zum siebsehnten Jahrhundert*. Halle: Niemeyer, 1921.

'Tochmarc Étaíne', ed. Osborn Bergin and R. I. Best, *Ériu*, 12 (1938): 137–96.

Togail bruidne [*sic*] *Da Derga*, ed. Eleanor Knott. Dublin: The Stationery Office, 1936; rpt Dublin Institute for Advanced Studies, 1963, 1975.

Tóraigheacht Dhiarmada agus Ghráinne: The Pursuit of Diarmaid and

Gráinne, ed. and trans. Nessa Ní Shéaghdha. Irish Texts Society, vol. 47, Dublin: Educational Company of Ireland, 1967.

Triads, Trioedd Ynys Prydain. See Bromwich, Rachel.

Tymoczko, Maria (trans.), *Two Death Tales from the Ulster Cycle: The Death of Cú Roi and the Death of Cú Chulainn*. Dublin: Dolmen Press; Atlantic Highlands, NJ: Humanities Press, 1981.

Vendryes, Joseph, *La Religion des Celtes*, in *'Mana': introduction à l'historie des religions*, II, *Les religions de l'Europe ancienne*, pt. 3. Paris: Presses Universitaires de France, 1948, pp. 237–330.

Vouga, Paul, *La Tène*. Leipzig: Hiersemann, 1923.

Wilde, Sir William R., *Irish Popular Superstitions*. Dublin: McGlashan, 1852; rpt Dublin: Irish Academic Press, 1979.

Williams, Ifor, 'Rhagymadrodd [Introduction]', *Pedeir Keinc y Mabinogi*. Cardiff: University of Wales Press, 1951, pp. vii–lvi.

Wooding, Jonathan M. (ed.), *The Otherworldly Voyage in Early Irish Literature*. Dublin: Four Courts, 2000.

Yeats, William Butler, *The Celtic Twilight: Men and Women, Dhouls and Faeries*. London: Lawrence & Bullen, 1893.

Yeats, William Butler, *The Variorum Edition of the Poems of W. B. Yeats*, ed. Peter Allt and Russell K. Alspach. New York: Macmillan, 1957.

Leading Names and Terms in Celtic Mythology

PRONUNCIATION, A CAUTION

As with many languages, English speakers cannot expect to pronounce Celtic words and names without the extensive assistance of a tutor. It is much the same as with the French *r*, notoriously difficult for us to master. Our usual anglicized pronunciation of *hors d'oeuvres* as 'ohr **durvz**', for example, is likely to meet with incomprehension or derision from a native speaker of French. In the same way, most English speakers do not appreciate that Irish, Welsh and Breton present many greater challenges than does French, such as palatal and non-palatal (velar) consonants, broad and slender vowels, and an array of sounds not found in English, beginning with the velar fricative, the Welsh *-ll-* and the Welsh trilled *r*. Additionally, Modern Irish survives in three dialects; there is not a Standard Irish as there is a Standard English. Many names and terms survive in a wide variety of variant spellings. Scottish Gaelic, with different sound patterns, ranks almost as a fourth dialect. Complicating matters, some commentators prefer the uncertain pronunciations of Old Irish, Middle Irish and Classical Modern Irish (until the mid-seventeenth century). Thus the much-cited name of Ulster king Conchobar may be sounded in different contexts as '**kun**-ko-var', '**kun**-nă-khoor', '**kon**-khor', '**kru**-hoor' and 'kru-**hoor**'. The pronunciation of the hero Fionn's name, whose stories are more widely known, survives in even more variants. It is more than a matter of 'to-**mah**-toh' vs. 'to-**may**-toh'; pronunciation will be contentious for some readers. Suggestions given here are approximate and should not be considered sufficient for use in broadcasts or in addresses before learned bodies. Consult the Pronunciation Key at the end of this Appendix (pp. 348–9).

A handful of names, such as Deirdre, Fionn, Oscar, Suibne, are often cited with anglicized pronunciations while retaining their original spellings.

Classical Modern Irish spellings are preferred for most names here; other sources may employ Modern Irish or even anglicized spellings.

Abaris (ă-**bahr**-ĭs) Known as the 'Hyperborean', i.e. from beyond the north wind. Sixth-century BC figure who conversed with Pythagoras; may have been first known druid.

Áeb (ayv) Foster-daughter of Bodb Derg, wife of Lir, and mother of the swan children.

Áebhric (**ayv**-rik) Young, well-born hermit, perhaps a cleric, who records the story of the children of Lir.

Áed (i*th*) Twin brother of Finnguala among the swan children of Lir.

Aichlech mac Dubdrenn (**ahkh**-lekh mahk **duv**-dren) One of several possible assassins of Fionn mac Cumhaill.

Aífe (1) (**eef**-ĕ) Cruel stepmother of the swan children of Lir.

Aífe (2) (**eef**-ĕ) Amazonian warrior of the Isle of Skye, mother by Cúchulainn of Connla.

Ailbe (1) (**alv**-ĕ) Daughter of Cormac mac Airt.

Ailbe (2) (**alv**-ĕ) Large, ferocious hound owned by Mac Da Thó.

Ailech (**al**-yakh, **ĭl**-yakh) Prehistoric stone fortress of Co. Derry.

Ailill (**al**-yil) Father of the first Étaín in *Tochmarc Étaíne*.

Ailill Anglonnach (**al**-yil **ahng**-lon-ăkh) Brother of Eochaid Airem, smitten with Étaín.

Ailill mac Máta (**al**-yil mahk **mawd**-ĕ) Husband of Medb; their domestic quarrel begins the action of *Táin Bó Cuailnge*.

Aillén mac Midgna (**al**-yayn mahk **mi*th***-gĕnă) The 'burner' who harassed Tara until eliminated by Fionn mac Cumhaill.

Aillén Tréchenn (**al**-yayn **tray**-khĕn) Monster who wreaked havoc upon Ireland every Samain until eliminated by the poet Amairgin.

Áine (**aw**-nĕ; *ModIr.* **awn**-yĕ, **en**-yă) One of Fionn mac Cumhaill's many lovers.

Airgialla (ahr-ɣ**ahl**-ă, ahr-ɣ**eeal**-ă) A tribe or a people who held territory in the north of Ireland, living near Lough Foyle, in the first millennium AD.

Airmid (**ar**-vi*th*) Irish healing god, daughter of Dian Cécht.

Aitheachthuatha (**ath**-ekh-oo-ath-ă) 'Plebeian tribes', an underclass of subject tribes with no king of their own, dominated by the Tuatha Dé Danann.

Alba (**ahl**-ĕ-bă) An ancient name for Scotland.

Alésia (ahl-**ays**-ee-ă, ahl-**ay**-shă) Fortified settlement or proto-city of eastern Gaul, in what is now Burgundy.

Allen, Hill of Supposed residence of Fionn mac Cumhaill in Co. Kildare.

AM See Anno Mundi.

Amairgin (av-ăr-gin, av-ăr-γin, ah-măr-gin) Poet of the Milesians, often cited as the first poet of Ireland.

ambhrán (ahr-awn) Accentuated metre of early Irish poetry.

Ana (ahn-ă) Principal goddess of pre-Christian Ireland.

Andraste (ahn-drast-ě) Shadowy British war goddess invoked by Boudicca.

Aneirin (ă-nı-rin) Shadowy sixth-century Welsh poet, thought to be the author of the battle poem *Y Gododdin*. One of the two *cynfeirdd* [oldest poets] with Taliesin.

Angus (ang-us; cf. *Ir. Óengus*: oin-γus, ayn-eeas) Son of Áed Abrat, visits Cúchulainn on his sickbed.

Angus Óg (ang-us ohg) Irish god of poetry and son of the Dagda.

Anluan (ahn-looăn) Brother of Cet, beheaded by Conall Cernach.

Anno Mundi; AM (an-oh mun-dee) The year of the world, according to conflicting interpretations of the biblical story of creation. AM I was posited to be 5200 BC, 5198 BC, 5090 BC and 3952 BC.

Annwfn, Annwn (ahn-oovn, ahn-oon) The Welsh otherworld.

aos sídhe (ees shee) Irish for 'people of the *sídh*', i.e. fairies.

Apollo (ă-pol-oh) Classical name given by Romans to series of indigenous Gaulish gods, some of whom are distinguished by suffixes, e.g. Apollo Grannus, etc.

Arawn (ahr-awn) King of Annwfn; he and Pwyll agree to change places.

Arberth (ahr-berth) Residence or court of Pwyll in Dyfed, near the modern town of Narberth.

Arca Dubh [Black Arky] (ahrk-ă doov) Representative adversary of Fionn mac Cumhaill.

Arianrhod, Aranrhod (ahr-yahn-rhod, ahr-ee-ahn-rhohd, ahr-ahn-rhohd, ahr-ee-ahn-rhohd) Sister and lover of Gwydion, mother of Lleu Llaw Gyffes and Dylan.

Armorica (ar-mohr-ĭk-ă) Ancient name of Brittany.

Assal (ahs-ăl) King of the Golden Pillars; the sons of Tuireann must retrieve his magical pigs.

Áth Fhirdiad (awth-ir-dee-ăd; *ModIr.* ah-ir dee-ă) Ford on the River Dee where Cúchulainn duels with Ferdiad; the modern name is Ardee, 14 miles north of Drogheda, Co. Louth.

Áth Luain [ford of the loins] (awth-loo-ĭn, ah loo-ĭn) Principal ford of the River Shannon, coextensive with the modern town of Athlone.

Badb (bahv, bıv, bowv, bah*th*v) Evil early Irish war goddess who delights in slaughter, much associated with crows. One of the trinity Mórrígna with Macha and Mórrígan.

badhbh chaointe [*Ir.* weeping crow] (bahv, bıv kheen-tyě) Mournful scavenger of death in modern Irish folk tradition.

ball seirce (bal **shirk**-yĕ) 'Love spot' of Diarmait Ua Duibne that makes him irresistible to women.

Balor (**bah**-lor) Monstrous Fomorian leader whose evil or baleful eye can annihilate all upon whom he casts it.

Banba (**ban**-vă, **ban**-bă) One of a trio of wives of Tuatha Dé Danann chiefs, along with Ériu and Fodla, who encounter the invading Milesians. Her name was later an alternative poetic name for Ireland (Éire).

banshee (**ban**-shee) Woman of Irish and Scottish Gaelic folk tradition who foretells misfortune and death but does not cause it.

Barbarossa (bar-bar-**ohs**-ă) Name in Teutonic legend for Frederick I (1123?– 1190), the Holy Roman Emperor.

bard (bahrd) Generic name for a class of esteemed poets who went under different names in different countries. Of lower status than a druid or *vates* or Irish *filid*.

bean nighe (ben, ban **nee**-ĕ) Scottish Gaelic name for the washer at the ford.

Bébinn (**bay**-veen) Name of several great Irish beauties.

Bebo (**bev**-ŏ) Queen of the fairies in the thirteenth-century *Echtra Fergusa maic Léite*.

Bé Chuma (bay-**khoom**-ă) Beautiful but wicked adulteress whose liaison with Gaidiar, son of Manannán mac Lir, causes her to be banished.

Bedwyr (**bed**-weer) Welsh member of King Arthur's court.

Belenus (bel-ĕn-ŭs, bel-**ayn**-ŭ) Gaulish god whose cult stretched from Italy to Britain; perhaps an aspect of Apollo.

Belgae (**bel**-jee) Ancient P-Celtic people of the continent and Britain. The modern nation of Belgium may be named for them, but Belgians are not necessarily identical with the Belgae.

Beli Mawr (**bel**-ee mawr) Welsh ancestor deity, mate of Dôn.

Beltaine (bel-tin-ĕ, **bal**-tin-ĕ) Celtic spring festival, usually around 1 May.

Ben Bulben (ben **bul**-bĕn) Peak, 1,722 ft, 10–12 miles NW of Sligo town, Co. Sligo, rich in heroic and legendary associations.

Bendigeidfran, Brân the Blessed (ben-di-**gɪ**-vran, brahn) Celtic sea deity, later described as a king of Britain. A leading figure of early Welsh literature, including the *Mabinogi*.

Bibracte (bĭ-**brahk**-tĕ) Fortified Gaulish city atop Mt Beuvray, near the modern town of Auton in eastern France. Findings here argued for a more sophisticated and complex society than previous records had implied.

Birog (**bir**-ohg) Druidess who helps Cian seduce Eithne.

Bladma (bla*th*-vă) Minor Milesian invader for whom the Sliab Bladma [Slieve Bloom] mountains are named.

Blaí (blah-ee) Alternative name for Sadb.

Blái Briuga (blah-ee bree-ooγă) Hospitaller of Ulster, one of Cúchulainn's seven foster-fathers.

Bláithíne, Bláthnat, Blanid (blaw-ĭ-ně, blaw-nid) Wife of Cú Roí who betrays her husband for an affair with Cúchulainn.

Bleiddwn [wolf cub] (blɪth-oon) Lupine offspring of a transformed Gwydion and Gilfaethwy.

Blodeuedd (blo-di-eth, blo-dɪ-weth) Leading female figure in the Fourth Branch of the *Mabinogi* whose beauty brings much ill.

Boadach (both-ăkh) Sometimes cited ruler of the otherworldly Mag Mell.

Boand, Bóinn (boh-ănd, bohn, boh-ĭn) Goddess of the River Boyne, an anglicization of her name.

Bodb Derg (bohv, bohthv jer-ĕg) Son of the Dagda, foster-father of the children of Lir.

Bodhmall (bohγ-mal) Druidess aunt of Fionn mac Cumhaill, also his nurse.

Bodua (boh-dwă) Gaulish battle goddess.

Borba [harsh, arrogant] (bohr-vă) Representative adversary of Fionn mac Cumhaill.

Borvo, Bormo, Bormanus (bohr-vo) Gaulish healing god, often portrayed with Damona.

Boudicca (boo-dik-ă, boo-deek-ă) Historical British queen (first century AD) who led a rebellion against the Romans.

Brahan Castle (brah-ăn) Fifteen miles northeast of the city of Inverness.

Brahan Seer (brah-ăn) Legendary, gloomy, seventeenth-century Scottish Gaelic prophet, perhaps known in life as Coinneach Odhar Fiosaiche.

Bran (brahn) One of Fionn mac Cumhaill's favoured dogs; the other is Sceolang.

Brân the Blessed See Bendigeidfran.

Bran mac Febail (brahn mahk fev-ĭl) Protagonist of the eighth-century Irish *Imram Brain*, the oldest surviving story of a voyage to the otherworld.

Branwen (brahn-wen) Daughter of Llŷr, title character of the Second Branch of the *Mabinogi*.

Breaga (bree-aγă) Lesser Milesian invader, an uncle of Míl Espáine, for whom the medieval petty kingdom of Brega/Bregia was named.

Brega (bre-ghă) The plain between the Liffey and Boyne Rivers.

Brehon Laws (breh-ohn) Native Irish law in widespread use before Norman invasion, 1169–70.

Breizh (brez) Breton name for Brittany.

Brendan, St (brend-ăn) Historical Irish monk (d. 577), the story of whose voyage across the Atlantic, possibly to the New World, was composed 300 years after his death.

Breogan (bre-oγ-ăn)   Milesian leader who built a high tower at Brigantium (modern La Coruña), Spain, allowing his son Íth to see Ireland.

Bres (bres)   Vain king of the Tuatha Dé Danann at the Second Battle of Mag Tuired.

Brí Léith (bree lay)   Sídh in Co. Longford, residence of Midir, lover of Étaín.

Brian (bree-ăn)   Most prominent of the three sons of Tuireann.

Brian Bórama, Boru (bree-ăn bohr-ă-vă, bohr-oo-wa, bohr-oo)   Powerful Irish *ard rí* who defeated the Norsemen at Clontarf, AD 1014.

Briccriu Neimthenga [bitter-tongued] (**brik**-roo **nev**-theng-ă)   Sharp-mouthed troublemaker of the Ulster Cycle.

Brigantia (bri-**gahnt**-eeă)   Tribal goddess of north Britain.

Brigantium (bri-**gahnt**-eeŭm)   Old name for La Coruña, Spain, where Breogan builds a tower allowing Íth and the Milesians to see Ireland.

Brigid, St (breed, breej, *ang.* **brij**-id)   The 'Mary of the Gael', one of the three principal saints of Ireland, thought to have lived *c.*460–*c.*528.

Brigit (breed, **bree**-γid)   Pre-Christian fire-goddess of Kildare.

Brocéliande (broh-**sayl**-ee-ahnd)   Actual forest in eastern Brittany, 24 miles southwest of Rennes, scene of many episodes in the Arthurian legends.

Brug na Bóinne [*Ir.* hostel of the Boyne] (broogh, brooγ, broo-; nă-**boi**-nyă, nă-**bohn**-ă)   Early literature implies this is the Irish language name for the passage-grave of Newgrange in the Boyne valley. At the contemporary Visitor Centre the Modern Irish **Bru na Boinne** denotes three neighbouring passage-graves, Newgrange, Knowth and Dowth, as well as some forty smaller ones.

Bruidhean . . . [hostel, banqueting hall] (**brooth**-ăn)   First word in titles of Fenian stories in which the fighters find themselves trapped in enchanted dwellings.

Búanann (booă-ăn)   Amazon-like martial tutor of Fionn mac Cumhaill.

Buide mac Báin (**booth**-ĕ mahk **bawn**)   He is driving Dunn Cuailnge when Cúchulainn finds him and kills him.

Cáer (kayr)   Swan maiden loved by Angus Óg; nicknamed Ibormeith [yew berry].

Caer Feddwid [*W.* court of intoxication or carousal] (kɪr ve**th**-id)   Alternative early name for Annwfn.

Caer Siddi (kɪr si**th**-ĭ)   Alternative name for the Welsh otherworld, Annwfn.

Cahirconree (ka-hir-**kon**-ree)   Iron Age ruin on the Dingle Peninsula, Co. Kerry, possibly the site of Cú Roí's fortress.

Caicer (**ko**-her, **ka**-her)   Milesian druid who predicts his people will live in Ireland.

Cailb (kahl-ĕv) Ugly, haggish seer of early Irish literature.

Cailitin (kah-lit-ĭn) Irish wizard, friend of Medb, who does battle with Cúchulainn.

Cailleach Bhéirre (kol-yukh, kahl-yukh; vɪ-rŭ, vay-rĕ) Ugly Irish sovereignty figure, associated with the Province of Munster, especially the Beare Peninsula; often called the 'Hag of Beare' in English.

Caílte mac Rónáin (keel-tĕ mahk rohn-awn) Best runner of the Fianna Éireann, a companion and possible nephew of Fionn; he survives to tell St Patrick of heroic pre-Christian days. *ModIr.*: Caoilte (**kweel-tĕ**).

Cairbre Cinn-Chait (kor-bray, kahr-bray, kahr-ĕ-bray, kahr-bir-ĕ; kin-khaht) Plebeian usurper of Milesian hegemony.

Cairbre Lifechair (kor-bray, kahr-bray, kahr-ĕ-bray, kahr-bir-ĕ; lif-ohkh-ĭr, lif-ekh-ăr) Son of Cormac mac Airt.

Cairbre Nia Fer (kor-bray, kahr-bray, kahr-ĕ-bray, kahr-bir-ĕ; nee-ă-fer) Elder brother of Ailill mac Máta who is killed by Cúchulainn. His son Erc avenges his father's death.

Cairpre (kor-bray, kahr-bray, kahr-ĕ-bray, kahr-bir-ĕ) Satirist of the Tuatha Dé Danann.

Caitlín, or Céthlionn (kath-leen) Ugly, crooked-toothed wife of Balor.

Caladbolg (kahl-ăth-bohl-ĕgh) Widely cited sword of early Irish literature, usually attributed to Fergus mac Róich and Fergus mac Léti.

Calan Mai (kahl-ăn mɪ) Welsh name for May Day.

Caledonia (kal-ĕ-dohn-ee-ă) An ancient name for Scotland.

Cáma (kawv-ă) Female Fenian chief and custodian who survives the general destruction of the Fianna Éireann.

Camel (kahv-ĕl, kahm-ĕl) Co-gatekeeper, with Gamel, of Tara.

cantred **(kahn-tred)** A region of approximately 100 townships in medieval Wales; also *cantref* (**kahn-trev**).

Caoilte (kweel-tĕ) Modern Irish for Caílte.

castros **(kahs-trohs)** Small, defended Celtic-era towns in Spain; homes of the *mouros*, Galician fairy folk.

Cathach Chatutchenn [bellicose, hard-headed] **(kahth-ăkh kahd-ud-khen)** Female warrior in love with Cúchulainn.

Cathbad (kahth-vahd, kahth-vahth, kahf-ă) Chief druid in the court of Conchobar mac Nessa who predicts Deirdre will cause enmity leading to the destruction of Emain Macha and other calamities.

Caw (kow) Member of Culhwch's party who shaves the giant Ysbaddaden.

Céadach (kɪ-dukh, kay-dukh) Comic, unwanted 'helper' in Fenian tales from oral tradition.

Cei (kɪ)   Welsh member of King Arthur's court, anticipation of Sir Kay.

Céis Chorrain [Keshcorran] (kaysh **khohr**-awn)   Hill, 1183 ft, in Co. Sligo, with many Fenian associations. Longtime residence of Diarmait and Gráinne.

Celtchair mac Uithechair (**kelt**-khar mahk **uth**-ekh-ĭr)   Ulster warrior held as a guarantee in Conchobar's bargaining with Fintan.

Celyddon Wledig (kel-**uth**-ŏn oo-**led**-ig)   Princely but shadowy grandfather of Culhwch.

Ceridwen (ker-**id**-wen)   Ugly, shape-shifting witch in north Wales who keeps a cauldron of knowledge at the bottom of Lake Bala; her children are fair Creirwy and hideous Morfran. She also gives birth to Taliesin.

Cernunnos (ker-**noon**-ŏs, ker-**nun**-ŏs)   Stag-horned deity of the continental Celts, portrayed on the Gundestrup Cauldron; widely worshipped.

Cesair (**kes**-ĭr)   Leader of the first invasion of Ireland, according to *Lebor Gabála Érenn*.

Cet mac Mágach (kat, ket mahk **mah**ɣ-ăkh)   Boastful Connacht hero challenged by Conall Cernach.

Cethern mac Fintain (**keh**-arn, **keth**-ern mahk **fin**-tawn)   Ulster warrior who steps forward while Cúchulainn lies stricken from the duel with Ferdiad. Also tutors Fionn mac Cumhaill.

Cian (**kee**-ăn)   A son of Dian Cécht who seduces Eithne to produce Lug Lámfhota; later humiliated and killed by the sons of Tuireann.

Cichol (**kikh**-ŏl)   Rapacious leader of the Fomorians.

Cigfa (**kig**-va)   Wife of Pryderi in Third Branch of the *Mabinogi*.

Cilydd (**kil**-*eth*)   Father of Culhwch.

Cimbáeth (**kim**-bay, **kim**-bay*th*)   Ulster king, husband of Macha/Mong Ruadh.

Cináed mac Alpín [Kenneth MacAlpin] (**kun**-ay mahk **ahl**-pin)   Historical king of the Gaels who founded Scotland in 844.

cláenmíla (klɪn-**veel**-ă)   Untranslatable 'crooked beasts' or 'evil beasts' that Conaire Mór is forbidden to hunt; perhaps swans, as his mother had been impregnated by a bird man.

Claidheamh Soluis [sword of light] (kleev **sohl**-ush)   Also Cruaidin Catutchenn. Name for Cúchulainn's sword in oral tradition.

Clan Baíscne (klahn **bahsk**-ĭn-ĕ)   Family of Fionn mac Cumhaill.

Clan Morna (klahn **mohrn**-ă)   Goll's clan, rivals to Clan Baíscne.

Clettig (**klet**-ĭgh)   *Sídh* in the Boyne valley near Newgrange, residence of Elcmar.

Clothra (**kloh**-ră, **klohth**-ră)   Sister of Medb, killed by her while pregnant with Furbaide Ferbend.

Coímín, Micheál (kohv-een, mee-hahl) Irish poet (1688–1760) who composed the most polished version of the Oisín and Niam story, *c.*1750.

Coinneach Odhar Fiosaiche (kohn-yakh oh-ăr fis-ikh) Scottish Gaelic name for the Brahan Seer, the seventeenth-century prophet.

Coligny Calendar (kohl-een-yee) First-century AD bronze plates named for the place of their recovery in eastern France; they detail the Gaulish conception of time.

Colptha (kolp-thă) Second Milesian to go ashore at the invasion, leaving his name in Inber Colptha at the mouth of the Boyne.

Colum Cille, Columba (kul-am, kol-ŭm kil-ye; ko-lum-bă) Irish-born saint (d. 597) who founded Christianity in Scotland with his monastery at Iona.

Conaire Mór (kun-ir-ĕ, koh-nahr-ĕ mohr) Legendary early Irish king, leading figure of *Togail Bruidne Da Derga* [The Destruction of Da Derga's Hostel].

Conall Anglonnach (kun-al, kon-al ahng-lohn-ăkh) Ulsterman held as a guarantee by Cúchulainn.

Conall Cernach (kun-al, kon-al; kern-akh, kahrn-akh) Ulster hero, frequent companion of Cúchulainn and next to him in prestige.

Conarán (kohn-ahr-awn) A chief of the Tuatha Dé Danann whose three ugly daughters try to punish Fionn mac Cumhaill.

Conchobar mac Nessa (kun-nă-khoor, kun-ko-var, kon-khor, kru-hoor, kru-hoor; mahk nes-ă) King of Ulster in much of the Ulster Cycle.

Condere (kohn-*th*er-ĕ) Lesser Ulster champion sent to meet Connla.

Congal (kun-eeal) Foster-brother and compatriot of Máel Fhothartaig.

Conn (kun, kown) One of the four swan children of Lir.

Conn Cétchathach (kon kayd-khah-thahkh) Conn of the Hundred Battles, possibly second-century Irish king, cited in early chronicles and genealogies.

Connacht (kon-aht, kon-ăkht) Western province of Ireland, ruled by Ailill and Medb.

Connla (kon-lă) Son of Aífe (2) and Cúchulainn who meets his father in combat.

Corentin (kor-en-tin) Pious hermit who converts Gradlon to Christianity, made bishop of Quimper.

Cormac Connloinges (kur-mak, kor-mak kon-long-ăs) Turncoat son of Conchobar mac Nessa who joins Medb against Ulster.

Cormac mac Airt (kur-mak, kor-mak mahk ahrt) Possibly historical third-century Irish king, subject of *Echtrae Cormaic* [Adventures of Cormac]. Ruler during maturity of Fionn mac Cumhaill.

Cormac mac Cuileannáin (kur-mak, kor-mak mahk kul-ĕn-awn) Ninth-century bishop and scholar who compiled *Cormac's Glossary* or *Sanas*

Cormaic, which credulously treats mythical and legendary figures as historical.

Coventina (kov-en-**teen**-ă) Ancient British healing goddess.

Cráebruad (krɪv-roo-ă) A prime residence, with a distinctive red roof beam, at Emain Macha.

Credne (kred-ĭn-ĕ, kre*th*-nĕ) Bronze-working god of the Tuatha Dé Danann.

Creirwy (krɪr-ooee) Beautiful daughter of Ceridwen.

Crimthann Nia Náir (kree-făn, krif- hahn neeă nahr) Munster warrior who tries to kill Cúchulainn using the wiles of the female satirist Richis.

Crom Crúaich (krom krookh) 'Chief idol' of pagan Ireland, according to Christian scribes; evidence for its existence, e.g. the Killycluggin Stone, is disputed.

Crom Dubh (krom duv) Legendary pre-Christian Irish chieftain overcome by St Patrick.

Cruachain (kroo-akh-awn, kroo-ahk-ĭn) Fortress of Ailill and Medb in what is now Co. Roscommon.

Cruaidin Catutchenn See Claidheamh Soluis.

Crunniuc mac Agnomain (krun-yuk mahk **ag**-no-vahn) Rich landlord who forces his pregnant wife Macha into a footrace.

Cú Roí (koo-ree) Munster wizard and warrior whose castle may have been at Cahirconree, Co. Kerry; real identity of the giant in the beheading challenge.

Cualu (kul-ŭ) Area south of the River Liffey, coextensive with northern Co. Wicklow.

Cúchulainn (koo-**khul**-in) Leading hero of the Ulster Cycle and the epic *Táin Bó Cuailnge*. Hiberno-English: **Cucullin**.

Culann (kul-ĭn, kul-ahn) Smith whose watchdog is killed by Sétanta (later Cúchulainn).

Culhwch (kil-hookh) Welsh Arthurian hero, lover of Olwen.

Cumhall (kool, koo-ĭl, koo-val) Father of Fionn mac Cumhaill.

Cunebelinus (koon-ay-**bel**-in-ŭs) Historical leader in pre-Claudian Britain, first century BC.

curadmír (kur-a*th*-meer) Irish term for the champion's portion, i.e. favoured cut of pork.

Custennin (kus-ten-ĭn) Herdsman who warns Culhwch.

cwn annwfn (koon ahn-oon) Spectral Welsh dogs whose barks foretell death.

Cymidei Cymeinfoll (kum-id-ɪ ku-mɪn-vol) Ugly giantess who personifies the cauldron of regeneration; married to Llassar Llaes Gyfnewid.

Cymru (kum-ree) Welsh name for Wales.

Cynan Meiriadog (or Meriodoc), St (kun-**ahn** mɪr-yoh-dohk) Welsh saint who led the British to Brittany, according to legend.

Cynddylig Cyfarwydd (kun-*th*il-ig ku-**vahr**-ee*th*) Welsh member of King Arthur's court.

Da Derga (dah jer-ĕ-gĕ, dah der-gă) Owner of the hostel on the Dodder River where Conaire Mór is killed.

dà shealladh (dah **hahl**-ŭ) Scottish Gaelic phrase for second sight or clairvoyance.

Dabilla (dahv-il-ă) Lapdog of Boand.

Dagda (dahγ-*th*ă, dag-dă) The 'good god', divine leader of the Tuatha Dé Danann; often named with the definite article, 'the Dagda'.

Dahut (dah-ut) Corrupt, pleasure-loving daughter of King Gradlon.

Dáire (daw-rĕ) One of the many figures bearing this name is the king of Tír Tairngire; his queen is Rígru Rosclethan.

Dáire mac Fiachna (daw-rĕ mahk fee-ăkh-nă) Owner of Donn Cuailnge, the Brown Bull of Ulster, at the beginning of the *Táin Bó Cuailnge*.

Daithlenn (dath-len) One of Máel Fhothartaig's two prize hounds.

Dál gCais (dawl gash) Petty kingdom, home of Brian Bórama; anglicized Dalcass.

Dál nAraide (dawl nar-ath-ĕ) Historical early kingdom on the borders of Antrim and Down, ruled by Suibne before onset of his madness.

Dál Riada (dawl ree-ă-dă, ree-ă-*th*ă) Historical kingdom of early Scotland, the extension of a kingdom that originated in Ireland.

Damona (da-**mohn**-ă) Gaulish healing goddess, often worshipped with Borvo.

Danu (dahn-ŭ) Enigmatic mother goddess whose name may be preserved in genitive form in Tuatha Dé Danann. Suggested identification with Ana/Anu is not proven.

Dealgnaid (dyalγ-nă) Partholonian queen, the first adulteress in Ireland.

Dealra Dubh [dark sheen] (dyal-ĕ-ră duv) Representative adversary of Fionn mac Cumhaill.

Deichtine (dekh-tin-ĕ) Mother of Cúchulainn, daughter of the druid Cathbad.

Deirdre (der-drĕ; *Ir.* Deirdriu = dayr-drŭ; cf. *ang.* deer-drĕ) Tragic princess in one of the best-known stories of the Ulster Cycle; lover of Noíse.

Deirgderc (dyer-ĕ-g-derk) Another name for the Dagda.

Demne Máel (dem-nă, dev-nă mayl) Childhood name of Fionn mac Cumhaill.

Deoch (dyokh) 'Princess of the South', i.e. Munster, who, it is prophesied, will marry a 'prince of the North', Lairgnéan, in the story of the children of Lir.

derbfhine (der-veen-ĕ)   The descendants of a common great-grandfather.

Derbforgaill (derv-or-ɣal)   Swan maiden tragically in love with Cúchulainn.

Dian Cécht (dee-ăn kaykh, dee-ĕn kekht, dee-ĕn haht)   The Irish god of healing; his children include Cian, Miach, Airmid and possibly Tuireann.

Diarmait mac Cerbaill (deer-mid, dee-ăr-mid mahk ker-vil)   Last pagan *ard-rí* of Ireland.

Diarmait Ua Duibne (deer-mid, dee-ăr-mid; ooă duv-nĕ, ooă dı-nĕ)   Member of the Fianna, lover of Gráinne.

díchetal do chennaib [extempore incantation (?)] (dikh-ĕd-ăl do khen-ăv)   Power of divination possessed by Fionn mac Cumhaill and others.

díguin (dyeeɣ-ĭn)   Irish legal concept that demands compensation to a king or high nobleman for someone killed while under his protection.

Dindshenchas (din-hen-é-kas, din-hɣen-kas)   Twelfth-century Irish document giving heroic and poetic associations of rivers, fords, lakes, hills all over Ireland. The title means 'lore of prominent places'.

Diorruing (dir-ing)   Fenian hero gifted with second sight or clairvoyance.

Dis Pater (dis pat-er)   Aspect of the Roman god Pluto, ruler of the dead and the underworld; Julius Caesar (first century BC) found Gaulish counterparts for him.

Dobar (dov-ăr)   'King of Sicily'; Tuireann's sons must retrieve his steeds.

Doilín (dil-een)   One of Máel Fhothartaig's two prize hounds.

Domnall Mildemail [the warlike] (dov-nal, doh-nal; mil-*th*ĕv-ıl)   Teacher of the martial arts whom Cúchulainn meets on the way to join Scáthach.

Domnu (dov-nŭ)   Fomorian goddess, perhaps mother of all the Fomorians, and certainly the mother of the warrior Indech.

Dôn (dohn)   Welsh mother goddess, mate of Beli Mawr. Among her children are Gwydion, Gofannon, Arianrhod and Gilfaethwy in the Fourth Branch of the *Mabinogi*.

Donn (don)   Brother of Congal who avenges his murder in the Máel Fhothartaig story.

Donn Cuailnge (don kool-en-ĕ)   Irish name for the Brown Bull of Ulster in the *Táin Bó Cuailnge*. Also known as Dub [dark].

Donn mac Míled (don mahk meel-*eth*)   Malevolent son of Míl among the Milesians.

Donn Tétscorach [abounding in furious horses (?)] (don tayd-skor-ăkh)   God of the dead and ruler of the otherworld among the Tuatha Dé Danann.

Dord Fían (dor*th* feeăn)   War cry of Fionn and the Fianna Éireann.

Dorn (dorn)   Princess and mother of an assassin, later made a slave by Fergus mac Léti.

Dornoll (**dorn**-ol)   Scottish druidess, martial arts instructor, smitten with her student Cúchulainn.

Druim Derg (drum **dyer**-ĕg)   Burial mound in Co. Meath of Fionn mac Cumhaill.

Druim Ligen (drum **ligh**-ĕn)   Site of a battle between the Milesians and Tuatha Dé Danann in Co. Donegal.

Dub [dark] (duv)   Another Irish name for Donn Cuailnge.

Dubh Sainglenn, also **Saingliu** (duv **sahnγ**-len)   Less favoured of Cúchulainn's two horses.

Dubros (**duv**-ros)   Forest in Co. Sligo, containing rowan trees whose berries Gráinne craves.

Dubthach Dóeltenga [chafer-tongued] (**duv**-thakh, **duff**-akh **doil**-dĕng-ă) Fractious member of the Ulster court.

Dún Aonghusa (doon eenγ-ŭs-ă; *ang.* dun **ang**-ŭs)   Imposing archaeological site on Inishmore in the Aran Islands, fancifully named for a Fir Bolg leader.

Dún Dá Benn (doon **daw** ben)   Fintan's fortress in what is now Co. Derry.

Dún Delgan (doon **dyel**-ghĕn)   Fort of Delga, a Fir Bolg or Fomorian king; a fortified hill two miles west of modern Dundalk, where Cúchulainn made his home.

Dún Rudraige (doon **rohr**-ee)   Sumptuous residence of Briccriu at what is now Dundrum, Co. Down.

Dún Scáith [fort of shadow/fear] (doon **skawth**)   Hades-like realm thought to be on the Isle of Man, visited by Irish heroes; also identified with Scottish Hebrides.

Dún Sobairche (doon **sov**-ir-khĕ)   Northernmost extent of Medb and Ailill's campaign to the east, probably coextensive with the ruined castle of Dunseverick, west of Ballycastle, Co. Antrim.

Dúnlang (**doon**-lang)   Father-in-law of Cormac mac Airt.

Dyfed (du-**vid**)   Medieval kingdom occupying much of southern Wales. The United Kingdom resurrected the name for a newly constituted county in 1974.

Dylan [ocean, wave] (du-**lahn**)   Welsh sea deity, brother of Lleu Llaw Gyffes.

Éber (ay-văr)   Son of Míl Espáine who divides Ireland with his brother Éremón.

Echtra . . . (ekh-trĕ)   Old Irish for 'adventure', conventional first word in titles of travel narratives of voyages to shadowy lands.

Efnisien [unpeaceful] (ev-**nis**-eeĕn)   Malevolent, jealous half-brother of Branwen.

éiric (er-ĭg) 'Honour price' or fine paid for killing a noble person.

Éis Énchenn (aysh aynkh-ĕn) Grotesque hag who confronts Cúchulainn.

Eisirt (esh-ĭrt) Court poet of the fairies in the thirteenth-century *Echtra Fergusa maci Léite.*

Eithne (ayn-yĕ, eth-nŭ) Of the many women bearing this name, one is the mother of Lug Lámfhota; another is an alternative name for Boand; a third, of Munster, is the mother of Máel Fhothartaig.

Eithne Ingubai (ayn-yĕ inγ-uv-ı) Sometime wife of Cúchulainn, perhaps identical with Emer.

Eithne Tháebfhota (ayn-yĕ thıv-ŏd-ă) Wife of Cormac mac Airt.

Elatha mac Delbaíth (al-ă-ha, el-ath-ă mahk dyel-vath) Fomorian king, father of Bres.

Elcmar (elk-var) Foster-father of Angus Óg.

Elphin, Elffin (elf-ĭn) Maladroit Welsh prince who finds the baby Taliesin.

Emain Ablach [*Ir.* fortress of apples] (ev-in ahv-lahkh) A pleasant other-worldly realm in Irish tradition, residence of Manannán mac Lir, possible refuge of the Tuatha Dé Danann; linguistic cognate of Arthurian Avalon.

Emain Macha (ev-in ma-khă, va-khă; *ModIr.* eyaw-in, aw-in ma-khă) Royal seat or capital of Ulster in the stories of the Ulster Cycle. Identified with the 18-acre hill fort in Co. Armagh known as Navan Fort.

Emer (ay-ver, ee-mĕr) Usual wife of Cúchulainn.

Eochaid Airem (yohkh-ee, oh-khee, ekh-i*th*; ar-rev, ah-rem) Mortal *ard rí* of Ireland, paired for a while with Étaín.

Eochaid Bélbuide [yellow mouth] (yohkh-ee, oh-khee, ekh-i*th* byayl-vuid-ĕ) Nobleman murdered while under the protection of Fergus mac Léti.

Eochaid Feidlech (yohkh-ee, oh-khee, ekh-i*th*; fayl-ekh, fe*th*-lekh) Yet another husband ascribed to Étaín.

Eochaid, Echaid Iarlaithe (yohkh-ee, oh-khee, ekh-i*th*, ekh-a*th* yar-lath-ĕ) King Rónán's father-in-law.

Eochaid Inber (yohkh-ee, oh-khee, ekh-i*th* in-vĕr) Fearsome enemy of Labraid Luathlám.

Eochaid Iúil (yohkh-ee, oh-khee, ekh-i*th* yoo-ĭl) Otherworldly adversary of Labraid Luathlám.

Eochaid mac Eirc (yohkh-ee, oh-khee, ekh-i*th* mahk ayrk) Generous king of the Fir Bolg; husband of Tailtiu.

Eochaid Ollathair (yohkh-ee, oh-khee, ekh-i*th* ohl-ă-thir) Another name for the Dagda.

Eógan Inbir (ohn, oh-ĕn, eohγ-ăn in-vĭr) Husband of Bé Chuma, cockolded by Gaidiar.

Eógan mac Durthacht (ohn, **oh**-ĕn, eohγ-ăn mahk **durth**-akht) Retainer of Conchobar who kills Noíse.

Eórann (oh-rahn) Wife of Suibne.

Epona (ay-**pohn**-ă) Horse goddess of early Britain and Gaul.

Erannán (er-**ahn**-awn, er-**ahn**-awn) Milesian sailor killed in the invasion of Ireland.

Erc (ayrk) Son of Cairbre Nia Fer who wreaks vengeance upon Cúchulainn.

Éremón (**ayr**-ă-vohn) Son of Míl Espáine who divides Ireland with his brother Éber.

Ériu (**ayr**-ĕ, ay-roo) Eponymous goddess of Ireland (Éire), selected from a trio of eponyms, including Banba and Fódla; also the mother of the hateful Bres.

Ernmass (**ern**-vas) Attributed mother of the trio of war goddesses, Badb, Macha and Mórrígan; also the mother of the divine eponyms of Ireland, Ériu, Banba, Fódla.

Esus (**es**-ŭs) A leading god of the ancient Gauls. His cult may have required human sacrifice.

Étaín (**ay**-deen, ay-deen, ay-**thoyn**) Paragon of Irish beauty; the love object in *Tochmarc Étaíne* [The Wooing of Étaín].

Étar (**ay**-tar, ay-dar) A king of Ulster; his wife swallows Étaín in insect form.

Etarcomol (ed-ar **kov**-ol) Headstrong fosterson of Medb and Ailill, killed by Cúchulainn.

Eterscél (ed-ir-**skayl**) A king of Tara who marries the daughter resulting from Étaín's daughter's incest with her father, Eochaid Airem.

Ethal Anbúail (**eth**-al ahn-**vooïl**) Connacht prince, father of Cáer.

Fachan (**fahkh**-an) Grotesque supernatural character in Scottish Gaelic folklore.

Failinis (**fahl**-ĭn-ĭsh) Puppy of King Iruad, sought by the sons of Tuireann.

Fálias (fah-lee-ăs) One of the four magical cities of the Tuatha Dé Danann, source of the Lia Fáil, the Stone of Destiny.

Fand (fon, fown, fan) Beautiful wife of Manannán mac Lir; has an extended affair with Cúchulainn.

Fedelm (**feth**-elm fed-elm) Mysterious prophetess who foresees 'Crimson' at the beginning of Medb's campaign against Ulster.

Fedelm Noíchrothach (**feth**-elm, fed-elm **noi**-khrith-ăkh) Sometimes cited as the wife of Lóegaire. She is the wife of Cairbre Nia Fer when Cúchulainn has an affair with her in the *Táin Bó Cuailnge*.

Fedlimid (**feth**-lee-meeth, fel-ĭ-mee, fel-lee-meed) Chief poet of Ulster; father of Deirdre.

Femen (**fev**-in) *Sídh* of Co. Tipperary, residence of Bodb Derg.

Féni (fayn-ee) The earliest free inhabitants of Ireland, thought to be the purest strain, 'pure Gaels'.

Fenian Cycle (feen-ee-ăn) Third cycle of early Irish heroic literature, centring on Fionn mac Cumhaill.

Fenians (feen-ee-ănz) Alternative name for nineteenth-century Irish Republican Brotherhood, a revolutionary body.

Fénius Farsaid (fayn-yus far-să) Fanciful ancestor of the Irish, thought to have been present at the Tower of Babel. Grandfather of Goídel Glas.

fenodyree, phynodderree, etc. (fen-**ohd**-ĕr-ee, fin-ohd-ĕr-ee) Hairy-legged solitary fairy of the Isle of Man; also known as the uddereek.

Fer Caille (fer **kahl**-yĕ) Hooded, fearsome churl in Irish heroic narrative and in later folklore.

Fer Doirich (fer dor-ĕkh) Druid who transforms Sadb into deer form.

Fer Gair, Fer Lí, Fer Rogain (fer ɣar, fer lee, fer roɣ-an) Foster-brothers of Conaire Mór who plunder the Irish countryside.

Fer Loga (fer loɣ-ă) Charioteer for Medb and Ailill.

Ferdia (fer-dee-ă) Murdered servant of Fionn mac Cumhaill.

Ferdiad (fer-dee-ăd, fer-dee-ăth, fer-dee-ă*th*) Friend of Cúchulainn who nonetheless duels with him in the climax of the *Táin Bó Cuailnge*.

Fergus Lethderg (fahr-ees, fer-ɣus, **fer**-gus leth-der-ĕg) A Nemedian hero.

Fergus mac Léti (fahr-ees, fer-ɣus, **fer**-gus mahk lay-dĭ) Mythical king of Ulster, probably a double for Fergus mac Róich.

Fergus mac Róich (fahr-ees, fer-ɣus, **fer**-gus; mahk **roh**-ikh, mahk roy) Ulster hero, often a lover of Medb; sent as an emissary to the fugitives Deirdre and Noíse.

Fiachra (fee-akh-ră) One of the swan children of Lir.

fianna (pl.), **fian** (sing.) (fee-ă-nă, fee-ăn) Bands of militia-like armed men, also trained in poetry, in early Ireland.

Fianna Éireann (fee-ăn-ă ayr-an) Fionn's fianna.

fidchell (*fith*-khel) Chess-like board-game of early Ireland.

filid (pl.) (fil-ee) Class of poets in early Ireland, below the status of the druid but above that of the bard. Comparable to the ancient *vates*.

Fin M'Coul Hiberno-English form for Fionn mac Cumhaill.

Find (find, fyund) Early Irish personification of wisdom, likely anticipation of Fionn mac Cumhaill.

Findchóem (fin-khoo-ĕm) Mother of Conall Cernach, foster-mother of Cúchulainn.

Findias (fin-dee-ăs) One of the four magical cities of the Tuatha Dé Danann.

Finnabair (fin-av-ir, fin-av-ăr, **fyun**-oor) Daughter of Medb and Ailill.

Finnachad (fin-akh-ă*th*, fin-eh-ee) Famous *sídh* of Co. Armagh, residence of Lir, father of the exiled children.

Finnbennach (fin-ven-ăkh) Irish name for the White-horned Bull of Connacht in the *Táin Bó Cuailnge*.

Finnbheara (finn-**vahr**-ă) King of the fairies in Irish folklore.

Finnéces (fin-**ay**-ges) Druid who hopes to catch the Salmon of Knowledge.

Finnguala (fun-oo-ăl-ă, fin-**ool**-ă) Eldest of the swan children of Lir and sometimes their spokesperson.

Fintan mac Bóchra (fin-tăn mahk **bohkh**-ră) 'Husband' of Cesair who flees his conjugal duties in the form of a salmon.

Fintan, son of Niall Noígiallach Foster-son of Conchobar who shares a third of Ulster with him and Cúchulainn, achronologically.

Fionn mac Cumhaill (fin, fyun, foon, fawn; mahk **koo**-il, mahk **kuv**-ăl; *ang.* fin mahk kool) Leading hero of the Fenian Cycle, father of Oisín, grandfather of Oscar; Hiberno-English: Fin M'Coul.

fios (fis) Name for Fionn's esoteric wisdom.

Fir Bolg (feer **bohl**-ĭg, feer **bul**-ĭg) The fourth invaders of early Ireland in *Lebor Gabála Érenn*.

Fir Fálgae (fee **fawl**-γě) Warriors who contend with Cúchulainn and Cú Roí while they are in Scotland; speciously associated with the Isle of Man.

Fódla (**foh**-lă) One of the three eponymous goddesses of Ireland, along with Banba and Ériu, met by the invading Milesians; later an alternative poetic name for Ireland.

Follamain (fol-ă-măn) Leader of the martial boys' corps at Emain Macha.

Fomorians (fo-**mohr**-ee-ăns; cf. *Ir.* Fomoire = fuv-**oh**-rě) Malevolent euhemerized deities of the Irish pseudo-history, *Lebor Gabála Érenn*.

Forgall Manach (**fohr**-gal mahn-ăkh) Wily father of Emer; Cúchulainn's father-in-law.

Fothad Conainne (fu-hă **kon**-in-γě) Fenian warrior, a lover of the Cailleach Bhéirre.

Frecraid (**freg**-ră) Usual sword of Lug Lámfhota.

Friuch [boar's thistle] (**fryukh**) Swineherd whose squabble with his friend Rucht transforms them both into bulls. Friuch becomes Donn Cuailnge, the Brown Bull of Cooley.

Fuamnach (foo-am-năkh, **foo**-av-năkh) Jealous wife of Midir; changes Étaín into an insect.

Furbaide (**fur**-va*th*-ě) Son of Conchobar, foster-son of Cúchulainn, whose wailing chant helps to bring peace.

Furbaide Ferbend (fur-va*th*-ĕ fer-ven*th*)   Son of Clothra who avenges his mother's death by slaying his aunt Medb.

Gabalglinde (gav-ăl-γlin-*th*ĕ)   Blind seer at Temuir Luachra.

Gáe Assail (gay as-al)   Mighty spear of Lug Lámfhota.

Gáe Bulga (gay bool-gă, bul-gă)   Lethal spear of Cúchulainn, thrust with the foot.

gaesatae (gay-sat-ay)   Armed men in Gaulish times who protected populations of which they were not a part: possible anticipations of the fianna.

Gaidiar (ga*th*-yăr)   Son of Manannán mac Lir who commits adultery with Bé Chuma.

Gáirech or **Irgairech** (gaw-rĕkh, ir-gaw-rĕkh)   Site of the last battle in the *Táin Bó Cuailnge*, southwest of Mullingar in Co. Westmeath.

Gamel (gam-ăl, gav-ĕl)   Co-gatekeeper, with Camel, of Tara.

Gaulish Apollo One of several Gaulish gods known by classical names through *interpretatio Romana*; see under Apollo.

geis, (pl.) **gessa** (gesh, ges-ă)   The idiosyncratic taboo or prohibition placed upon heroes and prominent persons in early Irish narratives. The *geis* may be placed capriciously or unfairly, but breaking it can bring death or other calamity.

Genevra (jen-ev-ră)   Daughter of Tom, the Cornish giant.

gente buena [good people] (hen-tay bwayn-ă)   A name for the Asturian fairy procession.

Gilfaethwy (gil-vı*th*-wee)   Brother of Gwydion, rapist of Goewin.

Giraldus Cambrensis (jeer-**ahld**-ŭs kam-**bren**-sis)   Twelfth-century Welsh cleric and travel writer, known especially for closely observed but disdainful comments about Ireland.

Glen Bolcáin (glen **bolg**-awn)   Valley of the madmen, perhaps in both Counties Antrim and Kerry.

Glenasmole [*ModIr. Glean na smóil*: glen of the thrush, ember, small flame] (**glen**-ăs-mohl)   Glen at the headwaters of the Dodder River, in South Co. Dublin.

Glewlwyd Galfaelfawr (gloo-**loo**-eed gal-**vıl**-vawr)   Arthur's rude porter who deters Culhwch.

Glwyddyn Saer (gloo-*eth*-en sır)   Shadowy Welsh folk figure, a patron of the crafts.

Glyn Cuch [glen scowl] (glen kikh)   Valley where Pwyll meets and strikes a bargain with Arawn.

Goewin (goi-win)   Beautiful virgin foot-holder of King Math in the Fourth Branch of the *Mabinogi*.

Gofannon (go-**vahn**-ŏn)   Welsh divine smith, one of the children of Dôn.

Goibniu (gɪv-noo, giv-noo, gwiv-nĕ, gwiv-new)   Smith of the Tuatha Dé Danann.

Goídel Glas (gwith-ĕl, gɪth-ăl glahs)   Inventor of the Irish language, according to *Lebor Gabála Érenn*.

Goleuddydd (go-lɪth-eth)   Mother of Culhwch.

Goll mac Doilb (gul, gol mahk dolv)   Sometimes named as ruler of Mag Mell.

Goll mac Morna (gul, gol, mahk **mohr**-nă)   One-time adversary of Fionn mac Cumhaill who becomes his ally.

Goreu (gohr-ɪ)   Member of Culhwch's party who decapitates the giant Ysbaddaden.

Gorias (gohr-eeas)   One of the four magical cities of the Tuatha Dé Danann.

Gradlon (grahd-lon)   Virtuous king of Quimper, father of the debauched Dahut.

Gráinne (grahn-yă, grawn-yă)   Daughter of Cormac mac Airt, lover of Diarmait. She rejects Fionn, is pursued by him and later united with him.

Grampian Line (gramp-eean)   Range of mountains separating the Scottish Highlands from the Lowlands.

Grey of Macha (mahk-ă)   Cúchulainn's horse.

Gronw Pebyr (grahn-oo peb-eer)   Adulterer with Blodeuedd who plots to kill her husband Lleu.

Guaire (goo-ah-ir-ĕ)   One of many figures to bear this name becomes the lover of Eórann.

Guénolé (gwayn-ohl-ay)   Fifth-century ecclesiastic, cited in the 'Legend of the City of Ys'.

Gundestrup Cauldron (gun-des-trup)   Large silver vessel, richly decorated with Celtic art, named for place where found in Denmark but made elsewhere.

Gwawl (gooawl)   Suitor of Rhiannon favoured by her father but humiliated by Pwyll; a son of Clud.

Gwent Is Coed (gwent is koid)   Small, historical kingdom in what is now southeastern Wales. The child Pryderi, then known as Gwri, was raised here.

Gwern (gwern)   Child of the Welsh princess Branwen and the Irish king Matholwch.

Gwion Bach (gwee-on bahkh)   Name of the servant who is transformed into Taliesin.

Gwrhyr Gwastad Ieithoedd (goo-rheer gwas-tad ee-ɪth-oith)   Welsh member of King Arthur's court, an interpreter.

Gwri (goo-ree)   Substitute name for Pryderi while he is raised in exile.

Gwyddno Garanhir (gweeth-no gah-rahn-hir) Mythical Welsh ruler in whose realm baby Taliesin lands; father of Elphin.

Gwydion (gwid-eeon) Magician father of Lleu Llaw Gyffes who fashions Blodeuedd for him.

Gwyn Fryn [white mound] **(gwin vrin)** Hill near London where Bendigeidfran's severed head is placed.

Gwyn Gogoyw (gwin goh-goi-oo) Father of Cigfa, wife of Pryderi.

Gwynedd (gwin-eth) The medieval kingdom occupying northwest Wales; the reconstituted (1974) county that encompasses much of that kingdom.

Gwynn ap Nudd (gwin ap neth) King of the fairies, tylwyth teg, in Welsh tradition.

Hafgan [summer white] **(hav-gan)** Rival and enemy of Arawn, killed by Pwyll.

Hallstatt (hahl-shtaht) Style of earliest Celtic art, c.800–450 BC, named for archaeological site in Austria; often severely geometrical.

Harlech (hahr-lĕkh) Coastal town of north Wales, seat of Bendigeidfran.

Hebrides (heb-rid-ees) Islands off the west coast of Scotland.

Hesperides, Apples of (hes-payr-ĭ-dees) One of Heracles' twelve labours, reassigned to the sons of Tuireann.

Hochdorf (hohkh-dohrf) Site in southwestern Germany of a sixth-century BC burial of a wealthy Gaulish chieftain.

huestia [host] **(west-ee-ă)** A name for the Asturian fairy procession.

Hy Brasil (hɪ brahs-ĭl) An earthly paradise seen on the oceanic horizon west of Ireland.

Hychdwn Hir [tall piglet] **(hekh-doon heer)** Porcine offspring of a transformed Gwydion and Gilfaethwy.

Hyddwn (huth-oon) A fawn, offspring of the transformed Gwydion and Gilfaethwy.

Hywel Dda (hu-weel thă) Historical tenth-century Welsh king and law-giver.

Ibormeith [*Ir.* yew berry] **(iv-or-veth)** Nickname of Cáer, lover of Angus Óg.

imbas forosnai [poetic knowledge that illuminates] **(im-bas for-os-nɪ)** Power of divination possessed by Fionn mac Cumhaill and others.

Imbolc (in-bohlg, im-bohl-ĭk) Celtic winter festival, approximately 1 February on the modern calendar, later subsumed in St Brigit's Day.

Imram, Immram ... **(im-rahv)** Old Irish for 'rowing about', conventional first word in titles of travel narratives of visits to distant islands inhabited by human beings.

Ingcél Cáech (ing-gayl kɪkh) One-eyed British pirate who ravages Ireland.

Inis Fionnchuire (in-ĭsh **fyun**-kheer-ĕ)   Imagined island between Ireland and Britain; the sons of Tuireann must retrieve its cooking spit.

Iolo Morganwg (eeohl-oh mohr-**gahn**-oog)   Pseudonym of Edward Williams (1747–1826), poet, antiquarian and inventor of Welsh traditions such as the *gorsedd*.

Iona (ĭ-ohn-ă)   Island in the Inner Hebrides, site of the first Christian monastery founded by St Colum Cille.

Ír (eer)   Milesian sailor killed in the invasion of Ireland, one of many eponyms for Ireland.

Iraird Cuillen (ir-ard k[w]il-ĕn)   Site where Cúchulainn leaves his first warning to Medb's army, coextensive with the modern village of Crossakeel, Co. Meath.

Iseult (ĭ-**soolt**)   Lover of Tristan in the Arthurian legends.

Íth (eeth)   Milesian leader who sees Ireland from a high point in Spain; he is killed when leading an exploratory party to Ireland.

Iubdán (yuv-*th*awn)   King of the fairies in the thirteenth-century *Echtra Fergusa maic Léite*.

Iuchair (yukh-ar)   One of the three tragic sons of Tuireann.

Iucharba (yukh-ăr-vă)   One of the three tragic sons of Tuireann.

Jack Cornish giant; compared to Lug Lámfhota in 'Giants of Morvah'.

Joan Wife of Tom, the Cornish giant.

Keating, Geoffrey (*c*.1580–*c*.1645/50)   Irish-language historian, priest and poet. Irish name: Séathrún Céitinn (shah-**hroon** kɪ-tin, **kay**-tin)

Kêr Is (kayr ees)   Breton title for the 'Legend of the City of Ys'.

Kernow (**ker**-now)   Cornish name for Cornwall.

Knockmany (nok-**mahn**-ee)   Hill, 770 ft, near Augher, Co. Tyrone. Site of a passage-tomb but best known for citations in William Carleton (1794–1869).

korrigan (kohr-ee-gahn)   A lusty creature of Breton folklore, also adept at building.

Kristof (**krist**-ohf)   Small boy who removes the protective oak from the City of Ys.

La Tène (lah **ten**)   Style of Celtic art, *c*.500–200 BC and after, named for archaeological site in Switzerland; known for swirling patterns.

Labraid Luathlám ar Claideb (**lav**-ree, **lav**-ră; **loo**-ăth-lawm ar klɪ*th*-ĕv)   [Ir. swift hand on sword] Ruler of Mag Mell, husband of the beautiful Lí Ban.

Láeg (loygh)   Charioteer of Cúchulainn.

Lailoken (lɪ-loh-kĕn)   Scottish wild man of the woods.

Lallans (lal-ănz)   The language of the Scottish Lowlands, related to English.

Landévennec (lahn-day-ven-ĕk) Oldest abbey in Brittany, founded fifth century, 25 miles northwest of Quimper.

lavandeira nocturna [night washer] (lahv-ahn-**dayr**-ă nohk-**toorn**-ă) A Galician counterpart of the Irish and Scottish Gaelic washer at the ford.

Lebor Buide Lecáin (lev-or; ModIr. **lyow**-er; bui*th*-ĕ lek-awn) Early codex of Irish literature, compiled *c.*1390. Known in English as the *Yellow Book of Lecan*. Contains an early version of the *Táin Bó Cuailnge*.

Lebor Gabála (lev-or ga-vawl-ă; ModIr. *Leabhar Gabhála* = **lyow**-er ga-**wawl**-ă) The Irish pseudo-history.

Lebor Laignech (lev-or, ModIr. **lyow**-er; **lagh**-nekh) Twelfth-century codex of Irish literature. Known in English as *The Book of Leinster*.

Lebor na hUidre (lev-or; ModIr. **lyow**-er; nah **huth**-rĕ) Earliest codex of Irish literature, compiled before 1106. Known in English as *The Book of the Dun Cow*.

Leborcham (lowr-khahv, lev-or-khav) Poet and confidante of Deirdre.

Lairgnéan (largh-nay-ăn) 'Prince of the North', i.e. Connacht, who is prophesied to marry a 'Princess of the South', Deoch, in the story of the children of Lir.

Lendabair (len*th*-ăv-ar) Wife of Conall Cernach.

leprechaun (lep-rĕ-khawn) Solitary fairy, first seen as a water-sprite in the eighth-century *Echtra Fergusa maic Léite*.

Lí Ban [Ir. paragon of women] (lee von, lee bon) Woman of formidable beauty who seeks Cúchulainn's help in fighting the enemies of her husband Labraid Luathlám ar Claídeb.

Liath Macha [Grey of Macha] (lee-ăth, ModIr. lee-ă; **mahkh**-ă) The more favoured of Cúchulainn's two horses.

Liffey (lif-ee) River of eastern Ireland that runs through what is now Dublin.

Linn Féic [Fiac's pool] (lin **fayg**) Spot along the River Boyne where Finnéces waits for the Salmon of Knowledge.

Lir (lir) Tuatha Dé Danann king, father of the swan children; not identical with the Lir implied in the patronymic of Manannán mac Lir.

Llassar Llaes Gyfnewid (*ll*ahs-ăr *ll*ıs guv-nyoo-ĭd) Original possessor of the cauldron of regeneration; husband of Cymidei Cymeinfoll.

Lleu Llaw Gyffes (*ll*ı *ll*ow guf-es) Welsh hero, central figure of the Fourth Branch of the *Mabinogi*. Often compared with the Irish Lug.

Lloegyr (*ll*oi-gur) Welsh name for England.

Llwyd (*ll*ooeed) The enchanter who destroys the vegetation of southern Wales to avenge his friend Gwawl.

Llŷr (*ll*eer) Shadowy father of Bendigeidfran, Manawydan and Branwen.

Loch Rudraige (lokh **roo**-ăr-ee) Dundrum Bay, Co. Down.

Lochlainn (lokh-lahn)   Realm of dangerous invaders, often but not necessarily associated with Scandinavia.

Lóegaire Búadach [victorious, triumphant] (**loygh**-ĭ-rĕ, **lay**-ghee-rĕ, **lay**γ-ăr-ĕ, **lee**-rĕ; **boo**-ăkh)   Ulster hero who competes for the champion's portion with Conall and Cúchulainn.

Loingsechán (lin-shahkh-awn, **ling**-shahkh-awn)   Loyal friend of Suibne, possibly a half-brother or foster-brother.

Lomna (lum-nă, **lov**-nă)   Name borne by several fools in Irish literature, one of Conaire Mór, another of Fionn mac Cumhaill.

lón láith [light of the hero(?)] (lohn law)   Name for the beam of light that projects from the head of Cúchulainn.

Lough Derraverragh [*dairbhreach*: with an oak plantation] (lok, loch **der**-a-ver-ă)   Lake in what is now Co. Westmeath where the children of Lir were changed into swans.

Lough Lein (lok, loch layn)   A lake near Killarney, Co. Kerry.

Luchta (lukh-tă)   Carpenter god of the Tuatha Dé Danann.

Lug Lámfhota   [Long handed; of the long arm] (loo **lawv**-ohd-ă)   A chief of the Tuatha Dé Danann and leading hero of the Mythological Cycle. Often compared to the Welsh Lleu.

Lugaid (Looy-ă)   Son of Cú Roí who seeks vengeance upon Cúchulainn.

Lughnasa (loo-nă-să)   (*OldIr.* Lugnasad; *ModIr.* Lúnasa)   Celtic summer festival, approximately 1 August or 15 August on modern calendar.

Lugus, Lugos (loog-ŭs)   Likely Gaulish name for the god whom the Romans called Gaulish Mercury.

Mabon (mah-bon)   Abducted child of divine origin in the story of *Culhwch and Olwen*.

MacAlpin, Kenneth   See Cináed mac Alpín.

Mac an Lúin (mahk an **loon**)   Sword of Fionn mac Cumhaill.

Mac Cécht, Mac Cuill, Mac Gréine (mahk **kaykht**, mahk **kul**, mahk **grayn**-ĕ)   Three Tuatha Dé Danann kings who negotiate with invading Milesians. A hero named Mac Cécht is Conaire Mór's champion at Da Derga's Hostel.

Mac Da Thó (mahk **dah** thoh)   Host whose guests fight over the division of his huge pig.

Mac Glass (mahk **glahs**)   King Rónán's unfortunate jester.

Macha (mahkh-ă)   Ulster sovereignty goddess who appears in three manifestations, all linked with the establishment of Emain Macha; part of the trio Mórrígna with Badb and Mórrígan. (i) Ulster queen also known as Mong Ruadh. (ii) Queen of the Nemedians. (iii) Wife of Crunniuc who wins the footrace.

Macsen Wledig (**mahk**-sen oo-**led**-ig)   Roman emperor who, according to Welsh legend, favoured British migration to Brittany.

Máel Dúin (mayl doon)   Irish wayfarer to the otherworld in the eighth- to tenth-century narrative, *Imram Curaig Maíle Dúin* [The Voyage of Máel Duin's Boat].

Máel Fhothartaig (mayl **oth**-ar-dagh)   Handsome son of king Rónán, killed by his father.

Maelgwn Gwynedd (**mil**-goon **gwin**-*eth*)   Historical sixth-century Welsh king in whose reign the fanciful adventures of Taliesin take place.

Mag Dá Cheó [*Ir.* plain of two mists] (magh, maγ, *ModIr.* moi; daw khyoh)   Actual plain in Co. Roscommon, south of Medb's fortress of Cruachain.

Mag Mell [*Ir.* pleasant plain] (magh, maγ, *ModIr.* moi; mel)   An otherworldly realm in Irish tradition, a possible refuge for the Tuatha Dé Danann.

Mag Muirtheimne (magh, maγ, **mur**-hev-nĕ, **mur**-thev-nĕ)   Cúchulainn's home territory, a plain occupying much of present-day Co. Louth.

Mag Rath (magh, maγ, *ModIr.* moi; rath)   Scene of an Irish dynastic battle, AD 637, where Suibne goes mad.

Mag Slécht (magh, *ModIr.* moi shlaykht)   Plain in Co. Cavan, near present town of Ballymagauran thought to be site of worship of Crom Crúaich, perhaps a pagan idol.

Mag Tuired (*ang.* **Moytura**). (magh, maγ, *ModIr.* moi; **tur**-*eth*)   Old Irish name for at least two expanses of flat land in northwestern Ireland; one was the site of the battle between the Tuatha Dé Danann and the Fomorians in *Cath Maige Tuired* [The (Second) Battle of Mag Tuired].

Maignis (moy-**nay**-ish)   One of many wives of Fionn mac Cumhaill, reported deceased before he seeks out Gráinne.

Maine (**mah**-nyĕ, **mah**-nĕ)   Name borne by each of the seven sons of Medb and Ailill mac Máta.

Malaliach (mal-ăl-yakh)   A Partholonian thought to have brewed the first ale in Ireland.

Manannán mac Lir (mahn-**ahn**-awn, **mah**-naw-**nahn** mahk lir)   Principal sea-deity and otherworldly ruler in Irish tradition.

Manapii (mahn-ap-ee-ee)   A P-Celtic people of ancient Gaul.

Manawydan (mah-nah-**wud**-an)   Title character and protagonist of the Third Branch of the *Mabinogi*.

Manching (**mahn**-ching)   Fortified proto-city of the Vindelici people near what is today Ingolstadt, Bavaria. Its circular wall is four miles long.

Marie de France   Twelfth-century Anglo-Norman writer who introduced Breton *lai*.

Mark King of Cornwall in the Arthurian legends, betrothed of Iseult.

Math (mahth) King of Gwynedd, brother of Dôn, and a leading figure in the Fourth Branch of the *Mabinogi*.

Matholwch (math-**ohl**-ookh) The King of Ireland in the Second Branch of the *Mabinogi*.

Mathonwy (mahth-**ohn**-wee) Father of Math.

Matrona (mah-**trohn**-ă) Gaulish goddess of the Marne River in what is now eastern France.

Matroniae Aufuniae (mah-**trohn**-eeay owf-**oon**-eeay) Probably divine mother figures whose second-century icon survives in what is now Germany.

Medb (mayv, me*th*v) Vibrant warrior queen of Connacht (western Ireland) and a protagonist of the *Táin Bó Cuailnge*.

Mellifont Abbey (mel-ĭ-font) First Cistercian abbey in Ireland, founded 1142, 4.5 miles west-northwest of Drogheda, Co. Louth.

Men-an-Tol [holed stone] (**men**-an-tol) Annular standing stone at Morvah, Cornwall.

Menw (men-oo) Welsh member of King Arthur's court, an illusionist.

Mercury, Gaulish Name given by the Romans to the principal Gaulish divinity; probable name Lugus/Lugos.

Merlin Arthurian sorcerer, anticipated by the Welsh Myrddin (G)wyllt.

Mes Buachalla [cowherd's fosterling] (mes boo-ahkh-**ahl**-ă) Mother of Conaire Mór.

Miach (mee-akh) An Irish healing god, son of Dian Cécht.

Midac (mi*th*-ag) Adversary of the Fianna Éireann from Lochlainn.

Mide (mee*th*-ě) A kingdom of early Ireland, coextensive with Co. Meath and portions of neighbouring counties; it is named for the druid Mide, who lit the first fire at Uisnech.

Midir (mi*th*-ĭr, mid-ĭr, mĭ-yir, meer) Lover of the beautiful Étaín, much to the anger of his jealous wife, Fuamnach.

Míl Espáine (meel es-**pawn**-ě) 'Soldier of Spain', the leader of the Milesians, for whom they are named.

Milesians (mil-ees-yanz) The last and certainly mortal invaders of Ireland in *Lebor Gabála Érenn*; sometimes seen as synonymous with the early Gaelic people.

Miodhchaoin (mi*γ*-kheen) Chief who owns a hill in Lochlainn; the Sons of Tuireann have their most dangerous task here.

Mo Cháemóc (mu kh*ı*v-ohg) Disciple of St Patrick who baptizes the 900-year-old children of Lir.

Modron (**mohd**-rawn) Mother of Mabon in Welsh tradition, derived from the ancient goddess Matrona.

Moling, Mo Ling, St (mu-ling) One of the 'Four Prophets of Ireland', thought to have baptized mad Suibne.

Mongán (mong-awn) Historical early king in Ireland thought to have been sired by a liaison between his mortal mother, Caíntigern, and the sea god Manannán mac Lir. Sometimes thought to be a reincarnation of Fionn mac Cumhaill.

Mór Muman (mohr muv-ăn, moon) Early territorial goddess of Munster.

Morann (mohr-ahn, mur-ăn) Son of the usurper Cairbre Cinn-Chait who returns sovereignty to the Milesians.

Morfran (mohr-vrahn) Ugly son of Ceridwen.

Mórrígan (mohr-ee-ghan, mohr-ĭ-ɣan, mohr-ee-ĕn) The 'great queen', goddess of war fury in early Ireland; often named with the definite article, 'the Mórrígan'; one of the trio Mórrígna with Badb and Macha.

Mórrígna (mohr-eegh-nă) Collective name for the trio of war goddesses, Badb, Macha, Mórrígan.

Morvah (mor-vah) Archaeological site in western Cornwall, known for distinctive standing stones.

Morvarc'h [horse of the sea] (mohr-vahrkh) Gradlon's mighty steed.

mouros (moh-ros) Galician fairy folk associated with hidden treasure.

Moytura See Mag Tuired.

Mugain (muɣ-ahn, moon, moo-gahn) Lubricious wife of Conchobar mac Nessa, who bares her breasts to tempt Cúchulainn.

muirdris (mur-drish) Generic name for the sea monster of Loch Rudraige; later known as *sínach*.

Muirenn Mancháem (mir-en mun-khɪv) Mother of Fionn mac Cumhaill.

Murias (moor-eeas) One of the four magical cities of the Tuatha Dé Danann.

Myrddin (G)wyllt (mirth-ĭn [g]wiłlt) Wild man of the woods in Welsh tradition, an anticipation of the Arthurian Merlin.

Naísi Alternative spelling for Noíse.

Nantosuelta (nahn-tŏ-swel-tă) Cult partner of the Gaulish divinity, Sucellus.

Nechta Scéne (nekh-tă, nahkh-tă shkayn-ĕ) Mother of three supernatural sons who fight for Connacht and are killed by Cúchulainn the day he takes up arms.

Nechtan (1) (nahkht-ăn, nekh-tawn) Usual husband of Boand.

Nechtan (2) (nahkht-ăn, nekh-tawn) Sailor on Máel Dúin's otherwordly voyage who longs to return to the land of mortals.

Néit (nayd) Irish war god; cult partner of Nemain.

Nemain (nev-in) Irish war goddess; cult partner of Néit. May share identity with Badb.

Nemedians (nĕ-**meed**-ee-ans; cf. *Ir. Nemed*: nev-*ĕth*)   Third invaders of Ireland in *Lebor Gabála Érenn.*

Nemetona (ne-me-**tohn**-ă)   Shadowy Gaulish and British war goddess, a cult partner of Gaulish Mars.

Ness (nes)   Manipulative mother of Conchobar mac Nessa.

Newgrange   Passage-grave dating from *c.*3200 BC in the Boyne valley, five miles east of Slane, Co. Meath.

Niall Noígiallach (**nee**-al noi-γeeal-ăkh, noi-γahl-ăkh)   Niall of the Nine Hostages, probably historical fifth-century Irish king, eponym of the Uí Néill dynasty that dominated early Ireland.

Niam (1) (**nee**ăv, neev, cf. *ang.* **nee**ăm)   Beautiful maiden who lures Oisín to Tír na nÓg.

Niam (2) (**nee**ăv, neev, cf. *ang.* **nee**ăm)   Wife of Conall Cernach, mistress of Cúchulainn.

Nisien [peaceful] (**nis**-eean, **nis**yen)   Gentle, generous half-brother of Branwen.

Nodons (**noh**-dons)   Early British god worshipped at the healing sanctuary of Lydney Park, Gloucestershire.

Noíse (**nee**-shĕ)   Lover of Deirdre.

Nuadu Airgetlám [of the Silver Hand/Arm] (**noo**ă, **noo**-ă-hă, **noo**-ah*th*-ŭ ar-gad-lahv)   Wounded king of the Tuatha Dé Danann.

Nuadu Necht (**noo**ă, **noo**-ă-hă, **noo**-ah*th*-ŭ nekht)   Leinster double of Nuadu Airgetlám.

Nudd (ni*th*)   Legendary Welsh hero, one of the most generous men of Wales.

Ó Duibhgeannáin, Dáibhí (*ModIr.* oh **dayg**-nawn, oh **div**-ghan-awn, **dawv**-ee)   Scholar (d. 1696) who composed the manuscript version of the Diarmait and Gráinne story in 1651.

ogham, ogam (**oh**-ăm, ohm, oh*γ*-ăm)   An alphabet of incised parallel lines used to write early Irish; each figure is the equivalent of a Latin alphabet letter.

Ogma (o*γ*-mă, **ohm**-ă, ohm)   An orator and warrior, one of the three principal champions of the Tuatha Dé Danann, along with the Dagda and Lug Lámfhota.

Ogmios (**ohg**-mee-ŏs)   Gaulish god of eloquence.

Oisín (**ush**-een)   Son of Fionn mac Cumhaill of the Fenian Cycle; adapted by James Macpherson as Ossian (1760–4); father of Oscar; Hiberno-English: Usheen.

ollam (**ol**-av)   Poet of highest rank in early Ireland.

Olwen (**ohl**-wen)   Beautiful lover of Culhwch.

Oonagh (oon-ă) 'Wife' of Fin M'Coul in William Carleton's 'Legend of Knockmany' (*c.*1845).

Orlám (or-lawv) Son of Medb and Ailill killed early in the action of the *Táin Bó Cuailnge*.

Oscar (usk-ăr; cf. *ang.* osk-ăr) Hero of the Fenian Cycle, son of Oisín, grandson of Fionn mac Cumhaill.

Ossian (os-ee-ăn, osh-ăn) Adapted from Oisín by James Macpherson and made narrator of *The Poems of Ossian* (1760–4), bogusly claimed to be based on ancient texts.

Owain ap Urien (oh-wɪn ap eer-eean) Sixth-century Welsh king eulogized by Taliesin.

P-Celts Division of Celtic family of languages, including Gaulish, ancient British, Welsh, Cornish and Breton.

Partholonians (par-thoh-lohn-eeănz; cf. *Ir.* Parthalán = por-hu-lawn) The second invaders of early Ireland in *Lebor Gabála Érenn*; an industrious and beneficent people.

Patrick, St The fifth-century evangelist of Ireland is depicted in the Fenian Cycle as holding dialogues with pre-Christian survivors, Caílte and Oisín.

Pisear (pish-ăr) A 'king of Persia', original owner of Gáe Assail, retrieved by the sons of Tuireann.

pixie Mischievous folk creature, derived from the Cornish piskie.

Polybius (po-lib-ee-ŭs) Second-century BC Greek historian, commentator on the Celts.

Pryderi (prŭ-der-ee) Son of Rhiannon and Pwyll who appears in all four branches of the *Mabinogi*.

Ptolemy, Claudius Ptolemeus (tol-em-ee, klawd-eeus tol-em-ay-us) Important geographer of the ancient world, second century AD.

Puck Playful figure in English folklore, also in Shakespeare's *Midsummer Night's Dream*.

***púca*, pooka (pook-ă)** One of many Irish fairies.

Pwyll (pooi*ll*) Prince of Dyfed, south Wales, who falls in love with Rhiannon.

Q-Celts Division of Celtic family of languages, including Irish, Scottish Gaelic and Manx.

Redg (reth-ĕgh) Satirist of Medb and Ailill, killed by Cúchulainn, who jokes in death throes.

Reinheim (rɪn-hɪm) Burial site on the French–German border of a well-born fifth-century BC woman.

***remscéla* (rev-shkayl-ă)** Foretales, e.g. the tales found at the beginning of the *Táin Bó Cuailnge*, that anticipate, if not introduce, the beginning of the action in the epic.

Rhiannon (rhee-**ahn**-ŏn)   A female protagonist of the *Mabinogi*; portrayed as a mortal with suggestions of immortal antecedents.

Rhun (rhin)   Casanovian Welsh prince.

ríastrad (reeăs-tra*th*)   Name for Cúchulainn's empowering battle frenzy or fury, sometimes called warp spasm.

Richis (rikh-ish)   Female satirist of Munster who strips naked before Cúchulainn in a failed attempt to have him killed.

rigfhéinnid (rig-**hayn**-i*th*)   Captain or chief of a fianna.

Rígru Rosclethan (**righ**-rŭ ros-**kleth**-ăn)   Wife of Dáire and queen of the otherworldly realm of Tír Tairngire.

Robin Goodfellow   Playful spirit in English folklore; also known as Puck.

Roca Barraidh (**rohk**-ră **bar**-ră)   Scottish Gaelic name for an otherworldly realm lying near the Isle of Barra in the Outer Hebrides.

Rónán (**rohn**-ahn)   Fictional Leinster king who kills his son Máel Fhothartaig, probably based on the historical Rónán mac Aeda.

Rónán, St (**rohn**-ahn)   Evangelizing clergyman who curses Suibne.

Rosmerta (rohs-**mert**-ă)   Gaulish fertility goddess often linked with Apollo.

Ruad Rofhessa (roo-ă roh-es-ă, roo-ă*th* rohs-ă)   Another name for the Dagda.

Ruadchoin (rooă*th*-khon)   Brigands banished by Conaire Mór.

Rucht [boar's grunt] (rukht)   Swineherd whose squabble with his friend Friuch turns them both into bulls. Rucht becomes Finnbennach, the White-horned Bull of Connacht.

Sadb (sɪv, soy-ĭv)   The deer maiden, sleeps with Fionn mac Cumhaill to become the mother of Oisín.

Saingliu   See Dubh Sainglenn.

Sainrith mac Imaith (**san**-rith makh **iv**-ahth)   Mother of the Macha who wins the footrace at Emain Macha.

Saint   See under Saint's name, Brendan, Brigid, Patrick, etc.

Salmon of Knowledge   Swims in either the Boyne or Erne River. Fionn mac Cumhaill receives esoteric knowledge by touching the salmon with his thumb.

Samain (sow-ĭn, sa-vĭn)   Celtic New Year, 1 November on modern calendar.

Samildánach (saw-vil-**dawn**-ăkh, sahv-ĭl-**dahn**-ăkh)   'Master of all the arts', an epithet of Lug Lámfhota.

Santa Compaña [Holy Company] (**sahn**-tă kohm-**pahn**-yă)   The Galician fairy procession.

Scáthach (**skaw**-thakh, **skow**-hă)   Cúchulainn's amazon-like teacher of martial arts, living on the Isle of Skye

Sceolang (**skeeoh**-lahng, **shkeeoh**-lahng)   One of Fionn mac Cumhaill's favoured dogs; the other is Bran.

Scota (skoh-tă) Daughter of the Pharaoh of Egypt who gives her name to the Scoti in *Lebor Gabála Érenn*.

Scoti (skot-ĭ) Ancestors of the Irish who dwelt in Egypt, according to *Lebor Gabála Érenn*.

Scotia (skohsh-ee-ă) Roman name for Ireland, especially northern Ireland; after seventh century AD, Scotland.

Scotti (skot-tĭ) One of several Roman names for the early Irish.

Scythia (sith-ee-ă, sith-ee-ă) A historical land north of the Black Sea, coextensive with Ukraine, an object of fanciful speculation on Celtic origins in early Ireland.

Searbhán (shahr-vawn) Ugly churl who guards the rowanberries of Dubros.

Ségda Sárlbraid (shayg-thă sawrl-vră) Prince of the otherworldly realm of Tír Tairngire.

Sein (sen) Island off west coast of Brittany, home to pagan sisterhood.

Senach Siaborthe (shahn-ahkh shav-orth-ě) Otherwordly adversary of Labraid Luathlám.

Sencha mac Ailella (shahn-khă, shen-hă mahk al-el-ă) Conchobar's chief judge, the usual peacemaker in the Ulster court.

Senchán Torpéist (shahn-khawn tor-baysht) Chief poet of Ireland, who copied down the *Táin Bó Cuailnge* from the dictation of the spirit of Fergus mac Róich.

Sequana (se-kwahn-ă) Gaulish healing goddess associated with the river Seine.

Sétanta (shay-dan-dă) Birth name of Cúchulainn.

Setantii (say-tahnt-ee-ee) A P-Celtic people of ancient northwest Britain.

Shannon Principal river of Ireland, running north to south, dividing the island between east and west.

Sheela-na-gig (shee-lă nă gig) Possibly obscene medieval stone figure of woman exposing genitalia.

***sídh* (shee, sheeth)** Irish name for the distinctive, circular-topped man-made mounds found commonly in Ireland, thought to be routes to the otherworld; fairy mounds.

***sínach* (sheen-akh)** Later generic name for the sea monster of Loch Rudraige, earlier known as *muirdris*.

Sirona (sir-ohn-ă) Gaulish healing goddess.

Sliab Fúait [Slieve Fuad, mountain of the woods] (shlee-ăv foo-id) Highest point in the Fews Mountains, Co. Armagh, with rich heroic associations.

Sliab na mBan [Slievenamon, mountain of woman] (shlee-ăv nă mahn) Mountain, 2,368 ft, 10 miles east of Cashel, Co. Tipperary, sometimes called 'Ireland's Parnassus'.

sluagh sídhe, slua sí [fairy host]; ***sluagh/slua na marbh*** [host of the dead] (**sloo**-ă shee; **mahr**-ĕv)   Irish names for the fairy procession.

Snám Dá Én [Swim Two Birds] (snawv daw **ayn**)   Monastic site on the Shannon where Suibne once stopped.

Starn (starn)   Nemedian ancestor of the Fir Bolg.

Sualtam mac Róich (**soo**-al-dav mahk **roikh**)   Mortal stepfather of Cúchulainn.

Sucellus (soo-kel-ŭs)   Gaulish divinity known as the 'good striker'; cult partner of Nantosuelta.

Suibne Geilt (siv-nĕ, seev-nĕ, suv-nĕ, swiv-nĕ, cf. *ang.* swee-nee; gelt)   'Mad Sweeney', cursed king who sits naked in trees.

Sulis (sool-ees)   Ancient British healing goddess, worshipped at Bath.

taibhsear (tı-sher)   Scottish Gaelic term for seer or prophet.

Tailtiu (**tal**-tyĕ, tıl-tyĕ, **tal**-too)   Fir Bolg queen, wife of Eochaid mac Eirc and foster-mother of Lug Lámfhota. An annual festival was established in her honour. The townland named for her, modern Teltown [*Ir.* Taillten], Co. Meath, is also the site of a battle between the Milesians and Tuatha Dé Danann.

Taliesin (tal-ee-es-in)   Divine or divinely inspired poet of early Wales, often thought to be historical (sixth century). One of the two *cynfeirdd* [oldest poets] with Aneirin. Transformed from the servant Gwion Bach.

Tara (tar-ă)   Hill in Co. Meath where the high king was crowned in pre-Norman conquest times. Cited as a capital in many early Irish narratives.

Taredd Wledig (**tahr**-e*th* oo-**led**-ig)   Shadowy father of monster-boar Twrch Trwyth.

Tech Duinn (tekh dun)   Rocky islet at the end of the Beare Peninsula, reputed home of Donn, and thus the realm of the dead.

Tech Moling (tekh **mul**-ing)   Monastery of St Moling in Co. Carlow, now called St Mullin's.

Tegid Foel (**teg**-id voil)   Husband of Ceridwen who gives his name to Llyn Tegid, now known as Bala Lake.

teinm laida [breaking open of the pith] (ten-ĕm lı*th*-ă)   A power of divination possessed by Fionn mac Cumhaill and others.

Temuir Luachra (tev-ŭr **loo**-ăkh-ră)   Fictional residence of Munster kings, presumed in Co. Kerry.

Tethra (teth-ră)   One of the most threatening of the demonic Fomorians.

Teutates (tyoo-**taht**-es)   One of the three principal gods of ancient Gaul, according to Roman poet Lucan (first century AD), along with Taranis and Esus.

Teyrnon Twrf Lient (tir-non toorv lı-ent) King of Gwent Is Coed who raised the child Pryderi, then known as Gwri.

Thomond (*th*oh-münd) Anglicized name for northern Munster, coextensive with the modern counties of Clare and Limerick.

Three Sorrows of Storytelling, [*Trí Truagha na Sgéalaigheachta*] (i) The Deirdre Story, told under two titles, *Longas mac nUislenn* [Exile of the Sons of Uisnech] and *Oided mac nUisnig* [Death of the Sons of Uisnech]; (ii) *Oidheadh Chlainne Tuireann* [The Tragic Story of the Children of Tuireann]; (iii) *Oidheadh Chlainne Lir* [The Tragic Story of the Children of Lir].

Tír Chonaill (tyeer, teer khon-al) Early kingdom coextensive with modern Co. Donegal.

Tír fo Thuinn (tyeer, teer fŭ thun) The Land Under Wave, an Irish otherworld.

Tír na mBan (tyeer, teer nă mahn) The Land of Women, an Irish otherworld.

Tír na mBéo (tyeer, teer na may-oh) The Land of the Living, an Irish otherworld.

Tír na nÓg (tyeer, teer nah nohg) The Land of Youth, an Irish otherworld.

Tír Tairngire (tyeer, teer tahrn-γir-ĭ) The Land of Promise, an Irish otherworld.

Tom Cornish giant, protagonist of the 'Giants of Morvah'.

Tor Conaind (tor kohn-ănd) The Fomorian tower on Tory Island, off the coast of Donegal.

Tracht Esi (trakht esh-ee) Beach in Co. Louth where Connla fights Cúchulainn.

Tuan mac Cairill (also mac Stairn) (too-awn mahk kahr-ĭl; makh star-ĕn) Partholonian thought to have survived to the time of St Colum Cille (sixth century) to tell the story of the invasions.

Tuatha Dé Danann (too-hă, too-ă-hŭ, too-ăth-ă day dahn-an) Race of immortals who precede the mortal Milesians in the Irish pseudo-history, *Lebor Gabála Érenn*.

Tuireann (tur-ĭn) King of the Tuatha Dé Danann whose three sons meet a tragic fate in one of the best-known stories in the Mythological Cycle.

Tuis A king 'of Greece' (tooish) Retrieving the skin of his pig is a task of the sons of Tuireann.

***tunnerez noz* (tun-er-ez noz)** Breton name for the washer at the ford.

Twrch Trwyth (toorkh trooeth) Ferocious great boar, hunted by Culhwch.

tylwyth teg [W. fair folk] **(tul-weeth teg)** Name for the fairies in Welsh tradition.

Úamain (ooăv-ahn) *Sídh* of Connacht, home of Cáer, swan-lover of Angus Óg.

Uathach [spectre] (**ooăth-ăkh**) Ugly daughter of Scáthach, smitten with Cúchulainn.

uddereek (**ud-ĕr-eek**) Alternative name for the fenodyree, a Manx fairy.

Uí Fháilghe (**ee-al-γĕ**) Leinster dynasty favouring the worship of Find, personification of wisdom.

Uí Néill (**ee-nayl**) Powerful, multi-branched dynasty in medieval Ireland from fifth century forward, named for assumed progenitor, Niall Noígiallach [of the Nine Hostages]. Not identical with the later O'Neills, who derive from but one branch.

Uisnech (**oosh-nĕkh**) Hill thought to be the centre of Ireland where the druid Mide lit the first fire.

Ulaid (**ul-ee**) Historical people of early northern Ireland for whom Ulster is named.

urco (**oor-koh**) Fierce-looking black fairy dog of Galician tradition.

Urien Rheged (**eer-ee-ĕn, eer-yen, rheg-ĕd**) Sixth-century Welsh king eulogized by Taliesin.

Usheen Hiberno-English for Oisín.

vates (**vaht-ĕs, vaht-ees**) Latin name for the diviners as seers of ancient Gaul, of lower status than the druids but above the bards. The word is an exact cognate of the Irish *faith* [prophet, seer] and a near cognate of the Welsh *gwawd* [poet].

Ventry Harbour Four miles west of Dingle, Co. Kerry, site of the Fenian epic *Cath Fionntrágha*.

Vindabona (**vind-ă-bohn-ă**) Celtic settlement along the Danube in Roman times, site of modern Vienna.

Vindonnus (**vin-dohn-ŭs**) The 'fair god' of the continental Celts.

washer at the ford Generic name for a banshee-like figure known in all Celtic traditions; her washing of bloody garments presages the death of the onlooker.

xana (var. *inxana*) (**shahn-ă**) The fairy woman responsible for changelings in Galicia and Asturias.

Ynys Afallon [*W*. apple island] (**un-us ă-vah*ll*-ŏn**) Welsh otherworldly island in the western ocean, a place of feasting, pleasure and perpetual youth.

Ynys Prydain (**un-us pri-dɪn**) Welsh name for the Isle of Britain, implicitly the realm of the Welsh.

Youdic (**yoo-dik**) Dismal entrance to the infernal regions in Breton tradition.

Ys (**ees**) Legendary Breton city inundated by the sea.

Ysbaddaden (**us-bah*th*-ahd-ĕn**) Welsh giant, father of Olwen; gives Heraclean tasks to Culhwch.

PRONUNCIATION KEY

γ		See note on sounds not found in English, below
a	*as in*	act, bat, marry
ă	*as in*	ago, suitable
ah	*as in*	father
ahr	*as in*	arm, cart, bar
air	*as in*	air, dare, scary
aw	*as in*	all, walk, law
ay	*as in*	age, veil, say
b	*as in*	boy, habit, rib
ch	*as in*	chin, teacher, beach
d	*as in*	dog, ladder, head
e	*as in*	egg, bed, metal
ĕ	*as in*	taken, nickel, lawyer (the *schwa* vowel)
ee	*as in*	eat, fee, tier
f	*as in*	fat, effort, puff
g	*as in*	get, wagon, big
gh		An aspirated g. See note on sounds not found in English, below.
h	*as in*	hat, ahead
i	*as in*	if, give, mirror
ĭ	*as in*	pencil, credible
ɪ	*as in*	ice, eye, vine, spy
j	*as in*	jam, magic, edge
k	*as in*	king, token, back
kh	*as in*	Loch Lomond, das Buch (Ger.). See note on sounds not found in English, below.
l	*as in*	leg, alley, tell
ll		Welsh double l. See note on sounds not found in English, below.
m	*as in*	me, common, him
n	*as in*	no, manner, tan
ng	*as in*	bring, singer, tank
o	*as in*	odd, box, hot
ŏ	*as in*	official, lemon, ardour
oh	*as in*	oat, show, sew
ohr	*as in*	board, adore, four
oi	*as in*	oil, join, toy
oo	*as in*	ooze, rood, too
ow	*as in*	out, mouse, owl

p *as in*	pin, caper, cap
r *as in*	red, carry, near
rh	See note on sounds not found in English, below.
s *as in*	sit, lesson, nice
sh *as in*	she, ashen, rush
t *as in*	top, butter, hit
th *as in*	thin, method, path
th *as in*	this, mother, breathe
<u>th</u>	See note on sounds not found in English, below
u *as in*	up, cut, come
ŭ *as in*	suppose, circus, feature
uu *as in*	book, full, woman
v *as in*	van, river, give
w *as in*	will, awoke, quick
y *as in*	yes, you
z *as in*	zebra, lazy, tease
zh *as in*	vision, pleasure

Sounds Not Found in English

γ   The voiced velar fricative, similar to the more familiar unvoiced velar fricative kh with the voice added. Heard in Spanish *agua*.

gh   The lightly voiced velar fricative, as in German magen.

kh   The voiceless velar fricative found in many European languages, Loch Lomond, Johann Sebastian Bach, Das Buch, etc.

<u>ll</u>   Welsh unvoiced lateral fricative, approximately the l in *antler*, with more aspiration. Put the tip of the tongue behind front teeth and aspirate on the side or sides.

rh   Emphatic h sounded before and eliding with the r sound.

<u>th</u>   The aspirated t heard in some British pronunciations of Antony, about one third the sound of the unvoiced th.

Index

Aarne, Antti, 24
Aarne-Thompson catalogue, motif
    index, xxv, 24, 65, 112, 113, 166,
    184, 201, 222, 233, 240, 253, 263,
    268
Abaris the Hyperborean, 4
Aberystwyth, 267
Abhainn na Life, 14
Abraham, the Patriarch, 131
Acallam na Senórch, 237–9, 240
Achilles, xxvi, 229
Act of Union, Scotland and England,
    290
Adonis, 18, 96, 234
Adrian IV, Pope, 49
adultery, 14, 87, 121–2, 131, 137, 156,
    157–8, 166, 189, 197, 206, 215,
    282–3, 289
'Adventure of Fergus mac Léti, The',
    see Echtra Fergusa maic Léite
Áeb, 163
Áebhric, 165
Áed (son of Lir), 17, 163
Áed (son of Miodhchaoin), 155
Áed Abrat, 213
Áedán, 252
Aedui, 4
Aeneas, 192
Aericura, 40
áes sídhe, 116, 149
Aesculapius, 34, 73
Aesir, 144

Afagddu, 266
*Afinidades Culturais entre Galicia e
    Irlanda*, 303
Africa, xx, xxvi
*Agallamh na Seanórch, see Acallam na
    Senórch*
Agricola, 146
Ahé, Ahés, alternative forms for Dahut
    (q.v.)
Aichlech mac Dubdrenn, 233
Aided Maíl Fhothartaig Maic Rónáin,
    250
Aided Óenfhir Aífe, 200–201
Aífe (stepmother of swan children), 17,
    163–4, 165
Aífe (Amazonian teacher), 198–9, 200,
    201
Aífe (lover of Ilbrec), 16
Ailbe (Cormac's daughter), 253, 255
Ailbe (Mac Da Thó's hound), 174–5,
    176–7
Ailbe, St, 114
Ailech, 146
Ailill (father of Étaín), 156
Ailill (ring-thrower), 24
Ailill Anglonnach, 157–8
Ailill mac Máta (husband of Medb),
    86, 87, 170–71, 174–5, 180–81,
    188, 189, 194, 203, 205, 208, 211;
    'pillow talk with Medb', 203
Aillén mac Midgna, 56, 99, 226–7
Aillén Tréchenn, 99

Áine (deity of Cnoc Áine), 9
Áine (lover of Fionn), 228
Ainnle, 45, 81, 186
Airgialla, 46, 244
Airmid, 138
Aislinge Meic Con Glinne, 100, 184
Aislinge Oenguso, 17, 166–7
Aitheachthuatha, 148
Alba, 286
Alcides, 195, 224
Alcmene, 42
Alésia, xix, 4, 5, 7, 20, 72
Alexander III of Scotland, 290
Alise-Sainte Reine, 5
alius orbis, see orbe alio
All Saints' Day, 97–8
All Souls' Day, 98
Allantide, 97
allegory, 228
Allen, Hill of, 192, 223, 228, 229, 242
Alps, xiv, 4, 19, 39
Amaethon, 44, 71
Amairgin, 24, 62, 99, 147, 170, 194
amazonians, 67, 68, 75, 121, 197–8, 226
Amen (Welsh cauldron), 266
American Federation of Labor, 104
amhrán, 240
Ammianus Marcellinus, 67, 83
Ana, Anu, xiv, 8–9, 14, 71, 136, 153
anaon, 119
Anatolia, *see* Asia Minor
Ancient Celts, The, 302
Ancient Irish Tales, 243
Ancient Order of Druids, 30
Andraste, 83
Aneirin, xxiv, 261, 262–3, 265
Angles, 265, 286
Anglesey, 26, 29
Anglo-Normans, 49, 52, 57, 68, 116, 148, 298; *see also* Hiberno-Normans, Normans
Anglo-Saxons, 49, 129; *see also* Saxons
Anglo-Welsh literary tradition, xiii, 265

Angus (son of Áed Abrat), 213
Angus Óg, 7, 14, 17, 35, 99, 118, 137, 138, 152, 156, 165–7, 188, 194, 235, 236, 288; conception and birth, 166; epithets of, 138; narrative of, 165–7; variant forms for, 138
Angus Óg agus Cáer, 166–7
animal, imagery and symbolism, *see* individual animals
Anluan, 176
Anlwdd Wledig, 268
Anna Livia Plurabelle, 14
Annals (Irish), 115, 128
Annals (Tacitus), 26
Anno Mundi, 129
Annwfn, 79, 119, 266, 271, 272–3; etymology of, 119; 'king' of, 119–20, 272, 273
antiquarianism, xiii
Antiquité de la nation et la Langue des Celtes, xii
Antrim, County, 123, 132, 133, 169, 207, 231, 246, 247, 249, 250
Anu, *see* Ana
Anwyl, Edward, 31
aos, áes sídhe, 116
Aphrodite, 3, 96, 137
apple, apples, 97, 123, 154, 253; *see also* Emain Ablach, Ynys Afallon
Apollo, xxi, 21, 31, 32, 33, 34–5, 72, 102, 262
Apollo Citharoedus, 35
Apollo Grannus, 33, 72
Apollo Moritasgus, 34, 72
Aquae Sulis, 12–13, 39
Arabian Nights, 115; *see also* Sinbad
Aran Islands, 47, 122, 133
Arausio, 9
Arawn, 119, 271, 272–3
Arberth, 273, 278, 279
Arca Dubh, 227
archaeology, xiii, xv–xvi, xviii, xix, 7, 33, 42, 133, 169, 223, 296, 302
Archaeologia Britannica, 295

Ardan, 44, 81, 186
Ardennes Forest, 18
Ardfert, 114
ard rí, 13, 50, 52–7, 157, 159, 221, 226, 245; alternative names for, 54; ceremonies of, 55–6; origin of term, 54–5
Ardagh, 156
Ardee, 209
Arduinna, 18
Ares, 36
Argyll, Argyllshire, 129, 148, 291
Arianrhod, 71, 80, 281–2
Aristophanes, 185, 229
Aristotle, xx
Arizona, 265
Armagh, County, town of, 17, 46, 85, 118, 132, 163, 168, 169
Armorica, 297
Arnold, Matthew, xxvi
Arrée mountains, 120
Artemis 3, 45
Arthur, King, 56, 120, 199, 200, 233, 234, 245, 246, 264, 268–9
Arthuriana, Arthurian legends, tradition, 75, 123, 149, 168, 184, 239, 249, 253, 263, 264, 295, 298
Arvernii, 5
Asclepius, 34, 73
Ashmolean Museum, xii
Asia, 6, 27; central Asia, xiv; Asia Minor, Anatolia, xi, 145
Assal, Easal, 16, 154–5
Assaroe, 11, 22, 131, 225
Asturias, 302–4
Áth Fhirdiad, 209
Áth Luain, 212
Áth Tolam Sét, 207
Athena, 32, 39
Athlone, 13, 177, 212
Atholl, 10
Atlantic Ocean, 119, 303
Atlantis, 122
Aubrey, John, 30

Audacht Morainn, 51
Augusta (epithet), 12
Augustinians, 49
Augustus, 105
Australia, 287
Austria, xiv, xv, xviii, 39, 42, 46, 68, 109
Avalon, 123, 149
Aztecs, 96

Baal, 102
Babel, Tower of, 128, 130, 145
Babylonians, 47, 96
Badb, 32, 44, 75, 83, 84, 140, 218, 303; crow, linked with, 84; etymology of, 84
'badger-in-the-bag', 274, 279
badhbh chainte, 84
Baile in Scáil, 62–3
Baile's Strand, 200
Baíscne, Clan, 224, 227
Bala Lake, 75–6, 266–7
Balkans, the, 37, 40
Ballyjamesduff, 98
Ballymagauran, 98
Ballynascorney, 232
Balor, Balor of the Evil Eye, xxvii, 8, 43, 135, 138, 140–42, 246, 269
ball seirce, 235
banais ríghe, 59–60
Banba, 10, 46, 61–2, 130, 147
Bann, River, 164, 248
Bannockburn, Battle of, 290
bannocks, 103
Banqueting Hall, 53
banshee, 84, 149
Bantry Bay, 61, 76, 130
baptism, 113, 165
barbarians, xx, 3, 58
Barbarossa, 233
Barc Bresail 122
bard, bards, xxi, 23–4, 26, 81, 267
'Bard, The' (Gray), xiii
bardi, 26

Barkway, 37, 42

Barra, Isle of, 123

Barrow, River, 176

Bartholomew, St, 131

Barzaz Breiz, xiii, 298–9

Bath, 12, 31, 36, 39, 73, 83

Battersea Shield, 10

battle frenzy, fury [*ríastrad*], *see* Cúchulainn

Bavay, 44

Bé Chuma, 121–2, 124

bean nighe, 303

bean sídhe, 149

Beare Peninsula, 41, 61, 64, 76, 118, 139

Bebo, 258

Bébinn, 13–14

Bede, the Venerable, 129

'beds of Diarmait and Gráinne', 234

Bedwyr, 269

beheading contest, 177, 183–4

Belenus, 21, 34, 35, 102

Belgae, 4, 133, 192

Belgium, Belgians, the, xxiii, 4; *see also* Low Countries, Spanish Netherlands

Beli Mawr, 71

Belisama, 39

Beltaine, May Day/Eve, xix, 35, 59, 93, 95, 100, 101–104, 131, 135, 146; alternative forms, 102; cakes/ bannocks, 103; customs of, 102; etymology of, 102

Ben Bulben, 229, 236

Bendigeidfran, 38, 76, 120, 275–7

Benedict of Nursia, St, xvii

Benedictines, 49

Benén, 19

Beowulf, 168

Berkert, Walter, xxix

Berne Commentaries, 37, 40–41

Besançon, 33

Bettystown, 53

Bhreathnach, Edel, 54

Bible, 24, 128, 129–31, 134, 136, 145, 171, 252–3; *see also* Hebrew mythology, New Testament, Old Testament

Biblical exegesis, 127–8

Bibracte, 4

Binchy, D. A., 54

bird, birds, symbolism, 15–17, 160, 181, 194, 200, 203, 206, 212, 247, 276; *see also* cormorant, crane, crow, duck, eagle, egret, owl, raven, swan

Birog, 141

Birren, 130

bishop, 279, 300

Bith, 130

Black Book of Carmarthen, The, xxiv

'black Irish', 145–6

Black Isle, 289

Black Sea, 37

Blaí, *see* Sadb

Blái Briuga, 194

Bláithíne, 182, 189–90, 199

Bleiddwn, 281

Blessed Virgin and All Martyrs, church of the, 97

Blodeuedd, 74, 79, 80, 264, 282–3

Boadach, 124

Boaldyn, 102

Boand, 13–14, 98, 137, 138, 156, 166

boar, imagery and symbolism, xix, 15, 17–19, 96, 170, 226, 235, 236–7, 270, 278, 281; *see also* pig

Bod Fheargais, 170

Bód fo Bregaigh, 170 n.

Bodb Derg, 118, 149, 163–4, 167, 203

Bodhmall, 224

Bodua, 84

Bohernabreena, 161

'Bold Fenian Men, The', 220

Bolg, Bolga, 133

Bolivia, 47

Bollard, J. K., 271

Bolsheviks, 104

Boniface IV, Pope, 97

Bonn, 70

'Bonnie Prince Charlie', 287
Book of Aneirin, The, xxiv
Book of Armagh, The, xxiii
Book of Ballymore, The, xxiii
Book of Common Prayer, The, 293–4
Book of Deer, The, 288
Book of Durrow, The, xxii
Book of Fermoy, The, xxiii
'Book of Invasions', see Lebor Gabála
    Érenn
Book of Kells, The, xxii, 50
Book of Lecan, The, xxiii
Book of Leinster, The, xxiii, 128, 185,
    189, 202, 250
Book of Taliesin, 265
Book of the Dean of Lismore, The,
    xxiv, 288
Book of the Dun Cow, The, xviii, xxii,
    xxiii, xxiv, 185, 189, 202
Book of Uí Maine, The, xxiii
Borba, 227
Bormo, 35, 72
Bormana, 72
Bormanus, 35, 72
Boswell, James, 287
Borvo, 35, 72
Bottrell, William, 295
Boudicca, 5, 66–7, 83
Bourbonne-les-Bains, 35
Boyne River, Valley, 6, 11, 13–14, 19,
    23, 86, 118, 137, 147, 148, 160,
    166, 167, 169, 192, 194, 224, 225,
    233, 236, 238
Boys' Own Paper, 219
Brahan Castle, 289
Brahan Seer, 285, 289–91
Brân, 76
Bran (Fionn's dog), 226, 229
Bran mac Febail, 110–13, 117, 122,
    124
'Bran's Journey to the Land of
    Women', see Imram Brain
Bran the Blessed, see Bendigeidfran
Branwen (character), 46, 275–7

Branwen, Daughter of Llŷr, 76, 120,
    264, 266; summarized, 275–7
Brazil, naming of, 122
Breaga, 148
Brega, 105, 148, 160, 161, 170
Bregenz, 42
Brehon Laws, xxii, 49, 54, 68, 69,
    220–21
breithem, xxii, 54, 68
Breizh, 298
Brendan, St, 114–15, 121
Brendan Voyage, The, 115
Brent, River, 12
Brentford, 12
Breogan, 146, 302
Bres, 90, 140, 141–4
Bresail, 122
Bresal Etairláim, 156
'Breton Bards,' xiii
Breton language, xi, xvi, xxiv, 15,
    32, 97, 102, 119, 285, 295, 298,
    304
Breton literature, 299
Breton people, xii, 297–8
Brí Léith, 118, 156, 157, 158, 159
Brian (son of Tuireann), 153–5
Brian Bórama (Boru), 48, 50, 244, 245
Briccriu Neimthenga, 175, 177–82,
    189, 211
'Briccriu's Feast', see Fled Bricrenn
Brigando, 12, 90
Brigantes, 12
Brigantia (deity), 12, 39–40, 90
Brigantia (place name), 146
Brigid, St, 11, 40, 89–92, 101;
    biographies of, 91; cross of, 92
Brigidine Sisters, 91
Brigit (fire goddess), 12, 40, 46, 89–92,
    101, 140, 153
Bristol, 12
Britán Máel, 132
Britain, xvi, xvii, xx, 4–5, 12, 13, 20,
    25, 31, 35, 36, 37, 39, 45, 60, 61,
    71, 72, 73, 83, 132, 146, 154, 168,

192, 246, 249, 261, 270, 275, 286, 293, 297, 298
British Isles, xi, xii, xvi, 8, 21, 93, 102
British language, 261
Britons, 4–5, 161, 244, 261–2, 286, 297, 298
Brittany, xvii, xxv, 6, 8, 11, 15, 18, 25, 32, 34, 36, 44, 68, 94, 108, 120, 261, 284; history of, 297–8; traditions of, 297–302
Broccan, 91
Brocéliande, 298
Brocolitia, 12
Bronze Age, xiv, xv, 6, 10, 22, 96, 168, 293
Brooke, Charlotte, xiii
Brown Bull of Ulster, see Donn Cuailnge
brownie, 294
Bruford, Alan, 245
Brug na Bóinne, 7, 137, 156, 166, 167, 194, 236
Bruidhean tale type, 228
Bruidhean Chaorthainn, 228
bruidne, 78
Brythonic, xvi, 262, 295, 297
Búanann, 226
Buchanan, George, xii
Buide mac Báin, 207
Buile Suibhne, 243; summarized, 246–50
bull, imagery and symbolism, xx, 15, 16, 22–3, 81, 203
bull-feast, bull-sleep, 22–3, 56
Bumstead, Dagwood (comic-strip character), 230
Burghead, 22
Burgundy, 36, 70, 72
burial customs, 109
'burner, the', see Aillén mac Midgna
Byrne, F. J., 48, 54, 55, 58, 59

caduceus, 33, 71
Caer Feddwid, 120

Cáer Ibormeith (lover of Angus Óg), 17, 99, 165–7
caer siddi, 118–19
Cahirconree, 182
Caicer, 146
Cailb, 74–5, 161–2
Cailitin, 87, 216–17
Cailleach Bhéirre, 61, 64, 76–7; Christianized, 76; divine origin, 76; progeny of, 64; Scottish variant, 77; sovereignty of, 64
Cailleach Bheur, 77
Caílte mac Rónáin, 219, 238–9
Cairbre Cinn-Chait, 148
Cairbre Lifechair, 223, 233, 253–4
Cairbre Nia Fer, 205, 217
Cairpre (satirist), 141, 143
Caitlín, Céthlionn, 135, 143
Cala' Mē, 102
Caladbolg, 170, 199, 256
Caladhcholg, 256
Calan Awst, 105
Calan Gaeaf, 97
Calan Mai, Dydd Calan Mai, 102, 267, 274
Caledonia, 286
Caledonian Canal, 290
calendar, xix, 21, 37, 40, 90, 93–106; Jewish, 96; lunar, 94–5; numbering of, 96; solar, 93–4; see also Coligny, Gregorian
Callow, Edward, 294
Calvary, 171
Cáma, 238
Cambrian Peninsula, 261
Cambrian Superstitions, xxv
Cambridgeshire, 7
Camonica Valley, 19
Campbell, Archibald, xxv, 288
Campbell, John Francis, xxv, 288
Cambridge School, 51
Camel (doorkeeper), 142
Camross, 135
Camulodunum, 36

Canada, xvii, 220, 287, 291
Candlemas Day, 101
Canterbury Tales, The, 64–5
Cape Breton Island, *see* Nova Scotia
'Capers', 291
Carey, John, 121, 136
Carleton, William, 231–3
Carlow, County, 249
Carn Fróich, 59
Carnfree, 59
Carnac, 25
Carney, James, 234
Carnutes, 27
Carrawborough, 12, 74
Carré Alvarellos, Leandro, 303
Cashel, 10, 61, 245
Caspian Sea, 145
Castille, 47
castration, 232
castros, 146, 302–3, 304
Cath (classification of narrative), 151
Cath Fionntrágha, 222
Cath Maige Rátha, 246
Cath Maige Tuired, 43, 90, 128, 134,
    148, 152, 268; summarized, 140–44
Cathach, 199
Cathbad, 81, 193, 210, 216
Cathédrale engloutie, La, 302
Catholicism, Roman, xxiii, 40, 49, 69,
    89, 98, 103, 231, 246, 249, 303;
    St Brigid, explanation for, 89–90,
    91
Catobodua, 84
cattle, 13, 22, 81, 90, 100, 101, 102,
    114, 124, 131, 157, 175, 251; *see
    also* bull
'Cattle Raid of Cooley', *see Táin Bó
    Cuailnge*
Caturis, 36
cauldron, cauldrons, xix, 7, 17, 75–6,
    120, 121, 136, 137, 173, 266; of
    regeneration, 275–7
Cauth Bova, 84
Cavan, County, 40, 44, 90, 98, 169

cave, caves, 8, 123, 134, 151
Caw of Britain, 270
Céadach, 230
Cei, 269
Céis Chorrain, 236
Celt, Celtic, xii, xiii, 93; etymology of,
    xi; pronunciation of, xi
Celtae, xi
Celtchair mac Uithechair, 186
Celtic art, xv–xvi, 10, 15, 22
Celtic Christianity, *see* Christianity
Celtic deities (general), xix, 10
Celtic fringe, xiii, 286
Celtic Heathendum, xxvii
Celtic Heritage, xxix, 144
Celtic Ireland (MacNeill), 50–51, 52
Celtic languages (general), xi, xiv, xvi,
    xvii, xviii, 6, 47, 146; P–Q split, xvi
Celtic Mythology (MacCana), 66
'Celtic Olympus, the', 303
Celtic religion, xiii, 17, 19, 25–46
Celtic Religion in Pre-Christian Times,
    31
Celtic Revival (eighteenth century), xiii
Celtic society, 4
Celtic Twilight, The, 122
Celts (people), xi, xii, xiv, xviii, xix, xx;
    3–4, 8, 12, 44, 96; character of, xx;
    dress, xx; physical appearance, xiv
Celyddon Wledig, 268
Cenél Conaill, 58
ceo sídhe, ceol sídhe, 118
Cerberus, 40, 41
Ceridwen, 75–6, 266–7
Cerna, 161
Cernenus, 38
Cernunnos, xx, 18–19, 38, 41
ces nóinden Ulad, 21, 85, 172
Cesair, 130–31
Cet mac Mágach, 175–6
Cethern mac Fintain, 209–10, 226
Céthlionn, 135
cétmuinter, 50

Cétshamain, 102
Ceylon, 108
champion's portion, hero's portion, xxi, 18, 174, 177, 178–9, 180, 181, 183–4, 200
changelings, 303–4
Channel Islands, 44
Chants populaire de la Basse-Bretagne, xxv
Charlemagne, 233, 245
Charles Edward Stuart, Prince, 287
Chaucer, Geoffrey, 64–5
China, xiv, 108
Chrétien de Troyes, 264
Christian (literary character), 113
Christian fundamentalism, 93; creation of bogus deity Samhan, 98–9
Christianity, xvi, xvii, xviii, xxii, xxiii, xxvi, xxvii, xxviii, 7, 11, 16, 19, 24, 29, 30, 32, 33, 41, 46, 49, 50, 55, 56, 57, 67, 82, 88, 93, 94, 97, 103, 105, 117, 119, 134, 137, 146, 149, 167, 171, 219, 228, 237, 266, 288, 299–300; Celtic Christianity, 49, 69, 237; Christian legends, 57, 82, 89; didacticism, 110, 111; Lughnasa, adaptations of, 106; otherworld, beliefs of, 108; pilgrimage, 146; women, attitudes towards, 68–9; *see also* Catholicism, Eastern Orthodox, Irish monasticism, monasticism, Protestantism, sainthood
Christmas, 262
Christopher, St, 89
Chronicles (Holinshed), 129
Chyndonax, 30
Cian (father of Banba), 62
Cian (father of Lug Lámfhota), 153
Cian (son of Dian Cécht), 141
Ciar, 87
Ciarraí, 87
Ciarán, St, xxiii
Cichol, 134
Cigfa, 277–80

Cil Coed, 279
Cill Dara, 91
Cilydd, 268
Cimbáeth, 85, 173
Cimbri, 28
Cináed mac Alpín, 286
circular time, 96
Cistercians, xxii, 49
Citharoedus, 34
Civil War, America, 104, 220
cláenmíla, 160, 161
Claidheamh Soluis, 199
clairvoyance, 288
Clare, County, 107, 123, 164, 244
classical commentators, xi, xiii, xviii, xx, 20, 22, 25–7, 28, 31, 39, 42, 67, 83, 97
classical mythology, 3, 31, 96, 136–7, 155, 169, 170, 269, 294
'Clay' (James Joyce), 99
Clearances of Highlanders, 287, 289, 291
Clettig, 118
Cliffs of Moher, the, 123
Cloch nan Tarbh, 23
Clocharfarmore, 218
Clonfert, 114
Clonmacnoise, xxii, xxiii, 248
Clontarf, Battle of, 49, 244, 245
Clothra, 86, 87–8
Clud, 273
Cnoc Áine, 9
Cnámros, 135
Cogitosus, 91
Cóelrind, Well of, 11
Cóic Conairi Fuigill, 50
Coimín (also Comyn), Micheál, 20, 123, 240
Coinneach Odhar Fiosaiche, Scottish Gaelic phrase for the Brahan Seer (q.v.)
coins, coinage, 7, 10, 12
Colchester, 5, 36
Coligny calendar, xix, 95, 104

Collas, Three – Fo Chríth, Menn and Uais, 46
Collbran, 112
collective unconscious, xxviii
'Colloquy of the Elders, The', *see* Acallam na Senórch
Colmán, 246
Colooney, 84
Colptha, 147
Colum Cille, St, 29, 90, 132, 288
Columbus, Christopher, 115, 146
comedy, 184–5
Comyn, Micheál, *see* Coimín, Micheál
Conaire Mór, 56, 159, 160–62, 171; lineage of, 159; narrative of, 160–62
Conall Anglonnach, 186
Conall Cernach, 162, 170–71, 177, 178, 179, 180–81, 182, 183, 186, 194–5, 198, 200, 211, 216, 218; characterized, 170–71, 176; etymology of, 170–71; lineage of, 170–71
Conand, 132, 134
Conarán, 75
Conchobar mac Nessa, 21, 78, 81–2, 86, 169, 171, 172, 174–5, 177, 178, 180, 181–2, 184, 185–7, 189, 193, 194, 195, 198, 200, 202, 204, 210, 213, 216, 234, 243, 245; characterization of, 169; love for Deirdre, 81–2; pronunciation and spelling of name, 169
Condere, 200
Confessio (St Patrick), 7
Cong, 140
Conga, 140
Congal, 251–2
Conmac, 87
Conmaicne Mara, 87
Conleth, 90
Conn (son of Lir), 17, 163
Conn (son of Miodhchaoin), 155
Conn Cétchathach, 40, 48, 62–3, 86, 244, 245, 253, 256

Connacht, xix, 23, 55, 56, 59, 61, 85, 87, 118, 148, 161, 163, 167, 169, 170–71, 173–7, 181, 188, 203–9, 227, 244; bogus etymology of, 176
Connemara, xiv, 87
Connla, 199, 200–201, 202, 232
Connla's Well, 11, 14
Constance, Lake, 42
Constantinople, xxii
Conwy River, 267
cooking-spit of the women of Inis Fionnchuire (or Findchuire), 154–5
Cooley Peninsula, *see* Cuailnge
Corbridge, 42
Corc (son of Miodhchaoin), 155
Corentin, 299–300
Cork, County, 41, 64, 76, 118, 233
Corleck Hill, 40, 44, 90
Cormac Connloinges, 204
Cormac mac Airt, 56, 86, 151, 223, 233, 234, 236, 244, 245; narratives of, 253–5
Cormac mac Cuilennáin, 90, 100–101
Cormac Ua Cuinn, *see* Cormac mac Airt
Cormac's Glossary, *see* Sanas Cormaic
cormorant, imagery and symbolism, 15
Cornish language, xi, xvi, xvii, xxiv, 97, 102, 105, 133, 295, 296, 298
Cornish mystery plays, 295, 298
Cornwall, xviii, xxv, 11, 102, 234, 261, 284; duchy of, 295; traditions of, 294–7
Corotiacus, 36
corpán sídhe, 118
Corpre, Corpres, 161
Corrbolg, 16
cosmology, 70, 127, 292
Coventina, 12, 72, 73
cow, imagery and symbolism, 13, 22, 166, 170, 175; *see also* cattle
Cráebruad, 169, 182
Creation (Biblical), 129
Crete, 22

crane, imagery and symbolism, 15–16, 38

crane bag, 16

Crane Bag, The (journal), 16

Credne, 43, 46, 139, 143

Creirwy, 76

Crimthann Nia Náir, 189

Críth Gablach, 54

Croker, Thomas Crofton, xxv, 256

Crom Crúaich, 98

Crom Dubh, 106

Cromm Darail and Cromm Deróil, 188

Cromwell, Oliver, xxiv

Cross, T. P., and C. H. Slover, 185, 243; quoted, 78

Crossakeel, 204

crow, imagery and symbolism, 45, 84, 216

Cruacha, 86

Cruachain, 59, 86, 124, 169, 180, 203, 211, 212

Cruaidhin Catutchenn, 199

Crunniuc mac Agnomain, 21, 85, 172–4

Cú Roí mac Dáiri, 182, 184, 187–8, 189–90, 199, 217

cù sìth, 304

Cualu, 161

Cúchulainn, xxvi, xxvii, 17, 21, 38, 75, 78, 87, 99, 121, 122, 124, 139, 150, 152, 168, 169–70, 177, 178, 180–82, 183–4, 185–7, 188–90, 191–218, 222, 223, 224, 228, 229, 232, 245, 256, 288, 292; artistic representations of, 191; in beheading contest, 183–4; birth name Sétanta, 192, 195–6; boyhood of, 195–7; characterizations of, 192, 197; conception of, 193–4; courtship of Emer, 197–8, 199; death of, 215–18; described, 180, 188, 196; domain of, 192, 256; dreams of being whipped, 213; exempted from Macha's curse, 174; his fool, of Ethiopian appearance, 188; fosterage of, 194–5; horses of, 199; names, interpretation, 192–3, 195–6; origins of, 192–3; *ríastrad* [battle fury, etc.], 179–80, 195, 196–7, 208, 211, 214; salmon leap of, 197, 198; 'wasting sickness', 213–14; wife of, 199

cuckoldry, 111, 166, 190, 234

Cuculain, Cucullin, Hiberno-English forms for Cúchulainn (q.v.)

Cuculain and His Contemporaries, xxiv

Cuailnge, 195, 203, 204, 205–6, 216

Culann, 192, 195–6

Culhwch, 24, 44, 77, 267–70; birth, origin of name, 268

Culhwch and Olwen, 44, 70, 77, 120, 262, 264; summarized, 267–70; critique of 267–8

Culloden Moor, 287, 289

Cumberland Strait, 291

Cumhall, 224

Cunliffe, Barry, 302

Cunobelinus, 193

cup of truth, 253, 254–5

Custennin, 269

cŵn annwfn, 120, 266

Cycles, literary, heroic, classification of, *see* Irish literature

Cycles of the Kings, 17, 150, 233; critique of, 245–6; narratives of, 243–58

Cymidiei Cymeinfoll, 76, 275

Cymru, 262

Cynan Meiriadog, St, 298

Cynddylig Cyfarwydd, 269

cynfeirdd, 265

Cyntefin, 102

Czech Republic, xiv

D— (cryptic deity), 9

DIL, see Royal Irish Academy Dictionary of the Irish Language

DNA, 115, 302

Dá Chich Anann, 9, 71

Da Derga, 74, 161–2; *see also Togail Bruidne Da Derga*

dà shelladh, Scottish Gaelic phrase for 'second sight' (q.v.)

Dabilla, 13, 137

Dagda, (the), 14, 42, 84, 90, 98, 118, 136, 137, 138, 139, 141, 143, 149, 156, 166, 188; cauldron of, 136

Dahut, Dahud, 285, 299–301

Dáire (ruler of Tír Tairngire), 121

Dáire Donn, 222

Dáire mac Fichna, 203–4

Dál Cais, Dál gCais, 244–5

Dál nAraide, 246, 248, 249

'Dalcassian Cycle', 245

Dalcassians, 245

Dalmatia, 33

Dalorto, Angelinus, 122

Damona, 34, 35, 72

Dana, *see* Danu

Danaher, Kevin, 104

Danann, 9

dance, 7

Dancing at Lughnasa, 105

Danes (invaders), 50; *see also* Denmark, Vikings

'Daneforts', 304

Dante, 120

Danu, xiv, 8, 9, 71, 136, 262

Dānu (Sanskrit), 9

Danube, Danube Valley, xiv, 4, 9

Danuv, 9

daoine sìth, 118

Dea Matrona, 8, 262

Dea Sequana, 8, 72–3

Dealgnaid, 131

Dealra Dubh, 227

'Death of the Sons of Uisnech', *see* Oided Mac nUisnig

De Bello Gallico, xxi

Debussy, Claude, 302

Dee River, 209

deer, doe, fawn, stag, 19–20, 38, 170, 226, 228, 241, 272, 281

'Deer's Cry, The', 19

Deganwy, 267

Deichtine, 193–4

Deirdre, xxvii, 45, 66, 151, 155, 163, 168, 169, 170, 186, 202, 204, 234, 284, 288; as Deirdire in Nova Scotia, 292; narrative of, 80–82

Deirgderc, 137

Dela, 133

Delphi, 4, 34, 45

deluge, *see* flood

Delvin River, 256

Demne Máel (Fionn's birth name), 224–5

Denmark, xiii, xix, 6, 17; *see also* Danes (invaders)

Deoch, 165

derbfhine, 50–51

Derbforgaill, 199

Derry, County (London-), 169, 187

'Destruction of Da Derga's Hostel', *see* Togail Bruidne Da Derga

devil (Christian), 41, 303

Devon, 295

Dialogues (Lucian), 41–2

Dian Cécht, 138, 141, 143, 153; powers of, 138

Diana, 3, 19, 37

Diarmait mac Cerbaill, 55, 57, 59, 239

Diarmait Ua Duibne, 18, 82, 138, 151, 166, 222, 292; narrative of, 234–7

díchetal do chennaib, 29, 225–6

Dictionary of Celtic Mythology (Oxford), 90

díguin, 256, 258

Dijon, 5, 30, 72

Dillon, Myles, 155, 243

Dindshenchas, 152, 237

Dinéault, 68

Dingle Peninsula, 62, 182, 222, 247

Dinoding, 282

Dio Cassius, 83

Dis Pater, 33, 37, 40–41, 97, 139
divination, 22–3, 26, 29, 56, 99–100
Dillon, Myles, xxvii
Diorruing, 288
Diodorus Siculus, xxi, 67, 83
Dobar, 154
Dodder, River, 161, 242
doe, see deer
dog, hound, imagery and symbolism, 12, 13, 29, 40, 41, 120, 137, 153, 154–5, 174, 192–3, 195–6, 217, 226, 241, 251, 272, 278, 304; Irish breeds, 193
Doged, 268
Doílín, 251
dolmen, 30, 234
dolphin, imagery and symbolism, 23
Dominicans, xxii
Domhnach Chrom Dubh, 106
Domnall Mildemail, 198
Domnu, 143
Dôn, 9, 44, 71, 262, 269, 280, 281
Donegal, County, 58, 59, 112, 132, 134, 146, 147, 148, 169, 225, 247
Donegal Bay, 131
Donn (Congal's brother), 252
Donn (Diarmait's father), 18
Donn (takes form of deer), 19
Donn Cuailnge, 23, 86, 87, 202, 203, 206, 207, 211–12
Donn Désa, 161
Donn mac Míled, 41, 139
Donn Tétscorach (Irish ruler of dead), 41, 117, 139
Donnybrook, 161
Dord Fían, 226
Dorn, 256, 257–8
Dornoll, 75, 198
Dorsetshire, xviii, 22
Douarnenez, Bay of, 299, 301
Down, County, 169, 177, 215, 246, 257
Dowth, 13, 166
dragon, dragons, 170, 203

'Dream of Angus, The', see Aislinge Oenguso
Drogheda, 13, 53, 192, 209
'druidical circles', 30
druids, xiii, 4, 25–30, 40, 47, 91, 108, 135, 136, 143, 146, 153, 156, 162, 164, 180, 188, 204, 210, 216, 224, 225, 226, 227, 228–9, 292; Bresal Etarláim, 156; Cathbad, 81, 188, 210, 216; cats, druidical, 180–81; comic druids, 188; etymology of, 28; female, 26, 67, 141, 224; Finnéces, 225; modern, 29–30; Order of, 30; orders/strata of, 26; Tara ceremony, 56
'druids' table', 30
Druim Derg, 234, 238
Druim Ligen, 147
Druim Tairb, 212
Drumeague, 40, 90
Drunemeton, 28
Duanaire Finn, xxiii, 222, 229–30, 237
Dubh Sainglenn, Saingliu, 21, 199, 218
Dublin, xiv, 14, 49, 131, 133, 161, 163, 191, 215, 232, 233, 239, 240, 245
Dublin Penny Journal, 232
Dubliners (Joyce), 99
Dubros, 235
Dubthach Dóeltenga, 181, 182–3
duck, imagery and symbolism, 15
Dumézil, Georges, xxviii–xxix, 45, 85, 144
Dumuzi, 60
Dún Aonghusa, 133
Dún Dá Benn, 187
Dún Delgan, 187, 192, 216, 217
Dún na mBarc, 130
Dún Rudraige, 177–8, 179
Dún Scáith (Irish), 120–21, 293
Dùn Scàith (Scottish Gaelic), 121
Dùn Sgàthaich, 121
Dún Sobairche, 207, 249, 250, 251, 252

Dunaverney, 15
Dundalk, 91, 187, 192, 218
Dundrum, 177, 257
Dúnlang, 254
Dunquin, 61
Dunseverick, 207, 249
Dürer, Albrecht, 42
Dursey Island, 41, 118
Dydd Calan Mai, see Calan Mai
Dyfed, xvi, 21, 22, 79–80, 119–20,
    271, 272, 277, 278, 279, 280, 281;
    borders, ancient vs modern, 272
Dying Gaul (statue), the, 19
Dylan, 44, 265, 281

eagle, 282–3
Earl, William, xxv
Early Irish History and Mythology,
    xxviii, 144
Early Medieval Ireland, 52
Easal, see Assal
Easter Rising (1916), 191, 222
Eastern Orthodox, 97
Eastern religion, 27
Éber, 147
Echaid Iarlaithe, see Eochaid of Dún
    Sobairche
Echtra Fergusa maic Léite, 255–8
Echtra Mac nEchach Muigmedóin,
    63–4
Echtra Nerai, 87
Echtrae, 109
Echtrae Cormaic, 244; summarized,
    253–5
Eddas, xxvi, 127, 144
Edinburgh, xiv, 182, 261, 287
eel, imagery and symbolism, 23, 84,
    207
Efnisien, 275, 276–7
egret, imagery and symbolism, 15, 38
Egypt, 129, 145; Egyptians, 47, 108
Eil Ton, 281
Éire (name), 62
éiric, 153

Éis Énchenn, 75
Eisirt, 258
eisteddfod, xiii
Eithlinn, see Ériu
Eithne (alternative name for Boand),
    14, 166
Eithne (mother of Lug), 141
Eithne (mother of Máel Fhothartaig),
    250
Eithne Ingubai (double of Emer?), 199,
    212
Eithne Tháebfhota, 254, 255
Elatha mac Delbaíth, 140, 141
Elcmar, 14, 118, 137, 156, 166
Ellan Vannin, 293
Elphin, 267
Elysian Fields, Elysium, 120, 122
emain, 85, 110; etymology of, 174
Emain Ablach, 110, 111, 113, 117,
    123, 124, 149, 293
Emain Macha, 17, 45, 46, 82, 85, 86,
    99, 168, 169, 170, 171, 177, 181,
    182, 185, 186–7, 193, 194, 195,
    198, 199, 208, 210, 213, 216, 217,
    257; etymology of, 174
Emer, 79, 179, 182, 184, 197–8, 199,
    201, 202, 213, 214, 215, 216, 217,
    228
Emigrant Experience: Songs of
    Highland Emigrants in North
    America, The, 291
England, 23, 25, 30, 106, 107, 277,
    287, 295
English Channel, 290–91
English domination, xxiii, 257
English language, xvi, xxiv, 230, 295
English people, 262
Eochaid/Eochu, name glossed, 21
Eochaid of Dún Sobairche, Echaid
    Iarlaithe, 250–51, 252
Eochaid Airem, 157, 158, 160
Eochaid Bélbuide, 256
Eochaid Bres, see Bres
Eochaid Feidlech, 46, 86, 160

Eochaid Inber, 213
Eochaid Iúil, 124, 213, 214
Eochiad mac Eirc, 133
Eochaid Mugmedón, 63
Eochaid Ollathair (alternative name for
    the Dagda), 14, 137, 166
Eógan Inbir, 124
Eógan mac Durthacht, 82
Eólas, 131
Eórann, 246, 248, 249
Ephorus, xx
Epidaurus, 73
Epona, 20, 21, 79, 274
Eponabus, 20
equites, xxi, 26–7
Érainn, 61
Erannán, 146
Erc, 205, 217–18
Éremón, 147–8
Erin, 62, 147
Ériu, 10, 41, 46, 61–3, 141, 147;
    mother of Bres, 141; stories of, 62–3
Erne waterway, 23, 225
Ernmass, 85, 173
Erriapus, 34
Erris, 164, 165
esoteric knowledge, *see* knowledge
    (esoteric)
Espérandieu, Émile, xix
Esus, 15, 16, 37, 38, 46, 192
Esuvii, 38
Étang de Laval, 302
Étaín, 77–8, 118, 152, 155–9, 160,
    165
Étar, 156
Etarcomol, 206
Eterscél, 159, 160
Ethal Anbúail, 167
Euhemerus, euhemerism, xxvii
Euphrates, 60
Euripides, 252
Eusebius, 128
Evans, E. Estyn, 223
Excalibur, 199

'Exile of the sons of Uisnech, The', *see*
    Longas mac nUislenn
Exodus (Biblical), 129
Expugnatio Hibernica, 57

Fachtna, 157–8
Fáilbe Finn, 214
Failinis, 154–5
fairy, fairies, 32, 88, 107–8, 113, 120,
    134, 149, 254, 256–7, 294, 304;
    Galician equivalents, 303–4; 'king
    of', 149, 263; procession of, 303;
    'queen of', 88, 290; solitary and
    trooping, 294, 303
*Fairy and Folk Tales of the Irish
    Peasantry*, 231
*Fairy Legends and Traditions of the
    South of Ireland*, 256
fairy mound, *see* sídh
Faughart, 91
Fál, 55; *see also* Inis Fáil, Lia Fáil
Fálias, 136
family, Irish concepts of, 50–52
Fand, 79, 199, 213–15
'Farewell to Alba', 82
Feast of Lughnasa, The, 105–6
Fedelm (the prophetess), 204
Fedelm Noíchrothach, 179, 205
Fedlimid, 81
feis, xiii, 98
feis Temrach, Temro, 59–60
Femen, plain of, *sídh* of, 64, 118
feminism, 66, 77
Féni, 220
Fenian (word), etymology of, 219–20
Fenian Cycle, xxiii, 18, 20, 76, 78, 82,
    113, 122, 123, 136, 150, 152, 166,
    228, 243, 245, 288; alternative
    names for, 150, 219–20; critique of,
    222; narratives of, 223–42
Fenians (nineteenth-century political
    group), 220
Fénius Farsaid, 129–30, 145
fenodyree, 294

Fer Caille, 134, 161
Fer Doirich, 228–9
Fer Gair, 161
Fer Lí, 161
Fer Loga, 176–7
Fer Rogain, 161, 162
Ferdia (Fionn's servant), 233
Ferdiad, 87, 199, 208–9; combat at the ford, 209
Fergus (Niall's brother), 63
Fergus Caisfiaclach, 170
Fergus Lethderg, 132
Fergus mac Léti, 255–8
Fergus mac Róich, 82, 86, 87, 170, 182–3, 194, 195, 197, 202, 203, 204, 205, 206, 208, 210–11, 255, 256, 288; characterized, 170; etymology of, 170; model for Fergus mac Léti
Fermanagh, County, 169
Fertedil, 205
fertility, 6, 10, 34, 40, 71, 72, 92, 98, 123
féth fíada, 19, 149
Fiacclach mac Conchinn, 224
Fiachna ('father' of Mongán), 111
Fiachra (child of Lir), 17, 163
Fiachra (Niall's brother), 63
fianna (general), 100, 220; battle tactics of, 226; chief of, 227; reality of, 220–21; word, relative to 'Fenian,' 220; requirements for, 221
Fianna Éireann, 219, 220, 235, 238, 240, 288
Fianna Fáil, 221
fibula, fibulae, 12
fidchell, 143, 158, 181, 213, 236
filid (pl.), fili (sing.), 26, 247
Fin M'Coul, Fin-Mac-Cool, Hiberno-English for Fionn mac Cumhaill (q.v.)
Fínán Cam, Saint, 24
Find (early deity), 224, 225
Findchóem, 170

fine, 50
Fingal (Macpherson and Marryat's approximation of Fionn), xii, 232, 288
Fingal Rónáin, summarized, 250–53
'Fingal's Cave Overture', xiii
Fíngean mac Áeda, 10, 61
'fingerstones', 228
Finistère, xiv, 120
Finn Cycle, see Fenian Cycle
Finn Emna, 46
Finnabair, 180, 188, 196, 208, 212
Finnachad, Sídh, 118, 137, 163, 165, 226
Finnbennach, 23, 86, 87, 202, 203, 211–12
Finnbheara, 149
Finnéces, 23–4, 225; gloss of name, 225
Finnegans Wake, 14, 233; links to Fenian lore
Finnguala, 17, 163–5
Finnian of Moville, St, 18
Fintan, son of Niall, 185–7
Fintan mac Bóchra, 24, 130
Fionn mac Cumhaill, xviii, xxv, xxvii, 11, 16, 20, 21, 23, 29, 46, 56, 75, 82, 99, 139, 152, 191, 200, 219, 220, 221, 222, 239, 240–41, 242, 245, 246, 263, 266, 284, 288, 291, 293; as buffoon, 230–33; character, flexibility of, 229–30; date of death, 237; as Demne Máel, 224–5; as Manx hero Finn McCooil, 293; historicity of, 223; Gwynn ap Nudd, ties to, 263; lineage of, 224; name, etymology and spellings of, 223; narratives of, 223–39; portrait of, 227; quoted verse of, 239; thumb of knowledge, 24, 225; villainous cuckold, 234–7; women, relations with, 228, 234
Fios (the Partholonian), 131,
fios, 225, 226

Fir Bolg, 105, 130, 132–4, 135, 140, 148; etymology of, 133; pronunciation of, 133

Fir Fálgae, 293

fir flathemon, 51

fire goddesses, 12, 39–40, 46; *see also* Brigit

First Battle of Mag Tuired, 133, 141

Fís (classification of narrative), 151

fish, imagery and symbolism, 11, 23–4, 299, 300; *see also* salmon

Fisterra, 303

Flaithius, 63–4

flāmines, 27

Flavius Vopiscus, 67

Fled Bricrenn, xxiii, 87, 188; summarized, 177–84

Fled Dúin na nGéd, 246

Fled Goibnenn, 43–4, 139

Flidais, 19

Flood (Biblical), 24, 128, 129, 130–31; dating of, 129; Ireland, relative to, 130–31

flood legends, 299, 300

Flora, Floralia, 103

Florida, 115

Fochmarc, 131

Fódla, 10, 46, 61–2, 147

folklore, folktale, xviii, xxv, xxvii, 84, 134, 222, 223, 268, 270, 302; 'folk' element in, 286; theories of, 286; *see also* oral tradition

Folk-Lore of the Isle of Man, 294

Folktale, The, xxv

Follamain, 195

Fomorians, 84, 98, 99, 124, 130, 131–2, 134–5, 138, 139, 140, 141–4, 149, 153, 216; described, 134; members, 134–5; origins of, 134

Fontainebleau, 52

Fontes Sequanae, 72

foot-holder, 280–81

Foras Feasa ar Éirinn, 59

ford, fords, 8, 303

Ford, Patrick K., 128, 264

Ford of the Brea, 233

'Ford of the Overwhelming Gift', *see* Áth Tolam Sét

Forgall Manach, 192, 197

formalism, xxix

'Fortress of Apples', *see* Emain Ablach

Fortuna, 71

fosterage, foster parents, 14, 17, 81, 111, 137, 156, 161, 163–4, 166, 170, 186, 188, 194–5, 224, 248, 251, 252, 267

Fothad, 46, 76

Fráech, 24, 58–9

France, xi, xii, xvii, xix, xxvi, 4, 8, 9, 11, 21, 22, 30, 31, 33, 34, 36, 39, 43, 44, 61, 72, 106, 277, 290, 297, 298; *see also* Brittany, Burgundy

Franks (ancient people), 298

Frazer, James, Sir, 27–8, 51, 52

Frecraid, 122

French language, xxiv, 49, 232

French people, xi

'Frenzy of Suibhne/Sweeney, The', *see* Buile Suibhne

Freud, Sigmund, xxviii

Friel, Brian, 105

Friuch, 202–3

Frogs, The, 229

Fuamnach, 78, 156, 158

fuiríg, 54

Furbaide (son of Conchobar), 187, 212

Furbaide Ferbend, 87–8

Gabalglinde, 188

Gáe Bulga, 136, 192, 198, 199, 201, 209

Gáe Assail, 154–5

Gaels, 57, 61–2, 152, 157, 220, 286; *see also* Irish people

Gaelic, *see* Irish language, Scottish Gaelic

Gaelic Scotland, *see* Hebrides, Scottish Highlands

gaesatae, 221

Gàidhealtachd, 291

Gaidiar, 122, 124

Gáirech, 210

Gairloch, 291

gal- (phoneme), xii

'Galahad of the Cycle, the', 229

Galatia, xii

Galatians, xi, 28

Galicia (Poland), xii, xvii

Galicia (Spain), xii, xvii, 12, 35, 146;
traditions of, 302–4

Gallaeci, Gallaecia, xi, 302

Gallia, xii

Gallia Narbonensis, 42

Gallic War, xxi, 26, 31

Galway, City, County, 106, 114, 123,
140, 146, 169

Gamel, 142

Gantz, Jeffrey, 185

Garden of Remembrance (Dublin), 163

Garland Sunday, 106

Garlic Sunday, 106

Garonne, 34

Garristown, 233, 240

Gaul, xi, xxi, 8, 19, 20, 25, 26, 27,
30–31, 37, 39, 45, 60, 67, 72, 74,
262, 270

Gaulish Apollo, xxi, 21, 31, 33, 34–5

Gaulish Dis Pater, 33

Gaulish Jupiter, xxi, 21, 33, 38–9

Gaulish language, xvi, xix, 31–2, 95,
223

Gaulish Mars, 21, 33, 35–7, 71

Gaulish Mercury, xxi, xxvii, 31, 33–4,
44, 61, 104, 139, 192

Gaulish Minerva, 31, 33, 39–40

Gaulish religion, xx, xxi, 15, 31, 137

Gaulish pantheon, xxi, 41

Gaulish Vulcan, 41, 42

Gauls, xi, xii, xix, xxvii, 4, 7, 18, 22,
32, 41, 67, 127, 174, 192, 197, 221,
244, 247, 298

Gavrinis, 6, 7, 94

Ge, 33, 70, 71

Geilt, see Suibne, Suibhne

geis, gessa, 160–61, 210, 215, 217,
235, 236

gender, 60–61, 66–7, 68–70, 77, 83,
85, 87, 91, 211, 212–15

Genesis, Book of, 252–3

Genevra, 296–7

Genii Cucullati, 46

genome studies, 115, 145–6, 262, 302

gente buena, 303

Gentle Land, 110

Geoffrey of Monmouth, 264

George, St, 170

Gerald de Berri, 57

Germania, 31

Germanic languages, xiv, xvi

Germany, xiii, xiv, xix, xxv, 4, 22, 30,
39, 42, 44, 60, 70, 71, 83, 109;
language, xii; scholarship, xxiv, 150

gessa, see geis

Ge-Themis, 33, 70

Giant's Causeway, 231

'Giants of Morvah, The', 296–7

Giants of the Earth, 39

Gilbert, W. S., 107, 294

Gilfaethwy, 18, 71, 262, 280–81

Gimbutas, Marija, 70

Giraldus Cambrensis, 16, 21, 57–9, 91,
249, 298; quoted, 58

glam dícenn, 16

Glanicae, 12

Glanis, 11–12

Glanum, 11, 22

Glasgow, 24, 287

Glen Alden, 294

Glen Bolcáin, 247

Glen of the Deaf, 216

Glen Roy, 228

Glenasmole, 242

Glenbuck, 247

Glewlwyd Galfaelfawr, 268

Glwyddyn Saer, 43, 44, 139

Gloucester Castle, 270

Glyn Cuch, 272
Gobbán Saor, 43, 44
gobae, 43
God (Christian), 7, 238, 247, 248, 277
Goddesses and Gods of Old Europe, 70
Goethe, Johann von, xii
Goewin, 280–81
gof, gofan, 43
Gofannon, 43, 44, 71, 139, 262
Goibniu, 43, 44, 46, 139, 143
'Goibniu's feast', *see Fled Goibnenn*
Goídel, xvi
Goídel Glas, 130, 145
Goídelc, 130
Goidelic languages, xvi, 145, 220
Golden Bough, The, 27–8, 51
Golden Legend, 245
Golden Pillars, king of the, 154–5
Goleuddyd, 268
Goll, King (W. B. Yeats's creation), 250
Goll mac Doilb, 124
Goll mac Morna, 224, 227, 233
Gone with the Wind, 52–3
'good god', *see* Dagda
Goreu, 270
Gorias, 136
Gorsedd Beirdd Ynys Prydain, xiii, 30
Gospels, xxii, 88, 89, 111, 113, 165, 237, 288, 295; *see also* New Testament, Old Testament
Gradlon, Gralon, 285, 299–301
Graeco-Roman tradition, 12
Grail, 75
Grail Castle, 252
Gráinne, 80, 151, 222; narrative of, 234–7
Grampian Mountains, 10, 287
Grannus, 34
Grassholm, *see* Gwales
Graves, Robert, 51, 52
Gray, Thomas, xiii
Great Britain, *see* Britain
'Great Queen', 10, 83
Great Saint Bernard's Pass, 39

Greece, 136, 154, 286
'Greece, prince of', 131
Greek art, xv
Greek commentators, xi, xviii, 26, 41
Greek language, xi, xxii, 285
Greek mythology, *see* classical mythology
Greeks (people), xviii, 4, 11–12, 41, 47
Gregory, Augusta Lady, xxv, 66
Green, Miranda, 71, 280
Greenan Hill, 88
Greene, David, 202
Grey of Macha, *see* Liath Macha
Grianán Meidbe, 88
Grimm, Jakob and Wilhelm, 286
Gronw Pebyr, 80, 282–3
Groundhog Day, 101
Gruffydd, W. J., xxvii
Guaire, 248
Guatemala, 33
Guénolé, 299, 300–301
Guest, Lady Charlotte, xxiv, 264, 267, 299
Guinevere, 295, 296
Gulliver's Travels, 258
Gundestrup cauldron, xix-xx, 7, 17, 22, 23, 37, 38, 68, 75
Gwales, 120
gwawd, 26
Gwawl, son of Clud, 273–4, 279
Gwenhwyfar, 295
Gwent Is Coed, 274
Gwern, 276
Gwion Bach, 76, 266
Gwrhyr Gwastad Ieithoedd, 269
Gwri, 274
Gwyddno Garanhir, 267
Gwydion, 18, 71, 80, 262, 280–81
Gwyn Fryn, 277
Gwyn Gogoyw, 277
Gwynedd, 280, 283
Gwynn ap Nudd, 120, 223; etymology of, 263; Fionn mac Cumhaill, ties to, 263

Haakon the Good, 58
Hades, 40, 108, 121
Hadrian's Wall, 12, 46, 74
Hafgan, 119–20, 272–3
Hag of Beare, see Cailleach Bhéirre
Hallowe'en, 93–4, 97–8; etymology of, 98; see also Samain
Hallstatt, xv, xviii, 17, 22, 47, 109
Ham (Biblical), 134
Hamel, see van Hamel
Hamp, Eric, 35, 119
Hanes Taliesin, 266–7
Harlech, 275, 276
harp, 35, 142
'Harp That Once Through Tara's Halls, The', 52
Harrison, William, xxv, 294
hazel trees, nuts, 11, 23, 138, 221, 254
healing, 6, 12, 15, 21, 27, 34, 35, 36, 43, 72, 73–4, 90, 138, 139, 154–5, 157, 210
heaven (Christian), 111, 119
Hebrew Bible, see Old Testament
Hebrew language, 131
Hebrew mythology, 128; see also Bible
Hebrews (ancient), 129
Hebrides, xiv, xvi, xvii, 8, 47, 50, 121, 134, 142, 198, 223, 233, 287, 289, 291, 293
Hebrides Overture, xiii
Hecate, 45
hell (Christian), 41, 119, 120, 270; linked to Annwfn, 120; Welsh name for, 120
Helvetia, Helvetii, 4
Henkin, Elissa R., 89
Henry II, 49, 57
Henry VIII, xviii, 48
Hephaestus, 3, 43–4
Hera, 70, 71
Heracles, Hercules, xxvi, 41–2, 155, 192, 193, 195, 224, 229; labours of, 155, 156, 269; Tower of, 302
Hermes, 41

hero's portion, the, see champion's portion
Herodotus, xx
Hesiod, 70, 127, 128
Hesperides, Garden of the, 154–5
Hibernia, 145–6, 148
Hiberno-English, 122, 230, 231
Hiberno-Latin, 114
Hiberno-Normans, 49; see also Anglo-Normans, Normans
hierogamy, 60
high king, see ard rí
Highlands, see Scottish Highlands
Hippolytus, 246, 252
Hippolytus (Euripides), 252
Historia Brittonum, 262–3
Historia Regnum Britanniae, 264
Historical Cycle, see Cycles of the Kings,
History of Ireland: The Heroic Period, xxiv
'History of Taliesin', see *Ystoria Taliesin*
Hochdorf, xix, 109, 113
Hogonange, 20
Holinshed, Raphael, 129
Hollantide, 97, 99–100
Holy Roman Emperor, 222
Homer, 63, 202, 227
homosexuality, 68
horse, imagery and symbolism, 6, 7, 12, 20–22, 39, 58, 62, 68, 154–5, 164, 170, 173–4, 179, 230, 242, 267, 273, 274, 275, 301; mutilated, 275
'Hostel of the Quicken Trees, The', see *Bruidhean Chaorthainn*
'Hosting of the Sidhe, The', 116
'How Rónán Killed His Son', see *Fingal Rónáin*
Howells, William, xxv
Howth, 161
huestia, 303
human sacrifice, xx, 10, 26, 28–9, 37, 38, 51–2, 97, 98, 99, 228

'Hundred Battles', *see* Conn
    Cétchathach
Hungary, xiv, 34, 67–8
Hunt, Robert, xxv, 295
Hurle, Henry, 30
hurling, 195, 224–5
Hy Brasil, 122, 123
Hychdwn Hir, 18, 281
Hyddwn, 281
Hyfaidd Hen, 273
Hyperboreans, 4
Hywel Dda, xxii, 68

Ibar Cinn Chon, 176
Iberian Peninsula, Iberia, xi, 145–6,
    302
Ibor Cind Trácha, 215
Iceland, xxvi, 114, 127; Irish settlement
    there, 114
Iceni, 5, 83
Icovellauna, 11
Ilbrec, 16
Iliad, the, 32, 44, 63, 137, 168, 169,
    229
imbas forosnai, 29, 226
Imbolc, 40, 90, 95, 100–102, 105;
    ewes' lactation and, 100; variant
    forms, 100
Immram, 109
Imram, 109, 151
Imram Brain, xxiii, 109–14, 124, 150,
    243; Christian intrusions, 110, 113;
    summarized, 109–12
Imram Curaig Maíle Dúin, 112–13,
    115
Inanna, 60
Inber Colptha, 147
Inber Domnann, 133
Inber Scéne, 131, 147
incest, 159, 194
Inchcleraun, 88
Indech, 98
India, 30, 40, 58, 60, 166, 253
Indians (Native Americans), 30, 115

Indo-European languages, tradition,
    xiv, xxviii, 9, 13, 40, 44, 60
Industrial Revolution, 285
Ingcél Cáech, 161–2
Inis Clothrand, 88
Inis Fáil, 55, 130
Inis Fionnchuire (or Findchuire),
    154–5
Inishglora, 164, 165
Inishmore, 133
Inishowen Peninsula, 112
interment, *see* burial customs
International Socialist Congress, 104
interpretatio Celtica, 32–3
interpretatio Romana, xxi, 31, 39, 41
Into the West, 123
'Intoxication of the Ulstermen, The',
    see Mesca Ulad
Inverness, 228, 289, 291
inxana, 303–4
Iolanthe, 107
Iona, 50, 288
Ír, 146–7
Iraird Cuillen, 204
Ireland, xvi, xvii, xviii, xxi–xxii, xxiii,
    xxv, 6, 8, 9, 10, 16, 18, 21, 24, 25,
    40, 43, 44, 46, 61, 90, 98, 108, 112,
    113, 121, 124, 139, 143, 154, 164,
    166, 171, 185, 223, 226, 235, 239,
    242, 244, 249, 275–7, 285, 288,
    293, 297, 302; chronology of, 50;
    division of, 131, 133, 147, 148, 185;
    as Éire, 62; history, of, 48–50;
    personifications of, 10, 61–3, 130;
    poetic names for, 55, 62, 147;
    Republic of, 62, 169, 203, 221;
    Spain, links to, 145–6, 302
Irgairech, 210
Irish art, 7
Irish Comic Tradition, The, 258
Irish Fairy Tales, 222
Irish Folklore Commission, xxv
Irish Free State, xvii
Irish Heracles, xxvi

Irish language, xi, xiii, xvi, xvii, xxiii, xxiv, 44, 105, 116, 122, 131, 145, 238, 240, 291, 293; mythic invention of, 129–30, 145; *see also* Old Irish

Irish literature, xxi, 131, 243; Cycles of, classification, 150–51, 243; early, xxi, xxvi, 127–8, 137, 147, 191–2, 200, 209, 220, 233, 262; native modes of categorization, 151

Irish Melodies, 52

Irish monks, monasticism, xvii, xxii, xxviii, 49, 109, 114, 237, 285–6, 295

Irish people, xvi, xxi–xxii, 114, 115, 135, 220; genome studies of, 145–6; Giraldus's disdain for, 57–8; Welsh people, links to, 263; *see also* Gaels

Irish Popular Superstitions, 104

Irish Republican Brotherhood, 220

Irish Sea, 13, 124, 192, 293

Iron Age, xiv, xv, 7, 15, 20, 22, 44, 96, 108–9, 146, 182

Iruad, Ioruaidh, King, 154–5

Irving, Washington, 113

Isaiah, Book of, 96

Iseult, 234, 295

Ishtar, 96

Isidore of Seville, 128, 131

Island of Joy, 111, 112

Islay, 291

Isle of Man, *see* Man, Isle of

'Isle of the Mighty', Welsh phrase for Britain (q.v.)

Israel (ancient), Israelites, 129, 136, 145; 'lost tribe of', 129

Italy, Italian peninsula, xv, xx, 19, 102

Íth, 146, 147

Iubdán, 258

Iuchair, 153–5

Iucharba, 153–5

Iuchra, 16

Jack (Cornish giant), 296–7

Jackson, Kenneth H., 28

Jacobite Rebellion, 287

Jacobus de Voraigne, Archbishop, 245

Japheth, 132, 145

Jasconius, 114

Jefferson, Thomas, xii

Jennifer, 295, 296

Jeremiah, 300

Jerome, St, 131

Jesus Christ, 7, 91, 110, 111, 113, 171, 248, 277

Jewish calendar, *see* calendar

Jewish religion, *see* Judaism

Joan (Cornish narrative figure), 296

Johnson, Samuel, 287

Jones, Gwyn, 264

Jones, Thomas, 264

Joseph (Old Testament), 253

Jove, *see* Jupiter; cf. Zeus

Joyce, James, 14, 99, 233; *see also* *Finnegans Wake*

Judaism, 95, 129

Judas, 115

judges, xxii

Julius Agricola, xx

Julius Caesar, xi, xxi, 5, 16, 26–7, 31, 33, 34, 38, 39, 40, 67, 97, 127, 139, 192

Jung, Carl Gustav, xxviii

Jutland Peninsula, xix

Jupiter, Jove, xxi, 7, 21, 31, 33, 37, 38–9, 97; Beissirissa, 39; columns, 39; Partinus, 33; Poeninus, 39; Uxellinus, 39

Jutes, 261

Kala Goañv, 97

Kala Hañv, 102

Keating, Elizabeth Frances, 303

Keating, Geoffrey, xxvii, 59, 100, 103, 128, 174, 223

Keaton, Buster, 230

Kelleher, John V., 129, 227

Kelly, Oisín, 163

kelpie, 32

Keltoí, xi, xiv

Kenecunill, 58

Kenmare estuary, peninsula, 61, 147
Kennedy, Patrick, 231
'Kenneth, Sombre', *see* Brahan Seer
Kenneth Oaur, Owir, alternative forms for the Brahan Seer (q.v.)
Kentigern, St, 24
Kêr Is, summarized, 299–302
Kernow, 295
Kerry, County, 9, 61, 62, 64, 114, 117, 131, 147, 182, 233, 240, 247
Kildare, County, town, 13, 40, 89, 90, 91, 192, 223
Killaloe, 163–4, 244
Killarney, 9, 240
Killycluggin Stone, 98
Kincora, 244
King Kong, xxvi
King Lear, 129
'King of Greece, The', 227
'king of Sicily', 154–5
'king of the fairies', *see* fairy, Finnbheara
'king of the world, the', 222, 227, 228
Kings, Book of, 98
kingship, 22–3, 48–65, 243–4, 257, 280; definition, 48; gender of, 60; initiation, 57–60
kinship, Irish concepts of, 50–52
Knights of Labor, The, 104
Knockadoon Island, 123
Knockainy, 9
Knockaulin, 91
Knockmany, 231
Knocknarea, 88
knowledge (esoteric), 11, 14, 24, 25, 76, 131, 225
Knowth, 13, 166
Korentin, *see* Corentin
korrigans, 300, 301
Krause, David, 230
Kristof, 300–301

La Cathédrale engloutie, 302
La Coruña, 146, 302

La Tène, xv–xvi, xviii, 44, 98
La Villemarqué, Théodore Hersart de, xiii, 298–9
Laa Luanistyn, 105
Labraid Luathlám ar Claideb, 124, 213–14
Láeg, 79, 178, 181, 187, 189, 199, 209, 210, 213–14, 217–18
lai, lay (literary form), 298
Lailoken, 246, 263
Lairgnéan, 165
Laius, 230
Lallans language, xvi, 287
Lammas Day, 93, 106
Lancelot, 264
'Land of –': alphabetized under subject, e.g. 'Women, Land of'
land of youth, *see* Tír na nÓg
Land's End, 296
Landévennec, 299
Laoi Oisín i dTír na nÓg, 20, 123, 240; summarized, 240–42
Laois, County, 135
Laon, 34
Larzac Inscription, 31–2
Lascaux, 22
Latin, xi, xvii, xxi, xxii, xxiii, 5, 12, 14, 32, 42, 48, 91, 95, 108, 114, 128, 136, 145, 148, 169, 192, 234, 262, 285, 288, 302
lavandeira nocturna, 303
Lavoye, 7
law, legal systems, xxii, 44, 49, 54, 68–9
lay, see lai
'Lay of Oisín in the Land of Youth', *see* *Laoi Oisin I dTír na nÓg*
Le Châtelet, 8, 38
Lebor Gabála Érenn, Leabhar Gabhála, xxiii, 10, 18, 24, 29, 41, 55, 57, 61, 85, 102, 127–49, 151, 152, 155, 163, 166, 173, 192, 302; historicity of, 128; summarized, 129–40, 144–9; title translations, 127

Lebor na hUidre, xxii

Leborcham, 81, 185

legal systems, *see* law

legend, legends, xxvi; definition and etymology of, 245

'Legend of Knockmany, The', 231–2

'Legend of Fin-Mac-Cool, The', 232

'Legend of the City of Ys', 285; summarized, 299–302

Legendary Fictions of the Irish Celts, 231

legende, 245

Leiden, 34

Leinster, 50, 56, 62, 90, 160, 174, 204, 224, 242, 250, 251, 252, 254, 293

Leitrim, County, 107, 169

Lendabair, 179

Lenihan, Eddie, 107

Lenus, 36

leopard, leopard imagery, xx

leprechaun, 246, 256–7, 258, 304; etymology of, 256; Galician equivalent, 304

Lévi-Strauss, Claude, xxix

Lewis, Isle of, 289

Lhuyd, Edward, xii, 295

Lí Ban, 24, 79, 124, 213–15

Lia Fáil, 53, 55, 136, 170, 244

Liath Macha [Grey of Macha], 21, 179, 199, 218

Libyans, xx

Liegnitz, 34

Life of Brigid, 91

Liffey, River, 14, 89–90, 148, 160, 161, 224, 238

Lilliputians, 258

Limerick, City and County, 9, 13, 49, 62, 123, 245

Lincolnshire, 33

Lindow Man, xix, 28, 37

linear time, 96

Linn Féic, 11, 23, 225

Lir (father of swan children), 118, 137, 163

Lir (patronym of Manannán), 137, 163

Lisconner Bay, 123

L'Isola Brazil, 122

literacy, 285–6

'Little Britain', 297

Living, Land of the, *see* Tír na mBéo

Livy, xx

Llanes, 304

Llassar Llaes Gyfnewid, 76, 275

Lleu Llaw Gyffes, xxvii, 7–8, 34, 47, 80, 140, 280, 281–2; name explained, 282

Lloegyr (Welsh name for England), 278

Llwyd, 80, 279

Llyn Llyw, 24

Llyn Tegid, 266

Llŷr, 275

Llŷr, Children of, 71, 275–7

Labor Day, 104

Loch Lomond, 23

Loch Ness, 290

Loch Rudraige, 257–8

Lochaber, 19

Lochlainn, 16, 154, 155, 227, 228

Lóegaire Búadach, 177, 178, 179, 180–81, 182, 183, 186, 198

Loingsechan, 248–9

Loire, River, Valley, 21, 27, 67

Loki, 24

Lomna, 162

lón láith, 197

London, 5, 10, 90, 277

Longas (or *Longes*) *mac nUislenn*, 81–2, 171

Longford, County, 118, 156

'lost tribe of Israel', 129

Loucetious, 36

Loudon, 34

Lough Arrow, 140

Lough Derraveragh, 164

Lough Foyle, 244

Lough Gur, 9, 123

Lough Lein, 240

Lough Neagh, 24, 293

Lough Ree, 88, 212
Louis XIV, 8, 48
Louth, County, 46, 53, 91, 187, 192, 200, 203, 209
Louvain, xxiii
'love spot', see ball seirce
Low Countries, xix, 61; see also Belgium, Spanish Netherlands
Lowlands, see Scottish Lowlands
Lucan, 8, 32, 37, 38, 46, 108, 119
Luchta mac Luachada, 43, 46, 139, 142, 143
Lucian, 41–2
Lucifer, 267
Lug Lámfhota, xxvii, 7–8, 16, 34, 40, 41, 43, 47, 62–3, 105, 106, 122, 136, 138, 139–44, 151, 153–5, 174, 191, 192, 193–4, 207–8, 246, 268, 296, 297; Christian linkage to Michael, 106; epithet of, 139
Lugaid (son of Cú Roí), 217–18
Lughnasa, 34, 95, 104–6, 133, 296; alternative forms, 105; celebrations, 105; Christianization of, 106; dates of, 105–6; Feast of Lughnasa, The, 105
Lugnasad, 105
Lugos, Lugus, xxvii, 34, 47, 104, 139
Lug(u)dunum, 34, 104
lunar calendar, see calendar
Lúnasa, see Lughnasa
Lunasduinn, 105
Lupercalia, 101
Luzel, François Marie, xxv
Lydney Park, 36, 138
Lyon, 34, 43, 104

Mab, Queen, 88
Mabinogi, xxiii, 9, 18, 21–2, 35, 38, 46, 66, 71, 76, 79–80, 119, 120, 262, 263, 266, 271–83, 284, 303; critique of, 271; preferred to spelling Mabinogion, 264; summarized, 271–83; texts included in, 264;

themes of, 271; title, significance, 264, 271; see also branches: Branwen, Manawydan, Math, Pwyll
Mabinogion, Lady Guest's, xxiv, xxvi, 264, 267, 299; bogus etymology of, 264
Mabon, 24, 35, 70, 262, 268, 269
mac –: family names with the lower case patronymic mac signal that the figure is alphabetized under the given name, e.g. Fionn mac Cumhaill
MacAlpin, Kenneth, 286
Mac an Lúin, 226
MacCana, Proinsias, 66, 90–91, 115–16, 271
Mac Cécht (of Tuatha Dé Danann), 10, 147
Mac Cécht (ally of Conaire Mór), 162
McCone, Kim, xxviii
Mac Da Thó, 174–6, 177
MacDonell, Margaret, 291
MacGregor, James, xxiv
Mac Gréine, 8, 147
Macha (general), 32, 45, 140; parentage of, 83–5, 173; triad, identifying, 85, 173
Macha (Ulster queen), 85, 173
Macha (Nemedian queen), 85, 132, 173
Macha (wife of Crunniuc), 21, 32, 45, 83–5, 172–4; cursing with birth pangs, 85, 173–4, 202, 204, 206; parentage of, 85, 173
Mac Cuill, 62, 147
Mac Glass, 252
Macgnímartha Find, 224–5
Mac-ind-Óc, 35
MacKenzie, Kenneth, 289
MacKinnon, Clan, 18
MacMathúna, Séamus, 110–12
MacNeil, Joe Neil, 292
MacNeill, Eoin, 50–51, 52, 54, 98
MacNeill, Máire, 95, 105–6
Mac Óc, 35

Macpherson, James, xii, xiii, xxiv, 20, 219–20, 229, 232, 288, 299

Macsen Wledig, xxvii, 298

Mad Sweeney, see Suibne, Suibhne

'Madness of King Goll, The', 250

Máel Dúin, 112–13, 122

Máel Fhothartaig, 250–52

Máel Sechnaill, 55

Maelgwn Gwynedd, 266, 267

Mag Cruchna, 213

Mag Dá Chéo, 124

Mag Ítha, 148

Mag Mell, 124, 149, 213

Mag Muirtheimne, 153, 192, 193, 195, 212, 217, 256

Mag nAilbe, 176

Mag nElta (Moynalty), 131

Mag Rath, Battle of, 245, 247, 248

Mag Slécht, 98

Mag Tuired, 84, 149, 153; etymology of, 140; locations of, 140; see also Cath Maige Tuired, First Battle of Mag Tuired

magic, magicians, 14, 16, 18, 25–6, 43, 75, 80, 111, 118, 136, 137, 142, 146, 152, 154–5, 156, 182, 215, 245, 246, 247, 263, 266, 267, 273, 281, 283, 300–301

Magog, 131, 132

Maia, 34

Maiden Castle, xviii, 22

Maignis, 234

Maine (seven sons), 87, 161

Maistre Pierre Pathelin, 232

Malachy I, 55

Malahide Bay, 133

Malaliach, 131

'male gaze', 77

Mamers, 36

Man, Isle of, xvi, xxv, 7, 43, 44, 64, 76, 105, 121, 124, 171, 226, 284; Manannán mac Lir, links to, 137, 293; Manx names for, 293; traditions of, 293–4

'Man Who Dreamed of Faeryland, The', 107

Manapii, 192

Manannán mac Lir, 16, 110–11, 122, 124, 137, 141, 151, 163, 166, 213, 215, 255, 263, 293; etymology of name, 137, 293; Manawydan, compared with, 263

Manavia, 293

Manawydan fab Llŷr, 22, 80, 263, 275, 277–9; Manannán mac Lir, compared with, 263

Manawydan, Son of Llŷr, 18, 263, 264; summarized, 277–80

Manching, 4

Mannin, 293

manteis, 26

Manx language, xi, xvi, xvii, xxiv, 97, 105, 230, 293–4, 295

Maponos, 35, 270

Marie de France, 298

Mark, King of Cornwall, 234, 295

Marne, 8, 35, 38, 70, 262

marriage, practice, customs, law, 67, 68–9, 101, 103, 156, 165, 272, 273–4; sacral, ceremonial, 60–61, 71, 98, 280

Marryat, Frederick, 232, 233

Mars, 31, 33, 38, 83, 97, 234; Camulos, 36; Corotiacus, 36; Lenus, 36; Loucetious, 36; Mullo, 36; Nabelcus, 36; Olloudius, 33; Rigonemetis, 33; Teutates, 33, 37, 97; Toutatis, 37; Vesontius, 33; Vorocius, 36; see also Gaulish Mars

Marseilles, xi

Mary, Blessed Virgin, 101, 103

'Mary of the Gael', 90

Masons, Masonic Order, 30

materialism, xiv

Math, Son of Mathonwy (Branch Four), 18, 264; summarized, 280–83; critique of, 280

Math Vab Mathonwy (character), 80, 280–83

Math Vab Mathonwy (Gruffydd), xxvii

Matholwch, 38, 76, 275–7

Mathonwy, 280

Matres, 46

Matrona, Dea, 8, 262

Matoniae Aufuniae, 70

Mavers, Mavors, 36

May Day/Eve (non-Celtic), 103–4; *see also* Beltaine, Calan Mai

Mayo, County, 106, 140, 164, 169

maypoles, 103

Meath, County, 6, 13, 29, 46, 53, 62, 105, 116, 133, 147, 161, 166, 204, 234, 239

Medb, Queen, xix, xx, 56, 59, 61, 66, 85–8, 124, 156, 161, 169, 170, 174–5, 180–81, 188, 194, 197, 203, 204–12, 216, 245, 246; appearance of, 86; character, 86; death of, 87–8; etymology of, 85; lineage of, 86–7; cf. Medb Lethderg, 86; 'pillow talk with Ailill', 203

Medb Lethderg, 56, 86

Medb's Lump, 88

Medb's Sun Porch, 88

Mediterranean culture, peoples, 12, 39, 51, 67, 73, 192

Mediterranean Sea, xiv, 12

Mellifont Abbey, 238

Melor, St, 11

Men-an-Tol, 296

Mendelssohn, Felix, xii–xiii

Menw, 269

Mercia, 261

Mercier, Vivian, 258

Mercury, xxi, 18, 31, 33, 28, 41, 71–2

Mercury Moccus, 34

Merlin, 246, 249, 263, 298

mermaid, 301

Mes Buachalla, 160

Mesca Ulad, summarized, 184–90; translations of, 185

metalwork, 4

metempsychosis, 27

Metz, 11, 72, 73

Mexico, 96

Miach, 138

Michael, Archangel, St, 106, 120

Michaelmas, 106

Midac, 228

Midcháin, *see* Miodhchaoin

Middle East, 60, 130

Mide (druid), 29, 132, 292

Mide (province, petty kingdom), 29, 132

Midir, 17, 78, 118, 155–9, 160, 165

Midsummer Night's Dream, A, 107

Míl Espáine, 41, 145–6, 148

Milesians, 10, 24, 41, 57, 61–2, 102, 122, 128, 130, 135, 144–9, 157, 163, 170, 185; origins of, 144–5

Miletus, 145

Milky Way Galaxy, 127, 292

Milladoiro, 303

Milton, John, xii

Minerva 12, 13, 31, 33, 39–40, 73, 90

Minotaur, 245

Miodhchaoin, Midcháin, 154–5

Mioscgán Méabha, 88

Miscaun Maeve, 88

mistletoe, 27–8, 262

Mitchell, Margaret, 52–3

Mo Cháemóc, 165

Moccus, 18

mòd, xiii

Modron, 70, 262, 270

Modrun, Saint, 70–71

Moher, Cliffs of, 123

Moira, Battle of, *see* Mag Rath, battle of

Moling, Mo Ling, St, 249–50

Moloch, 98

Mona, 293

Mona Miscellany, xxv, 294

Monaghan, County, 46, 169

monasticism, xvii, xviii, 46, 88, 109, 242, 249, 285–6, 299; see also Irish monks, monasticism
Mong Ruadh, 85, 173
Mongán, 17, 111, 233
monogamy, 228
monster, monsters, 19, 39, 59, 99, 249, 257–8; see also Fomorians
Monte Pindo, 303
moon, 93–5
Moore, Arthur, 294
Moore, Thomas, 52
Mór Muman, 9, 61, 83–4, 85
Morann, Testament of, 51
Morann (son of Cairbre Cinn-Chait), 148
Morfran, 76, 266
Morganwg, Iolo, xiii, 30, 299
Moritasgus, 34, 72
Morna, Clan, 224
Mórrígan, 10, 19, 44, 61, 83–4, 85, 98, 140, 143, 152, 206, 207, 210, 218, 246, 303
Mórrígna, 32, 44, 83
Morvah, 105, 296–7
Morvarc'h, 301
Moselle River, Valley, 11, 20, 36, 39
Moses, 129, 145
mother-goddesses, 8, 9, 12, 33, 46, 70–71, 73, 85–6
motif index, see Aarne-Thompson catalogue
Motif-Index of Folk-Literature, 112; see also Aarne-Thompson catalogue
Mound of the Hostages, 53
Mourne Mountains, 216
mouros, 304
Moville, 18
Movilly, 36
Moyle, Strait of, Sea of, 148, 164
Moynalty, see Mag nElta
Moytura, see Cath Maige Tuired, Mag Tuired
Mugain, 78

Muileartach, 77
muirdris, 257–8
Muirenn Muncháem, 224
Mull of Kintyre, 164
Mullingar, 210
Mullo, 36
Mummers' May Day, 104
Munremur mac Gerrcind, 183
Munster, 9, 41, 61, 118, 165, 182, 187, 215
Murias, 136
Murphy, Gerard, xxvii, 229–30
music, 226–7, 253, 254, 303
Myrddin (G)wyllt, 249, 263
mystery plays, 295
Mythological Cycle, 128, 136, 150–67, 228, 243, 245; characteristics of, 152; naming of, 152
mythology, xxv, xxvi; definition, xxvi–xxvii, 152
mythos, xxvi

na trí dé dána, 43
Nabelcus, 36
Nagy, Joseph, 238
Nantosuelta, 41, 72
Narbonensis, 42
Narbonne, 12
National Museum of Ireland, 98
Natural History (Pliny), 22, 27
Navan, 53
Navan Fort, 85, 168
Navigatio Sancti Brendani Abbatis, 114–15
Nechta Scéne, 197
Nechtan (Boand's husband), 14, 118, 137, 166
Nechtan mac Collbrain, 112, 113
Néit, 83
Nemain, 83
Nemausicae, Nemausus, 9
Nemed, 85, 132–3; lineage of, 132
Nemedians, 130, 132–3, 135, 136, 145
nemeton, 28, 33

Nemetona, 83

Neptune, 14

Nera, 87

Ness, 169, 170

Neuchâtel, Lake, xv

New Catholic Encyclopedia, The (quoted), 89–90

New Comparative Mythology, xxix

New Testament, xxii; *see also* Gospels

New World, xvii, 292; *see also* North America

New Year's Day, 60, 95; *see also* Samain

Newell, Mike, 123

Newgrange, 6–7, 13, 93, 94, 137, 156, 166

Newman, Conor, 54

Newry, 215

Niall Noígiallach, 40, 48, 63–4, 185, 244, 245; name, meaning of, 244

Niam, Niamh (of the golden hair), 20, 78, 113, 123, 216, 222; described, 241; narrative of, 241–2

Niam (often seen as wife of Conall), 216

Ní Dhomhnaill, Nuala, 108

'Nine Hostages', *see* Niall Noígiallach

Nisein, 275

Niúl, 145

Noah, 128, 130, 134, 145

Nodons, 23, 36, 138

noínden, see ces noínden Ulad

Noíse, 45, 81, 151, 170, 186; as Nois in Nova Scotia, 292

Normandy, 36, 38

Normans, xvi, 50, 116, 221, 239, 262, 264, 271; *see also* Anglo-Normans, Hiberno-Normans

Norse language, 169, 286, 290, 293

Norse religion, mythology, 24, 137, 144, 290

Norsemen, 49, 50, 114, 134, 221, 244, 245, 286, 290, 293

North America, 6, 27, 30, 115, 146, 265, 291; *see also* New World

North Carolina, 291

North Channel, 164

Northern Ireland, 24, 133, 220, 244, 246

Norway, 58

Nostradamus, 290

Nova Scotia, xvii, 115, 127, 223, 230, 284, 291–2; traditions of, 291–2

Nuadu Airgetlám, 136, 137, 140, 141–3, 153, 224, 268; sword of, 136

Nuadu Necht, 224

Nudd Llaw Erient, 138

numerology, 44–5, 110–11

numinosity, 8

nymph, nymphs, 12, 20

oak, 27, 28, 29, 38, 39, 80, 91, 164, 204, 216, 282, 301

O'Brien (literary character), 232

Ochall Ochne, 203

Ó Cléirigh, Micheál, 128

Ó Conchobhair family, 59

O'Connell, Daniel, 57

O'Connell Street, 14, 191

O'Connor, Rory, 55

O'Conor, Charles, 128–9

Ó Corráin, Donnchadh, xxviii

Ó Cróinín, Dáibhí, 52

Ó Duibhgeannáin, Dáibhi, 234

Odysseus, 227, 233

Odyssey, 227

Oedipus, xxvi, 230, 232

O'Faolain, Sean, 222

Offa, King, 261

Offaly, County, 13

O'Flaherty, Roderick, 128

ogham, xvii, 16, 29, 42, 115, 138–9, 154, 205

Ogma, 42, 138–9, 141, 143

Ogmios, 42, 47, 139

O'Grady, Standish James, xxiv, 168, 229

O'Hara family (fictional), 52–3
Ohio River, 115
Ó hÓgáin, Dáithí, 193, 224
Ó hUiginn, Tadhg Dall, 10
Oided Mac nUisnig, 82, 171
Oidhheadh Chlainne Lir, 17, 83, 113, 118, 152, 155; dating of, 152, 163; summarized, 163–5
Oidhheadh Chlainne Tuireann, xxiii, 83, 163; summarized, 153–5
Oisín, 20, 78, 123, 216, 219, 220, 221, 222, 229, 230, 232, 234, 235, 236, 238–9; etymology of name, 20, 229; as Manx hero Oshin, 293; narrative of, 240–42
Old English, *see* Anglo-Saxons
'Old English' in Ireland, 49
Old Irish, xi, xiii, xxiv, 37, 45, 48, 51, 74, 128, 130, 150, 165–6, 220, 233, 287, 293
'Old North, the', 261, 265
Old Testament, Hebrew Bible, 96, 98, 300; *see also* Gospels
Old Welsh, xi, 74
Olimpo Celta, 303
ollam, 226
Olloudius, 33
Olmstead, Garrett, xx
Olwen, 77, 267, 268, 269
Olympians, Olympian deities, xxvi, 3, 32, 70, 136–7, 149
omphalos, 62, 292
Ong, Walter J., 285
'Only Jealousy of Emer, the', *see* Serglige Con Culainn
Ontario, 291
Oonagh, 231–2
O'Rahilly, Thomas, F., xxviii, 8, 117, 144, 244
oral tradition, xviii, xxv, 7, 8, 10, 19, 32, 76, 88, 102–3, 122, 123, 134, 149, 166, 171, 191, 232–3, 237, 238, 249, 256, 263, 284–6, 295–6, 299, 302, 303; *see also* folklore

Orality and Literacy, 285
Orange (France), 9
Orastie (Romania), 17
orbe alio, alius orbis, 108, 117, 119
Orc Triath, 18
Orci, 17
Orlám, 205–6
Orosius, 128
Orpheus, xxvi
Oscans, 36
Oscar, xiii, 221, 229, 236, 240–41, 292
Oshin, 293
Ossian, xii, xiii, 20, 220, 288
Ossianic Cycle, *see* Fenian Cycle
Ossianic fashion, xii
Ossianic Society, xxiv
otherworld, otherworlds, 11, 17, 18, 20, 43, 79, 99, 107–24, 139, 152, 157, 207, 213, 225, 240, 256, 263, 272, 293; names for, 119–24; *sídh* and, 116–19; voyages to, 109–16
Owain ap Urien, 265
owl, imagery and symbolism, 80, 283
Oxford University, xii

P-Celtic, xvi, 97, 102, 133
Pagan Celtic Britain, 8, 17, 41, 66
Pagan Past and Christian Present in Early Irish Literature, xxviii
'pagan survival' theories, xxvii–xxviii, 192, 262
Palace Beautiful, 113
Palila, 102
Pallas, 32
Pantheon (Rome), the, 97
papacy, 49, 58, 91, 97, 237
Paps of Ana, the, 9, 71, 117
par Ys, 302
Paradise Lost, xii
Paraguay, 108
'Parallel Roads', 228
Parilia, 102
Paris, xiv, 22, 38, 302

Partholón, 131
Partholonians, 102, 130, 131–2, 134–5
passage-graves, tombs, 6, 13, 116, 166
Passover, 95
Patai, Raphael, 230
Patterson, Nerys, 101, 103, 104
Patrick, St, xvii, xxiii, xxvii, 7, 19, 29, 50, 90, 106, 165, 219, 226, 237, 238–9, 240, 244
Paul the Hermit, 115
Pennant, Thomas, 289
Pentecost, 98
Perceval, 253, 298
Peronnik, 298
Perseus, 170, 193
'Persia, king of', 154–5
Persians, xx, 201, 232
Perthshire, 233
petasus, 33
Peter Simple, 232
Pezron, Paul-Yves, xii
Phaedra, 246, 252
phallic symbolism, 17, 19, 34, 44, 46, 53, 55, 103, 170, 232
phantom funeral, 303
'Phantom's Frenzy, The', 62–3
Pharsalia, 108
Philomena, St, 89
Phoebus, 31
Phoenicia, 102
phynodderree, 294
Phynodderree, The, 294
physical evidence (archaeological), xviii, xix, 7, 42
Picts, 132, 265, 286
pig, imagery and symbolism, 153, 154–5, 161, 166, 170, 175–6, 202–3, 226, 254, 280–81
Pilgrim's Progress, 113
Pirates of Penzance, 294–5
Pisear, 154–5
pixie, piskie, 295–6
Plain of Delights, 111
Plain of Sea, 110

Plain of Sport, 110, 111
Plebes Dei, 136
Pliny the Elder, 22, 27
Pluto, see Dis Pater
'Poem Book of Fionn', See Duanaire Finn
Poems of Ossian, The, xii, xxiv, 20, 220, 299
poetry, 7, 14, 16, 26, 40, 53, 64, 137, 138, 142, 147, 156, 170, 221, 222, 224, 235, 247, 265, 266, 267
'poet's execration', 16
poisoned spear of Pisear, 'king of Persia', 154–5
Poland, xii, xvii
Polybius, xx, 221
polytheism, 8
Pomona, 97
'popular antiquities', 286
Popular Romances of the West of England, xxv, 295
Popular Tales of the West Highlands, xxv, 288
portal tomb, 30, 234
Portugal, xii
Poseidon, 137
Posidonius, xxi, 26, 174, 247
Potiphar's wife, 253
Powys, 265
Prasutagus, 5
pre-Columbian travel to North America, 115
primogeniture, 50
Pritona, 11
Procolitia, 12
Profane Book of Irish Comedy, The, 230
programmes of action, xxix
'Promise, Land of', see Emain Ablach, Tír Tairngire
Propp, Vladimir, xxix
Prose Eddas, xxv
Protestantism, 231, 240
Provençal troubadours, 74

Provence, 11, 22, 36
Pryderi, 18, 22, 80, 272, 274, 277–81; death of, 281
pseudo-history, defined, 127–8
Ptolemy (geographer and astronomer), xxi, 128, 171, 192, 224, 293
púca, 304
Puck, 296
Purification (Christian feast day), 101
Puritans, 103
'Pursuit of Diarmait and Gráinne, The', *see Tóraigheacht Dhiarmada agus Ghráinne*
Pwyll (character), xxvii, 21, 79, 271–4, 278, 279
Pwyll, Prince of Dyfed, 119, 264; summarized, 271–4
Pyrenees, 39
Pythagoras, 4, 27, 45

'Q' (*nom de plume*), 232–3
Q-Celtic, xvi, 97, 145
Quaker's Island, 88
'Quarrel Between Finn and Oisín, The', 230, 232
Queen Mab, 88
'queen of the fairies', *see* fairy
quicken tree, *see* rowan
Quimper, 299, 300

ram, imagery and symbolism, xix, 19, 228
Rasharkin, 247
Rath of the Synods, 53
Rathcrogan, 203
Rathlin Island, 123, 133
raven, imagery and symbolism, 15, 81, 199, 206, 207, 214, 218
Red Book of Hergest, The, xviii, xxiv, 264
Red Branch Cycle, *see* Ulster Cycle
Redg, 207
Rees, Alwyn and Brinley, xxix, 99, 128, 144

Reims, 44
Reinheim, 109, 113
Reliques of Irish Poetry, xiii
remscél, remscéla, 81, 171, 202
Republicanism, Irish, 220
Researches in the South of Ireland, xxv
Revue Celtique, xxiv
Rhea, 70, 71
Rheged, 286; *see also* Uiren Rheged
Rhiannon, xxvii, 21–2, 66, 79–80, 264, 265, 272, 273–4, 277–80; antecedents of, 79; etymology of, 79
Rhiannon (Gruffydd), xxvii
Rhine, 39
Rhineland, 70
Rhône, Rhône Valley, 9; Upper Rhône, 221
Rhun, 267
Rhŷs, Sir John, xxvii
rí benn, 54
rí buiden, 54
rí bunaid cach cinn, 54
rí cóicid, 54
rí Temro, Temrach, 54
rí tuaithe, 53
Richis, 189
Rigantona, 21, 79
rígdomna, 51, 52
rigfhéinnid, 227
Rígru Rosclethan, 121
ring, symbolism, 24
ringforts, xviii, 22, 293, 304
Rinnal, 133
Risco, Vicente, 302
Ritona, 11
river deities, 8, 11, 13–14, 23
Riverdance, 7
Rivros, 104–5
Robin Goodfellow, 296
roc, 123
Roca Barraidh, 123
Roi Soleil, Le, 8
Roman alphabet, script, xvii, xxii
Roman de Brut, 264

Roman empire, xiv, xvii, xviii, xxii, 4, 19, 20, 26, 88, 146, 223, 298
Roman Catholicism, *see* Catholicism
Roman commentators, *see* classical commentators
Roman legions, xvii
Roman religion, xxi, xxix, 20, 30–31, 33, 34, 36, 234
Roman roads, xvii
Romanesque art, 69
Romance languages, xiv
Romania, 17, 40
Romano-Celts, 7, 11, 18
Romans (people), xi, xii, xvi, xviii, xxi, xxii, xxvii, 3, 5, 7, 10, 12, 20, 30–31, 32, 47, 67, 129, 261, 293, 302; in Ireland, 49
Rome, 4, 30, 39, 97, 286
Romeo and Juliet, 88
Rónán, Rónán mac Aeda, 246; narrative of, 250–53
Rónán, St, 246–7, 249
Roscommon, County, 59, 86, 88, 99, 124, 162, 169, 203, 212, 213
Rosh Hashanah, 95
Rosetta Stone, 75
Rosmerta, 34, 61, 71–2
Ross, Anne, 8, 17, 38, 41, 66, 228
Ross-shire, 289, 291
Round Table, 221
rowan (mountain ash, quicken tree), 29, 156, 217, 228, 229, 235–6; berries of, 235–6
Royal Irish Academy Dictionary of the Irish Language (DIL), 51, 54
Ruad Rofhessa, 137
Rúadán, 43, 44
Rúadán, Saint, 57
Ruadchoin, three, 161
Ruaidrí Ua Conchobair, 50, 55
Rucht, 202–3
Rudiobus, 20–21
ruirí, 54

Ruirteach, 14
Russia, 104

Saarbrücken, 109
Saba, *see* Sadb
Sabbath, 95
Sabines, 36
Sablon, 11
Sadb, 20, 228–9
saga, sagas, xxvi
Sages, Saints and Storytellers, xxviii
Saingliu, *see* Dubh Sainglenn
Sainrith mac Imaith, 173
St –: alphabetized under saint's name, e.g. Patrick, St
St Bride's Church, 90
St Brigid's Day, 90, 93
St Ives, 297
St Just, 296
St Michael's Day, 106
St Mullins, 249
'St Patrick's Breastplate', 19
sainthood, 88–92, 115
saints' legends, 89, 245
Salisbury Plain, 30
salmon, imagery and symbolism, 11, 15, 23–4, 116, 124, 130, 225, 244, 254, 266
salmon leap, 197, 198
Salmon of Knowledge, 225
salt mining, xv
Salthill, 123
Salzburg, xv
Salzkammergut, xv
Samain, Samhain, 21, 37, 80, 95, 96–100, 132, 167, 185, 212, 213, 226, 227; etymology of, 97; related forms, 97; *see also* Hallowe'en
Samhain (bogus deity), 98–9
Samildánach, 34, 139, 142, 297
Samonios, xix, 95
samurai, 100, 221
Sanas Cormaic (Cormac's Glossary), 8, 46, 90, 100–101, 102

Sancta (epithet), 12
Sanskrit, 9
Santa Comaña, 303
Santiago de Compostela, 146
saol eile, an, 108
Saône, 8
Sarrebourg, 72
satyr, 294
Saxons, xiii, 244, 261, 298
scaltae, 114
Scandinavia, xiii, 6, 227, 290
Scáthach, 68, 75, 121, 197–9, 200,
    201, 202, 208, 212
Scéla mucce Meic Dathó, 87;
    summarized, 174–7
Sceolang, 226, 229
Scholia Berensia, 37
Scota, Scotia, 129, 145, 147–8
Scoti, 129; *Lebor Gabála* name for
    Irish people, 148
Scotia (person), *see* Scota
Scotia (place), 148
Scotland, 16, 19, 22, 35, 43, 44, 56, 81,
    82, 98, 102, 115, 120, 124, 129,
    133, 164, 197–9, 200, 216, 235,
    246, 251, 291; history of, 286–8;
    traditions of, 286–91
Scots language, xvi, xxiv, 287
Scotti (people), xvi, 129, 148, 286;
    origin of term, 148
Scottish Gaelic, xi, xii, xvi, xvii, xxiv,
    15, 19, 22, 23, 44, 62, 97, 98, 99,
    127, 134, 219, 223, 230, 240, 284,
    285, 293, 295, 304; links to Old
    Irish, 286–7; traditions in Nova
    Scotia, 291–2; traditions in Scotland,
    286–91
Scottish Highlands, xii, xvi, xvii, xxv,
    8, 10, 18, 40, 43, 76, 148, 192, 222,
    226, 228, 233, 284, 287; Clearances
    of, 287, 289, 291; history of, 287–8
Scottish Lowlands, xvi, xxiv, 261, 287
Scottish Parliament, 291
Scottish people, 148, 244

Scythia, 129, 132, 144, 182
Scythian Diana, 37
Scythians, xx, 37
sea deities, 14, 137, 255, 275; *see also*
    Lir, Manannán mac Lir, Neptune
Seaforth, Earl of, 289, 290
Sean-bhean Bhocht, 64
Searbhán, 235
Sechnesach, 10, 61
'second sight', 285, 288
Ségda Sárlbraid, 121
Segais, Well of, 11, 14
Segomo, 36
seideán sídhe, 118
Sein, isle of, 300
Seine, 8, 27, 72
Selene, 45
Semion, 133
Semitic peoples, 60
Sencha mac Ailella, 178–9, 181,
    185–6, 187, 188, 194
Senchán Torpéist, 90, 170, 202
Senach Siaborthe, 213, 214
Sennett, Mack, 187
Septuagints, 129
Sequana, *see* Dea Sequana
Serglige Con Culainn, 78–9, 124;
    summarized, 212–15
Sétanta (Cúchulainn's birth name),
    192, 195–6, 224
Setantii, 192
seven pigs of Assal, king of the Golden
    Pillars, 154–5
severed heads, speaking, 210
Severin, Tim, 115
Severn River, 23, 24, 36, 138
Seville, 304
sexual intimacy, 10, 17, 20, 24, 48, 56,
    59, 60–61, 84, 86, 90, 98, 111–13,
    121, 141, 157–8, 159, 166, 170, 172,
    198, 206, 215, 235, 241, 251, 252,
    267, 270, 272, 273, 277, 281, 282,
    300, 301, 303; *see also* marriage,
    sacral

sexuality, human,17, 19, 21, 67, 73, 78, 79, 80, 81, 82, 86, 89, 101, 105, 130, 170, 189, 280, 294, 300

Sgrìob Chlann Uisnich, 292

Shakespeare, William, 88, 129

shaman, shamanism, 19, 27

Shan Van Vocht, 64

Shannon River, xxii, 11, 13, 169, 177, 228, 235, 244, 248, 276

Shaw, John, 127, 292

Shee (Manx), *see sídh*

Sheela-na-gig, 69–70

Sheppard, Oliver, 191, 215

Sheridan, Jim, 123

Shorter Oxford English Dictionary, quoted, 245

Shrove Tuesday, 101

sí, see sídh

sianach, 19

Sicily, xxvii, 154–5

'Sickbed of Cúchulainn, The', *see Serglige Con Culainn*

sídh, 7, 116–19, 149, 152, 155, 159, 163, 164, 166, 203; archaeology of, 116; etymology of, 117; famous examples, 118; spelling of, 116; variant forms, 118–19

sídh chóra, sídh ghaoithe, 118

Sídh Nechtain, 14, 118

Siegfried, 193

Sile na gCioch, 69–70

Silent Valley, 216

silver branch, 110

Silver Cloud, plain of, 110

Silvery Land, 110

Simon Magus, 46

Sims-Williams, Patrick, 108, 117, 118–20, 121

sínach, 258

Sinann, 13, 14

Sinbad the Sailor, 114

Siôn, Llywelyn, 266

Sir Gawain and the Green Knight, 184

Sirona, 34, 72, 192

sìth, sìthean, 118

skin of the pig of King Tuis 'of Greece', 154–5

sky, symbolism and worship, 6, 8, 21, 38, 39

sky deity, 8

Skye, Isle of, 68, 75, 121, 198, 289

Slane, 6

slavery, xxi

Slavic languages, xiv

Sleeping Army motif, 233

Sliab Bladma, 148

Sliab Fúait, 226

Sliab Mis, 147

Sliab na mBan, 225

Slieve Bloom, 148

Slieve Felim, 62

Slieve Fuad, 226

Slieve Mish, 62, 147

Sligo, County, 84, 88, 107, 140, 169, 229, 235, 236

Slovakia, xiv

Slover, C. H., *see* Cross, T. P.

sluagh sídhe, slua sí, 303

sluagh/slua na marbh, 303

smith, smithing, 43–4, 90, 114, 139, 142, 195–6

Snám Dá Én, 247–8

Sohrab and Rustum, 201

solar calendar, *see* calendar

solar imagery, *see* sun

Solinus, 39

solstices, 94; summer, 30; winter, 6, 94

'Sombre Kenneth', *see* Brahan Seer

Somerset, 12, 295

Sopron-Varhély, 67–8

Souconna, 8

sovereignty, 9, 21, 48, 60–65, 280; drink of, 63; Flaithius, 64; gender of, 60–61, 280; personifications of, 61–4

Spain, xii, xvii, 35, 74, 145; Ireland, links to, 145–6, 302–3; *see also* Galicia

Spanish language, 47, 302–4
spear, spears, 136, 154–5, 192, 198, 199, 201, 209, 224, 247, 249, 252, 268, 269, 282
spirals, symbolism, 6
spirituality, xiv, 27
Sri-Lakshmi, 60
Srúb Brain, 112
stag, *see* deer
standing stones, 6
Starn, 132–3
Stephens, James, 222
Stone Age, 6
Stone of Destiny, 53
Stonehenge, xiii, 25, 30, 94–5
'Story of mac Da Thó's Pig, The', *see Scéla mucce Meic Dathó*
Strabo, xx–xxi, 28, 67, 127
Strathglass, 291
Strettweg, 68
Stroove Point, 112
structuralism, xxix
Stukeley, William, 30
Styx, Stygian, 120
Sualtam mac Róich, 194, 204, 205, 210
suan sídhe, 118
Sucellus, 41, 72, 137
Suetonius Paulinus, 26
Suibne, Suibhne, 243, 246–50, 263
Sulevia, Suleviae, 39
Sulis, Sul, 12–13, 31, 39, 73; healing deity, 73
Sullivan, Arthur, Sir, 107, 294
Sul-Minerva, 12–13, 31, 39
Sumer, Sumerians, 46, 60
sun, 93–5; imagery, symbolism and worship, 6–8, 9, 13, 15, 19, 21, 34, 38, 62
sun deity, 7, 135
sunwise turn, 147, 160
Sutherland, Elizabeth, 289
swan, imagery and symbolism, 17, 99, 113, 138, 152, 159, 163–5, 165–7; swan as maiden, 167

swastika, 6
Swift, Jonathan, 258
Swim Two Birds, 247
Switzerland, the Swiss, xv, xviii, 4
sword, swords, 122, 136, 138, 164, 170, 189, 199, 209, 226
syncretism, 33
Synge, John Millington, 66
Syria, xxi, 41

taboo, 14, 16; *see also* geis
Tacitus, 5, 26, 31
taghairm, 22–3
taibhsear, 288, 289
Tailtiu, 105, 133, 147, 163
Táin (classification of narrative), 151, 202; pun on, 211
Táin Bó Cuailnge, xx, xxiii, 21, 23, 56, 81, 84, 85, 87, 90, 151, 152, 168, 169, 170, 171, 177, 191, 195, 200, 215, 224, 245, 284, 303; boy troops, 208; bulls' duel to the death, 211–12; critique of, 201–2; dating of, 201–2; *remscéla* to, 202–3; summarized, 201–12; title interpreted, 202
Táin Bó Flidais, 202
Táin Bó Fraích, 58–9, 202
'Tales of the Traditional Kings', 243
Tales Until Dawn, 292
Taliesin, 24, 76, 262–3, 264, 265–7; historicity of, 265; name explained, 267; narrative of, 265–7; poems ascribed to, 265
Taliesin West, 265
Tallaght, 131
Tammuz, 96
Tánaise, tánaiste, tánaiste, 51–2; *tánaise ríg*, 52
tanist, 51–2; rival definitions, 51
Tara, xxiii, 13, 19, 22, 52–7, 62, 63, 86, 98, 99, 139, 142, 158, 159, 160, 170, 177, 218, 226–7, 239, 244, 245, 253, 255; Christian legends

of, 57; described, 53; etymology of, 57

Tara Brooch, 53

Taran, 38

Taranis, 8, 37, 38, 40, 46, 97

tarbh uisge, 23

tarbfheis, 22–3, 56

Taredd Wledig, 270

taroo ushtey, 23

Tarvos Trigaranus, 22

taxes, xxi, 26, 143

Téa, 57

Tech Duinn, 41, 117, 139

Tech Moling, 249

Tegid Foel, 266

teinm laida, 29, 226

Telamon, 4

Teltown, 105, 116, 147

Temair, 57

Temuir Luchra, 187–9

Tennyson, Alfred Lord, xxiv

territorial goddesses, 9–10, 86

Terryglass, xxiii

Tertullian, 69

testing cup of truth, motif of, 253, 254–5

Tethra, 124

teutā, 32, 37

Teutates, xx, 32, 33, 37, 46, 97

Teyrnon Twrf Liet, 274

Thames, River, 10, 12, 66–7

Themis, 33, 70

Theogony, 127

Theseus, 245

Thomas the Rhymer, 290

Thomond, 161

Thompson, Stith, xxv; *see also* Aarne-Thompson catalogue

Thor, 137

Three Exalted Prisoners, 46, 270

Three Finns of Emain Macha, 46

Three Generous Men, 46

three shouts on the hill of Miodhchaoin, 154–5

'Three Sorrows of Storytelling, The', 83, 155, 163

thumb of knowledge, 24, 225

thunder, 8, 37–8

Thurneysen, Rudolf, 42, 79, 139

Tiber, 34

Tigh Mhóire, 61

Tigris, 60

timpán, 226

tinkard (defined), 297

Tintagel, xviii

Tipperary, County, xxiii, 10, 11, 61, 64, 118, 225

tipra sláine, 138

Tír Chonaill, 247

Tír fo Thuinn, 122

Tír na mBan, 111, 122

Tír na mBéo, 122

Tír na nÓg, 11, 78, 113, 123, 149, 241–2

Tír Tairngire, 114, 121–2, 235, 253

Titans, 70

Tlachtga, 46, 98

Tochmarc (classification of narrative), 151

Tochmarc Étaíne, xxiii, 17, 77–8, 152; summarized, 155–9

Togail Bruidne Da Derga, 56, 74–5, 150, 171, 228; summarized, 160–62

tóin (pun), 211

Tom (Cornish giant and hero), 296–7

Tophet, 98

Topographia Hibernia, 21, 57–8

Tor Conaind, 132, 134

Tóraigheacht Dhiarmada agus Ghráinne, 151; summarized, 234–7; differences from Deirdre story, 234; origins, 234

Torc Triath, 18

Tory Island, 132, 134

Tour in Scotland, A, 289

Toutain, 18

Toutatis, 37

Tower of Babel, 128

Tracht Esi, Trácht Éisi, 200
Traditions and Hearthside Stories of West Cornwall, 295
'Tragic Death of Aífe's Only Son, The', *see Aided Óenfhir Aífe*
'Tragic Story of the Children of Lir, The', *see Oidheadh Chlainne Lir*
'Tragic Story of the Children of Tuireann, The', *see Oidheadh Chlainne Tuireann*
Transalpine War, xxi
transhumance, 101–2
Traveri, 36
trees, sacred, x, 29; *see also* hazel, oak, rowan, yew
trefoil, 44
Trépassés, Bay of, 302
Trier, 11, 22, 36
Trinobantes, 5
Trioedd Ynys Prydain, 44–5, 270, 271
triplism, 15, 20, 22, 29, 32, 34, 37, 38, 39, 40, 43, 44–46, 70, 84, 85, 90, 91, 92, 99, 215, 253, 270, 271
triskele, 7, 44
trispiral, 6
Tristan, 234, 295
troisième Souverain, Le, xxix
trout, imagery and symbolism, 23
Troy, 169
Trundheim Chariot, 6
Tuan man Cairill, mac Stairn, 18, 24, 132
tuath, 32, 51, 53–4, 59, 117, 136
Tuatha Dé Danann, 9, 10, 42, 43, 84, 90, 122, 123, 130, 132, 133, 135–40, 148, 152, 153, 155, 156, 157, 163, 164, 166, 185, 224, 226; arrival in Ireland, 135; etymology of, 136; four cities of, 136; members of, 136–40; treasures of, 136
Tuireann, 153
Tuis 'of Greece', King, 154–5
Tulsk, 169
tunnerez noz, 303

Twelfth Night, 101
Twrch Trwyth, 18, 77, 270
tylwyth teg, 120
Tynwald, the, 293
Tyrconnell, 58
Tyrone, County, 46, 169, 231

Ua –: people with this patronymic are alphabetized under their given names, e.g. Ruaidrí Ua Conchobair
Úamain, 118
Úath (classification of narrative), 151
Uathach, 198
uddereek, 294
Uffern, 120
Uffington White Horse, 20
Uí Fháilghe, 224
Uí Néill, 49, 50, 55–6, 63, 224, 239, 244
Uisnech, 62, 81 103, 186; fire at, 103, 132, 204; as Uisneach in Nova Scotia
Ukraine, 129
Ulaid, 168–9, 171
Ulster, 21, 23, 54, 58, 80–82, 85, 87, 129, 148, 156, 173–7, 178, 185, 187, 193, 194, 203, 217, 220, 231, 233, 234, 255, 256, 293; etymology of, 169; geography of, 169
Ulster Chronicles, 148, 250
Ulster Cycle, 52, 54, 56, 80–82, 85, 136, 150, 160, 222, 228, 243, 245, 292; alternative names for, 150, 168–9; heroes of, 169–71; introduction to, 168–71; narratives from, Part I, 168–90; narratives from, Part II, 191–218; status of, 168
Ultonia, *see* Ulster
Ultonain Cycle, *see* Ulster Cycle
Ulysses (Joyce), 233
unified imagination, theory of, xxviii
Union Army, 220
United Irishmen (1798 rebellion), 53, 57, 64

United Kingdom, 169, 220, 265, 293
United Order of Druids, 30
United States, 104, 220
Unshin, 84
Uranus, 70
urco, 304
Urien Rheged, 265, 266
Urnfield culture, xiv–xv, 15, 16, 17
Usheen, Hiberno-English form for Oisín (q.v.)

Vaison-la-Romaine, 9
Vallancey, Colonel Charles, 220
Valley of Grief, 270
van Hamel, Anton, 42
Van Winkle, Rip, 113
Vanir, 144
Vanity Fair, 113
Vannes, 6
Varhély, 40
Vasio, 9
vates, 26
Vatican, the, *see* papacy
vellum, xxii
Vendryes, Joseph, 32, 33, 37, 45
Ventry, 222
Venus, 3, 96, 234
Vercingetorix, 4–5
Verín, 304
Verity, Bill, 115
vernacular evidence, xviii
Vesontius, 33
Vestmannaejar, 114
Vichy, 35, 36
Vienna, 223
Vikings, 49, 50; *see also* Danes, Lochlainn, Norsemen
Vindabona, 223
Vindonnus, 34, 223
Virgil, xiv, 28
Vishnu, 60
'Vision of Angus, The', *see Aislinge Óenguso*

Vorocius, 36
votive materials, 11
'Voyage of Bran, The', *see Imram Brain*
'Voyage of the Abbott Saint Brendan', *see Navigatio Sancti Brendani Abbatis*
Vulcan, 3, 41, 42, 43, 44

Wace, 264
Waifs and Strays in Celtic Tradition, xxv, 288
Waldelgesheim, 98
Wales, xvi, xvii, xviii, 5, 8, 11, 21, 26, 32, 46, 75–6, 108, 115, 261–83, 285, 288; etymology of, 261–2; history of, 261–4
Wanborough, 7
'Wanderings of Oisin, The', 123, 240
war deities, 10, 35, 45, 61, 83–7
warp spasm [*ríastrad*], *see* Cúchulainn
'washer at the ford, the', 303
'Wasting Sickness of Cúchulainn, The', *see Serglige Con Culainn*
water, symbolism, properties, 10–11
water deities, 8, 11, 137; *see also* sea deities
waterfalls, cataracts, 8, 11, 32
Wave, Land under, *see* Tír fo Thuinn
wells, holy, sacred, 10–11, 14, 88, 91, 106
Welsh language, xi, xiii, xvi, xxiv, 133, 262–3, 291, 295, 298; *see also* Old Welsh
Welsh Legends, xxv
Welsh literature, xxi, 18, 169, 249; early, xxi, xxii, xxiii–xxiv, 298
Welsh people, 261–2, 286; Irish people, links to, 263
Welsh Triads, *see Trioedd Ynys Prydain*
Westmeath, County, 62, 164, 210, 292
Wexford, County, 104
whale, 114
wheel, symbolism, 6, 7, 37–8, 84

whelp or puppy Failinis of King Iruad, 154–5

White Book of Rhydderch, The, xxiv, 264

White-horned Bull of Connacht, *see* Finnbennach

White Silver, plain of, 110

wicker execution, 29

Wicker Man, The, 29

'Wife of Bath's Tale, The', 64–5

'Wild Man of the Woods' theme, 263

Wilde, Sir William, 104

Williams, Charles, 265

Williams, Edward, xiii

Williams, Ifor, 119, 265

Willingham Fen, 7

Wiltshire, 30

Windsor Castle, 52

Wisconsin, 265

witches, witchcraft, 79, 103, 143, 216, 270, 289, 304; witches' Sabbath, 304

'Women, Land of', 110, 111, 112–13; *see also* Tír na mBan

'Wonders, The Land of', 110

'Wooing of Étaín, The', *see Tochmarc Étaíne*

Works and Days (Hesiod), 128

Wright, Frank Lloyd, 265

xana, 303–4

Y Gododdin, 261

yannig, 32

Yeats, William Butler, xxv, xxvi, 88, 107, 116, 122, 123, 222, 231, 240, 250

Yellow Book of Lecan, The, xxiii, 202

Yeun, Yeun-Elez, 120

yew tree, 29, 167, 176, 215, 247

yn foldyr gastey, 294

Ynys Afallon, 123

Ynys Prydain, 261

yoga, yogi, xx, 18

Yorkshire, 12, 39, 43, 90, 261

Youdic, 120

Ys, City of, 285; described, 300

Ysbaddaden Bencawr, 77, 135, 268, 269–70

Ystoria Taliesin, 266–7

Zeus, 33, 42

zoomorphic figures, 18, 20